THE COOK'S DICTIONARY GUIDE

DENISE GREIG

THE
Cook's
Dictionary
GUIDE

NH
NEW
HOLLAND

FOR MY SON, ALEXANDER FALLOWS, WITH LOVE.

FOREWORD

The Cook's Dictionary Guide is a welcome addition to both the professional chef's and the home cook's bookshelf because it encompasses the influences made by many diverse ethnic groups on the worldwide culinary scene—influences both old and new. From good old-fashioned dishes and ingredients to wonderful new tastes and the abundance of herbs, spices and fresh vegetables previously unavailable, this book opens our eyes to the riches we now have on our doorstep.

If you're in doubt about any of these ingredients or their origins, the various techniques used in the kitchen or the implements required, let *The Cook's Dictionary Guide* be your guide.

Enjoy!

Tetsuya Wakuda

AOC *see* APPELLATION D'ORIGINE CONTRÔLÉE.

à la carte | FRENCH | Restaurant term meaning that each item on the menu is priced individually, and not a set meal at a fixed price.

abaisser | FRENCH | To roll out pastry with a rolling pin.

abalone (*Haliotis* spp.) Marine mollusc with a single ear-shaped shell lined with mother-of-pearl. Found along the coasts of the northern Pacific Ocean, Australia and South Africa. Available dried, canned and fresh. The best abalone are live, and the greenlip abalone (*H. laevigata*) is often considered to have the best taste. The white flesh should be shiny and crisp and briefly sautéed. Dried abalone requires extensive soaking and cooking. Abalone is a delicacy of Japanese cuisine and is often eaten raw in sashimi, also seasoned with sake and steamed, barbecued or braised.

abalone mushrooms *see* OYSTER MUSHROOMS.

abattoir Slaughterhouse where animals are killed for both their edible and by-products.

abbacchio | ITALIAN | Suckling lamb that has been milk-fed. Abbacchio al forno is a speciality of Rome where it is cooked in several different ways, such as roasted whole in an oven or outdoors on a spit, and served with an anchovy sauce containing olive oil, vinegar and garlic. Essential herb used is rosemary.

abbocatto | ITALIAN | Generic term for sweet wine.

Aberdeen Angus | SCOTTISH | Also known as 'Angus'. Breed of black, polled cattle originating in north-eastern Scotland; considered a leading breed of beef.

abiu (*Pouteria cainito*) Also known as 'caimito'. Tropical fruit from South America in regions of Peru and northern Chile, now cultivated in tropical Queensland. It is a yellow, oval-shaped fruit about the size of a large lemon with very juicy, off-white flesh. Eaten fresh, often with ice-cream.

aboukir almonds Glazed petits fours. Almonds are embedded in green or pink almond paste and dipped in caramelised sugar.

absinthe Green bitter alcoholic liqueur with hints of aniseed. Composed of aromatic plants and high-proof spirit. Absinthe contains dangerous oils obtained from the plant wormwood (*Artemisia absinthium*) which have a serious effect on the nervous system. Its manufacture and sale are prohibited in most countries. In France, Pernod and other pastis are used in its place.

aburage | JAPANESE | Thin sheets of deep-fried tofu, sold frozen. An essential ingredient in making inari-zushi (small pouches of tofu stuffed with sushi rice). *see also* SUSHI.

acacia blossoms | AUSTRALIAN | (*Acacia* spp.) Fluffy yellow flowers used to flavour fritters and liqueur (ratafia).

acacia gum Gum arabic or gum exudation of certain species of Acacia used as a stabiliser in pickles, bottled sauces and confectionery.

acacia seed | AUSTRALIAN | (*Acacia* spp.) Traditional food of Aborigines. Ripe seeds are typically high in protein, fat and carbohydrate. Roasted and milled acacia seeds produce a nutritious flour used in modern Australian cuisine. Flour is incorporated into damper, breads, cakes, pastries, desserts and beverages.

accolade (en) | FRENCH | The presentation on a serving plate of two similar types of food arranged back to back; usually poultry and game birds.

accompaniment Food or sauce served separately with a dish.

acerola *see* BARBADOS CHERRY.

acetic Like vinegar or sour.

acetic acid Clear, pungent liquid used industrially and in diluted solutions; the chief component of vinegar.

aceto | ITALIAN | Vinegar. Aceto balsamico is balsamic vinegar.

aceto-dolce | ITALIAN | Condiment made of fruit and vegetables pickled in vinegar and preserved in honey and mustard. Served with antipasto.

acetomel Sweet-and-sour syrup made of honey and vinegar used for preserving fruits which then become aceto-dolce. Derived from the Latin *acetum*, meaning vinegar, and *mel*, meaning honey.

achar | INDIAN | Strongly spiced, salted relish, made from fruits such as mango or lime, which may be spicy hot, pungent or sweet depending on the seasoning added.

achiote *see* ANNATTO.

acid drop Hard, white sweet made from boiled sugar and cream of tartar.

acidophilus (*Lactobacillus acidophilus*) Friendly bacteria added to yoghurt to help restore intestinal bacteria balance and commonly used to make yoghurt more easily digestible.

acidulate To add vinegar, lemon or lime juice to a dish to make it slightly acid; or to add to water in which freshly peeled raw foods, such as apples, artichokes, pears and potatoes, are soaked in order to prevent browning.

acini di pepe | ITALIAN | Small, round pasta the size and shape of peppercorns. Used in soups.

ackee *see* AKEE.

acorda | PORTUGUESE | Garlic soup with softened bread, poached eggs and chopped coriander leaves.

acorn squash (*Cucurbita maxima*) Also known as 'Des Moines squash'. Small, acorn-shaped winter squash with dark green or yellow skin and yellow flesh.

acra / akra | CARIBBEAN | Savory fritter made by mixing salted fish and other ingredients such as puréed vegetables, dipped in batter and fried in olive oil. Served as cocktail food and appetizer.

additives Substances added to foods for preserving, coloring, emulsifying, stabilizing, enriching or replacing vitamins. All additives must be approved by law and their use is strictly controlled.

ade Beverage consisting of sweetened water and citrus juice, such as lemonade.

adobo | FILIPINO | National dish consisting of chicken or pork (or a combination of both) marinated in garlic, vinegar and pepper, simmered in water and sometimes coconut milk, then fried.

adobo sauce | MEXICAN | Thick chili sauce made with vinegar and highly seasoned with herbs and spices. Used as a marinating paste or served as a condiment.

advocaat | DUTCH | Golden liqueur made with beaten egg yolks, sugar and spirit, served both before and after meals. An ingredient of the cocktail 'snowball'.

adzuki beans (*Phaseolus angularis*) Small, dried red beans with a sweet taste. Popular in Japanese and Chinese cooking. Used in desserts, cakes and confectionery in the form of a sweet paste called 'yokan'. They need only a short soak, before cooking. Also used as a sprouting vegetable.

aemono | JAPANESE | A cooked salad. Cooked vegetables are tossed together with dressing, often made with miso or puréed tofu. A well-known aemono dish is spinach dressed with sesame paste mixed with soy and sugar.

aerate (1) To incorporate air into food to make it lighter. **(2)** Kitchen technique of changing the water of soaked food daily to prolong freshness of certain produce such as seaweed, sweetbreads and other offal.

aerated water (1) Distilled water with purified air added. **(2)** Carbonated mineral water.

Affine *see* KERVELLA CHEESE.

africaine (à l') | FRENCH | North African style. Dish containing potatoes, egg- plant, cucumbers or zucchini seasoned with herbs, spices and tomato.

African horned cucumber (*Cucumis metuliferus*) Cultivated and promoted under the name of 'kiwano' in New Zealand. An oblong cucumber with golden orange skin and thick spines; the flesh is bright green. Used in salads.

agar-agar Processed gelatin-like product primarily obtained from red seaweed (*Gelidium* and *Gracilaria*) species. It is made into unscented transparent bars or strands, shaved into fine flakes, or powdered. Principally used in the food industry as a stabilizer in canned foods and thickening agent in ice creams, desserts and confectionery. Agar-agar is fast setting and is used by vegetarians as a substitute for gelatins made with animal products. Popular in Japanese cooking. It is the preferred gelatin for gelling pineapple, which will not set in animal gelatin.

agaric Any member of the family of field and woodland mushrooms (both edible and poisonous), typically with a white cap, pink then brownish gills, and a stalk bearing a single or double ring. The common cultivated mushroom is a member of this family.

agave Genus of succulent plants found in the southern states of North America, Mexico and Central America. The pulp of certain species is fermented to make alcoholic beverages such as mescal, pulque and tequila.

agedashi | JAPANESE | Deep-fried tofu served with a mirin and soy dipping sauce seasoned with bonito flakes, grated ginger and daikon.

agemono | JAPANESE | Any deep-fried food, the best-known of which is tempura. *see also* TEMPURA.

aglio e olio | ITALIAN | Translates to 'garlic and olive oil'.

agneau | FRENCH | Lamb.

agneau de lait | FRENCH | Milk-fed baby lamb.

agnolotti | ITALIAN | Crescent-shaped pasta with a variety of fillings, similar to ravioli.

agraz | NORTH AFRICAN | Sorbet made from ground almonds, verjus and sugar.

agrodolce sauce | ITALIAN | Sweet-and-sour sauce made with vinegar, sugar and pan juices and various additives which might include ground pepper, almonds, candied peel, sultanas, capers or bitter chocolate. Served with duck, pork and game.

aguardiente | SPANISH | Clear, high-alcohol spirit made from the residue of pips and skins left from the last wine-pressing. In some Spanish-speaking Latin American countries it is made from distilled sugarcane molasses.

aïgo boulido | FRENCH | Garlic soup. Specialty of Provence.

aigre-doux | FRENCH | Sweet-and-sour.

aiguille à brider | FRENCH | Trussing needle.

aiguille à piquer | FRENCH | Larding needle.

aiguillette | FRENCH | Long, narrow slice of under-fillet, cut from the breast of poultry. It is also a thin strip of any meat or fish.

aile | FRENCH | The wing (including the breast) of poultry or game birds.

aïoli | FRENCH | Garlic mayonnaise served with cold poached fish, hard- boiled eggs, snails, vegetables or cold meats. Specialty of Provence.

Ajinomoto | JAPANESE | Brand name for chemical seasoning, monosodium glutamate (MSG).

ajishio | JAPANESE | Seasoning mix of salt and monosodium glutamate. Served with tempura prawns.

ajowan | INDIAN | (*Carum ajowan*) Light brown seeds with thyme-like taste. Used as a spice in Indian cooking, mainly in chutneys, curries and lentil dishes.

akajiso | JAPANESE | Red perilla. *see also* SHISO.

akamiso | JAPANESE | Red soya bean paste that is high in protein and salt. *see also* MISO.

akebia | JAPANESE | Sausage-shaped, purple fruit that ripens in autumn. It has a white, pulpy flesh with a fairly insipid taste. Eaten raw or puréed into a cream or drink.

akee | CARIBBEAN | (*Blighia sapidia*) Named after William Bligh of the *Bounty* fame. Three-angled, bright red fruit with a soft, creamy white flesh that is edible when ripe; the large black seeds and unripe flesh are poisonous. It is an important part of the Jamaican diet and is traditionally cooked with salt fish, usually cod.

akra *see* ACRA.

akudjura | AUSTRALIAN | (*Solanum centrale*) Finely ground form of the native bush tomato. Used in soups, sauces and casseroles.

al dente | ITALIAN | Literally 'to the teeth', referring to the correct degree of cooking pasta so that it is tender, but still firm to the bite. Now also commonly refers to vegetables which are served while still slightly crunchy.

al fresco | ITALIAN | Eating outside, as in a garden, courtyard, plaza, piazza or street.

albacore (*Thunnus alalunga*) Deep-sea fish of the tuna family with white to pale pink, mild flesh, often referred to as 'chicken of the sea'. Sold in steaks or sliced off the bone. Used raw in sushi and sashimi; also briefly pan-fried or grilled.

Albert sauce | ENGLISH | Sauce made with white stock, grated horseradish, breadcrumbs, cream and egg yolks. Traditionally served with joints of braised beef. Named after Prince Albert, husband and consort of Queen Victoria.

albondigas | SPANISH | Small spicy meatballs, usually served as a tapas or appetizer. Also popular in Mexico where they are usually served in a tomato sauce.

Albufera sauce | FRENCH | Béchamel sauce with red capsicums.

albumen powder Powder used as a substitute for egg whites to make meringues or royal icing.

albumen/albumin Soluble protein found in egg whites, milk, animal blood and plants.

alcarraza | SPANISH | Water cooler made of porous earthenware.

alcazar | FRENCH | Cake made with a pastry base topped with apricot jam, almond meringue and decorated with almond paste.

alcohol Clear, intoxicating liquid obtained from the fermentation or distillation of various fruits, grains, roots and stems.

alcool blanc | FRENCH | Translates to 'white alcohol'. White, fruit brandy distilled from fruit other than grapes and aged in crockery, rather than casks.

ale Alcoholic beverage brewed from malt and hops. It is fuller-bodied and more bitter than beer.

alecost *see* COSTMARY.

alewife (*Pomolobus* spp.) Important North American fish of the herring family.

alexander (*Smyrnium olusatrum*) Also known as 'alisander' and 'alexander parsley'. Aromatic biennial herb resembling both lovage and angelica. Young leaves used as a salad ingredient; also used in soups and stews. Leaves, stems, flower buds and upper parts of the root often appear in medieval recipes.

alfabeto | ITALIAN | Pasta shaped as tiny letters of the alphabet. Used in soup.

alfalfa sprouts (*Medicago sativa*) Perennial clover-like plant of the pea family, native to Europe and widely grown for cattle feed. Popular as a nutritious sprouting vegetable. The seed has a high germination rate and the very fine sprouts are ready to eat when between 2.5–5 cm (1–2 inches) long. Used as a garnish, in salads and on sandwiches.

Alfredo sauce | ITALIAN | Rich, creamy pasta sauce originating in Rome and named after restaurateur Alfredo di Lello. Contains butter, double cream, grated Parmesan cheese and freshly ground black pepper. Traditionally served with fettuccine.

algae *see* SEAWEED.

algérienne (à l') | FRENCH | Algerian style dishes garnished with sweet potato, tomatoes and garlic.

alginic acid Gelatinous substance, extracted from seaweed and used in processed food such as jellies, puddings, soups and meat pastes to improve their texture or consistency.

aligot | FRENCH | Potato purée, stirred vigorously with the fresh curds of Cantal cheese and crushed garlic. Specialty of the Auvergne.

alisander *see* ALEXANDER.

all-purpose flour | AMERICAN | Plain flour.

allemande (à l') | FRENCH | German style. Dishes served with allemande sauce.

allemande sauce | FRENCH | Velouté sauce enriched with cream and egg yolks. Served with offal, poached chicken, veal and vegetables.

alligator pear *see* AVOCADO.

allspice (*Pimenta officinalis*) Also known as 'pimento' or 'Jamaica pepper'. Small sun-dried berries obtained from a tropical tree cultivated mainly in Jamaica. They have a combined aroma of cinnamon, cloves and nutmeg. Whole berries are used in preserves, pickles and chutney. Ground allspice is used in baked goods and desserts.

allumettes | FRENCH | Translates to 'match'. **(1)** Puff pastry strips topped with a spread and baked in the oven. **(2)** Fried matchstick potatoes.

almejas | SPANISH | Translates to 'clams'. The classic almejas à la marinara is a dish made with clams, white wine, garlic, onions and tomatoes, seasoned with a little chili and garnished with chopped parsley.

almond These creamy-hued, oval nuts are the most popular nuts used in cooking. Almonds are an excellent source of vitamin E, dietary fiber and riboflavin (vitamin B2); also high in mono-unsaturated fat, the good fat with cholesterol-reducing properties. Two varieties are used: the **sweet almond** (var. *dulcis*), eaten as a snack or used in cooking and baking, and the **bitter almond** (var. *amara*), which contains prussic acid and is never eaten raw. Used to make a strong extract for liqueurs and bittersweet confections. Sweet almonds are sold in their shells or skins, smoked, salted or blanched whole, halved, slivered, flaked or ground and used extensively in many dishes. *see also* ALMOND ESSENCE, ALMOND MEAL, ALMOND OIL *and* ALMOND PASTE.

almond cream Cold dessert made from ground almonds, butter, sugar and eggs.

almond essence Very strong taste extracted from the bitter almond and mixed with alcohol. Used to season liqueurs, confectionery and biscuits, including the classic Italian amaretti.

almond meal Ground almonds made from dried, sweet almonds. Used as an alternative to flour to thicken sauces and to coat meat or fish for frying; also used in many types of cakes, pastries, desserts and confectionery, including marzipan.

almond milk (1) Thick liquid made by boiling nuts in a small amount of water and puréeing in a blender. Used as a base for desserts. **(2)** Also a medieval soup made from ground almonds, onions, wine and spices.

almond oil Mono-unsaturated oil obtained by pressing sweet almonds. Used as a cooking oil, in salad dressing or drizzled over certain vegetables such as asparagus.

almond paste Mixture of sugar and ground almonds bound together with a little glucose syrup or egg yolk. Used to cover cakes and as a filling for pastries and in confectionery. *see also* MARZIPAN.

almond, sugared Almonds coated with hard sugar. Mostly manufactured commercially. It is a very old tradition to distribute sugar-coated almonds to celebrate a birth or wedding, still practiced in Europe and the Middle East.

Alsace Important gastronomic and wine-producing region of north-eastern France on the German border. The cuisine combines the robust foods of Germany, the culinary traditions of France and the Jewish spice influence. Noted food products and dishes include fresh and cured pork, various sausages, pâté de fois gras, gefilte fish, bacon-and-onion tart, frog soup, sauerkraut, red cabbage with chestnuts, and many baked specialties such as Kugelhopf, savarin and gingerbread.

alsacienne (à l') | FRENCH | Alsace style. Dishes garnished with sauerkraut, sausage, ham or foie gras.

aluminite Heat-resistant porcelain used for cooking utensils.

aluminium/aluminum Lightweight, silvery white metal used for cooking utensils and for canning. It is an excellent heat conductor and, because of its light weight, is popular for large cooking saucepans. The heavier the gauge the more evenly it cooks. Pure aluminium/aluminum blackens in contact with alkaline food such as potatoes and spinach, but lightens again when exposed to acids such as citrus fruit and vinegar. This effect is harmless.

aluminium/aluminum foil Lightweight, silvery white, thin sheets of aluminium/aluminum used to wrap foods for covering, packing, freezing and cooking food. Withstands high temperatures very well in conventional ovens, but cannot be used for microwave cookery. Available in different gauges and sold in a roll.

amandine | FRENCH | **(1)** Several types of pastry made with almonds. **(2)** Food served with almonds.

amaranth (*Amaranthus* spp.) Wild or cultivated spinach-like annual vegetable with green leaves tinged with purple or red. Leaves and stems are rich in iron and vitamin C. Used much like spinach in Oriental dishes, stir-fries and soups. In Central America the seeds were an important cereal crop among the Aztecs. A canned pickle version is sold in Asian shops.

amaretti | ITALIAN | Almond biscuits or macaroons made from almonds, egg whites and bitter almond essence.

Amaretto | ITALIAN | Liqueur made from bitter almonds, apricot kernels and aromatic extracts. Used to enrich fruit salads, trifle and whipped cream. The best known is Disaronno Amaretto.

amaro | ITALIAN | Bitter. Generic term for various bitter alcoholic drinks reputed to have excellent digestive properties.

Amarone | ITALIAN | Quality dry red wine from Verona, Veneto.

amatista chili Small, purple, sweet chili usually pickled and used as a garnish in salads.

amazake | JAPANESE | Hot drink made by steeping rice with water and rice inoculated with mould. It is sweetened with ginger and consumed to treat colds.

ambarella (*Spondias dulcis*) Also known as 'Otaheite apple' or 'hog plum'. Gold plum-like fruit, native to Tahiti and now widespread in tropical Asia. Related to the mango, the yellow flesh is eaten raw and used in curries or preserves.

ambigu | FRENCH | Buffet meal where the meat, desserts and fruit are served at the same time.

ambrosia | GREEK | (1) Mythical food of the gods of Mount Olympus giving them immortality. (2) The name given to an American dessert of chilled orange segments sprinkled with sugar and grated fresh coconut.

Ambrosia | SWEDISH | Semi-firm cow's-milk cheese with cream-hued, open-textured interior with tiny irregular holes. Served mainly as a snack or sandwich cheese. Mass-produced in large dairies and widely available throughout the world.

amchur (*Mannigifera indica*) Seasoning made from dried unripe mango ground to a powder. Used as a tart seasoning in many Indian dishes, also to tenderize meat, poultry and fish.

Amer Picon | FRENCH | Bitter liqueur drunk as an aperitif and often used in cocktails.

américaine (à l') | FRENCH | American style. Sauce of white wine, tomatoes, garlic, butter and cognac, traditionally served with lobster.

americano Cocktail of Italian vermouth, Campari, slice of lemon and splash of soda.

amino acids Organic molecules containing at least one amino group (–NH2) and one acid group (COOH). Some 20 different naturally occurring amino acids make up proteins most of which are manufactured in the human body. Eight must be provided by our diets and these are known as 'essential amino acids'.

amontillado | SPANISH | Pale, dry sherry, originating in Spain.

amoroso | SPANISH | Medium-dry dessert sherry.

amourette | FRENCH | Spinal marrow of beef, mutton or veal. Usually cut in strips and crumbed.

amphora | GREEK | An early Greek two-handled pottery jar used to store and transport olives, oil and wine.

anadromous fish Fish that migrate from their saltwater habitat to spawn in fresh water.

anago | JAPANESE | Conger eel. Long, sea eel that is filleted and flattened butterfly-style. It is grilled while being basted with a thick mirin and sugar sauce; or braised in equal parts of soy sauce, sake, mirin and sugar until a strong tasting dark sauce results. The anago is formed into rectangles with sushi rice and brushed with the sauce.

Anaheim chili | AMERICAN | Also known as 'chili California'. Mild to medium- hot, elongated, hot chili once grown extensively on the site of what is now Disneyland in Anaheim, California. Used in sauces, soups and stews, also stuffed and pickled.

ancho chili | MEXICO | Mild mahogany heart-shaped chili. The most used of the dried red chilies in Mexican cooking. When fresh and green, it is known as 'poblano chili'.

anchoïade / anchoyade | FRENCH | Sauce that is a blend of anchovies, olive oil and garlic, usually served as a dip with raw vegetables, or spread on toast or bread. Specialty of Provence.

anchovy (*Engraulis australis*) Tiny, silvery saltwater fish occurring in large schools in shallow coastal habitats. They are usually filleted and sold canned in olive oil, or salt-cured and available flat or rolled. They have a strong taste and small quantities are used for pizza, sauces, salads and garnishing. Also made into anchoïade, tapenade and anchovy paste.

anchovy butter Anchovies pounded to a paste then mixed with softened unsalted butter and a dash of lemon. Used as a spread for canapés and hors d'oeuvres; also served with meat or fish.

anchovy paste Commercially prepared mixture of anchovies, vinegar, spices and water. Mainly used as a spread for bread and toast.

ancienne (à l') | FRENCH | In the old style. Often refers to braised dishes in which the garnishes include sliced onions and button mushrooms.

ancient egg *see* PRESERVED EGG.

andalouse sauce | FRENCH | Mayonnaise mixed with tomato purée and fine julienned red capsicums. Served with vegetable salads or cold seafood.

andouille | FRENCH | Large smoked sausage made from the tripe, small intestines, and various other parts of the pig, highly seasoned with pepper and spices, often encased in black skin. Usually served cold, cut in thin slices as an hors d'oeuvres. Also used in Cajun specialties such as gumbo and jambalaya.

andouillette | FRENCH | Smaller version of andouille sausage, usually grilled or fried and traditionally served with mustard.

anelli | ITALIAN | Small pasta rings used in soups or salads. Anellini are smaller.

angasi oyster *see* OYSTER, AUSTRALIAN FLAT.

angel's hair (1) Type of jam made from the fibrous part of a large mature pumpkin or squash. (2) Ultra fine, long strands of pasta. 'Capelli d'angelo' in Italy.

angelica (*Angelica archangelica*) Candied hollow stem from a robust biennial herb native to Eurasia. Used to enrich pastries, confectionery and ice-cream; also for decoration. The crushed stems and seeds are used in the manufacture of gin, vermouth and Chartreuse.

angels on horseback | ENGLISH | Oysters wrapped in thin slices of bacon and grilled. Served as an appetizer or on pieces of hot toast as an after dinner snack.

anglaise (à l') | FRENCH | English style. (1) Food cooked simply in water or white stock. (2) Deep-fried food coated with milk and flour.

angled loofah (*Luffa acutangula*) Also known as 'silk squash' and 'Chinese okra'. Long thin green vegetable with longitudinal ridges. It is native to India and is cultivated and eaten throughout much of Asia for its crisp texture and refreshing, slightly sweet taste. The ridges are trimmed and the vegetable sliced in cross-section; usually stir-fried or used in soups.

angler fish *see* MONKFISH.

Angola pea *see* PIGEON PEA.

Angostura Trade name of a reddish-brown bitter extract made in Trinidad. Used mainly to enhance cocktails and aperitifs; a few dashes of Angostura bitters in gin makes a pink gin.

Angus *see* ABERDEEN ANGUS.

animal crackers | AMERICAN | Animal-shaped arrowroot biscuits.

animelles | FRENCH | Term for sheep, calf or bull testicles. Usually soaked, split, flattened and fried. In Spain, fried bull testicles (criadillas) are served as an appetizer.

anis | FRENCH | Generic term for pastis.

anisbrod | GERMAN | Bread seasoned with aniseed.

anise (*Pimpinella anisum*) Annual herb native to Middle Eastern countries and cultivated chiefly for its strong licorice tasting seeds called aniseed. Seeds used for seasoning bakery goods, confectionery and cheeses. Essential oil obtained from the seed is the main additive for aniseed based aperitifs of Mediterranean regions, such as Pernod, ouzo and arak. Medicinally the seeds are used to aid digestion.

anise pepper *see* SZECHWAN PEPPER.

anise, star (*Illicium verum*) Small, dry, brown seed-cluster, shaped like an eight-pointed star, obtained from small evergreen tree of the Magnolia family native to China, Japan and Vietnam. Strong aniseed-like taste. Widely used in Asian cuisine either whole or ground as a spice. Most commercial oil of anise is distilled from this spice. Used chiefly for seasoning liqueurs, aperitifs and confectionery.

aniseed *see* ANISE.

aniseed myrtle | AUSTRALIAN | (*Backhousia anisata*) Shiny green leaves with a pleasant aniseed-like taste. Used in sauces accompanying white meats, desserts, bread and vinegar. Available fresh, dried whole or dried and ground.

anisette | FRENCH | Aniseed-flavoured liqueur.

Anjou pear Large, yellowish-green winter pear, with red blush. It is one of the best eating pears and is also suitable for cooking. *see also* PEAR.

Anna potatoes *see* POMMES ANNA.

annatto (*Bixa orellana*) Also known as 'achiote'. An orange or red natural food-staining agent obtained from the red waxy coating surrounding the seed of the annatto tree, native to Central America. When ground, the seeds are used to enhance Mexican, Caribbean and some Asian dishes. Commercial annatto powder or paste is used in margarine, the rind of various cheeses and smoked fish. A cooking oil enriched with annatto seeds is used in many Caribbean dishes.

antelope Grazing animals belonging to the cattle family, found mainly in Africa and Asia. Prepared in the same way as venison.

antioxidants Compounds that protect the body from damage caused by free radicals. Free radicals are unstable molecules which cause oxidation and attack cells which can ultimately result in ageing, degeneration of sight, cancer and heart disease. Major antioxidants include vitamins C and E, betacarotene, selenium and zinc, found in fresh fruit and vegetables (particularly the cabbage family), green tea, wine and mono-unsaturated fats such as olive oil.

antipasto | ITALIAN | Translates to 'before the meal'. Hot or cold appetizer served at the beginning of an Italian meal. Typical antipasti (plural) include olives, bruschetta, marinated or pickled vegetables, prosciutto and other cured meats, salads, fish and many other ingredients.

antojitos | MEXICAN | Translates to 'little whims' and refers to small portions of food served as appetizers.

anu | PERUVIAN | (*Tropaeolum tuberosum*) Important root vegetable grown in the High Andes and eaten after boiling.

Anzac biscuit | AUSTRALIAN | Crunchy round biscuit made with rolled oats, flour, sugar, butter, coconut and golden syrup. Given this name during World War I when, due to the fact that they don't contain eggs, which were rationed at the time, the biscuit became a popular treat to send to the ANZAC troops overseas.

ao nori | JAPANESE | Dried, flaked version of nori seaweed. Used primarily as a condiment over dishes such as soups, rice or noodles.

ao noriko | JAPANESE | Dried, powdered form of nori seaweed. Used as a seasoning agent and sold in bottles.

aojiso | JAPANESE | Green perilla. *see also* SHISO.

apéritif | FRENCH | 'Aperitivo' in Italian. Alcoholic drink served before meals to stimulate the appetite and cleanse the palate.

appareil | FRENCH | Culinary term for blending together various ingredients necessary for a particular dish.

Appellation d'Origine Contrôlée (AOC) | FRENCH | French legal system that protects the regional names of traditional wines and foods with a high reputation by disallowing them to be duplicated elsewhere and still called by the same name: for example, Roquefort, which was the first cheese to be protected by an AOC in 1926.

Appenzeller | SWISS | Name-controlled firm cow's-milk cheese with ivory-hued interior, some small round holes and pebbly, golden-brown rind. It is steeped in cider or white wine and spices during maturation, giving a pronounced fruity taste. Used as a table cheese and to replace Gruyère in cooking.

appetiser Food served before meals to stimulate the appetite, such as hors d'oeuvre, canapés or nibbles such as salty nuts; also a first course of a meal.

apple (*Malus* spp.) With some 25 species and thousands of known varieties, the apple is the most widely cultivated tree fruit. Fruits vary in size and shape, taste and crispness according to species and variety, ranging from small, wild crab-apples, to universally cultivated dessert and cooking apples. Dessert apples such as Fuji, Red Delicious and Jonathan have crisp, sweet flesh and are eaten raw, often in fruit and vegetable salads. Apples with a tart, acid taste like the Granny Smith and Golden Delicious are usually cooked and used in sauces, pastries, desserts, puddings, pies and tarts, etc. Some apples are suitable for cider-making and for distilling (Calvados), others for drying. Apples provide vitamins A and C, and are an excellent source of dietary fiber. *see also* CRAB-APPLE, GOLDEN DELICIOUS, FUJI, GALA, GRANNY SMITH, JONATHAN, PINK LADY, *and* RED DELICIOUS.

apple bonne femme | FRENCH | Cored apples stuffed with mixture of butter and caster sugar and baked in a little water in the oven.

apple brandy *see* CALVADOS *and* APPLEJACK.

apple brown betty | ENGLISH | Baked pudding consisting of sliced apples, buttered breadcrumbs, brown sugar and spices.

apple corer Small tubular kitchen utensil used for removing apple cores.

apple mint (*Mentha suaveolens*) Popular culinary herb with the combined aroma of spearmint and apples. Used in drinks, sauces, jellies, fruit and meat dishes.

apple pandowdy *see* PANDOWDY.

apple strudel *see* STRUDEL.

applejack | AMERICAN | An apple brandy with a high alcohol content and a minimum maturation period of two years in wooden casks.

apricot (*Prunus armeniaca*) Aromatic stone fruit with velvety, golden-yellow skin and rich yellow or orange flesh. Native to China, the apricot is cultivated throughout the temperate regions of the world. It is eaten fresh, stewed or poached or cooked in a variety of sweet dishes and pastries; also preserved in syrup or brandy, or made into jam, jellies, wines and liqueurs. Dried apricots are a rich source of vitamin A and iron and make an excellent snack. They can be reconstituted by soaking in hot water for 30 minutes and are used in baked goods, compotes, stuffing, preserves and ice-creams.

apron Small European river fish belonging to the perch family. Served fried.

aqua | ITALIAN | Water. Aqua minerale is mineral water.

aquaculture Fish farming. The rearing of fish, shellfish and some sea vegetables under controlled conditions to supplement the natural supply. Oysters, clams, scallops and mussels are farmed successfully throughout most of the world, as are carp and trout. In recent decades many different species have been raised successfully including prawns, marron, abalone, trout, Atlantic salmon, tuna and barramundi. Salmon is also raised in the United States, Canada, Scotland and Norway. The sturgeon of caviar fame is raised in Russia.

aquavit | SCANDINAVIAN | Derived from the Latin *aqua vitae* (water of life). Potent clear spirit distilled from grain or potatoes, usually infused with caraway seeds, cumin or aniseed. Served icy cold as a short drink. Also known as 'schnapps'.

aragosta | ITALIAN | Spiny lobster.

arak / arrack Potent and coarse alcoholic spirit that may be distilled from grapes, palm sap, rice, dates or cane. In the Middle East arak is distilled from dates and infused with aniseed.

arame | JAPANESE | (*Eisenia bicyclis*) Dried seaweed with large, firm fronds that turn dark brown when cooked. It is rinsed thoroughly with plenty of cold water to remove any grit. It will expand considerably in cooking and is usually simmered in soups.

arbol chili Tiny hot green chilies used fresh in Mexico, Japan, Thailand and India.

arborio rice | ITALIAN | Variety of short-grained rice which absorbs the cooking liquid well, while still retaining its shape and creamy texture. Used to make risotto. Superfino arborio rice has a larger grain and is considered the best for risotto.

arbutus berry (*Arbutus unedo*) Also known as 'strawberry tree'. Red berry-like fruit obtained from a small, bushy tree cultivated in the south of France for its rather tart berries. Used to make wine, spirits and the liqueur Crème d'Arbouse.

archiduc | FRENCH | Name given to dishes with a Hungarian influence, served with a rich creamy onion sauce cooked in butter and paprika.

ardennaise (à l') | FRENCH | Generally a dish of game birds or meat with juniper berries.

Argenteuil | FRENCH | (1) District in France famous for the cultivation of asparagus. (2) Name given to dishes garnished with asparagus or served with a sauce of puréed asparagus.

arista | ITALIAN | Roast loin of pork.

arlésienne (à l') | FRENCH | In the style of Arles, a town in Provence. Dishes are garnished with tomatoes, fried onion rings and eggplant.

Armagnac | FRENCH | Name-controlled high quality brandy aged in special black oak. Produced in the Armagnac area in Gascony, south-western France.

aromates | FRENCH | Any aromatic herb, spice or vegetable used to enhance the taste and aroma of food and drinks.

aromatic ginger | *see* KENCUR.

arrabbiata sauce | ITALIAN | Hot pasta sauce made with tomatoes, tomato purée, garlic, fresh red chilies, white wine and chopped parsley. Traditionally served with penne and sprinkled with grated Pecorino.

arrosto | ITALIAN | Roast of meat.

arrowhead (*Sagittaria sinensis*) Starchy edible corm obtained from a swamp plant with leaves shaped like arrowheads. Cultivated extensively in China and Japan. The vegetable is peeled, sliced and always cooked. Traditionally eaten on Chinese New Year's Eve with pork and hoi sin sauce.

arrowroot (*Maranta* spp.) An easily digestible and nutritious starch obtained from tubers of several tropical plants, sold as a very fine powder. Used as a thickener in soups and sauces, and in making puddings, desserts and biscuits.

arroz | SPANISH | Rice. Arroz con huevos is rice with eggs, arroz con pollo is chicken with rice, and arroz con azafran is saffron rice.

artichoke, globe (*Cynara scolymus*) Large, thistle-like, perennial plant grown for its edible, immature flower heads. Native to Europe it has been grown in its present form since the 15th century. Edible parts include the tightly clinging flower leaves and the fleshy base or heart. When preparing artichokes brush with lemon juice or drop into acidulated water to prevent browning. They are usually steamed and eaten with a dipping sauce, stuffed, or served cold as a salad.

artichoke, Jerusalem (*Helianthus tuberosus*) Fleshy, irregularly shaped, tuberous rhizome related to the sunflower. Cultivated by the American Indians and introduced to Europe in the 16th century. During preparation, Jerusalem artichokes are dropped into acidulated water to prevent browning. They are a good source of iron and are sautéed, roasted, baked, puréed and used in soup.

arugula *see* ROCKET.

asafoetida (*Ferula foetida*) Gum resin obtained from a large fennel-like plant. Reddish-brown with a pungent, garlic-like scent, it is sold as a powder or in lumps. Used mainly in Iran, Afghanistan and India as a condiment in curries, meatballs and pickles; traditionally used to prevent flatulence.

ascorbic acid Also known as 'vitamin C'. An essential vitamin present in citrus fruits, some other fruits and some vegetables. It is vital in the formation and maintenance of collagen, bones, blood vessels and connective tissue, particularly skin, and for the healing of wounds and burns. Humans cannot make their own vitamin C and it must be included in the diet.

ash (*Fraxinus* spp.) The leaves of certain ash trees used for a type of tea or a low alcohol fermented drink.

Asiago | ITALIAN | Granular, cheddar-style, partially skimmed cow's-milk cheese with a smooth, reddish-brown rind. Firm and slightly granular when young, very hard, granular and sharp-tasting when aged. Used as a table cheese when young and for grating and cooking when aged. From the Veneto region.

Asian pear *see* NASHI PEAR.

asparagus (*Asparagus officinalis*) Young, fleshy, spear-like shoots obtained from a spreading perennial plant native to many parts of Europe and western Asia. Used as a vegetable for thousands of years. There are two main forms available: the fleshy white asparagus (grown in darkened conditions to prevent greening), and the slender green variety which is richer in vitamin C and has the best taste. There is also a purple-tipped variety. Fresh asparagus is cooked for the shortest possible time until just tender.

asparagus bean *see* SNAKE BEAN.

aspartame An artificial sweetener sold under the brand name 'Nutrasweet'. Used in 'diet' products such as cola drinks, yoghurts, chewing gum and table sweeteners.

aspic jelly Clear, jelly made from clarified meat stock, rendered gelatinous with calf's feet, shank, veal knuckle or gelatin, and infused with wine or spirits. Also made with fish or vegetable stock. Used for glazing or setting cold cooked food; also cubed or cut into other geometric shapes as a garnish.

Assam tea Full-bodied black tea from a region of north-eastern India.

assiette anglaise | FRENCH | Translates to 'English plate'. Assorted cold meats arranged on a plate, usually served as a first course accompanied by mustard and condiments.

Asti Spumanti | ITALIAN | Slightly sweet, sparkling white wine with moderate alcohol made from white muscat grapes. Produced around Asti, a town in the Piedmont region of north-western Italy.

ataif | MIDDLE EASTERN | Pancakes traditionally dipped in syrup and sprinkled with pistachios, eaten with thick cream. They are served sweet, stuffed with a mixture of chopped nuts, sugar and cinnamon; or filled with Haloumi cheese, Gruyère or feta, then fried until golden brown.

atemoya (*Annnona hybrid*) This close relative to the custard apple is a hybrid between the tropical cherimoya (*A. cherimola*) and sugar apple (*A. squammosa*). Its commercial importance is that the tree will produce fruit in less tropical areas where its parents fail to do so. *see also* CUSTARD APPLE.

Atlantic salmon (*Salmo salar*) Also known as 'salmon trout'. This large, silvery fish with firm, orange flesh is mostly raised on fish farms in south-eastern Australia. It is sold whole or in steaks, cutlets or fillets. The traditional method of cooking whole salmon is to poach it in a court bouillon. Steaks, cutlets and fillets are chargrilled, grilled or pan-fried. Fresh Atlantic salmon can be sliced very thinly and served raw in sashimi or carpaccio. Also smoked and cured (gravlax). The large bright orange roe is a popular sushi topping.

atole | MEXICAN | Sweet milk drink made in various ways, but always thickened with masa (corn dough).

atta | INDIAN | Fine, soft, wheat flour, low in gluten, used to make flat unleavened breads such as chapati.

attereau | FRENCH | Hot hors d'oeuvre of food placed on skewers, coated with a thick sauce and breadcrumbs, and fried. The principal ingredient is usually offal, but an attereau can also be made with vegetables, meatballs or seafood. Served hot.

au bleu | FRENCH | To poach live or freshly killed whole fish (usually trout) in court bouillon or boiling water; the natural slime on the skin will turn a blue shade.

au choix | FRENCH | Of your choice. De choix means 'prime quality'.

au four | FRENCH | Baked in an oven.

au gratin | FRENCH | Food browned under a grill or salamander.

au jus | FRENCH | Meat served with its natural, unthickened pan juices.

au lait | FRENCH | Served or prepared with milk. Café au lait is coffee with warmed or steamed milk.

au naturel | FRENCH | Food served in its natural unadorned state.

aubergine | FRENCH | Eggplant.

aurore sauce | FRENCH | Béchamel sauce with tomato purée, served with eggs and chicken.

auslese | GERMAN | Translates to 'selection'. Wine made from specially selected, perfectly ripened grapes.

Australian flat oyster *see* OYSTER, AUSTRALIAN FLAT.

Australian salmon (*Arripis trutta*) Young fish are also known as 'salmon trout', a name also given to Atlantic salmon. In New Zealand it is known by the Maori name of 'kahawai'. This southern saltwater fish is not a true salmon or trout but is a species of sea perch. The flesh tends to be rather dry and coarse and is not really used as a table fish; it is mostly canned.

autoclave Thick-walled vessel with a tight-fitting lid in which foods are cooked under pressure so that the temperature rises above boiling point. Designed for sterilizing and preserving food.

Auvergne | FRENCH | Region in France noted for its high quality charcuterie, freshwater fish, vegetables, fruit, walnuts, chestnuts and mushrooms. The potato dish 'aligot' is a specialty of the region. Famous cheeses include Bleu d'auvergne, Cantal, Bleu des Causses, Fourme d'ambert and Saint-Nectaire.

avgolemono | GREEK | Classic soup made with chicken stock, egg yolks, rice and lemon juice. The same ingredients are also made into a thick sauce and served with poached or baked fish.

avocado (*Persea americana*) Round to pear-shaped fruit with a smooth, buttery flesh and nut-like taste. Avocados vary in size and shape and the skin may range from the smooth, light green of the **Fuerte**, to the pebbly, dark green or black of **Hass**; **Reed** has a large, round shape with thick, smooth skin and creamy yellow flesh of excellent taste. Little **cocktail** avocados are stoneless. Avocado has a high content of mono-unsaturated fat and is rich in vitamin E and other vitamins and minerals. Avocado is almost always served cold and is popular in salads. Lemon juice sprinkled over cut flesh prevents browning. Avocado is the basis of Mexico's famous dish, guacamole.

awabi | JAPANESE | (*Nordotis* spp.) Abalone.

ayam | INDONESIAN / MALAYSIAN | Chicken.

ayu | JAPANESE | (*Plecoglossus altivelis*) Trout-like freshwater fish with a distinct sweetish taste. Usually salt-grilled. Traditionally ayu were caught from fishing boats by trained cormorants and flares at night. The birds, held on long leashes, have neck rings to prevent them from swallowing. When taken aboard, the ayu is disgorged and transferred immediately to accompanying restaurant boats. Today ayu is mainly caught by rod or trapped.

azuki beans *see* ADZUKI BEANS.

baba ghanoush | MIDDLE EASTERN | Creamy dip of puréed roasted eggplant mixed with garlic, lemon juice and tahini (sesame seed paste) and garnished with chopped parsley and a few black olives. Served with flat bread as an appetizer.

baba / rum baba / baba au rhum Yeast cake studded with raisins or currants and, after cooking, steeped in rum or kirsch. It is baked in tall individual casings (dariole) or as a large cake in a ring (savarin). The origin of rum baba is attributed to the Polish King Stanislas who dipped a kugelhopf in rum, and named the dessert after the fabled Ali Baba.

babaco (*Carica pentagona*) Golden-yellow, oblong fruit with an aromatic and very juicy, creamy flesh. It is believed to be a natural hybrid of two varieties of pawpaw. The taste has been variously described as a blend of pineapple and banana, or pawpaw with a hint of strawberry. Babaco is a good source of vitamins A and C and is best eaten raw when fully ripe.

babmi goreng *see* NASI GORENG.

baccalà | ITALIAN | Salted, dried cod. In France it is called 'morue', in Spain 'bacalao', and in Portugal 'bacalhau'. This dried fish is extremely popular in Mediterranean countries and forms part of many regional dishes. Before cooking it is always soaked overnight with several changes of water, and rinsed thoroughly to remove the salt. *see also* COD, SALTED.

bacon Cured and smoked meat from the back and sides of the pig. It is sold in slices of varying thickness and cuts depending on which part of the animal it comes from. **Slab bacon** is sold in one piece. **Streaky bacon**, cut from the tail-end of the loin, has alternate streaks of fat and lean meat and is frequently used for larding. Bacon pieces, off-cuts and bacon bones are used enhance beans and lentils, soups and stews.

bagel | JEWISH | Doughnut-shaped yeast roll, with a chewy texture and varnished crust that is boiled before being baked. Traditionally served in New York with cream cheese and thinly sliced lox (a type of salted smoked salmon).

bagna cauda | ITALIAN | Hot, buttery sauce consisting of garlic, olive oil, unsalted butter and anchovy fillets and fresh herbs. Served warm or simmering over a small flame and used as a dip for slices of various vegetables. Specialty of Piedmont.

baguette | FRENCH | Classic long thin loaf of bread with a crisp crust.

baharat | MIDDLE EASTERN | Aromatic spice mixture used in marinades, made from paprika, black pepper, ground cumin, cinnamon bark, cloves, coriander seeds, cardamom and nutmeg.

bain-marie Water bath in the form of a bowl or saucepan placed over a larger saucepan or pan of simmering water. Used on top of the stove for keeping mixtures warm, for melting ingredients or to maintain slow, even cooking; used in the oven to cook pâté, meat loaves, mousse, egg dishes, caramel custard and other things that require gentle and even cooking.

bake To cook in an oven by dry heat. Often modified by the presence of water in the form of a water bath or bain-marie.

bake blind To bake an empty uncooked pastry case which is pricked over with a fork, lined with paper and filled with dried beans, rice or special weights before baking.

baked Alaska A dessert of sponge cake topped with a thick slab of firm ice-cream and completely covered with meringue. It is then baked quickly in a hot oven until lightly browned and served immediately.

baked beans | AMERICAN | Also known as 'Boston baked beans'. Slow-cooked dish of dried beans and onions, with molasses, brown sugar, mustard and salt pork. This old Bostonian dish was traditionally cooked on Saturdays to be eaten that evening and the following day.

baking powder Powdered combination consisting of bicarbonate of soda, an acid such as cream of tartar, and a small amount of starch. Used as a raising agent when making cakes and breads.

baking sheet Flat, thin metal sheet with slightly raised sides used for baking biscuits and breads.

baking soda | AMERICAN | Term for bicarbonate of soda.

baklava | GREEK / TURKISH | Very sweet pastry dessert consisting of many thin layers of buttered filo pastry filled with a spicy nut mixture. Immediately after baking, a honey and lemon syrup is poured over the baklava in the pan and left to stand. It is then cut diagonally into diamond shapes to serve.

balacan *see* BLACHAN.

ballottine | FRENCH | Parcel of boned meat, poultry or fish that is stuffed, rolled up (often in cheesecloth) and tied, then braised, poached or roasted. Served hot or cold (when it is often weighted and set or glazed with aspic).

balm *see* LEMON BALM.

Balmain bug (*Ibacus peronii*) Broad, flat-bodied crustacean found in southern Australian waters. The closely related Moreton Bay bug (*Thenus orientalis*) is found in northern coastal waters. Both are also known as 'shovelnose lobsters', 'sand lobsters' and 'bay lobsters'. Sold alive, raw or cooked. Live bugs are placed in the freezer until they die, but not long enough to freeze the flesh. They are then put in cold water which is brought to the boil and cooked for no more than five minutes, then plunged into icy cold water to prevent further cooking. Bugs are served cold in their shells, or alternatively the flesh is extracted from the tail and tossed in a salad dressing. Raw bug meat can also be quickly stir-fried or braised in a wok.

balouza | MIDDLE EASTERN | Blancmange-style chilled pudding made of cornflour, sugar and water, with rose or orange blossom water and chopped almonds or pistachio nuts.

balsam pear *see* BITTER MELON.

balsamic vinegar | ITALIAN | Produced around Modena, this is one of the best-known vintage vinegars. It is made from local trebbiano grapes and aged in a succession of small barrels made of different woods, from five years up to 30 years or more. Genuine aged (for 12 or more years) balsamic vinegar is labelled 'Aceto Balsamico Tradizionale di Modena'. It is a rich, dark shade and has a sweet, mellow taste. Used in salad dressings, marinades and sauces.

Balthazar Large bottle of champagne containing the equivalent of 16 standard bottles.

Baltic herring *see* BISMARCK HERRING *and* ROLLMOP.

bamboo shoots (*Dendrocalamus latiflorus*) Young, tender, ivory shoots with a pointed tip, widely used in Chinese cooking. Sometimes available fresh in produce markets. A parboiled variety in vacuum-sealed plastic packs can be found in Asian specialty shops. Prized for their rich aroma and crunchy texture. Used to add crispness to soups and stir-fried dishes. Canned bamboo shoots have a softer texture; they should be washed well before use.

banana (*Musa paradisiaca*) One of the world's highly valued fruits, the banana is rich in potassium and vitamins A, C and B-group, is high in carbohydrates and low in fat. The best-known eating banana is the **Cavendish**, which has large, almost straight fruit and fragrant, creamy-white soft flesh. Others include the smaller and plump **Lady Finger** and the **sugar banana**, which is short, thin-skinned and also very sweet. The banana is mostly eaten fresh with the thick skin peeled back. Freshly cut banana for fruit salads and side dishes should be brushed with lemon juice to avoid browning. Uncooked they are included in a huge variety of desserts. They are also used in many baked goods and can be barbecued or baked whole in their skin. Ground, **dried banana** is used as a type of flour in baked goods. **Banana leaves** are used as a food wrapping in South-East Asia, the Caribbean and some Latin American countries. The flower is also eaten in South-East Asia and India. The plantain is a green cooking banana. *see also* BANANA FLOWER *and* PLANTAIN.

banana chili *see* HUNGARIAN WAX CHILI.

banana flower (*Musa paradisiaca*) The fat, purple, male flower of the banana plant is appearing more often in fruit markets. It can be cooked in boiling water for about 20 minutes, then stripped of the outer leaves and the tender fleshy part eaten like artichoke leaves; also the pale inner part can be boiled for 15 minutes then sliced and simmered in coconut milk and served hot.

banana passionfruit (*Passiflora mollissima*) Elongated tropical fruit with a slightly downy, yellow skin and rich yellow flesh with a banana-like taste. Used in the same way as passionfruit.

banana split Ice-cream dessert consisting of a banana cut in half, lengthways, topped with ice-cream, coated with a sweet syrup such as chocolate sauce, and decorated with whipped cream and maraschino cherries.

bananas Foster | AMERICAN | A classic dessert created at Brennan's Restaurant, New Orleans. It consists of bananas, cut in half and sliced lengthwise, quickly sautéed in a mixture of butter, brown sugar, banana liqueur and cinnamon. When slightly browned, rum is added to the dish and, when hot, flamed. Served on top of vanilla ice cream.

Banbury cake | ENGLISH | Small, oval pastry made from flaky pastry filled with dried fruit and spices.

bangers and mash | ENGLISH | Sausages served with mashed potato.

Bannock cake | SCOTTISH | Thick, flat cake made of oatmeal and/or barley meal that is generally cooked on a griddle.

Banon | FRENCH | Soft to semisoft cow's- or goat's-milk cheese with a soft natural rind. Usually wrapped in chestnut or grape leaves that have been steeped in white wine or brandy, and tied with raffia. Used as a table cheese. Named after Banon, a village in the Alps of Provence.

bara brith | WELSH | Rich, yeast bread made with currants, raisins, mixed candied fruit peel and spices.

bara cierch | WELSH | Thin, round oatcake, cooked on a griddle or heavy frying pan. Served spread with butter.

Barbados cherry (*Malpighia glabra*) Also known as 'acerola'. Deep red to almost black, cherry-like fruit with thin skin and red, pulpy, sweet flesh when fully ripe. Excellent source of vitamin C. Used in jams, jellies and preserves; also desserts and drinks.

Barbados sugar Moist, fine-textured brown sugar made from the residual syrup after white sugar has been refined out.

Barbaresco | ITALIAN | Full-bodied red wine from Piedmont.

barbecue (1) To cook food (usually outdoors) directly over an open fire of hot charcoal, gas or electricity. **(2)** The name of the cooking apparatus used to cook such food. **(3)** An outdoor social gathering at which barbecued food and salads are served.

barberry (*Berberis* spp.) Elongated berries that are usually red, although some varieties produce black or purple fruit. They are pleasantly acid tasting and a few may be added to fruit salads or compotes, but they are mostly used in pies and preserves. Green berries can be pickled and eaten as capers.

barbouille | FRENCH | Casserole of rabbit or chicken cooked in red wine, with the blood of the animal added at the end of cooking to thicken the sauce.

barbounia *see* RED MULLET.

bard Thin strips of pork fat or bacon which are wrapped around poultry or game birds to keep them moist during roasting. Also used to line pâtés and terrines.

barding To wrap pork-back fat around poultry or game birds to keep them from drying out during roasting.

Bardolino | ITALIAN | Dry, light red wine from around Verona, Veneto.

barfi | INDIAN | Fudge-like confection made from milk and sugar, with various kinds of nuts added.

barley (*Hordeum vulgare*) Cereal grain with only the outer husk removed. It is the most nutritious form of the grain and is most often found in health food stores. Usually added to soups, stews and casseroles, bread, muffins and other baked goods; also used to make beer and whisky. Pearl barley is a polished milled form of the grain, mostly added to soups and stews; also used to make barley water. Rolled barley is steamed and flattened barley used to make porridge, in muesli and baked goods, or as a thickener.

barley sugar | ENGLISH | Twisted stick of confectionery originally made from sugar boiled in barley water.

Barolo | ITALIAN | Quality, full-bodied red wine from Piedmont.

baron A large joint made up of two legs including the saddle, still joined at the backbone; usually from lamb and occasionally from beef. It is roasted in a large oven or spit-roasted.

barquette | FRENCH | Boat-shaped filled pastry tartlet.

barracuda (*Sphyraena* spp.) Generic name given to a number of aggressive fish. The great barracuda (*S. barracuda*) of the tropics is not usually eaten because of the risk of ciguatera (tropical fish poisoning). The smaller Pacific barracuda (*S. argentea*) is a popular eating fish in California where it is usually cut into steaks for grilling or barbecuing.

barramundi (*Lates calcarifer*) Also known as 'giant perch'. This popular sporting fish has a mild-tasting, white flesh with large flakes and fine bones. Sold whole, in fillets or cutlets. Can be grilled, poached, fried, barbecued or baked. The barramundi season is mainly spring and summer. It is also farmed.

Bartlett pear *see* WILLIAM PEAR.

basbousa | MIDDLE EASTERN | Sweet semolina cake baked in the oven, after which it is soaked with a sweet lemon syrup and cut into diamond shapes.

basella (*Basella rubra*) Also known as 'Malabar spinach'. Tropical climber grown for its fleshy leaves. Used as a green vegetable and eaten like spinach.

basil (*Ocimum basilicum*) Also known as 'sweet basil'. Native and annual herb of India and Iran and cultivated in Europe for around 2000 years. Fresh basil leaves feature prominently in Mediterranean cuisine and several varieties are used in South-East Asia and India. They are a key ingredient in pesto and pistou and are renowned for their affiliation with tomatoes. Also used with egg dishes of all kinds, mushrooms, pasta sauces, green vegetables and salads. Basil makes excellent vinegar, the reddish-purple variety will turn the vinegar deep pink.

basil, hoary (*Ocimum canum*) Known as 'manglak' in Thailand. Dwarf annual herb with tiny, slightly hairy, peppery leaves. Used in Thailand sprinkled over salads and in soups; the seeds when soaked develop a gelatinous coating and are used to garnish sweet cool drinks and desserts.

basil, sacred (*Ocimum sanctum*) Native and sacred herb of India, but more often used in Thai cookery. The narrow leaves have a reddish-purple tinge and are used in meat and fish curries, leaving a hot taste on the palate.

basmati rice | INDIAN | White, long-grain rice with a light texture and distinct scented aroma and taste; served on its own or in pilaf.

bass Also known as 'sea bass'. Generally refers to a highly desirable and expensive European fish caught in Mediterranean waters. Prized for its delicate white flesh with few bones. Usually sold whole, it is poached, baked, grilled or braised and is also used raw in sashimi. In the south of France, bass is known as 'loup de mer' (meaning sea wolf) and is used in the classic provençal dish, loup de mer au fenouil, in which the grilled bass is flamed with alcohol over a bed of dried fennel stalks.

baste To moisten meat or vegetables during cooking, often by spooning over the cooking liquid from the dish.

bastela / bastilla | MOROCCAN | Also spelled and pronounced 'pastilla'. Large, flat pie made with fine layers of pastry stuffed with spiced chicken, egg and stock sauce, sautéed almonds, sugar and cinnamon. It is baked until golden brown and cut into diamonds to serve. Traditionally made with pigeon.

bâtarde pain | FRENCH | Translates to 'bastard bread' and refers to a long thin loaf of white bread, larger than a baguette.

Batavian endive (*Cichorium endiva var latifolia*) Called 'escarole' in the United Sates and 'scarole' in France. Broad-leaved form of endive. Used mostly as a salad green.

Bath bun | ENGLISH | Large, rich bun flavoured with candied peel, caraway seeds and sometimes saffron and sprinkled with sugar. Originated in the health resort of Bath.

bâton | FRENCH | Small stick of white bread, smaller than a baguette.

bâtonnet | FRENCH | Vegetables cut into thin strips, about the size of a match-stick. Used as a garnish and in cooking.

battara-zushi *see* SUSHI.

batter Mixture usually based on flour, eggs, milk or water. Used for fritters, pancakes or waffles; can also be used to coat food, such as fish and vegetables before frying.

batterie de cuisine | FRENCH | Cooking equipment and utensils.

battuto | ITALIAN | Mixture of finely chopped vegetables, garlic and parsley, browned in olive oil or butter. Used as a base for soups and stews.

Bavarian cream *see* BAVAROIS.

bavarois | FRENCH | Also known as 'Bavarian cream'. Chilled dessert made from custard, gelatine and whipped cream.

bay (*Laurus nobilis*) Dark green, spicy leaves obtained from a medium-sized tree native to the Mediterranean region. The taste of bay leaves becomes more pungent when dried and they are best used fresh. Used to infuse marinades, soups, sauces, stuffing, stews, many vegetable and meat dishes; also used in white sauces and infused in milk for making custard and other desserts. A bay leaf is an essential part of the classic bouquet garni.

Bayonne ham | FRENCH | Mildly smoked raw ham that has been cured with a mixture of salt, sugar and herbs and dried for up to six months. It is sliced very thinly and served raw as an hors d'oeuvre. Also used in cooked dishes.

bean curd | CHINESE | Highly nutritious, white, custard-like product made from ground soya beans and used extensively in Chinese cooking. Available in a soft form and firm blocks sold in plastic tubs of water. Firm bean curd can be tossed, stir-fried and deep-fried. Soft bean curd requires gentle treatment and is used in soups or late in the cooking. There are also deep-fried bean curd puffs that can be stuffed and bean curd sheets or skins which are used for wrapping. Preserved or fermented bean curd is also available. Japanese-style bean curd is known as 'tofu'. *see also* TOFU.

bean curd, fermented | CHINESE | Cheese-like form of marinated bean curd which may be packed in rice wine and brine, sometimes with various additions such as sesame oil, chili or red rice wine. It is sold in small square cakes in jars and is used for enhancing meat, poultry, vegetarian dishes or as a side dish with rice. Once opened, fermented bean curd will keep for months in its brine or oil if refrigerated.

bean paste *see* BEAN SAUCE *and* MISO.

bean sauce | CHINESE | Also known as 'bean paste'. Rich, pungent sauce made from whole or ground fermented soya beans in many varieties such as yellow, brown or black, sweet, salty or very hot and spicy. Used in marinades, or as a seasoning when cooking meat or vegetables, or as a condiment.

bean sauce, red | CHINESE | Thick, reddish-brown, sweet paste made from puréed red or adzuki beans. Used as a filling for cakes and buns.

bean sprouts | ASIAN | The green type of mung bean is commonly used to sprout. They are cream with green hoods and a crunchy texture. They are high in protein and a good source of vitamin C. When allowed to grow longer and thicker they are called 'bean shoots'. Usually sold by the weight or pre-packed in cellophane bags. Although they can be eaten raw in salads, in most Asian dishes they are briefly cooked or dropped into soup just before serving.

bean thread noodles | CHINESE / SOUTH-EAST ASIAN | Also known as 'green bean vermicelli', 'cellophane', 'transparent' and 'glass' noodles. Very fine, thread-like white noodles made from green mung bean starch. They are sold dried in neat, small or large, tied bundles. Cut them in shorter lengths with scissors, then soak briefly in hot water before using in stir-fries and salads. If adding to soups, hotpots or deep-frying, use straight from the pack. When fried they instantly puff up and become crisp.

beans, dried *see* PULSES. Also adzuki beans, black kidney beans, black-eyed beans, borlotti beans, broad beans, cannellini beans, flageolets, great northern beans, lima beans, haricot beans, pinto beans, red kidney beans, soya beans.

beans, green (*Phaseolus vulgaris*) Also known as 'French beans'. There are many varieties of these slender green vegetables. Fresh green beans are sold mainly by shape, such as round, flat and baby. Most are stringless and need only be topped and tailed. Butter or yellow beans are round yellow beans. They are a good source of vitamin C and other vitamins and minerals and should be cooked briefly until just tender.

beard To remove the hair-like filaments which may be attached to oysters or mussels.

béarnaise | FRENCH | Classic sauce made with egg yolks and butter, with vinegar, shallots and tarragon. Usually served with meat, fish and egg dishes.

beat To stir an ingredient or mixture vigorously to modify its consistency or appearance.

Beaufort | FRENCH | Firm, Swiss-style cow's-milk cheese with smooth, pale interior without holes and thick, natural brushed rind. Used as a table cheese; also excellent for melting. From Savoy Mountains, France.

Beaujolais | FRENCH | Light, fruity red wine, usually drunk when fairly young.

béchamel | FRENCH | Basic white sauce of white roux (flour and butter) to which milk is added. Used for egg, vegetable and gratin dishes and as the base for many other sauces.

bêche de mer *see* SEA CUCUMBER.

beef The meat obtained from adult cattle. When the carcass is butchered it is divided into sides, each of which is again divided into a hindquarter and a forequarter. The forequarter has the following cuts: neck; shoulder, which contains chuck and blade steak; rib section, which is cut into spare ribs, rib roasts, steaks and rib eye (Scotch fillet); brisket, which is below the rib section and is suitable for salting and pot roasts. The hindquarter has the best quality meat and includes the sirloin which contains the fillet, and the rump; the tail end includes topside, round and assorted boneless steaks and roasts such as silverside. The shin and flank which come from both fore and hind legs are usually used in slow-cooked dishes. *see also* BRISKET.

beef Stroganoff / Stroganov | RUSSIAN | Thinly sliced fillet of beef, onions and mushrooms quickly sautéed in butter and coated in sauce made from the pan juices and sour cream. Served with rice.

beef Wellington Fillet of beef that has been coated with pâté de fois gras or duxelles, wrapped in pastry and baked.

beefsteak plant *see* SHISO.

beefsteak tomato *see* TOMATO.

beer Pale amber to dark brown, low-alcohol beverage made from grain, mostly malted barley, hops, yeast and sugar. In cooking, beer is sometimes used as a marinade, as a basis of soups, to lighten batter and to enhance bread and stews. *see also* ALE, LAGER, PILSNER *and* STOUT.

beetroot (*Beta vulgaris*) Dark red, bulbous root which varies in shape from round to oblong according to variety. There are also orange and deep-yellow varieties. Used in the classic borsch, as a vegetable and in salads. To reduce bleeding during cooking leave some stalk attached and do not peel. The fresh leafy tops are also edible and can be cooked like spinach.

beignet | FRENCH | (1) Translates to 'fritter' and refers to food dipped in batter and deep-fried. (2) Spoonfuls of choux pastry cooked like fritters and then dusted in icing sugar.

Bel Paese | ITALIAN | From the Lombardy region. Semisoft cow's-milk cheese with a smooth, creamy interior and washed crust wrapped in yellow wax. Used as a table cheese; also melts well.

belacan *see* BLACHAN.

Belgian endive *see* WITLOOF.

belila | MIDDLE EASTERN | Wheat or barley pudding, sweetened with sugar and lemon syrup with rose or orange blossom water, and decorated with nuts.

bell pepper | AMERICAN | Alternate name for capsicum.

Belle-Hélène | FRENCH | Classic dessert of poached fruit (usually pears) served on vanilla ice cream and coated with hot chocolate sauce.

Bellelay *see* TÊTE-DE-MOINE.

bellevue, en | FRENCH | Term applied to an elaborate presentation of whole fish, lobster, poultry or ham decoratively garnished and usually glazed with aspic.

Bellini Cocktail made with champagne and peach juice and garnished with a slice of peach.

beluga caviar *see* CAVIAR.

Benedictine | FRENCH | Amber, cognac-based liqueur infused with a variety of herbs and parts of plants. It was first made in the 16th century at the Benedictine monastery at Fecamp in Normandy.

beni shoga | JAPANESE | Thinly sliced, red, pickled ginger. *see also* SHOGA.

bento | JAPANESE | Boxed lunch or picnic food often packed in lacquer boxes divided into compartments. The food must be able to be served at room temperature, easy to eat and hold up well when prepared ahead of time. Bento bought at railway stations in Japan is called 'ekiben'.

berceau | FRENCH | Hand-held chopping utensil with a wide curved blade and upright handle at each end.

Bercy sauce | FRENCH | Fish stock based, velouté sauce with white wine, shallots and finely chopped parsley. Traditionally served with poached fish. Bercy butter is made with beef marrow, butter, chopped shallots, lemon juice, parsley and seasoning; served with grilled meat or fish. Named after a district in Paris.

bergamot (*Monarda didyma*) Leaves obtained from a perennial herb native to North America. Used sparingly in salads and stuffings, but mostly used in a herbal tea. The tea was used by the Oswego Indians and early colonists for its soothing and relaxing effect.

bergamot orange (*Citrus bergamia*) Variety of bitter orange cultivated for its oil. Used in perfumery. Its highly aromatic peel is used in Earl Grey tea; it is also candied.

Berlin doughnut Ball-shaped doughnut filled with jam and coated with sugar.

berliner Devon-style, soft-textured sausage made from veal and pork, pepper and nutmeg.

berries Small edible fruits from various species of plants often associated with trailing, bramble-like plants (*Rubus* spp.), but mulberries grow on trees, blueberries and gooseberries come from bushes and strawberries are produced on low-spreading ground covers. Berries are usually sold in punnets and should be firm and dry, with their natural bloom still evident. Being highly perishable they should be used as soon as possible. Wash just before using. Berries are eaten as a fresh fruit, in fruit salads, mousses, ice cream, pies and summer puddings; also made into sauces and coulis, jams and preserves. *See also* ARBUTUS BERRY, BARBERRY, BILBERRY, BLACKBERRY, BLACKCURRANT, BLUEBERRY, BOYSEN- BERRY, CAPE

GOOSEBERRY, CRANBERRY, ELDERBERRY, GOOSEBERRY, JUNIPER BERRY, LOGANBERRY, MULBERRY, RASPBERRY, REDCURRANT, STRAWBERRY, YOUNGBERRY.

besan | INDIAN | (*Cicer arietinum*) Also known as 'chickpea flour'. Flour made from a small variety of chickpea. Used in a batter for fritters and as a thickener for sauces and stews.

betacarotene A form of vitamin A that causes fruit and vegetables to be orange, yellow and red. It is an excellent anti-oxidant. Found in the carrot, mango, pawpaw, persimmon and sweet potato.

beurre | FRENCH | Butter.

beurre blanc | FRENCH | Classic white sauce reduction of vinegar, white wine and shallots with cold butter whisked in. Served warm with fish, poultry and vegetables.

Beurre Bosc Also known as 'Bosc'. Tall, tapered pear with light brown skin. It has a fine juicy texture with a sweet tart taste. A good eating pear that holds its elegant shape well when poached or baked. *see also* PEAR.

beurre compose | FRENCH | Translates to 'compound butter'.

beurre fondue | FRENCH | Melted butter, sometimes with lemon juice added when served with fish.

beurre manié | FRENCH | Paste made from well-blended equal parts of softened butter and flour. Used to thicken sauces and stews.

beurre noir | FRENCH | Sauce of browned butter, lemon juice or vinegar, capers and parsley. Served with poached fish and brains.

beurre noisette | FRENCH | Simple, hot sauce for poached fish, vegetables and sweetbreads, made by cooking butter over a low heat until a light golden brown.

bhel puri | INDIAN | Snack of chickpea chutney served on miniature deep-fried puris. Often sold in India from stalls in bazaars and on beaches.

bicarbonate of soda Also called 'sodium bicarbonate'. An alkaline powder used as a raising agent when combined with batters containing an acid ingredient such as buttermilk. It is an ingredient of baking powder. Bicarbonate of soda was once added to the cooking water to keep beans or peas bright green, but it destroys their vitamin C content and is not recommended.

Bierkäse | GERMAN | Translates to 'beer cheese'. *see* WEISSLACKERKÄSE.

bigarde sauce | FRENCH | Bitter orange sauce consisting of a rich, brown sauce infused with the zest and juice of Seville oranges. Served with duck and game.

bigos | POLISH | Slow-cooked one-pot casserole consisting of layers of sauerkraut, sausages and other cooked meats.

bilberry (*Vaccinium myrtillus*) Also known as 'huckleberry'. Small variety of blueberry grown wild in the UK and other parts of Europe. Used in tarts, jams, wine and confectionery; also stewed and served with cream.

billy by / bilibi | FRENCH | Creamy mussel soup. Served hot or cold with fresh cream.

biltong | SOUTH AFRICAN | Dried strips of lean beef or game, with a strong taste, that can be sliced and eaten raw. *see also* JERKY.

bind To thicken with flour or other starch; also to hold stuffing together with cream or beaten raw egg.

Bintje potato *see* POTATO.

bird's nest | CHINESE | Expensive, dried, shallow nest made from the white gelatinous saliva secreted by Asian swiftlets and used by the birds to coat and attach their nest to deep crevices and dark cave walls. A less expensive grade are bits of pieces of bird's nest known as 'dragon's teeth'. Used in the classic speciality bird's-nest soup. They are soaked overnight and cleaned before use.

birds' eye chili | SOUTH-EAST ASIAN | Also known as 'pequín'. Very hot, oval-shaped, tiny, bright red chili. Used in condiments and stir-fries.

biriani / biryani | INDIAN | Dish made with spiced saffron rice steamed with a layer of curried lamb, chicken or beef.

biscotto | ITALIAN | Twice-cooked biscuit first baked in a loaf shape, cooled, sliced and rebaked in the oven. The result is a crisp, porous biscuit. Biscotti (plural) are designed to be dipped into espresso coffee or sweet dessert wine.

biscuit Small, dry flat cake that is usually baked.

Bismarck herring Also known as 'Baltic herring'. Herring pickled in white wine vinegar and spices, sold as flat fillets. When rolled and secured with a toothpick it becomes a rollmop.

Bison potato *see* POTATO.

bisque Thick, rich seafood soup, made with lobster, crab or prawns, often infused with brandy.

bitter melon | CHINESE / SOUTH-EAST ASIAN | (*Momordica charantia*) Also known as 'balsam pear'. Pale yellowish-green, ridged and warty, cucumber-like vegetable with a tart taste. Usually sliced and the inner pith and seeds removed. Used in soups, stir-fried and braised dishes; also the rings are blanched then stuffed with a seasoned pork filling before braising. Bitter melon is also made into a pickle in India.

bitters Generic term for various alcoholic drinks and essences extracted from aromatic bark, roots and herbs. Those bitters used as a digestive aid or aperitif and taken with soda include Fernet Branca and Campari from Italy. Bitters used as an additive are Angostura from Trinidad and Peychaud from New Orleans.

blachan | SOUTH-EAST ASIAN | Also known as 'trasi'. Strong-smelling paste made from salted and fermented dried shrimps. Sold in jars, packages or cans. Should always be fried before use. Used frequently in South-East Asian cooking. It is a rich source of protein and vitamin B and when cooked there is no trace of the smell.

black beans, salted | CHINESE / SOUTH-EAST ASIAN | (*Glycine max*) Also known as 'fermented black beans'. Small black soybeans that are fermented with salt and spices (often ginger) and sold in sealed plastic bags or cans. Lightly chopped or crushed they are used in steamed, braised and stir-fried dishes. Once opened, they will keep in a covered container in the refrigerator for up to a year. Blackbean paste or sauce has a smoother consistency and is used in the same way.

black bream *see* LUDERICK.

black bun | SCOTTISH | Rich spice and fruitcake mixture that is enclosed in a pastry cake. Cooked at least a week in advance and is traditionally served on New Year's Eve.

black cumin *see* NIGELLA.

Black Forest cake | GERMAN | Schwarzwalder Kirschtorte. Rich, elaborate cake made with three layers of chocolate sponge soaked in Kirsch syrup and filled with whipped cream with Kirsch and cherries. The sides and top are covered with more whipped cream and decorated with cherries and chocolate curls. It originated in the Black Forest area of Bavaria in southern Germany.

black fungus *see* WOOD EAR FUNGUS.

black kidney beans (*Phaseolus vulgaris*) Medium-sized, black, kidney-shaped dried beans. Robust, sweet taste. After soaking overnight they are simmered for about an hour. Used in Mexican dishes.

black pudding Also known as 'blood sausage'. Thickish black sausage made from seasoned pig blood, fat, oatmeal and a range of different seasonings. Traditionally fried or grilled and served with mashed potatoes.

black rice | SOUTH-EAST ASIAN | Long-grain, dark brown rice with a bran coating which gives it a sticky texture when cooked and imparts a dark hue to the dish. Often served as a dessert combined with freshly grated coconut or coconut milk and sugar.

black Russian Cocktail made with two parts vodka to one part coffee liqueur such as Kahlúa, served on ice.

black salsify *see* SALSIFY.

black salt | INDIAN | Coarse, almost black, mined salt. Used in masalas and herb pastes.

black sapote *see* SAPOTE.

black tea (*Camellia sinensis*) Fully fermented tea producing a dark brown brew. The main type used in Western blends.

black truffles *see* TRUFFLES.

black trumpet mushroom *see* TROMPETTE DE LA MORT.

black velvet Cocktail made with half champagne and half Guinness.

black-eyed beans (*Vigna sinensis*) Medium-sized, creamy, kidney-shaped dried beans with a black, circular splotch. After soaking they are simmered for about 45 minutes. Used in soups, casseroles or salads.

blackberry (*Rubus fruticosus*) Also known as 'bramble'. Shiny black berries with small hard seeds. They are a good source of calcium, vitamins B and C and minerals. Eaten raw or in fruit salads, tarts and summer pudding. When used as a purée or sauce, the pulp is strained and the seeds discarded.

blackcurrant (*Ribes nigrum*) Small round black berry valued for its high vitamin C content. Its taste is generally acid and it is often mixed with other berries or used in a variety of desserts such as summer pudding or pies; also made into jams, syrups, cordials and liqueurs, such as cassis.

blackened fish | CAJUN AMERICAN | Highly spiced fish fillet cooked very quickly at a very high temperature. The surface should be well charred and crispy on each side, and the interior just cooked and moist. Served with unsalted butter and lemon sauce.

blackfish *see* LUDERICK.

blade steak Cut of beef that comes from the animal's shoulder blade.

blanch (1) To cook raw ingredients in boiling water (often for a very short time) which are then plunged into cold water, or simply drained. Blanching removes bitterness (in onions) or saltiness (in bacon) or loosens the skins for easy peeling or skinning (in almonds or tomatoes). Also lightly cooks and helps retain brightness of green vegetables such as asparagus and green beans. **(2)** Growing technique which excludes light from vegetables in order to prevent greening. Used for white asparagus, leeks, witlof, etc.

blancmange Chilled almond milk pudding.

blanquette | FRENCH | Classic stew of white meat or poultry, thickened with a roux and enriched with cream and egg yolks.

blend To mix ingredients together until well combined.

blender Small electrical appliance with a set of whirling blades in a heat-proof glass goblet used to grind, purée, chop and mix ingredients to make a paste. A hand-held blender is useful to take to the pot used for cooking to purée soups such as pumpkin and vichyssoise.

Bleu d'Auvergne | FRENCH | Blue vein cow's-milk cheese with a firm whitish interior with well-spaced veins and naturally formed crust. Used as a table cheese at the end of a meal. Produced mainly in dairies and on some farms in the province of Auvergne.

Bleu de Bresse | FRENCH | Factory-produced blue vein cow's-milk cheese with a soft, creamy-white interior with blue streaks, and a thin natural crust. Best consumed when young. Used as a table cheese at the end of a meal. From the Bresse area in the Rhône-Alps region.

Bleu de Corse | FRENCH | Blue vein sheep's-milk cheese similar to Roquefort, but not cured in the cellars of Aveyron and not considered as fine. Used as a table cheese at the end of a meal.

Bleu de Gex *see* BLEU DE HAUT-JURA.

Bleu de Haut-Jura | FRENCH | Also known as 'Bleu de Gex' and 'Bleu de Septmoncel'. Highly regarded blue vein cow's-milk cheese with a creamy, white interior with heavy, blue veining and a thin, natural crust. Used as a table cheese at the end of a meal. Made in only a few small dairies and farms in the Departments of Ain and Jura.

Bleu de Septmoncel *see* BLEU DE HAUT-JURA.

Bleu des Causses | FRENCH | Blue vein, unpasteurised cow's-milk cheese with a semisoft, ivory-white interior with blue-green streaks, and a natural, salty crust. Used as a table cheese at the end of a meal. Mainly from commercial dairies in southern Auvergne.

blini | RUSSIAN | Small yeast pancake made with a mixture of wheat and buckwheat flour. Traditionally served with caviar or smoked fish and sour cream.

blintz | JEWISH | Thin pancake that is cooked on one side only; it is then rolled around a filling and then fried.

bloaters | ENGLISH | Golden, lightly salted smoked herrings, larger than kippers but with a milder taste.

blondir | FRENCH | To shallow-fry in butter, oil or fat to a very pale brown .

blood orange (*Citrus sinensis*) Variety of sweet orange with juicy aromatic flesh that can vary from bright red to ruby-red. It is eaten fresh or used in salads. The juice and shredded blanched zest of the Maltese blood orange is added to hollandaise sauce to make maltaise sauce. Served with poached fish and cooked green vegetables.

blood sausage *see* BLACK PUDDING.

bloody Mary Cocktail made with vodka and tomato juice, with lemon juice, Worcestershire sauce, Tabasco sauce, pepper and celery salt.

Blue Castello | DANISH | Brie-like, blue vein cow's-milk cheese with a soft, whitish interior with a few large, blue veins and a faint, reddish-brown rind. Served as a table cheese at the end of a meal.

blue cheese Any of the many varieties of cheese marbled or streaked with blue or green veins. Most are made from cow's milk, although the most famous blue cheese of France, **Roquefort**, is made from sheep's milk. Spores of *Penicillium roqueforti* (*P. glaucum* in Italy) are added either during coagulation, or more frequently during curding. This fungus gives the blue veining. The mold, during varying periods of ripening, grows both in small irregular natural openings in the cheese, and in fine perforations that are made by the cheesemaker either with a long, slender needle or, more commonly, by machine. Roquefort and some Gorgonzolas **in** Italy are ripened in damp caves or cellars, the atmosphere of which imparts a distinctive character to the cheeses. A good blue cheese may be soft and creamy or firm and crumbly in texture, ivory or cream with a characteristic sharp, tangy taste and a hint of salt; the veins should be evenly distributed. Blue cheeses are usually wrapped in foil. Well-known blue cheeses in addition to those mentioned above include **Bleu de Bresses** and **Bleu d'Auvergne** (French), **Danish Blue** (Danish), **Blue Stilton** and **Blue Cheshire** (English), **Edelpilz** (German). Blue cheese is served mostly at the end of a meal.

Blue Cheshire | ENGLISH | Firm, blue vein cow's-milk cheese with a yellow-orange interior with bluish-green veins and traditionally cloth-wrapped with a natural rind. Used as a table cheese, as a snack with fresh fruit or at the end of a meal. From the Cheshire area and nearby counties.

blue mackerel *see* MACKEREL.

blue manna crab *see* BLUE SWIMMER CRAB.

blue mussel *see* MUSSELS.

Blue Orchid *see* TARAGO RIVER CHEESE COMPANY.

blue swimmer crab (*Portunus pelagicus*) Also known as 'sand crab'. This medium-sized blue, purple and white crab is widely distributed in Australian waters. The sweet white meat is often considered the finest-tasting of the Australian crabs. It is sold whole, dead or cooked. After cooking it is served whole with the shell cracked, or the flesh extracted from the body and tossed in a salad dressing. *see also* CRABS.

blue warehou *see* WAREHOU, BLUE.

blue-eye / blue-eye cod (*Hyperoglyphe antarctica*) Also known as 'blue-eye trevalla' and 'deepsea trevalla/trevally'. Large, silvery-grey, deep-bodied fish found in deep water in southern Australia. It has firm, pale-pink flesh with a few large bones and is usually sold in cutlets and fillets. Smaller fish are sometimes available whole. Can be grilled, pan-fried, barbecued, poached or steamed.

blueberry (*Vaccinium* spp.) Small, black or dark blue, rounded berries with a natural waxy bloom. Several varieties are grown in Australia and they are available from late spring to early autumn. They are low in kilojoules, an excellent source of vitamin A and have high levels of vitamin C. They are eaten fresh or used in muffins, pancakes, summer pudding, ice cream, cheesecake, pies and cakes; also stewed or made into preserves, jams, or sauces.

bocconcini | ITALIAN | Translates to 'little mouthfuls'. Small balls of mozzarella often displayed floating in bowls of whey. When fresh they should have a moist, springy, yielding texture and be able to slice neatly. Served as an antipasto, often sliced, topped with a slice of tomato and fresh basil and drizzled with olive oil, known as 'insalata caprese'.

boeuf | FRENCH | Beef. Boeuf bourguignon is a beef stew made with red wine, mushrooms, small whole onions and pieces of bacon.

bohémienne (à la) | FRENCH | Gypsy style; often with tomatoes, capsicums and garlic served with plain rice.

boil To cook food submerged in a rapidly boiling liquid at 100°C (212°F).

bok choy | CHINESE | (*Brassica chinensis*) Also known as 'pak choy' and 'Chinese chard'. Green vegetable with long, white, fleshy stems topped with dark green crinkly leaves. There are a number of types of bok choy available including ones with pale green stems, also known as '**Shanghai bok choy**' or '**baby bok choy**', and an even smaller version sold as '**moon bok**'. Both the stems and the leaves are used, but are sometimes separated before cooking as the leaves will cook much more quickly. Used in stir-fried dishes or cooked as a vegetable. Small bok choys can be steamed or braised whole.

bok choy, rosette | CHINESE | (*Brassica chinensis* var. *rosularis*) Also known as 'tat soi'. Leafy green vegetable with small, dark green, puckered leaves in a perfect flat rosette. The individual leaves are steamed, braised or used in soup or stir-fried dishes.

boletus *see* CEPS.

bollito misto | ITALIAN | Classic mixed meat stew originating in Piedmont. It consists of various meats, such as beef, veal knuckle, ox tongue, chicken, pork sausage (cotechino) or a zampone, cooked together in a stock with onions, carrots, celery, herbs and seasoning until all the meats are tender. Served hot with salsa verde, a green sauce made with oil, lemon juice, parsley, capers and garlic.

bologna *see* MORTADELLA.

Bolognese sauce | ITALIAN | Rich, meat pasta sauce originating in Bologna in northern Italy where it is known as 'ragu'. Traditionally served with tagliatelle and topped with grated Parmesan cheese. *see also* RAGU.

boloney | AMERICAN | Mortadella.

bombay duck | INDIAN | This is not duck, but dried salted fish used to enhance curry dishes. When deep-fried or grilled in small pieces it is eaten as a snack or served as an accompaniment to a meal.

bombe Alaska Dome-shaped baked Alaska that is baked quickly in a hot oven until the meringue surface is golden brown.

bombe glacée | FRENCH | Dome-shaped frozen dessert layered and packed in a bombe mold. The sides of the chilled mold are lined with a firm plain ice-cream, then the inside filled with a softer mousse-like or custard mixture, often with fruit, nuts or liqueur.

bonbon | FRENCH | Piece of confectionery.

bonbonniere | FRENCH | Small, ornate box with lid for holding sweets. Dated from 19th century in France.

bone marrow Soft, fatty substance found inside long bones.

boning Removal of bones from meat, poultry, fish, etc.

bonito (*Sarda* spp.) This elongated, silvery fish with dark grey stripes along the body is a member of the large mackerel family and has firm oily flesh with a strong taste. It can be baked with herbs or barbecued. The belly section of the bonito is considered the best part and when very fresh is used as sashimi. Many Japanese dishes used shaved flakes of dried bonito called 'katsoubushi'.

bonito flakes Known as 'katsoubushi' in Japan. Dried, smoked and then shaved flakes of the bonito, a member of the mackerel family. Used together with kombu seaweed and water to make the basic stock, dashi. Also sprinkled on soups as a garnish and as a condiment.

bonne femme | FRENCH | Home-style cooking or simply cooked; often includes white wine sauce with shallots and mushrooms.

bookmaker sandwich Cold, toasted steak sandwich, spread with English mustard.

borage (*Borage officinalis*) Decorative annual herb grown for its wrinkled, cucumber-scented leaves and edible blue flowers. Only the young leaves are used in salads, added to cool summer drinks or cooked as a vegetable and eaten like spinach. The pretty star-shaped flowers are used to garnish salads or for cake decoration.

bordelaise sauce | FRENCH | Wine sauce made with bone marrow and shallots and red or white wine, depending on the food it is to accompany.

borek | MIDDLE EASTERN | Small pastries made with sheets of filo pastry filled with white cheese, spinach or minced meat, made into triangles or rolls and deep-fried or baked. Served hot as an appetizer or first course.

borlotti beans (*Phaseolus vulgaris*) Also known as 'cranberry beans'. Large, pale brown beans speckled with reddish markings. Available fresh in their pods and shelled like peas; also in dried form. Used in Italian dishes, particularly soups and bean salads. The red markings fade with cooking. Dried borlotti beans must be soaked overnight before cooking.

borsch / borscht | RUSSIAN | Hot or cold soup made with fresh beetroot. There are many versions with greatly differing ingredients. Some are made with beef, chicken or vegetable stock and may also include meat. Traditionally served with sour cream; the meat is always served separately.

Bosc *see* BEURRE BOSC.

boscaiola sauce | ITALIAN | Rich pasta sauce made with fresh or dried mush- rooms, butter, onions, garlic, tomatoes, dry white wine, sage leaves and seasoning. Sometimes mascarpone cheese and crumbled Gorgonzola cheese are added to the sauce before serving. Any Italian dish with the name boscaiola includes mushrooms in some form.

Boston baked beans *see* BAKED BEANS.

Botrytis cinerea Also called 'noble rot'. A grey mold which develops on the skins of ripening grapes and gradually dehydrates the fruit, intensifying both the concentration of sugar and taste. The grapes are used to make naturally sweet white wines such as Sauternes in France.

bottarga | ITALIAN | Cured, pressed tuna roe from Sardinia. Served as an appetiser or shaved over pasta.

bottle gourd (*Lagenaria siceraria*) Also known as 'calabash'. Closely related to pumpkins and squashes, gourds are cooked in much the same way. The bottle gourd, which resembles a large, bottle-shaped cucumber, is so-called because when dried, with the pith removed, it is used as a container. Popular in India and the West Indies where immature gourds are used in curries and stews; also used in Chinese stir-fries and soups.

botvinia / botvinya | RUSSIAN | Cold green vegetable soup with fish and added horseradish and lemon juice.

bouchée | FRENCH | Small, bite-sized pastry case filled with various cream fillings. Served hot as an hors d'oeuvre. Also refers to a petit four.

boudin blanc | FRENCH | Translates to 'white pudding'. Fine-textured, white- meat sausage made from minced chicken, veal or pork, fat, cream, eggs, flour and seasonings. It is poached or gently sautéed, baked in the oven or wrapped in buttered paper and grilled.

boudin noir Translates to 'black pudding'. *see* BLACK PUDDING.

bouillabaisse | FRENCH | Classic Mediterranean fish soup made with a variety of the freshest local fish and shellfish cooked in a broth of water, olive oil, onions, garlic, tomatoes, herbs, dried orange peel and saffron. Traditionally the fish is served separately from the soup, which is poured over slices of dry garlic-rubbed French bread and accompanied by rouille sauce. The scorpion fish (or rascasse) is considered an essential ingredient of bouillabaisse.

bouillon | FRENCH | Strong, clear stock made from meat, vegetables or fish.

Boulette d'Avesnes | FRENCH | Strong-tasting, soft cow's-milk cheese traditionally made by mixing visually defective Maroilles cheese with parsley, tarragon and spices. This is shaped by hand into a cone and tinted red with paprika. Served as a snack or at the end of a meal. *see also* MAROILLES.

bouquet garni | FRENCH | Small bunch of fresh herbs tied with a long thread, used in stocks, soups, stews, casseroles and sauces. It is discarded before serving. Classic herbs are two sprigs parsley, one sprig thyme and a bay leaf, but marjoram, rosemary and sage are sometimes included. In Provence a strip of orange peel is sometimes added for beef and pork dishes.

bourbon | AMERICAN | Kentucky whisky distilled from fermented corn.

bourgeoise (à la) | FRENCH | Family-style braised dish containing carrots, small onions, braised lettuce and bacon.

bourguignon (à la) | FRENCH | Burgundy style. Often with red wine, onions, mushrooms and bacon, boeuf bourguignon for example.

bourride | FRENCH | Mediterranean fish dish containing a variety of white sea fish, and sometimes shellfish. The fish are poached in a fish stock that is thickened with egg yolks and aïoli. Served with fresh bread, plain boiled potatoes and extra aïoli.

bowles mint *see* MINT.

boxty | IRISH | Fried, crispy pancakes made with grated raw potatoes, flour, salt and milk. Served with fried or grilled bacon.

boysenberry (*Rubus* spp.) Elongated, dark red berry thought to be a hybrid of the blackberry, loganberry and raspberry. Popular in the United States, but also grown in Australia. It is served fresh with cream or used in pies, summer pudding, ice-cream, jams, syrups and cordials.

brains The best brains are obtained from calves, but those from lamb, pork and beef are also eaten. They are washed well and soaked in cold water for one or two hours. The fine membrane is then removed under cold running water to dissolve any blood. They are then simmered in acidulated water for 15 minutes, after which they are ready for further cooking, such as gently frying in butter, poaching or baking.

braise To cook whole or pieces of meat, fish, poultry or vegetables that have been first seared on all sides in oil and/or fat, and then cooked slowly in a tightly covered vessel containing a small amount of liquid, on the stove or (more usually) in the oven.

bran The thin outer layers of wheat or other grains removed during the early stages of milling. An excellent source of dietary fiber, used in breakfast cereals, in cakes, breads and biscuits.

brandade | FRENCH | Smooth, rich paste of salt cod (that has been soaked overnight) olive oil and milk or cream and sometimes crushed garlic and/ or lemon juice. Served with triangles of fried bread. Brandade de morue is a speciality of Provence. *see* COD, SALTED.

brandy Distilled spirit made from fermented fruit juice or wine.

brandy butter | ENGLISH | Sweetened, beaten butter with brandy and a little grated orange rind. Traditionally served with Christmas pudding.

brandy snap Crisp, wafer-thin biscuit that is shaped in a roll, cone or basket while still hot.

brassado | FRENCH | Small cake shaped like a doughnut that is poached in boiling water, then baked like a bagel. Speciality of Provence.

brasserie | FRENCH | Licensed cafe or informal restaurant where some meals are served at any time of the day or night.

bratwurst | GERMAN | Type of sausage made from pork and veal and seasoned with herbs and spices. Usually sold raw, and fried or grilled before eating.

brawn Also known as 'head cheese'. Loaf-shaped terrine traditionally made from pig's-head meat with various seasonings and set in its own aspic. When cool it is unmolded and cut into slices.

Brazil nut (*Bertholettia excelsa*) Creamy, three-sided nut with a dark brown skin enclosed in a tough, angular, grey-brown shell. Rich in vitamin E and thiamin. Eaten raw or roasted as a snack or in salads; also used in cakes, slices, fruit breads and confectionery; Brazil nut oil is used in salad dressings.

bread A universal staple food made from flour and water. European type breads usually contain yeast, are kneaded, shaped into loaves and baked in the oven. Unleavened or slightly leavened breads such as the flat breads of the Middle East and India are cooked on a griddle, shallow-fried or baked in a charcoal oven. *see also* ANISBROD, BAGUETTE, BARA BRITH, BATARDE, BATON, BRIOCHE, CHAPATI, CIABATTA, FLUTE, GRISSINI, NAAN, PANETTONE, PAPPADAM, PARATHA, PITA, PUMPERNICKEL, PURI, ROTI, STOLLEN, TORTILLA, *and* ZWIEBACK.

bread and butter pudding | ENGLISH | Baked pudding made with thin slices of buttered bread, eggs, milk, sugar, currants and sultanas.

bread sauce | ENGLISH | Thick sauce made with seasoned milk, breadcrumbs and butter with onion and cloves. Served with roast game birds, especially pheasant.

breadcrumbs Soft breadcrumbs, made from day-old bread that is rubbed through a sieve or processed in a blender, are used in cooking to thicken sauces, as a topping on casseroles or gratins and in some stuffings. Dry breadcrumbs, made from bread slices that have been dried in a warm oven then pulverized, are used to coat foods before frying.

breadfruit (*Artocarpus communis*) Large, round fruit with a rough, green skin, native to the Malay Archipelago, and one of the food plants that the Polynesians carried on their migrations to the Pacific Islands. The plant become famous when Captain Bligh was sent to Tahiti to collect and propagate specimens and take them to the West Indies. This expedition took so long it caused the well-known mutiny on the *Bounty*. Breadfruit is sometimes available in specialty fruit markets. It has a creamy flesh with a bland, bread-like taste and is cooked like a starchy root vegetable, such as roasted, boiled or steamed; when mashed with milk and sugar and served with syrup it is eaten as a dessert.

bresaola | ITALIAN | Lightly smoked, cured dried beef. It is dark red and similar to prosciutto, but less salty. Served in wafer-thin slices.

Breton sea salt *see* CELTIC SEA SALT.

brick cheese | AMERICAN | Factory-produced cow's-milk cheese with semisoft, pale interior with numerous small holes. Sold in brick-shaped loaves and popular in the midwestern United States. Used mostly as a table cheese as a snack or in sandwiches; also used in cooking.

Brie | FRENCH | Soft, ripened cow's-milk cheese originating in the Ile-de-France and other districts in France, now produced elsewhere in Europe and other countries, including Australia. Brie is made in the shape of a flat disc of variable diameter. The rind is thin and velvety-white, tinted with red and the thick ivory-yellow satiny interior bulges when ripe. Brie is served at the end of a meal; also used as filling in canapés.

Brie de Coulommiers *see* COULOMMIERS.

Brie de Meaux | FRENCH | The famous name-controlled Brie from Meaux just east of Paris, produced in a large, flat disc weighing about 2 1/2 kg (5 lb), sold wrapped in waxed paper and enclosed in a wooden box. Considered one of the best Bries.

Brie de Melun | FRENCH | Name-controlled Brie made with raw milk and molded by hand. It has a crackly brown/red rind and is slightly smaller than Brie de Meaux. Brie de Melun Frais is a fresh variation with a very white interior and pronounced milky taste.

brik | TUNISIAN | Filo pastry made with a spicy meat, fish or cheese filling with an egg broken over, then rolled into cylinders. It is gently deep-fried and served hot.

brill European marine flatfish, related to the turbot.

Brillat-Savarin | FRENCH | High fat cow's-milk cheese with soft, triple cream interior and white, velvety crust. It is best eaten as young as possible and is usually serve at the end of a meal with fruit. From Normandy and named after the celebrated 19th-century French gastronome, Jean-Anthelme Brillat-Savarin.

brine Solution of salt and water used for pickling or preserving foods. Sometimes sugar is added to the brine.

brinjal *see* EGGPLANT.

brioche | FRENCH | Light, sweet, yeast bread enriched with eggs and butter and baked in a variety of shapes and sizes. Served at breakfast, as a dessert or with tea. The dough is also used to enclose foods such as fillet of beef, sausages and other meats.

brisket Meat from the breast or under-section of the ribs of beef. It requires long, slow cooking and is usually pot roasted; also corned and boiled.

broad beans (*Vicia faba*) Large, slightly flattened, green, beige or light brown beans. When very young the whole pod is occasionally eaten, but usually they are shelled like peas. The dried varieties are soaked overnight before simmering for about 40 minutes. Known as 'fava' in Italy where they are often served with prosciutto or pancetta.

broccoli (*Brassica oleracea* var. *italica*) Dark green, compact heads of clusters of flower buds on stout edible stalks. Cultivated and eaten since ancient Roman times, broccoli is an excellent source of vitamin C and other vitamins, riboflavin, iron and calcium. It is cooked in boiling salted water until just tender, steamed or stir-fried.

broccolini This cross between gai larn and broccoli has long, thin stems and small florets. Suitable for steaming and use in stir-fried dishes.

brochette | FRENCH | Cubes of meat or seafood and vegetables threaded onto a flattened skewer and grilled or barbecued. Also the name for a metal or wooden skewer.

broil | AMERICAN | Word used for grill.

Brolio | ITALIAN | Classico Chianti wine estate-bottled at Brolio Castle, Tuscany.

bromelin The enzyme of fresh pineapple that is used for tenderising meat.

bronze-formed pasta | ITALIAN | Artisan pasta made using bronze rollers. This gives the surface a slightly rough, porous texture which helps trap more sauce.

brook trout *see* TROUT.

broth Strong stock made from vegetables, meat and bones.

brown sauce In classic French cooking known as 'espagnole sauce'. It is made with rich brown meat stock (usually veal) stirred into a brown roux and mirepoix of cooked vegetables and simmered gently for at least two hours. Additions might include shallots, parsley, bay leaf, thyme, mushroom trimmings or a little tomato paste. It is skimmed from time to time and strained when ready. Used as a basis for many other sauces.

brown sugar Coarse, moist sugar made from refined white sugar treated with molasses. Available in light or dark. Dark brown sugar has a stronger molasses taste.

brown sugar slabs | CHINA | Flat layered slabs of semirefined sugar with the taste of brown sugar.

brown trout *see* TROUT.

brownie | AMERICAN | Rich, fudge-like biscuit usually made with chocolate and cut into squares.

brûlé | FRENCH | Meaning burnt, as in crème brûlée. Usually refers to the caramelization of sugar on top of a custard, sweet omelette or fruit using a hot skewer, brûlée iron, blow torch or when placed under a grill.

brûlot | FRENCH | Alcohol that is flamed before being consumed or added to food.

brunch A meal that is a cross between a late breakfast and lunch.

brunoise | FRENCH | Tiny diced vegetables, often braised in butter and used as a garnish for soups and sauces, and for stuffings; also to enhance stews such as osso buco.

bruschetta | ITALIAN | Slices of crusty bread that is lightly toasted, rubbed with garlic, olive oil and seasoning. Toppings might include chopped fresh tomatoes, sun-dried tomatoes, shaved Parmesan cheese, mozzarella cheese or herbs. Served as an appetizer or part of antipasti.

Brussels sprouts (*Brassica oleracea* var. *gemmifera*) Bright green, miniature cabbages first grown near Brussels, Belgium in the 13th century. A good source of vitamins A and C. They should be bought when bright green and firm, with tightly closed leaves. Steamed and served whole or mashed with butter; also used in soups and stews or sliced raw and added to salads.

brut | FRENCH | Very dry or sugarless. Often used to describe the driest of champagnes.

bubble and squeak | ENGLISH | Left-over cold meat, cold, cooked potato and left-over vegetables (traditionally cabbage) mashed together and fried until brown and crisp on both sides.

bucatini | ITALIAN | Pasta similar to spaghetti, but tubular.

bûche de Noël | FRENCH | Traditional Christmas cake shaped and decorated like a log.

buckwheat (*Fagopyrum esculentum*) Hard, triangular seeds obtained from a perennial plant native to northern Europe and Russia. The kernels are eaten whole in pilaf or stuffings, or coarsely ground into granules which are roasted and called 'kasha'. Buckwheat flour is used to make blini and Japanese noodles called 'soba'.

buffalo cheese The huge water buffalo has been raised in southern Italy for centuries for its milk which is used to make mozzarella, bocconcini and other soft, fresh cheeses.

buffalo mozzarella *see* MOZZARELLA DI BUFALA.

buffet | FRENCH | Selection of a variety of dishes arranged on a large table where guests serve themselves.

Bugne | FRENCH | Large, deep-fried fritter in the shape of knotted pastry ribbons. Served hot, dusted with icing sugar. A specialty around Lyons and traditionally eaten at Easter.

buisson | FRENCH | Traditional method of arranging food in a cluster, bunch or pyramid. It is a classic way of presenting crayfish or lobster; also vegetables and shellfish.

bulgur | MIDDLE EASTERN | Also known as 'burghul'. Whole wheat that has been partially boiled, before cracking, then dried. Widely used by vegetarians and the basis of the Middle Eastern salad tabbouleh.

bully beef Military slang term for corned beef (usually canned).

bun Small yeast roll, often containing dried fruit.

bunuelo | MEXICAN | Crisp, deep-fried, round pastry puffs, sprinkled with sugar and cinnamon.

bunya nut | AUSTRALIAN | (*Araucaria bidwillii*) Large, egg-shaped nuts obtained from the huge pine cones of an enormous rainforest tree of south-east Queensland. The nuts were a highly prized food of the Aboriginal people, who ate them either raw or roasted, or ground and used as flour. Bunya nuts are sometimes available fresh at gourmet produce shops. They can be roasted like chestnuts and eaten hot, and boiled and used as a purée in soups or made into dumplings; also used in desserts, pastries and cakes.

burdock (*Arctium lappa*) Called 'gobo' in Japan. Long, tapering, brown root eaten as a vegetable mainly in Japan. To retain taste and nutrients the root is scrubbed rather than peeled, soaked in water and vinegar to remove any bitterness, then shaved or julienned. Used in a cooked salad dressed with soy sauce, sake and sugar, or formed in a clump and made into tempura; also used in soups and with other vegetables and in stews. The young shoots and leaves are also edible. Used as a medicine in China.

burghul *see* BULGUR.

Burgundy (Bourgogne) Large region in north-eastern France, known throughout the world for its excellent wines and regional dishes. Dijon is famous for its mustard, blackcurrant liqueur (cassis) and gingerbread. Specialties of the region include boeuf bourguignon, coq au vin and escargots à la bourguignon; also jambon persille, a dish of cold poached ham, cubed and layered with parsleyed gelatin, and salmon with Chablis. Distinguished cheeses include Epoisses, Montrachet, Langres and fresh goat's-milk cheese.

burnett (*Poterium sanguisorba*) Also known as 'salad burnett'. Perennial herb originating in Europe. The leaves have a mild, cucumber taste, similar to borage, and are used likewise in cool drinks, salads and sauces.

bush tomato | AUSTRALIAN | (*Solanum centrale*) This small, prickly shrub of arid inland areas bears small berries that are yellow when ripe, that turn brown and raisin-like when dry. They were an important food plant of Australian Aborigines, eaten fresh or dry. The bush tomato is available dried, packed in oil or ground as a spice. It has a strong, pungent taste and small amounts are used in chutneys, marinades, sauces and casseroles. Bush tomato sauce is sold in specialty shops.

butter Firm milk product made by churning fresh cream. The content of butter is chiefly saturated fat (80 per cent). It is available salted and unsalted. Salted butter has a slight percentage of salt added and has a longer shelf life. Unsalted butter contains no additional salt and is the preferred butter for everyday use and for baked goods in European cooking.

butter lettuce Small, round, loosely formed lettuce with soft, pliable leaves and with a mild, buttery taste. Used on its own or in mixed green salads.

butterfly To split a food, such as shelled prawns or piece of pork, down the center almost completely through, and flattening it out so that the food resembles a butterfly.

buttermilk Traditionally the low-fat liquid left after the cream has been removed when making butter. Commercial buttermilk is made from skim milk and milk powder and is cultured in the same way as yoghurt. Buttermilk is used in drinks, cakes and breads.

butternut pumpkin *see* PUMPKIN.

butterscotch Toffee-like piece of confectionery made with butter and brown sugar cooked to the hard crack stage.

button squash (*Cucubita pepo*) Also known as 'pattipan' or 'scallop squash'. Small cake-shaped marrow with scalloped edges in various shades of green and bright yellow. They are a good source of vitamin C and should be used soon after purchase, either steamed, boiled, sautéed or baked.

Byrrh | FRENCH | Proprietary brand name for an aperitif made from sweetened wine and quinine.

cabanossi Thin smoked sausage with a red skin, made from minced pork and beef, seasoned with garlic and spices.

cabbage (*Brassica oleracea* var. *capitata*) This group of vegetables includes the common green cabbage, red cabbage and the crinkly leafed savoy cabbage which is slightly milder. All are an excellent source of vitamin C and fiber and should be bought with the leaves firmly packed in heavy, compact heads. They can be finely shredded and used raw in salads or cooked for a minimum of time in a variety of ways.

Cabécou | FRENCH | Translates to 'little goat'. Small, round goat's-milk cheese, sometimes made with sheep's milk or a mixture of the two. Some cheeses are wrapped in chestnut or vine leaves. It has a soft to fairly firm, ivory interior and soft, white rind with a bluish tinge.

cabernet One of the main red wine-producing grapes, both in France and many other countries, including Australia. There are two main varieties: Cabernet Franc and the superior Cabernet Sauvignon, capable of producing top quality, full-bodied red wine.

cabinet pudding | ENGLISH | Traditional steamed pudding made with a decorative pattern of glacé cherries, angelica and raisins, then topped with layers of sponge-fingers and egg custard, infused with sweet sherry. The cooked pudding is turned onto a plate and served warm, sometimes with a wine sauce.

Cabrales | SPANISH | Semifirm blue vein cheese made by combining goat's, cow's and sheep's milk. It has a moist crumbly interior with intense purplish-blue veining and a pale, salty rind. A superior table cheese. Served as a snack, light meal with salad or fruit, or at the end of a meal.

cacao (*Theobroma cacao*) Tree cultivated for its beans, used to make chocolate and cocoa powder. The finest cacao comes from Venezuela and is known as 'Caracas cacao'.

cacciatore | ITALIAN | Translates to 'hunter-style'. Stew of rabbit or chicken cooked in a sauce of onions, garlic, tomatoes, mushrooms and wine.

cacciatoro | ITALIAN | Small, whole, soft-textured salami, made the same way as Milano salami but cured and matured for a much shorter time.

cachou Tiny silver aromatic confectionery. Used for sweetening the breath, also to decorate cakes.

cacik | TURKISH | Diced cucumber and yoghurt salad, seasoned with crushed garlic, chopped mint and salt and pepper. Served very cold. A popular mezze throughout the Middle East.

caciocavallo | ITALIAN | Gourd-shaped cow's-milk cheese made in southern Italy. Made by the pasta filata method where the curds have been pulled and molded by hand into shape. The interior is pale yellow and the taste sharp, tangy and mildly smoky. Used as a table cheese at the end of a meal; also grated and used in cooking.

Caerphilly | WELSH / ENGLISH | Semifirm cow's-milk cheese with a natural brushed rind and a white, crumbly interior that is creamy and moist. Used as a snack and table cheese.

Caesar salad | AMERICAN | Salad of cos (romaine) lettuce, garlic-rubbed croutons and Parmesan cheese, with a dressing of olive oil, Worcestershire sauce, lemon juice and coddled egg; sometimes anchovies are included.

café | FRENCH | **(1)** Coffee. **(2)** Also a place serving drinks (particularly coffee) and snacks.

café au lait | FRENCH | Espresso coffee with warmed or steamed milk, usually served at breakfast.

café brûlot | AMERICAN | New Orleans speciality of strong black coffee, flavoured with cloves, cinnamon and citrus peel, and ignited with brandy.

café noir | FRENCH | Plain black espresso coffee.

cafeteria Self-service restaurant.

caffè espresso | ITALIAN | Strong black coffee made by forcing steam through ground coffee.

caffè freddo | ITALIAN | Iced coffee.

caffè latte | ITALIAN | Espresso coffee combined with an equal amount of steamed milk.

caffè macchiato | ITALIAN | Espresso coffee marked with a dash of foamy milk.

caffè mocha | ITALIAN | Espresso coffee combined with chocolate syrup and steamed milk, usually served in a tall glass and often topped with whipped cream and a dusting of cocoa powder.

caffè ristretto | ITALIAN | Small serving of extra strong, espresso coffee.

caffeine An alkaloid present in coffee, tea, cocoa and cola with stimulating and diuretic properties. Caffeine is toxic in high doses.

caimito *see* ABIU.

Cajun | AMERICAN | Style of cooking developed by displaced French settlers in the bayous of Louisiana. Traditional French preparations, such as dark roux to thicken sauces and pork fat, are combined with local ingredients such as chilies, capsicums and spices and freshly caught seafood and game birds. Most cajun cooking is country-style, hearty and very spicy. Well-known dishes include gumbo, étouffée, jambalaya and, more recently, blackened fish.

Cajun spices | AMERICAN | Blend of herbs and spices used in Cajun cooking. Many different blends are sold in packets and may include garlic, onion, black pepper, cayenne pepper, chilies, mustard and thyme.

calabash *see* BOTTLE GOURD.

calabrese | ITALIAN | Medium-sized, spicy hot salami made from pork or a mixture of meats and pieces of white fat, seasoned with chili, spices and red wine.

calamari *see* SQUID.

calamondin *see* CUMQUAT.

Calasparra | SPANISH | Plump, short-grain rice used in paella.

calcium Essential mineral for the formation and maintenance of bones, teeth and nails. Milk, yoghurt and cheese are high in calcium.

caldo verde | PORTUGUESE | National soup made with potatoes, onions and shredded green cabbage, garnished with slices of spicy sausages.

California roll Non-traditional and relatively recent version of sushi in which the rice filling is hand-rolled in nori seaweed, usually in a cone shape. The ingredients are often more familiar to Western palates and might include avocado, cooked crab, smoked salmon or prawns, ham, chicken, cucumber or watercress. An inside-out sushi roll, where the rice is on the outside of the nori, is a more traditional type of California roll. *see also* SUSHI.

callaloo (*Calocasia esculenta*) These are the large, elephant's ear-shaped leaves of taro and other related plants. Used in cooked vegetable dishes. A soup dish called 'callaloo' is a specialty of the Caribbean islands.

callop *see* GOLDEN PERCH.

calorie Imperial measurement of the energy value of food. For example, 4.2 calories equal one kilojoule.

calrose rice | AUSTRALIAN | Medium-grain rice, often called short-grain. Served with Chinese and Japanese food as, when steamed, it produces moist plump grains that cling together and can be easily picked up with chopsticks; also suited to molded Japanese sushi, and for making puddings and sweet dishes.

Calvados | FRENCH | Name-controlled apple brandy distilled from cider apples and matured in oak casks. It is drunk chiefly as a short drink as a digestive. In cooking, Calvados is used in cream sauces, apple desserts and pastries.

calzone | ITALIAN | Crescent-shaped pastry made with pizza-dough filled with ham or salami, and mozzarella cheese, then baked in the oven. Panzerotti are similar but they are fried instead of baked.

Cambridge sauce | ENGLISH | Type of hollandaise sauce with anchovies and mustard. Served as an accompaniment to cold meats.

Camembert | FRENCH | Soft cow's-milk cheese with a supple, pale yellow interior and a white, velvety rind. Mass-produced throughout France and widely copied in other countries. Some very good Camembert-style farmhouse and artisan cheeses are made in Australia. Served almost anytime and at the end of the meal.

camomile *see* CHAMOMILE.

Campari | ITALIAN | Bittersweet, bright crimson aperitif usually served with soda water. Also used in some cocktails such as negroni and americano.

canapés Variety of small bite-sized pieces of food consisting of neat shapes of bread, toast, crackers or thin slices of vegetables, spread with various toppings and decoratively garnished. Canapés can be lightly glazed with a fine clear aspic. These days Asian titbits such as sushi and miniature fish-cakes are also served. Served with drinks before dinner or at a cocktail party.

candied fruit Also known as 'glacé fruit'. Whole, peel or pieces of fruit preserved in a heavy sugar syrup. The most common fruits that are candied are cherries, pineapple, apricots and citrus, as well as ginger and angelica stalks. Once the fruit is candied it can then be crystallized by giving it a coating of granulated sugar. Used as confectionery; when chopped added to cakes, buns, ice creams and other desserts.

candlenut | SOUTH-EAST ASIAN | (*Aleurites moluccana*) Cream, round nut, similar to the macadamia nut in texture. Usually sold shelled. When ground it is used to thicken sauces and curry pastes. Macadamia nuts can be used as a substitute.

candy | AMERICAN | Small piece of confectionery or lolly.

candyfloss Solution of sugar syrup (usually pink) that is cooked and spun by an electric machine to a floss which is then rolled around a stick.

canelling Technique of making grooves with a small knife (canelling knife), over the surface of raw vegetables and the rind of citrus fruit, which when sliced show decorative borders.

canistel (*Lucuma nervosa*) Also known as 'egg fruit' or 'yellow sapote'. Egg-shaped tropical fruit with orange-yellow skin and very sweet, yellow flesh when ripe. The fruit is eaten raw, or puréed and used in pies, puddings and as a pancake filling.

canister Metal box for holding tea, coffee or spices.

cannaroni | ITALIAN | Also known as 'zitoni'. Very wide, tubular spaghetti.

cannellini beans | ITALIAN | (*Phaseolus vulgaris*) Small, white kidney beans available in dried form. They are popular in Tuscan cooking, particularly in soups, in a salad with tuna, and with spicy sausages. Should be soaked overnight before cooking.

cannelloni | ITALIAN | Large tubes of pasta (or squares that can be rolled up into cylinders), stuffed with a savoury filling and baked with a tomato or cheese sauce.

cannery Factory or other establishment where foods are canned.

canola oil Oil obtained from rapeseed. Canola oil is largely mono-unsaturated and contains Omega-3 fatty acids, known to reduce harmful (LDL) cholesterol levels in the blood. Mild-tasting, it is suitable for both cooking and making salad dressing. Also used to make margarine-type spread.

Cantal | FRENCH | Semifirm, uncooked cow's-milk cheese with a moist, pale yellow interior and a darker, cloth-covered crust. Used as a snack with fruit or at the end of a meal; also used in salads and gratins.

cantaloupe *see* ROCKMELON.

canteen (1) Place where communal meals are eaten. (2) Small shop where food is bought, such as at schools. (3) Small, metal flask for hot water, coffee, etc. (4) Box containing a set of cutlery.

cantucci | ITALIAN | Hard, crunchy biscuits studded with almonds or hazelnuts and aniseed.

cape gooseberry (*Physalis* spp.) Round, many-seeded berry enclosed in a thin, lantern-shaped husk. The husk is easily peeled back and the berries are rinsed. They have a sweet, tart taste and are rich in vitamin C. Eaten raw or gently poached in syrup; also used in pies, jams and purée.

capelli d'angelo | ITALIAN | Translates to 'angel's hair'. Ultra fine, long strands of pasta.

caper (*Capparis spinosa*) Flower-bud of a shrub cultivated chiefly in the Mediterranean region. Capers are usually pickled in vinegar or preserved in brine and used in white sauces and condiments, as a pizza topping, in salads, to accompany smoked salmon and to with rice. Nonpareil is a small variety of caper from France.

caper berry (*Capparis spinosa*) Fruit of the caper shrub, often preserved with the stalks intact. Usually from Spain. Served as a cocktail snack or in a salad.

capon Young castrated rooster that has been fattened and sold before it is nine months old. It is tender, juicy and full-breasted with well-distributed fat. Cooked in the same way as chicken, particularly roasted.

caponata | ITALIAN | Sicilian dish of eggplant, celery, tomatoes and onions, cooked gently in olive oil and with capers, olives and anchovies. Usually served cold as an appetizer.

cappelletti | ITALIAN | Pasta in the shape of small peaked hats, usually stuffed and cooked like ravioli.

cappuccino | ITALIAN | Espresso coffee with hot steamed milk, topped with frothy milk, often dusted with cocoa powder or cinnamon.

Caprini | ITALIAN | Small, disc-shaped goat's-milk cheese made in southern Italy. It is rarely found outside of Italy.

capsaicin Heat-generating alkaloid present in chilies, which varies in strength according to variety. It is found mostly in the pale membranes and tiny seeds and can cause an intense burning sensation to the mouth, throat and eyes.

capsicum (*Capsicum annuum*) Also known as 'bell pepper' or 'sweet pepper'. These crunchy vegetables are native to tropical America and became known in Europe and Asia only after the voyages of Columbus and other early explorers. They can be green, red, orange, yellow, brown or purplish-black in several different shapes: squat and bell-like, rectangular or tapering. The riper the fruit, especially the red varieties, the higher the content of vitamin C, other vitamins and minerals. Capsicums are used raw in salads; also stir-fried, sautéed, baked, grilled or stuffed. Finely chopped they are used in salsas and sauces. Sliced capsicum is the main ingredient of the classic Italian peperonata.

carafe | FRENCH | Glass container with a wide base and narrow neck used to serve tap-water and house wine at the table. A full carafe contains one litre and a demi-carafe a half litre.

carambola (*Averrhoa carambola*) Also known as 'star fruit'. This glossy, yellowish-green fruit with five distinct wings is becoming more widely available. It has a crisp, refreshingly sweet flesh. When cut in cross-sections the slices are star-shaped, used in fruit salads or as a garnish.

caramel Sugar that has been melted and browned by heating. Used in desserts and sauces. Also base for confectionery.

caramelize Process of heating sugar slowly until it melts into a thick, clear and molten syrup. Used for glazing, candied fruit, pastries and nuts.

carapace Hard, bony, outer case on the back of various animals such as turtles, lobsters and crabs.

caraway (*Carum carvi*) Biennial plant native to Europe mainly grown for its aromatic seeds (see below). The root and leaves are also edible. Young leaves have a more delicate taste than the seeds and are used in salads, soups and as a garnish for cooked vegetables. The root is sometimes cooked as a vegetable.

caraway seeds Small, brown, aromatic seeds used chiefly in pickles, cheeses and bakery goods, particularly rye bread; also used with cabbage and other vegetable dishes, apple sauce, meat and fish. Oil obtained from the leaves and seeds is used in the liqueur Kümmel.

carbohydrates Found primarily in foods of plant origin, carbohydrates are the body's most important source of energy. Sugars of various kinds are the simplest form of carbohydrates and are absorbed by the body very quickly. Starches and fiber are complex carbohydrates found in whole grains and in vegetables such as potatoes, corn, legumes and pulses. These are broken down to sugars during digestion and provide more nutrients than simple carbohydrates.

carbon steel Iron with carbon and other elements added. Used for quality knives and cooking utensils.

carbonade / carbonnade | FRENCH | (1) Chargrilled meat. (2) Flemish speciality of beef and onions braised in dark beer or stout.

carbonara sauce | ITALIAN | Rich pasta sauce made from pancetta (or streaky bacon), finely chopped onion, garlic, egg yolks, double cream, Parmesan cheese and freshly ground black pepper.

cardamom (*Elletaria cardamomum*) Perennial herb native to India, valued for its small, dark brown, highly aromatic seeds enclosed in a three-sided creamy-white pod. Used as an ingredient in Indian curry blends and other forms of Indian cooking; also a principal spice in Scandinavian cakes and pastries; and used in Turkish coffee, iced beetroot and to spice wine.

cardinal Iced dessert that contains red fruit or is accompanied by a red sweet sauce made with raspberries or strawberries.

cardinal sauce Béchamel sauce with fish stock, cream, butter, lobster meat and roe, seasoned with a little cayenne pepper and garnished with chopped truffles. Served with fish or lobster.

cardoon (*Cynara cardunculus*) Related to the globe artichoke, but only the blanched inner stems and hearts are eaten. It looks like a large bunch of creamy-white celery. Once cut they should be dropped into acidulated water to prevent browning. Cardoons can be fried, boiled or blanched and baked in a white sauce sprinkled with cheese.

Carnaroli riso superfino | ITALIAN | Fat short-grain rice considered one of the finest for risotto.

carnitas | MEXICAN | Translates to 'little meats'. Small pieces of fatty pork boiled until tender, then fried until browned. Served as a snack.

carob (*Certatonia siliqua*) Also known as 'St John's bread'. The brown seed pod of a tree native to the Mediterranean region. The pulp is rich in sugar and when ground to a powder is used in baked goods, desserts and confectionery; often used as a substitute for those allergic to chocolate.

caroline | FRENCH | Small choux pastries filled with various mousses and served hot or cold as hors d'oeuvres.

carotene Natural, fat-soluble pigment which converts to vitamin A in the body. It is found in carrots, dark green vegetables and many fruits.

carp (*Cyprinus carpio*) Large freshwater fish of Asian ancestry, but now introduced throughout the Northern Hemisphere. In Asia and parts of Europe it is reared commercially on farms. Asian cooks stir-fry, braise or use carp in one-pot dishes. It is also suitable for Thai fishcakes and to make the Jewish dish, gefilte fish. Carp tend to acquire a muddy taste that can be eliminated by soaking the skinned fillets in vinegar and water. In Europe it is often stuffed and baked, deep-fried or grilled.

carpaccio | ITALIAN | First course dish of thinly sliced raw beef. Served cold, dressed with olive oil and lemon juice; sometimes garnished with shaved Parmesan cheese.

carpetbag steak Thick piece of fillet steak with a pocket cut into it and stuffed with fresh oysters. It is then grilled or pan-fried.

carrageen / carragheen *see* IRISH MOSS.

Carré de l'Est | FRENCH | Soft, ripened cow's-milk cheese with a creamy interior and white downy rind. Flat and squarish in shape and similar to Camembert in style, but milder in taste. Used as a table cheese.

carrot (*Daucus carota*) Bright orange root vegetable used for at least 2000 years and now cultivated and eaten throughout the world. Carrots are a rich source of betacarotene, which is converted to vitamin A in the body. There are baby carrots sold in bunches with their feathery leaves intact, and larger leafless varieties sold by the weight. Carrots are used in a multitude of ways, as a snack or juice, in salads, stews, soups, stir-fries, jams, cakes and as an important vegetable on their own.

casalinga Small, fine-textured salami made from finely minced lean pork and fat, seasoned with garlic and spices.

cascabel chili In Spanish, cascabel means 'rattle', alluding to the sound the seeds make when this chili is shaken. It is dried, dark red and round, with a medium heat and earthy taste. Used in salsas, sauces, soups and stews.

casein The protein of milk and the main substance of cheese.

cashew nut (*Anacardium occidentale*) Creamy-brown, kidney-shaped nut that is produced from the bottom of a reddish fruit called 'cashew apple'. The nut's shell is highly toxic and cashews are always sold pre-shelled. Because of their high fat content, cashews should be stored airtight in a cool place, refrigerator or freezer. Cashews are usually roasted and used as a snack, in cakes, biscuits, desserts and confectionery. Also widely used in Asian cooking.

cassareep | WEST INDIAN / LATIN AMERICAN | Seasoning agent made from the reduced juice of grated cassava root, with brown sugar, cinnamon and cloves.

cassata | ITALIAN | Dessert consisting of several layers of different ice creams, enriched with various ingredients such as candied fruits and pistachio nuts.

cassava (*Manihot utilissima*) Also known as 'manioc'. Dark brown, tuberous root with a dense, white flesh. There are two main types, sweet and bitter. The bitter cassava is poisonous unless cooked. Cassava is a staple food in many tropical countries. The root is peeled and boiled until tender. It is then grated and made into cakes or thinly sliced and fried; also used in soups and stews. Tapioca is extracted from the cassava root.

cassava flour *see* TAPIOCA.

casserole Ovenproof cooking dish made of earthenware, porcelain or metal, with handles and a tight-fitting lid. Designed for long, slow cooking. Also refers to the food cooked in a casserole.

cassia (*Cinnamomum cassia*) Dried bark from the cassia tree, native to China. Similar to cinnamon, only thicker, it is often sold as cinnamon; it is distinguished by its stronger taste and dark reddish- brown hue.

cassis (crème de) | FRENCH | Blackcurrant liqueur. Specialty of Dijon and the Côte d'Or.

cassolette | FRENCH | Small, heatproof cooking dish with short handles used to prepare, cook and serve a variety of hot individual dishes.

cassoulet | FRENCH | Famous casserole dish of haricot beans and including various combinations of sausages, pork, lamb and goose, usually layered in an earthenware dish and baked very slowly for a long time.

cast iron Hard, brittle, iron-carbon alloy used for making heavy cookware such as casseroles and frying pans.

Castello Blue *see* BLUE CASTELLO.

caster / castor sugar *see* SUGAR.

catnip (*Nepeta cataria*) Also known as 'catmint'. Perennial herb native to Europe and a member of the large mint family. Catnip is noted for its attractiveness to cats and was once used as a herbal tea to relieve upset stomachs and headaches.

cats' tongues Slightly sweet, thin narrow biscuits usually served with desserts. Known as 'langues-de-chat' in France.

catsup | AMERICAN | Another name for 'ketchup'.

caul Almost transparent, fatty membrane that encloses the stomach of animals, particularly pigs. Used to hold food together in charcuterie and when cooking other food preparations such as terrines.

cauldron Large kettle or boiler made of cast iron or copper with a detachable handle.

cauliflower (*Brassica oleracea* var. *botrytis*) Botanically related to broccoli and similarly cultivated for its tender underdeveloped flower heads which are high in vitamin C and are a good source of dietary fiber. Sprigs of cauliflower can be eaten raw in salads, coated in batter and deep-fried, or used in stir-fried dishes or curries. Whole cauliflowers (either baby or normal size) can be steamed whole and served coated in a rich mornay sauce or herb butter.

cavatelli | ITALIAN | Short and narrow, ripple-edged pasta shaped like a shell.

caviar The highly prized eggs (roe) of the female sturgeon (*Acipenser* spp.), sold fresh, very lightly salted, pasteurized or pressed. The main supply comes from the Caspian Sea; Russia and Iran are the main producers. The three main varieties take their names from the species of sturgeon they come from. The best and most expensive is **beluga**, which has large, light grey to black eggs with a soft shell and delicate taste. **Osietra** has medium-sized golden-grey eggs with a firm shell and oily, nutty taste. **Sevruga**, the least expensive, has the smallest eggs which are dark grey. Fresh unpasteurized caviar is extremely perishable and will keep under refrigeration for no longer than three weeks. **Pasteurized caviar** has been partially cooked and will keep under refrigeration for more than six months. **Pressed caviar** is composed of very ripe or damaged eggs and is salted and compressed. **Red caviar** comes from the salmon which has large bright-orange eggs with a fresh salty taste. **Lumpfish roe**, sometimes called caviar, are tiny eggs of the lumpfish that are dyed red or black. Caviar is always served cold as an hors d'oeuvre with blinis or toast, and often accompanied by iced vodka or champagne.

cayenne chili Very hot, long, curved, bright-red chili used in salsas, sauces and soups. Also dried and ground to produce cayenne pepper.

cayenne pepper (*Capsicum* spp.) Also known as 'chili powder'. Ground product made from various forms of dried red chilies. Cayenne pepper is extremely hot and is used sparingly in sauces, pickles, salad dressings, egg dishes and dips; also used in some curry powders and many Mexican dishes such as chili con carne.

cazuela | SPANISH | Traditional earthenware casserole glazed only on the inside, used both on the top of the stove and in the oven.

cebiche *see* CEVICHE.

ceci *see* CHICKPEAS.

celeriac (*Apium graveolens* var. *rapaceum*) Large, round tuberous root with numerous small bumps on the surface. The flesh is white and has a mild, celery-like taste. It is rich in calcium and phosphorus. Available during the cooler months. After peeling, soak in acidulated water to prevent browning. Grated raw and used in salads; also chopped and used in soups and stews or julienned and blanched then simmered in butter. The French dish, celeriac en rémoulade, is grated celeriac with mayonnaise and capers, mustard, herbs and anchovies.

celery (*Apium graveolens* var. *dulce*) The crispy stalks of celery are mainly used as a stir-fried or braised vegetable and for stock, soups and casseroles. The celery seed is also used as for seasoning. The more tender inner stalks are used as a snack, or for salads.

celery salt Blend of ground celery seed and salt.

celery seed (*Apium graveolens*) Small brown seeds of the celery plant with the same taste as the stalk. Widely used in pickling and chutneys; also crushed and added to tomato juice, egg, vegetable and fish dishes.

cellophane noodles *see* BEAN THREAD NOODLES.

celsius System of measuring temperature in which the freezing point of water is 0°C (32°F) and the boiling point is 100°C (212°F).

Celtic sea salt | FRENCH | Coarse, grey sea salt, harvested from the bottom of the same saltpans as fleur de sel, off the coast of Brittany. Also known as 'Breton sea salt' and 'grey salt'. It is sold in its natural state with no additives. Used mostly in cooking. *see also* FLEUR DE SEL.

cendre (sous la) | FRENCH | Cooked by being buried in hot embers. Some French cheeses are matured in wood ashes.

century egg *see* PRESERVED EGG.

cephalopod Class of marine molluscs, including the squid, octopus and cuttlefish, which have a clearly defined head, and tentacles attached to the head. An ink sac is found in the intestines.

ceps (*Boletus edulis*) Also known as 'boletus' and 'porcini' in Italy. Wild European mushroom with a creamy-brown to dark brown hemispherical cap and bulging stalk. This is rated as one of the best edible mushrooms. There are other kinds of wild boletus including the popular **slippery Jack** (*B. luteus*). Dried ceps retain their deep taste especially well and are available at specialty food shops. They are also preserved in oil. *see also* PORCINI.

cereals Edible starchy grains from certain plants of the grass family such as rice, wheat, corn, rye, barley and oats. They are high in carbohydrates, an excellent source of dietary fibre, valuable in protein and vitamins and make up the diet of most of the world's population. Also a term used for breakfast food made from cereal grain.

cervelas | FRENCH | Short, thick, garlic infused pork sausage. Usually heated before eating.

cévenole (à la) | FRENCH | Dish that contains or is garnished with chestnuts.

ceviche / seviche | LATIN AMERICAN | Very fresh, raw fish marinated in lime juice and other seasonings until the flesh turns opaque. Served with limes, sliced raw onions, tomatoes and capsicum.

Ceylon tea High quality black tea, originally grown at high altitudes in Sri Lanka.

Chabichou | FRENCH | Small goat's-milk cheese usually in the shape of a short cone or cylinder. It has a white, creamy interior and natural, thin, white rind with occasional mottling. Used as a table cheese. Produced by dairies and farms in the province of Poitou.

Chablis | FRENCH | A very dry white wine made from Chardonnay grapes. Produced in northern Burgundy and named after the town of Chablis.

chafing dish Portable cooking utensil with a flame underneath, used on the table to cook or to keep food warm.

chai | INDIAN | Spiced tea. Usually made with black tea and may contain cinnamon, cardamom, nutmeg, cloves, coriander seeds or ginger. In India it is infused with hot water and milk and served sweetened.

chakchouka | MIDDLE EASTERN | Traditional egg dish from Tunisia, comprising a mixture of onions, tomatoes and green capsicums, cooked in olive oil and seasoned with spices and harissa. When the vegetables are soft, eggs are broken in whole and cooked until set.

chakki | INDIAN | Large grindstone used to pound pieces of spices to a powder.

challah | JEWISH | Loaf of white bread, traditionally formed into a braid.

chamomile / camomile (*Chamaemelum nobile*) Perennial herb with finely cut apple-scented leaves and small white daisies with yellow centers. Since Tudor times chamomile has been used as a fragrant ground cover for lawns and paths, but today is extensively cultivated for its flowers which are dried and sold as a soothing herbal tea. The flowers are also used in a light Spanish sherry, Manzanilla.

champ | IRISH | Also known as 'thump' or 'stelk'. Hot mashed potatoes mixed with chopped spring onions, with a generous portion of melted butter poured into a hole in the middle of the mash.

Champagne | FRENCH | An outstanding sparkling white wine from the Champagne district of northern France.

champignon | FRENCH | Mushroom. Usually refers to the commonly cultivated small button mushroom. Champignon de bois are wild mushrooms.

chanterelle (*Cantharellus cibarius*) Known as 'girolle' in France. Trumpet-shaped bright yellow to orange mushrooms with frilly edges. Used in French cooking. They require longer cooking than some other mushrooms.

chantilly | FRENCH | Whipped fresh cream to which sugar and vanilla have been added. Used as an accompaniment to various desserts.

Chaource | FRENCH | Soft, ripened cow's-milk cheese with a creamy interior and edible, white, downy rind tinged with red mottling. It is cylindrical in shape and is similar to a rich Brie. Used as table cheese, usually at the end of a meal. Produced in small dairies in the province of Champagne.

chap chae | KOREAN | Traditional stir-fried dish of sliced beef, vegetables and sweet potato noodles (dang myun), with garlic, chili, soy sauce, sugar and sesame oil.

chapati | INDIAN | Flat, unleavened bread made from wholemeal flour.

chapon | FRENCH | Day-old slices of narrow French bread that are rubbed with garlic and sprinkled with oil and vinegar. Used in green salads.

char kway teow | MALAYSIAN | Famous stir-fried dish of rice noodles, barbecued pork, prawns, cheong sausage, bean sprouts, shallots, garlic and egg, with red chilies, soy sauce and oyster sauce.

charcuterie | FRENCH | Numerous preparations based usually on pork meat or offal such as sausages, pâtés, black puddings, cured meats, etc. Also the name of the shop where such products are sold.

Chardonnay French grape used for making superior dry white wines.

chargrill To cook meat, poultry, fish or vegetables on metal rungs directly over heat source. Also refers to food cooked in heavy iron pans or hot plate with raised ridges.

charlotte Classic hot or cold dessert. In the hot version a round mold is lined with crustless buttered bread and filled with a thick fruit purée with lemon and cinnamon and baked in the oven. For a cold charlotte the mold is lined with sponge fingers and filled with a bavarois cream, mousse or other filling and chilled before serving.

Chartreuse | FRENCH | Herby, brandy-based liqueur available in two forms: green which is highly aromatic and stronger in alcohol content, and yellow which is sweeter.

chasseur sauce | FRENCH | Brown sauce made with white wine, mushrooms, shallots, tomatoes and herbs. Served with various sautéed dishes such as chicken, veal and kidneys.

chat | INDIAN | Generic name for various salty snacks that are always bought, for example roasted chickpeas or puffed rice.

chats Small young potatoes of any variety. *see also* POTATO.

château potatoes | FRENCH | Small potatoes first blanched, then sautéed in butter and cooked gently with the lid on. Traditionally served with châteaubriand.

châteaubriand | FRENCH | Slice of double-thick fillet steak (usually for two) cooked more slowly than smaller steaks. Traditionally served with béarnaise sauce and château potatoes.

Châteauneuf-du-Pape | FRENCH | Full-bodied red wine from the Rhone valley.

chatni | INDIAN | Freshly prepared chutney made with various fruit, vegetables, herbs and spices. They are not designed to be kept for any length of time and are usually served chilled as an accompaniment to a meal.

chaud-froid | FRENCH | Cooked meat, game, poultry or fish dish that is chilled and then coated with aspic jelly. Served cold.

chayote *see* CHOKO.

cheddar | ENGLISH | Firm, pressed cow's-milk cheese with close-grained, creamy-yellow interior and natural, oily rind. Tangy and rich, it is sharp without bitterness; strong and nut-like when aged. Used as a table cheese, snack and shredded in cooking.

cheese Highly nutritious dairy product consisting primarily of a concentration of milk solids (curds) that have been separated from the whey. Cheese is a highly concentrated food and an excellent source of protein, calcium and some vitamins. It retains almost all the food value of milk and has better keeping qualities in a much more convenient form for storage—about 10 volumes of milk reduces to one volume of cheese. Hundreds of varieties of cheese are made mostly from the milk of cows, goats, sheep or buffaloes. The differences in character vary in time, temperature, the adjustment of fat content, the addition of enzymes or cultures of bacteria, molds or yeasts and the ripening and curing process. Following is a broad classification of cheese. *see* *also individual entries for descriptions.* **Fresh cheeses** are uncooked, unripened types without the addition of rennet and usually with a high water content. Some are blended with cream: examples include fromais frais, cottage cheese, Mascarpone and ricotta. **White-rind cheeses** such as Brie and Camembert are distinguished by their soft ripened satiny texture and thin, white, velvety mold-covered rinds. This group also includes Chaource, Neutchatel and Saint Marcellin. The **semi- soft cheeses**, usually with surface-ripened washed rind and a strong smell, include French Muster, Epoisses, Pont-l'Eveque, the Italian Taleggio and most monastery-type cheeses. **Blue vein cow's-milk cheese** (sheep's-milk in Roquefort) gets its characteristic blue veining by the addition of penicillin mold. Examples include Bleu de Bresses, Danish Blue, Blue Stilton and Blue Cheshire, Gorgonzola and Roquefort. *See also* BLUE CHEESE *and individual entries.* **Semihard pressed cheeses** with a relatively low moisture content include the large cheddars and Swiss types such as Beaufort, Gruyère and Emmentale, Dutch Gouda and English Cheshire. **Hard- cooked** or **granular cheeses**, mainly Italian in origin, are made from cow's milk mixed with rennet, are cooked at a high temperature, cut and then pressed. They are extremely hard with a low moisture content and are used for grating, typified by Parmesan. **Goat's-milk cheeses**, often made by ladling into molds, come in a large variety of shapes. The natural rind may have a bluish tinge or be dusted with ash, spices or herbs: examples include Cabecou and Chabichou. *See also* CHÈVRE (FROMAGE DE). **Sheep's-milk cheeses** include Broccio (fresh), Roquefort (blue vein) and Pecorino (hard cooked granular). **Stretch-curd** cheeses, sometimes referred to as 'pasta filata' cheeses are mainly from Southern Italy and include the fresh, uncured elastic-textured mozzarella and the harder, mature stretched-curd types such as Provolone and Caciocavallo, which is sometimes smoked. *See also* PASTA FILATA. **Processed cheeses** are mass-produced and are wholly uniform in shape, taste and texture. They are produced according to standardized recipes and techniques and usually have a bland taste and long shelf life.

cheesecake A rich cake, usually baked in a springform pan, served chilled and decorated with whipped cream, fruit or nuts. It may have a base of short-crust pastry or a biscuit crust and is made with fresh cheese, sugar, eggs, various additions and sometimes cream.

cheesecloth Loosely woven cloth used for straining liquids.

chef garde-manger | FRENCH | Member of the staff in a large kitchen who is in overall charge of cold items found on the menu.

chef's salad Tossed green salad that is topped with a combination of julienned chicken, ham, Swiss cheese and vegetables dressed with a vinaigrette sauce.

Chelsea bun | ENGLISH | Round, spiral-shaped bun made from a sweet yeast- dough sprinkled with currants, candied peel and spices, and glazed with syrup.

chemise (en) | FRENCH | Food wrapped in pastry. Also refers to food cooked in its natural covering such as potatoes in their skins.

chemiser | FRENCH | To coat or line the interior of a mold with a film of aspic, caramel, ice-cream or forcemeat to prevent the food from sticking and/ or to provide a coating for the main filling ingredient.

Chenin Blanc French grape used for making the aromatic dry white wines of the Loire Valley.

cherimoya *see* CUSTARD APPLE.

chermoula | MOROCCAN | Spicy marinade for preserving meat and seasoning fish, made with various ingredients which might include chopped skin of preserved lemon, garlic, small red chilies, crushed cumin and coriander seeds, coriander leaves, parsley, mint and basil, lemon juice, olive oil and salt. After cooking, the remaining chermoula can be served as a sauce.

cherry (*Prunus* spp.) They vary from yellow, to bright red, to a very dark red. There are both sweet and sour varieties: **sweet cherries** are eaten whole with the skin, added to fruit salads and compotes and used in pies, sauces, ice-cream and many sweet dishes; small **sour cherries** are derived from the bitter **Morello** variety and have a sharp, tart taste perfect for cooking and making Maraschino liqueur. Sour cherries are poached in syrup, puréed, made into jams or preserves, or used in pies and tarts. Vinegar flavoured with sour cherries and spices is used in sauces for meat, duck, turkey and game.

cherry tomato *see* TOMATO.

chervil (*Anthriscus cerefolium*) This annual herb, native to eastern Europe, has delicate, lacy leaves with a smell and taste a little like tarragon. Widely used in classical French cooking, chervil is one of the ingredients in *fines herbes*. It is best added at the end of cooking for the best taste. Used in flans, omelettes, salad dressings and fish dishes; also as a garnish for oysters, green salads and soups.

Cheshire | ENGLISH | Firm, pressed cow's-milk cheese with a crumbly interior and cloth-wrapped or waxed rind. There are three varieties: orange, stained organically with annatto, white, and blue (which is light-orange with blue veining). Used as a table cheese and for melting. *see also* BLUE CHESHIRE.

chestnut (*Castanea sativa*) Round, white, starchy nut with a shiny, reddish-brown outer shell romantically linked in the Northern Hemisphere with roasting over an open fire. Chestnuts contain very little fat. The shells are removed by making a slit in one side and placing them in boiling water for five minutes. They can also be roasted with a little hot water in a hot oven for about 10 minutes. When cool enough to handle, the shell and skin is peeled off. Peeled chestnuts can be boiled, poached or fried; also puréed as a thickening agent for soups, stews, stuffings and sauces as well as in desserts, cake fillings, soufflés and ice cream. When preserved whole in sugar or syrup they are called marrons glacés.

chestnut mushroom Small button-type mushroom with a rich brown skin. They are sold sold with partly opened or closed caps. They hold their shape well and are sautéed, grilled or baked; also used in soups, sauces and casseroles.

chèvre (fromage de) | FRENCH | Goat's-milk cheese. Usually small cheeses made in individual molds, available in a variety of shapes including flattened pyramids and cones, small barrels, balls, buttons and discs. Most are sold whole and often show a thin bluish mold on the natural rinds, others may have an ash coating or are dusted with herbs or spices.

chevrotin | FRENCH | Generic name referring to several goat's-milk cheeses produced in the Bourbonnais province. Usually shaped like truncated cones.

Chevrotin du Bourbonnais *see* CHEVROTIN.

Chianti | ITALIAN | Renowned red wine from Tuscany, usually seen in straw-covered flasks. Chianti Classico is produced in the legally defined region between Florence and Sienna and bears the neck label insignia of a black rooster. Chianti produced in nearby vineyards is labeled Chianti Putto with the emblem of a cherub.

chicken The young bird of the domestic fowl. **Battery-raised chickens** are mass-produced birds reared in small spaces and fed a regulated growth-enhancing feeding mixture. They are the most commonly available chickens and the most affordable. **Free-range chickens** are reared in large pens and should be set free to roam. They are fed a special organic diet and have a firm, tasty flesh. **Corn-fed chickens are** fattened on corn to give them their distinctive yellowish appearance and special taste.

chickpea flour *see* BESAN.

chickpeas (*Cicer arietinum*) Also known as 'ceci' and 'garbanzo'. Medium-sized, pale brown, wrinkled peas with a sweet, nutty taste. Used in many Mediterranean, Middle Eastern and Indian dishes. They are the main ingredient of hummus and besan (chickpea flour). Soak before simmering for about 45 minutes.

chicory (*Chichorium intybus*) Slightly bitter, leafy, green vegetable with dark green leaves, similar to the dandelion in appearance and sold in small bunches. The tough lower portion of the stems is removed and the young leaves sliced finely and used in salads; also blanched in acidulated water and braised in butter. The roots are ground and used as a coffee substitute. *see also* WITLOF.

chiffonade | FRENCH | Green leaves such as lettuce, sorrel or spinach cut into ribbon-like strips. Used raw or sautéed to garnish soups.

chilaca chili | MEXICAN | Long, wide, brown chili, often twisted or bent. Usually dried, and then it is called 'pasilla' or 'chili negro'.

chili Any of the 200 or so, small hot peppers derived mostly from *Capsicum annum* and *Capsicum frutescens*, native to Mexico and central America and introduced to Europe and Asia about 500 years ago. Chilies are one of the world's most commonly consumed spices and play an important part in the cuisine of Mexico, India, Malaysia, Thailand, Japan and parts of China. Fresh chilies of most varieties are green when young and ripen to degrees of yellow, orange, red and purple; red chilies are generally sweetest. Tiny green chilies eaten in Mexico, Japan and Thailand are usually hotter than the red. The degree of heat comes from alkaloids known as 'capsaicins' which vary according to variety and climate. Seeds and the pale membranes are hotter than the flesh and are often removed before use. Dried chilies, which are used whole, crushed or as a powder, can also be reconstituted in hot water until softened and either puréed for sauces or pounded for pastes. The availability of fresh chilies varies according to the season. *see* AMATISTA, ANAHEIM,

ANCHO, ARBOL, BIRD'S EYE, CASCABEL, CAYENNE, CHILACA, CHIPOTLE, DE AGUA, HABANERO, HUNGARIAN WAX, JALAPEÑO, JAMAICAN HOT, JAPANESE SHISHITO, MULATA, NEW MEXICO RED, PASILLA, PEQUIN, POBLANO, SCOTCH BONNETS, SERRANO, THAI CHILI *and* TABASCO.

chili con carne | AMERICAN | Mexican-style dish originating in Texas consisting of minced beef, simmered with onions, garlic, chilies, tomatoes, herbs and spices. Cooked red kidney beans may be added a short while before serving.

chili negro *see* PASILLA.

chili oil Hot, spicy oil made from dried red chilies seeped in vegetable oil. Used in Chinese cooking, usually combined with a milder oil; served as a condiment.

chimichurri | ARGENTINE | Traditional spicy sauce consisting of olive oil, red wine vinegar, finely chopped onions, garlic, parsley, oregano, cayenne pepper, salt and freshly ground pepper. Served with grilled and roasted meat.

chimney Small opening made in the pastry covering of a pie to allow steam to escape. After cooking, a small tube is inserted into which liquid jelly is poured.

chine The backbone of an animal carcass. Also a term referring to the removal of the backbone from a cut of meat.

Chinese artichoke (*Stachys affinis*) Also known as 'Japanese artichoke' and 'chorogi'. Small, white, knobbly root similar to Jerusalem artichoke in taste, and can be used in the same way. It can be boiled in salted water until tender, sautéed, baked or steamed.

Chinese black mushrooms *see* SHIITAKE *and* MUSHROOMS, DRIED.

Chinese broccoli *see* GAI LARN.

Chinese cabbage | CHINESE | (*Brassica rapa* subsp. *pekinensis*) Also known as 'Peking cabbage', 'wong bok' and 'pe tsai'. Round or elongated cabbage with a solid heart and pale-green crinkly leaves, crisp in texture and mild in taste. It requires little cooking and is not boiled. Cut into chunks or shreds it is used in stir-fried dishes or in soups towards the end of cooking. *see* GAI CHOY.

Chinese chard *see* BOK CHOY.

Chinese chives *see* CHIVES, GARLIC.

Chinese date *see* RED DATE.

Chinese five spices *see* FIVE SPICE POWDER.

Chinese flowering cabbage *see* CHOY SUM.

Chinese gooseberry *see* KIWI FRUIT.

Chinese kale *see* GAI LARN.

Chinese keys (*Kaempferia pandurata*) Known as 'krachai' in Thailand. Perennial plant widely cultivated in India, Sri Lanka, Thailand and Malaysia for its tapering, yellowish-brown rhizomes which are used as an aromatic, spicy seasoning for food and in pickles.

Chinese long bean *see* SNAKE BEAN.

Chinese mustard greens *see* GAI CHOY.

Chinese okra *see* ANGLED LOOFAH.

Chinese parsley *see* CORIANDER.

Chinese pepper *see* SZECHWAN PEPPER.

Chinese sausage *see* LAP CHEONG.

Chinese white radish *see* DAIKON.

Chinese zucchini *see* FUZZY MELON.

chinois Metal, conical sieve with extremely fine mesh used for straining sauces, purées, creams and broths.

chip butty | ENGLISH | Hot potato chips served in a white bread sandwich.

chipolata Small, fresh, spicy sausage made of beef, pork or chicken. Fried or grilled and served as an appetizer or as a garnish for stews or risotto.

chipotle chili | MEXICAN | Dried, smoked version of red jalapeños. It is medium-hot with a pungent, distinct taste. Used in stews and sauces requiring warmth. Also pickled or canned. *see* JALAPEÑO CHILI.

chirashi-zushi *see* SUSHI.

chirinabe | JAPANESE | One-pot dish cooked by diners at the table. Raw fish, tofu and vegetables are simmered in a kelp infused fish stock. Chirinabe is eaten with ponzu sauce and other spicy condiments served in individual bowls.

chitterlings Small intestines of animals, usually young pigs. After thorough cleaning they are simmered until tender, then usually sautéed in butter.

chives (*Allium schoenoprasum*) Small, perennial tufting herb grown for its grass-like, tubular leaves which have a mild onion-like taste. Leaves are chopped finely as a garnish for omelettes, potatoes, salads, soups, dips and vegetables; also blended with sour cream, mayonnaise and cream cheese.

chives, garlic (*Allium tuberosum*) Also known as 'Chinese chives'. Perennial herb with a clumping habit and flat, grass-like leaves with a mild garlic-like taste. Grown extensively throughout Asia where both the leaves and flower buds are used in cooking. The leaves are chopped finely and added to noodles, omelettes, stir-fried dishes, salads and many other dishes. The flower buds are stir-fried.

chocolate (*Theobroma cacao*) Food product made from the fermented, dried, roasted and ground beans of the tropical cocoa tree, native to Mexico and South America. Chocolate comes in several forms including powdered (cocoa), liquid and in blocks. The type of chocolate depends on how much cocoa butter (as the oil is known), milk powder, lecithin and vanilla are added. The more cocoa butter it contains, the smoother and creamier the chocolate. Couverture has a high proportion of cocoa butter and is used for dipping, molding and making professional quality chocolates with a high gloss finish. *see* COCOA BUTTER *and* COCOA POWDER.

chocolate caraque Long chocolate curls made by shaving a thin layer of almost- set chocolate with a large knife. Used to decorate cakes and desserts.

chocolate pudding fruit *see* SAPOTE.

chocolate truffle Chocolate confection made with melted chocolate, butter, egg yolks, castor sugar, rum or brandy and other ingredients. It is made into a truffle-like ball shape and rolled in cocoa powder.

choko (*Sechium edule*) Also known as 'vegetable pear' and 'chayote'. Pear-shaped, pale green vegetable with a thick, ribbed skin. Originating from Central America, it is widely used in the West Indies, Louisiana, parts of Asia and Australia. The round, flat seed is also edible. Chokos are peeled under running water, cut in half and boiled or steamed; also stuffed or cut into pieces and simmered in soups or stews. Young shoots and very small chokos can be used raw in salads or eaten like asparagus.

cholent | JEWISH | Slow-cooked meat casserole containing white beans, barley, onions, garlic and various other seasonings. Made on the day before the Sabbath and reheated after the synagogue service.

cholesterol Fat-like substance, normally present in the blood. Most cholesterol is produced by the body and is needed for the production of bile. High blood cholesterol is one of the risks of heart disease. The over-consumption of saturated fats raises the cholesterol levels in the blood leading to excesses being transported and deposited in the arteries, including those that supply the heart. Saturated fat is found in animal products, which also contain cholesterol. There is no cholesterol in vegetable oils or any other plant products, however coconut oil and palm oil are highly saturated and will raise blood cholesterol levels, as do animal fats. There are two types of cholesterol: low-density lipoproteins (LDL) is the harmful type that contributes to the cholesterol loading in the body; high-density lipoproteins (HDL) are known to help reduce the levels of LDL in the bloodstream. Olive oil, high in mono-unsaturated fats, is high in HDL.

chop suey | AMERICAN | Chinese-style, stir-fried dish adapted by Chinese immigrants at the end of the 19th century in America. It consists of strips of meat with chopped vegetables and is seasoned with soy sauce and garlic.

chorizo | SPANISH | Spicy, coarse-textured pork sausage, highly seasoned with garlic, chilies, herbs and spices. When sliced thinly it is served raw as a tapa; also grilled or cooked in soups or stews. Chorizos are also an important ingredient in Mexican cooking.

chorogi *see* CHINESE ARTICHOKE.

Choron sauce | FRENCH | Béarnaise sauce with added tomato paste. Served with grilled fish, steak or eggs. Developed and named by a French chef, Choron, who was head chef at the exclusive Parisian restaurant, Voison, in the late 19th century.

chou | FRENCH | Plural is 'choux'. Small pastry made from double-cooked choux pastry, often filled with cream and used for éclairs, profiteroles and other cream-filled pastries. Choux with savory fillings are served as hors d'oeuvres.

chow chow preserves | CHINESE | Ginger infused mixed fruit-and-vegetable pickle.

chow mein | CHINESE | Stir-fried dish of various combinations of meat and vegetables served over crispy fried noodles.

choy sum | CHINESE | (*Brassica chinensis* var. *parachinensis*) Also known as 'Chinese flowering cabbage'. Sparsely leafed green vegetable with small yellow flowers on slender, pale green stems. Both the leaves and stems are either steamed or stir-fried.

chrysanthemum leaves (*Chrysanthemum coronarium*) Known as 'shungiku' in Japan and 'tung hao' in China; also known as 'garland chrysanthemum'. Deeply dissected, dark green leaves with a strong distinct taste, commonly cultivated in China and Japan and used as a vegetable or in soups. Young, tender leaves are eaten raw, but they are more commonly blanched and quickly refreshed to prevent further cooking. Often used in one-pot dishes in Japan. The fresh petals of chrysanthemum flowers are used in Chinese cooking as a garnish to soups. Dried flowers are used as a tea.

chuck steak Inexpensive, boneless cut of beef from between the neck and shoulder blade. Usually cut into bite-sized pieces and used in slow-cooked dishes such as casseroles and curries, also minced.

churro | SPANISH | Linear, fluted doughnut cooked in hot oil and sprinkled with castor sugar.

chutney Sweet-and-sour, jam-like condiment made with various combinations of fruit and vegetables cooked in vinegar and sugar, with spices. Brown sugars are usually included in dark chutneys.

ciabatta | ITALIAN | Flattish, elongated loaf of bread made with olive oil, sold plain or sprinkled with herbs, olives or sun-dried tomatoes.

cider Beverage made from pressed apples. After fermentation alcohol is present, the strength of which can vary considerably. Cider is also made into vinegar.

cilantro *see* CORIANDER.

cinnamon (*Cinnamomum zeylanicum*) The inner bark of a tree native to Sri Lanka, sold in curled, paper-thin, brown sticks or quills. Used freshly ground in sweet dishes such as cakes, biscuits, pastries, puddings, stewed fruits and cooked apples. It is an ingredient of many curry powders and in Eastern and Middle Eastern dishes it appears quite frequently in meat and poultry recipes. Whole cinnamon is used in mulled wine, pickles, preserves, fruit compotes and as stirrers for beverages.

cioppino | AMERICAN | Stew made of shrimp, mussels, clams, white fish, garlic, tomatoes and white wine. Specialty of California.

citric acid White, crystalline, sour-tasting compound found in all citrus fruits and some other fruits and vegetables. Used in drinks, desserts and confectionery.

citron (*Citrus medica*) Large, thick-skinned, lemon-like fruit with a bitter flesh, grown for its fragrant thick peel that is processed into candied peel, often used in baking. Oil extracted from the peel is sometimes used in liqueurs. The zest of the Japanese citron (*Citrus junos*), called 'yuzu', is used to impart a citrus aroma in clear soups. The juice is also used in ponzu sauce.

citrus fruits (*Citrus* spp.) There are dozens of different types of citrus trees grown and loved throughout the world for their juicy fruit packed full of vitamin C. They are enjoyed fresh or made into drinks, jams, desserts or confectionery. The zest or peel may be used fresh or candied. Pectin, used in jam-making, is another citrus product. *see also* CITRON, CUMQUAT, GRAPEFRUIT, LEMON, LIME, MANDARIN, ORANGE, POMELO *and* TANGELO.

citrus peel This includes both the zest and the white pith of citrus fruit. Peel is included when making marmalade; also candied in a heavy sugar syrup. Dried mandarin peel is first soaked then used in Chinese cooking.

citrus zest The bright, oily rind or zest of citrus fruits, especially oranges, lemons and limes used for seasoning and garnishing drinks, desserts or salads. Unwaxed fruit can be finely grated or thinly pared using a potato peeler, taking care not to include any white pith. The strips can be left long, julienned or finely chopped. A special citrus zester with small, round cutting holes will create thread-like strips of peel. For some sweet dishes sugar cubes are rubbed on the skin to absorb the oil, then used as part of the recipe.

civet | FRENCH | Game stew, traditionally thickened with the animal's blood.

clafoutis | FRENCH | Custard dessert made with black cherries and baked in a shallow dish. Specialty of the Limousin region.

clams (*Dosinia* spp.) Small, hard-shelled bivalve molluscs sold live in their shells. Fresh clams should have tightly closed shells. They are soaked in cold water for several hours to rid them of any sandy residue in the gut. Clams are cooked gently over a low heat and removed as soon as they start to open. They are used in pasta sauce, risotto, paella, chowder or as an ingredient of seafood salad. Large clams can be grilled in the half-shell with garlic butter. *see also* ALMEJAS.

clarified butter Pure butter-fat that can be used to cook at high temperatures without burning. The butter is slowly heated until it liquefies. The foam on the surface is lifted off and the clear liquid is carefully poured through cheesecloth, leaving the sediment behind.

clarify To make clear stock, syrup or butter. Crushed egg shells, beaten egg-whites or minced beef are added to stock which is brought to the boil, then simmered. These absorb any particles that were making the liquid cloudy. The stock is then cooled and strained. Butter is clarified by heating until it liquefies. The clear liquid on top is removed and strained, leaving the sediment behind. Fruit syrups are clarified by slowly straining through a paper filter or cheesecloth.

cleaver Chopping knife with a strong, almost rectangular blade, usually made of carbon steel. Used for chopping large pieces of meat and bones; Asian cooks use cleavers for chopping, dicing and shredding meat, poultry and vegetables.

clobassi Mild-tasting, smoked, curved sausage made from pork or beef (sometimes both), herbs and spices.

cloche Dome-shaped dish-cover with a handle, made of stainless steel, silver or glass. Used mainly to keep food hot; also to cover cheese.

clotted cream Slightly cooked cream made by gently heating milk slowly until the cream has formed a thick layer on top. After cooling, the cream is skimmed off. Traditionally served with scones for Devonshire tea.

cloud ear fungus *see* WOOD EAR FUNGUS.

cloves (*Syzygium aromaticum*) Dried, unopened flower buds of tropical tree native to the Molucca Islands. Cloves are reddish-brown and resemble short nails. Whole cloves are used to stud ham, fruit, onions, in many stews and soups. Ground cloves are added to spice cakes, plum pudding, biscuits, some breads, various sauces and vegetable dishes.

club sandwich Double-decker sandwich consisting of three slices of bread or toast, held together with a toothpick and cut in half; can also be cut into finger lengths.

coat To cover any food with a protective coating such as dipping in batter, or completely covering in breadcrumbs, flour or sugar.

cobbler Deep-dish fruit pie with a thick top crust made with overlapping rounds or squares of dough.

cochineal Red food dye obtained from a dried, pulverized insect (*Dactylopius coccus*).

cock-a-leekie | SCOTTISH | Classic soup made with chicken, leeks and barley. Traditionally served with stewed prunes.

cockles (*Anadara* and *Katelysia* spp.) Small bivalve molluscs with a hard, fluted shell, found in bays and estuaries just below the surface, in sand or firm mud in southern Australia. Fresh cockles should have tightly closed shells. They are soaked for several hours in cold water to rid them of any sandy residue, then scrubbed thoroughly. Cockles are poached, steamed, grilled, roasted or barbecued and are ready as soon the shells open. A popular English dish is steamed cockles served with malt vinegar and pepper.

cocktail Cold, mixed alcoholic drink served before meals.

cockscomb Fleshy crest on the head of an adult male fowl. Used in classic French cooking chiefly as a garnish for extravagant dishes.

cocktail food Small hors d'oeuvres served with aperitifs and mixed drinks. All food is in bite-sized pieces that can be eaten while standing and do not require a plate. A variety of cocktail food might include spicy nuts, olives, canapés, caviar with blinis or toast, or small pastry cases filled with various mousses. Hot cocktail food might include miniature pizzas, quiches, fishcakes and meatballs.

cocoa butter Natural, pale yellow fat extracted from the oily paste produced when processing cocoa beans. Used in the preparation of chocolate. The percentage of the cocoa butter determines the quality and texture of the chocolate.

cocoa powder Powder obtained from the remaining cocoa paste after most of the cocoa butter has been removed. **Dutch cocoa powder** is processed to neutralise its natural acidity. Used for flavouring many desserts, cakes, biscuits, confectionery and some sauces; also as a drinking chocolate.

coconut (*Cocus nucifera*) The fruit of a tall tropical palm. Fresh coconut is usually sold whole, enclosed in its brown fibrous husk with three soft eyes at the pointed end. When shaken it should sound heavy with coconut water. The thin liquid is drained through the eyes which have been pierced. Coconut water can be used in drinks and cocktails, but is unsuitable for cooking. The white flesh can be eaten as a snack, or freshly grated or shredded, used in curries, fish dishes, fruit salads, cakes, desserts and confectionery; also used to make coconut milk and cream. Coconut flesh is grated or flaked and dried to produce desiccated coconut, and is used in many Asian dishes, for baking and confectionery.

coconut grater Rotary utensil with a number of curved, serrated blades. It is screwed onto the edge of a bench. Half a coconut is firmly held over the blades while the handle is turned. Especially useful when grating large quantities for making coconut milk and cream.

coconut milk and cream Readily available in cans or frozen packs and used instead of stock in many South-East Asian and Indian recipes. Coconut milk can be extracted from freshly grated coconut: it is covered with hot water and left to stand for 10 minutes, then strained and squeezed through cheesecloth and left to stand in the refrigerator. The cream is the thicker concentrated portion that rises to the top. Alternatively a rich coconut cream can be made using four parts grated coconut to one part hot water and let stand for 10 minutes, then strained ready for use. This process can be repeated, adding more hot water to the same coconut for a diluted batch of coconut milk. A third time will produce a thinner milk, but still suitable for use.

coconut oil Vegetable oil high in saturated fat (94 per cent) and considered to increase cholesterol levels much in the same way as do animals fats. It is widely used as the shortening medium in many baked goods and is used as a commercial frying oil; also used as an aromatic basting oil for satays and grilled dishes in Asian cooking.

cocotte | FRENCH | Flame-proof casserole with two handles and a lid. Used for slow-cooking dishes on the top of the stove or in the oven.

cod, salted For centuries this dried salted fish has been an important staple in Europe and Scandinavia. Before cooking it is always desalted by soaking overnight in several changes of fresh water. Salt cod is baked, poached, grilled or fried, seasoned in countless ways with many different sauces. It is creamed to a rich paste or made into soups, stews and codfish cakes, a Portuguese specialty. The popular French dish 'brandade' is a rich purée of salt cod, olive oil, milk or cream and sometimes garlic. In Italy it is known as 'baccalà'.

coddled eggs Soft-boiled eggs that have been lightly cooked slowly in the shell, or out of its shell in a special coddling container that has a tight fitting lid.

coeur à la crème | FRENCH | Dessert of whipped cream and cream cheese placed in individual heart-shaped perforated molds lined with moistened cheesecloth, then chilled. It is removed from the mold and served with fresh berries and sweetened fruit sauce.

coffee Two main species of coffee plants are cultivated for their raw beans which are roasted to various degrees, ground and brewed into a hot drink. *Coffea arabica*, grown at higher altitudes, has a mild, aromatic taste and is naturally lower in caffeine; it is considered the finest and is the most expensive. *Coffea robusta* is higher yielding and grows at lower altitudes; it has a harsher taste, double the caffeine and is commonly used in instant coffee and less expensive blends.

cognac | FRENCH | Fine, matured brandy distilled from white wine. Made in the Cognac region in western France.

Cointreau | FRENCH | Orange based triple-sec liqueur sold in a distinctive square bottle.

colander Bowl-shaped perforated strainer with a base for standing in the sink when draining liquid from food.

Colbert | FRENCH | Method of preparing fish in which the fillets are coated with egg and breadcrumbs and then fried. Served with Colbert butter.

Colbert butter Composite butter made from maitre d'hôtel butter, blended with melted meat glaze and chopped tarragon; served with fried crumbed fish and fried oysters. Colbert sauce is made with meat glaze, butter, wine and lemon juice, with nutmeg, cayenne pepper and chopped parsley; served with vegetables, grilled meat and fish.

Colby | AMERICAN | Mild, semifirm cheese originating in Colby, Wisconsin. Similar to cheddar, but has a softer and more open texture. All-purpose cheese.

colcannon | IRISH | Traditional dish made from boiled shredded green cabbage and mashed potatoes moistened with butter and milk and flavoured with spring onions and seasonings; garnished with finely chopped fresh parsley.

cold larder Department set aside in a large commercial kitchen for the storage and preparation of perishable food. Also the section of a kitchen where cold items are prepared and decorated. *see also* GARDE-MANGER.

cold-pressed oils *see* OILS

colère (en) | FRENCH | Method of presenting whole fish such as whiting in which the tail is inserted in the mouth.

coleslaw Shredded cabbage salad mixed with various other finely chopped ingredients such as onion, carrot, capsicum and herbs, tossed in a vinaigrette or mayonnaise dressing.

Colican potato *see* POTATO.

collard (*Brassica oleracea* var. *acephala*) Type of loose-leafed cabbage that does not form a head. Related to kale.

colombine Hot hors d'oeuvre consisting of a small pastry case with a savory filling, sprinkled with Parmesan cheese, coated with breadcrumbs and fried or baked.

colombo | CARIBBEAN | Type of curry powder or paste introduced to the French West Indies by migrant Ceylonese workers in the 19th century. It mostly consists of mustard seeds, garlic, coriander, chili, saffron, turmeric and black pepper. Named after Colombo, the capital of Sri Lanka. It is also the name given to a curry dish seasoned with colombo.

compote Fresh or dried fruits gently poached and served in sugar syrup, with various ingredients such as wine, liqueur, spices or citrus peel.

compound butter Butter with garlic, herbs, spices or other ingredients. Used on grills, breads and canapés.

Comte | FRENCH | Also known as Gruyère de Comte. Firm, Swiss-style cow's-milk cheese with a natural, brushed rind and pale yellow interior with small scattered holes. Used as a table cheese, also for cooking and melting. This name-controlled cheese bears the origin and date of manufacture stamped in green after the word 'Comte'.

concassé | FRENCH | Coarsely chopped: for example, shinned and deseeded tomatoes that have been chopped are known as 'tomato concassé'.

conchiglie | ITALIAN | Pasta in the shape of a shell. Conchigliette are tiny shells used in soups; there is also a larger version, conchiglioni.

condiment Sauce, relish, mustard or pickle that is served as an accompaniment rather than as an addition to food.

confectionery Also called 'sweets', 'candies', 'lollies' and 'sweetmeats'. Sweet food products based mainly on sugar, corn syrup, honey, molasses and maple syrup. To the sweet base are added chocolate, nuts, fruit, eggs or milk products. Typical confectionery includes chocolate, butterscotch, caramels and toffee, fudge, fondant, jellies, nougat, marzipan and boiled sweets.

confit | FRENCH | Preserve, generally of salted pieces of duck, goose or pork cooked in its own fat and preserved by being completely covered by the fat and stored in a pot. Also refers to fruit or vegetables preserved in sugar, alcohol or vinegar.

congee | CHINESE | Rice porridge, popular for breakfast and as a late-night supper. It is usually accompanied by a variety of small side dishes which might include cooked chicken or fish, chopped green onions, fried peanuts, coriander, preserved vegetables, fried garlic, soy sauce and sesame oil.

conger eel (*Conger* spp.) Large, scaleless saltwater eel. Used mostly in fish soups and stews. *see also* ANEGO.

conploy | CHINESE | Dried, amber-hued scallops available in Asian grocers. They are reconstituted in warm water for at least an hour before use. They fade on cooking. Used in soups and in slow-cooked dishes and rice.

conserve Type of thick jam made from whole or large pieces of fruit of two or more types, often with nuts added. May be used as a thick spread or served as a sauce with dessert.

consommé Clarified and reduced meat, fish or vegetable stock served hot, cold or jellied at the beginning of a meal. It may be infused with wine and garnished in many different ways.

Conti (à la) | FRENCH | Term applied to dishes containing or served with lentils.

convection Method of heating which involves the movement of air.

conversation | FRENCH | Puff pastry tartlet with sugar glazing and an almond or cream filling, decorated with thin strips of intertwined pastry.

cookie | AMERICAN | Biscuit.

copha Solidified coconut oil of mainly saturated fat. Used as a commercial frying oil and in Asian cooking; also a commercial product used for making uncooked confectionery such as coconut ice and chocolate crackles.

coppa | ITALIAN | Salted and dried sausage made from the neck or shoulder of pork, seasoned with salt and garlic and marinated in red wine. Served raw in very thin slices as part of antipasti or used as a pizza topping. In Rome, coppa is a type of pig's-head brawn.

coq au vin | FRENCH | Traditionally a dish of chicken pieces slowly cooked in red wine with whole onions and mushrooms, cubes of bacon, garlic and brandy.

coquille | FRENCH | Translates to 'shell'. Shell or ramekin in which food is served.

coquilles Saint Jacques | FRENCH | Scallops served in their shells. Sometimes refers to scallops topped with a mornay sauce and baked in their shells. *see also* SCALLOPS.

coral The orange or red roe of some shellfish such as scallops. It can be cooked with the scallop or separated and used in a sauce. Lobster coral is often used in a sauce served with lobster.

coral fungus *see* WHITE FUNGUS.

coral lettuce (*Lactuca sativa*) Decorative, non-hearting lettuce with tight frilly leaves in both red and green varieties. Popular in mixed green salads.

coral trout (*Plectropomus* spp.) Collective name given to four similar species of pinky-red medium-sized fish with a pattern of small bluish spots. They are found in coral reef waters of northern Australia and have a firm white flesh with a mild sweet taste and are highly regarded as table fish. Available whole or as fillets.

corallini | ITALIAN | Tiny, tube-shaped pasta used in soups.

Corella pear Small, squat pear with green skin and a generous pinkish-red blushing. Aromatic, with very little core and few seeds. An excellent eating pear that also holds its shape well when poached. Available mid-winter to spring. *see also* PEAR.

coriander (*Coriandrum sativum*) Also known as 'Chinese parsley' and 'cilantro'. Annual herb native to the Mediterranean and Middle East regions and used since earliest times. Leaves are widely used in Indian, Oriental, Latin American and Middle Eastern cooking. The whole of the plant is used in many Thai dishes. Dried mature seeds are roasted and ground and form an important ingredient of many curries. Also used in pickles, confectionery, charcuterie, bakery goods and in liqueurs.

corn, sweet (*Zea mays*) The pale-yellow, milky kernels on the cob, enclosed in a bright-green husk, are best eaten soon after harvesting. The husks and silky tops are removed and the cobs are cooked in boiling water for about five minutes and served immediately with butter and freshly ground pepper; also baked or barbecued in the husk. When taken off the cob, the kernels can be used in soups, vegetable dishes, salads, fritters and desserts. Baby corn cobs are eaten whole in some Asian dishes.

cornbread | AMERICAN | Unleavened bread made with cornmeal instead of, or in a combination with, regular flour. It can be baked in a shallow pan, cooked in a frying pan or deep-fried. Popular both in New England and the South.

corned beef Also known as 'salt beef'. Whole pieces of beef cured in a seasoned brine. Usually rolled brisket or silverside are used. In England it is simmered whole with small onions, carrots, bay leaf and spices and traditionally served with dumplings. Also served cold in slices for sandwiches.

cornet | FRENCH | Translates to 'small horn'. Usually refers to cone-shaped food such as a wafer ice-cream cone or puff pastry filled with cream, sometimes known as a 'cream horn'.

cornflour Also known as 'cornstarch' and 'maize flour'. Very fine flour milled from the starch of corn kernels. Used as a thickener and in baked goods; frequently used in Chinese cooking.

cornichon Tiny pickled gherkin, often served as an appetizer, or with cold meats, pâtés and fish.

Cornish pasty | ENGLISH | Individual folded pie containing a mixture of diced meat, potatoes and onions and other vegetables, then baked in the oven.

cornmeal (*Zea mays*) Dried white or yellow corn kernels ground to various thickness. Used in the United States to make cornbread. In Italy cornmeal is used to make polenta.

corn oil Also known as 'maize oil'. Polyunsaturated oil pressed from corn kernels. It can be heated at high temperatures and is suitable for frying and stir-fried dishes.

corn salad (*Valerianella locusta*) Also known as 'lamb's lettuce' or 'mâche' in France. Dark green, small, rounded leaves in a loose rosette. Individual leaves used mostly in mixed salads; ingredient of mesclun; also, lightly cooked, like spinach.

cornstarch | AMERICAN | Cornflour.

corn syrup Clear, sweet liquid derived from sweet corn. Used as a pancake topping and in baked goods; also popular in jams and preserves because it does not crystallize. Corn syrup also comes in a dark form.

cos lettuce (*Lactuca sativa*) Called 'romaine lettuce' in America. Elongated head of dark green, oval leaves with a crisp, pale green, slightly bitter heart which is the part used in salads and traditionally used in Caesar salad.

costmary (*Chrysanthemum balsamita*) Also known as 'alecost'. Perennial herb with strong-tasting toothed leaves. Used in small amounts in salads and to flavour soups, stews, stuffings and sausages.

côte | FRENCH | Chop or cutlet of any meat; also part of the rib section of beef.

cotechino | ITALIAN | Large, fresh pork sausage seasoned with nutmeg and cloves and salted for only a few days. It is simmered slowly for two to three hours, cut into thick slices and served on a bed of mashed potatoes, lentils or cooked dried beans. The pork mixture is similar to the stuffing of zampone and either can be used as a traditional ingredient of bollito misto (mixed boiled meats). *see also* BOLLITO MISTO *and* ZAMPONE.

cotelette | FRENCH | Thin chop or cutlet.

Côtes du Rhône | FRENCH | Generic name given to red, white and rosé AOC wines grown in the valley of the Rhône River in south-eastern France.

Some of the more specific wines are sold under their own appellation and include Chateauneuf-du-Pape, Côte-Roti, Crozes-Hermitage and Tavel.

cotignac | FRENCH | Pink confection made from quince purée and sugar.

cottage cheese Low-fat, unripened cow's-milk cheese high in calcium and popular with the diet-conscious. Moist, mild and perishable. Used in salads, with fruit, as a dip and in desserts.

cottage pie *see* SHEPHERD'S PIE.

coulibiac | RUSSIAN | Elaborate, oblong pie usually of layers of salmon, rice, mushrooms, hard-boiled eggs, onion, dill and parsley, wrapped in a yeast pastry and baked in a dish shaped like a fish.

coulis | FRENCH | (1) Smooth purée usually served as a small sauce made from raw or cooked fruit or vegetables. A fruit coulis is served as an accompaniment to hot or cold desserts. A tomato coulis is served with shellfish and pasta. (2) Thick seafood bisque.

Coulommiers | FRENCH | This Brie-style cheese takes its name from Coulommiers, Ile-de-France where it was first made. Available in small, flat discs with a whitish rind.

coupe Rounded dish made of glass or metal, often on a stem. Used for ice cream, desserts, fruit salads and sundaes. Also the name of a dessert served in a coupe.

courgette *see* ZUCCHINI.

court-bouillon | FRENCH | Seasoned stock used for poaching fish or vegetables.

couscous | NORTH AFRICAN | National dish of Morocco, Tunisia and Algeria. Hearty dish made with flour-coated granular semolina (also called 'couscous'). The couscous is steamed over a broth or stew of meat, vegetables, spices and sometimes chickpeas, broad beans and raisins. The grain couscous is available in supermarkets and instructions for cooking it are on the packet.

couscousière | NORTH AFRICAN | Two-part cooking pot, with a tall pointed lid, in which couscous is prepared. It consists of a large round pan in which the meat and vegetable stew is cooked, and a smaller upper pan pierced with small holes in which the couscous is steamed simultaneously.

couverture | FRENCH | Bittersweet chocolate high in cocoa butter. Used for dipping, molding and making the shiniest chocolates.

cozze *see* MUSSELS.

crab-apple (*Malus pumila*) Small, bitter, red or yellow apple with a rather hard flesh. It is high in pectin and makes an excellent jelly and preserve.

crab The four main species of crabs caught and eaten in Australia are the **blue swimmer crab** (*Portunus pelagicus*), the mud or mangrove crab (*Scylla serrata*), the **spanner crab** (*Ranina ranina*) and the **giant crab** (*Pseudo- carcinus gigas*). Crabs are sold live, dead and cooked. When buying a live crab ensure that it is active and all its limbs are intact. The claws should be tied so that it stays in good condition during transportation. Experts humanely and quickly kill a live crab by piercing the nerve centres between the eyes from the underside of the shell. Alternatively it can be killed by being placed directly in the freezer until it dies, but not frozen. The whole crab can then be placed in a large pot with cold water, brought to the boil and simmered for about 8 minutes per 500 g. It is then plunged into icy cold water to prevent further cooking. Alternatively the raw flesh can be first extracted from body, legs and claws and then sautéed, pan-fried or braised. To steam crab, pull off the top shell, lift and remove the tail flap from behind and discard the gills, then wash. Pull off the claws and chop the body into pieces. Crack the hard shell on the claws. Place the crab in a steamer and cook for about eight minutes. Crab pieces can also be stir-fried in a wok, then tossed and coated with an Asian-style sauce. *see also* BLUE SWIMMER CRAB, MUD CRAB, SPANNER CRAB *and* GIANT CRAB.

cracked wheat *see* BULGUR.

cracker Light biscuit used for snacks and often served with cheese.

crackling Crispy rind of roast pork that is usually scored and salted. Served with the meat.

cramique | FRENCH | Brioche with raisins or currants, eaten hot with butter. Speciality of northern France and Belgium.

cranberry (*Vaccinium macrocarpum*) Scarlet, slightly oval berry with a rather astringent taste when raw. Cranberries are a good source of vitamin C. Usually made into cranberry sauce, the traditional accompaniment to roast turkey, but also used in jams, jellies, pies, puddings and other desserts.

cranberry beans *see* BORLOTTI BEANS.

crapaudine (en) | FRENCH | Preparation of small poultry or game bird with backbone removed, flattened and cooked whole. It is usually coated with seasoned breadcrumbs, then grilled.

craquelin | FRENCH | Small, crisp biscuit.

crawfish Another name for freshwater crayfish often referred to in Cajun and Creole cooking.

crayfish Small freshwater crustaceans that look like tiny lobsters with large claws. They include the highly regarded Western Australian marron (*Cherax tenuimanus*), the redclaw (*C. quadricarinatus*) found in northern river systems of Queensland, and the smaller yabby (*C. destructor*). Crayfish are farmed commercially in Australia and are sold live and cooked. Species of saltwater crayfish are commonly known in Australia as 'lobsters' or 'rock lobsters'. *see also* LOBSTER, MARRON *and* YABBY.

cream Dairy product consisting of the fatty part of milk. It rises naturally to the surface of cow's milk and was traditionally skimmed by hand. Commercial cream is separated by centrifugal force. Most **pure cream** sold in Australia has been pasteurized and has a minimum of 35 per cent milk fat. It is sold in various forms and is classified according to fat content. **Thickened cream** is pure cream with gelatin added. **Sour cream** is pure cream soured by the addition of a bacterial culture to give it a slightly acidic tang. *see also* CRÈME FRAÎCHE.

cream cheese Fresh cow's-milk cheese with a soft, spreadable texture. It is mild tasting and sometimes has the addition of cream or herbs and spices. The best-known brand is Philadelphia Cream Cheese. Used as a spreadable snack or made into dips, desserts and cheesecake. Mascarpone is a triple cream cheese made from cream curdled with citric acid.

Crécy | FRENCH | A dish that contains or is served with carrots.

crème anglaise | FRENCH | Light custard sauce of egg yolks, sugar and milk. Used as a pudding topping, in other desserts and in patisserie.

crème brûlée | FRENCH | Translates to 'burnt cream'. Rich egg custard dessert with a hard caramelized top. This is produced by sprinkling a thin layer of sugar on top of the cold set custard and placing under a hot grill, or using a brûlée iron or small blowtorch.

crème caramel | FRENCH | Classic vanilla custard dessert that has been baked in a caramel-coated mold. When cool it is inverted onto a plate coated in its caramel sauce.

crème de banane Sweet, banana liqueur.

crème de cacao Sweet liqueur with chocolate and vanilla.

crème de cassis French liqueur made from blackcurrants.

crème de fraises Red French liqueur with strawberries.

crème de menthe Sweet peppermint liqueur. Available in clear form or green.

crème de mokka Light brown French liqueur with a coffee taste.

crème de noix French, walnut-based liqueur.

crème de noyeau Almond French liqueur made from peach and apricot kernels.

crème fraîche Velvety sour cream that is allowed to mature naturally until it thickens and develops a distinctive sharp flavour. It has a fat content of 48 per cent. As it does not curdle when boiled or reduced it is used in numerous sauces.

crème pâtissière | FRENCH | Custard filling used for pastries and cakes.

Creole cooking | AMERICAN | A sophisticated style of cooking, mostly practiced in Louisiana and derived largely from French, Spanish, African and American Indian influences. Creole cuisine is typified by the use of roux, freshly made stock, tomatoes and a subtle blend of seasonings.

crêpe | FRENCH | Thin savory or sweet pancake.

crêpes Suzette | FRENCH | Hot crêpe dessert flamed with orange liqueur.

crêperie | FRENCH | Restaurant specializing in serving various sweet and savory crêpes.

crépine | FRENCH | Pig's caul used to wrap around sausage meat and hold together certain ingredients such as pâté and forcemeat during cooking. *see also* CAUL.

crépinettes | FRENCH | Small flat sausage made of ground pork, lamb, veal or poultry, and chopped parsley, wrapped in caul (crépine). It is coated in melted butter and sometimes breadcrumbs before pan-frying or grilling. Served with mashed potatoes or lentils.

cress, garden (*Barbarea vulgaris*) Also known as 'winter' or 'land cress'. Small, shiny leaves with a strong taste used raw in salads, as a garnish or cooked in soups and purées. Not to be confused with watercress.

Crescenza *see* STRACCHINO.

crespelle Tiny pickled gherkin, often served as an appetizer, or with cold meats, pâtés and fish.

cresponi *see* MILANO SALAMI.

criadillas *see* ANIMELLES.

crimp To make a decorative pattern and to seal the dough around the edge of an unbaked pie.

crique | FRENCH | Potato pancake made with grated raw potato with garlic and parsley; sometimes with the addition of eggs.

crocodile | AUSTRALIAN | Two species of crocodiles are farm-bred for their meat in northern Australia. The white meat is taken mainly from the tail and it is usually sold in steaks. It is very low in fat and is similar to chicken and pork in taste and texture. Many chicken recipes can be adapted for crocodile meat, but it should be cooked lightly.

croissant | FRENCH | Light, crescent-shaped pastry consisting of layers of yeast-dough dotted generously with butter before baking.

croquant | FRENCH | Translates to 'crisp' or 'crunchy'. Confection of almonds and hazelnuts embedded in crunchy caramel.

croque-madame | FRENCH | Open-faced sandwich of ham and Gruyère cheese served with a baked egg on top.

croquembouche | FRENCH | Traditionally a tall conical tower made up of many small choux pastry rounds filled with crème pâtissière that are coated with a caramel glaze, and decorated with spun caramel, crystallized flowers, sugar-coated almonds, etc. Served at special events and as a wedding cake in France.

croque-monsieur | FRENCH | Hot sandwich filled with ham and Gruyère cheese and lightly fried or grilled on both sides.

croquette | FRENCH | Minced meat, fish, poultry or vegetables bound with eggs and shaped into various forms, coated with breadcrumbs and fried until they are crisp and lightly browned.

crostini | ITALIAN | Croutons or small pieces of toast.

Crottin de Chavignol | FRENCH | Small, flattened ball of goat's-milk cheese with a white, soft interior and a natural crust. Mild to tange when young, pungent and strong when aged. Served as a snack, after meals or grilled and served warm with a green salad. Mainly farm-produced in the Loire Valley.

croustade | FRENCH | Hot hors d'oeuvre, made from hollowed-out French bread or pastry shell with various fillings, which is fried or heated in the oven.

croûte | FRENCH | Thick slice of fried bread with the crusts removed, or a pastry case upon which various cooked toppings are served. A croûte is also a slice of toasted or fried bread served with or in a soup.

crouton | FRENCH | Small cubes of toasted or fried bread. Used as a garnish for soups, salads and other dishes.

crown roast Roasted racks of lamb or pork tied in a circle with the bones on the outside pointing upwards to form the shape of a crown. The centre is filled with vegetables or is garnished.

cruciferous vegetables Any vegetable belonging to the large cabbage family (*Cruciferae*) which might include broccoli, cabbage, cauliflower, radish, turnips and various leafy green vegetables known as Chinese mustard greens.

crudités | FRENCH | An assortment of raw vegetables generally cut into small pieces and served with a cold sauce; usually as an appetizer.

crumb tray Small tray with matching brush for brushing crumbs from the table, usually after the main course before dessert is served.

crumiri | ITALIAN | Sweet, elbow-shaped biscuits made with polenta and honey.

crumpet | ENGLISH | Small yeast-cake cooked on a hotplate inside a metal ring. As the crumpet cooks small holes appear on the top surface. Served toasted whole and spread with butter.

crustaceans Group of aquatic animals with hard or crust-like shells and segmented bodies. *see also* BALMAIN BUG, CRABS, CRAYFISH, LOBSTERS, PRAWNS *and* YABBY.

crystallized flowers Preserved edible flowers such as violets and the petals of roses that have been lightly coated in egg white, dusted in caster sugar and allowed to completely dry out. Used for decorating desserts and cakes, chocolates and ice creams. Leaves such as those of scented geraniums, mint, lemon verbena or lemon balm can also be crystallized.

crystallised fruit *see* CANDIED FRUIT.

csabai | HUNGARIAN | Dried, smoked irregular-shaped slender salami made from pork, or a mixture of meats, seasoned with paprika and peppercorns. Mild and hot varieties are available.

cucumber (*Cucumis sativus*) Closely related to gourds, the cucumber has been cultivated for several thousand years. Most varieties have green skins and some have warts or soft spines. The **Lebanese cucumber** is narrow with a smooth skin and the **telegraph** is long, thin, dark green and almost seedless. The almost round, **white apple** varieties have a smooth, whitish skin and flesh. Usually eaten raw as a salad vegetable; also made into pickles or lightly cooked. Sliced cucumber and yoghurt is a popular side dish in the Middle East and India. *see also* GHERKIN.

cuisine minceur | FRENCH | Specialized recipes developed by chef Michel Guérard for slimmers in the early 1970s at his health farm at Eugenie-les-Bains where the menu was served to spa guests.

culatello | ITALIAN | High quality raw ham that has been cured and soaked in wine. It is sliced thinly and served as an antipasto.

culotte | FRENCH | Rump, usually of beef.

Cumberland sauce | ENGLISH | Traditional fruity sauce made with fine strips of orange and lemon zest and juice, mustard, redcurrant jelly, port wine and seasoning; served at room temperature with venison, ham or duck.

cumin (*Cuminum cyminum*) Annual herb native to Egypt and now cultivated in many warm countries for its small but powerful, light brown seeds that are used in a variety of foods. The seeds constitute one of the ingredients of curry power and Mexican chili powder and is used in dishes in Asia, North Africa and Latin-America. Cumin is often used in rye bread, pickles and chutneys, and in cheese and liqueurs.

cumquat / kumquat (*Fortunella* spp.) Small, oval citrus fruit with thin, orange rind and sweet, acid pulp. The tear-drop **Nagami** is the sweetest variety and when fully ripe can be eaten raw, skin included, or mixed into fruit salads. It makes an excellent marmalade and may be preserved in brandy or gin. **Calamondin** is a round type of cumquat often grown as an ornamental container plant. Its sour fruit is used mainly for marmalade and brandied preserves.

Curaçao Sweet orange liqueur. Originally from the Caribbean island of Curaçao and made from the dried peel of bitter oranges.

curd The coagulated part of the milk which separates from the whey when the milk is curdled. Curdling is the first stage in the manufacture of cheese.

cure To preserve meat or fish by hanging in smoke, or by salting or drying.

curly endive (*Chichorium endivia*) Called 'frisée' in France. Slightly bitter, leafy green vegetable with extremely frilly leaves often sold in large bunches tied up so that the loose hearts are kept dark and less bitter. The tender, light green, inside leaves are used for adding a touch of bitterness to salads. Also cooked briefly like spinach. The broad-leaved form is known as 'Batavian endive', 'escarole' in the United States and 'scarole' in France.

currants (*Ribes* spp.) **(1)** Small summer berries widely used in fruit salads, preserves, cordials, purées and wine. **(2)** Also the name given to small, seedless dried grapes. *see* BLACKCURRANT *and* REDCURRANT.

curry | INDIAN | Anglicized form of the Tamil word 'kari', which means 'sauce'. Generally refers to a dish of meat, fish or vegetables that is cooked with a combination of spices to produce a spicy stew that is usually served with rice.

curry leaves (*Murraya koenigii*) Aromatic fresh or dried leaves used in dishes from southern India, Sri Lanka and South-East Asia.

curry paste | INDIAN | Aromatic mixture of ground spices and freshly chopped herbs blended with a liquid such as water, lime juice, coconut milk or vinegar to make a smooth paste.

curry paste, green | THAI | Mixture of ground, freshly roasted spices such as peppercorns, coriander seeds, cumin, nutmeg, mace, green chilies blended with shallots, garlic, lemon grass, galangal, coriander leaves and shrimp paste to form a smooth paste. Principal ingredient in green curries.

curry paste, Musaman *see* MUSAMAN CURRY PASTE.

curry paste, red | THAI | Mixture of ground, freshly roasted spices such as peppercorns, coriander seeds, cumin, nutmeg, mace and red chilies blended with shallots, garlic, lemon grass, galangal and shrimp paste to form a smooth paste. Principal ingredient in red curries.

curry powder Mixture of aromatic ground spices and seasonings, originally adapted by British settlers in India from the traditional mixtures (or masalas) of Indian cuisine. Commercial curry powders range in taste from hot to mild and vary according to the type of cuisine as well as the manufacturer. The basic dried ingredients usually consist of coriander, cumin, peppercorns, cloves, chilies, cinnamon, fenugreek and turmeric which imparts the characteristic yellow hue. *see also* MASALA.

custard apple (*Annona reticulata*) Also known as 'cherimoya'. Round, knobbly fruit with pale green, leathery skin enclosing a creamy-white, fleshy pulp with numerous large black seeds. A good source of vitamin B and some vitamin C. Used in fruit salads, creamy desserts, pies and ice cream.

cut in In pastry-making, to mix dry ingredients such as flour with cold butter or shortening, by using a knife, cool fingers or a food processor until the mixture resembles coarse breadcrumbs.

cutlet Thin slice of tender meat, taken from the rib section, with the bone attached.

cuttlefish (*Sepia* spp.) Closely related to the squid, the cuttlefish generally has a wider body, eight stubby tentacles, two long tentacles and a hard internal bone known as the 'cuttlebone'. Cuttlefish is prepared and cooked in the same way as squid, and similarly is most tender when cooked briefly.

cuttlefish, dried | SOUTH-EAST ASIA | Thin slices of cuttlefish are sold in clear plastic packs in Asian grocers. It is eaten as a snack or used in slow-cooked soups.

Cynar | ITALIAN | Very bitter aperitif made from artichokes. Usually served with soda water and ice.

cyrniki | RUSSIAN | Light cheese dumpling made with cottage cheese mixed with eggs, flour and seasoning. The dough is cut into small triangles and lightly browned in butter.

dacquoise | FRENCH | Almond and hazelnut meringue gâteau consisting of two or three layers filled with butter cream or fresh whipped cream.

daikon | JAPANESE | (*Raphanus sativus*) Also known as 'Chinese white radish', and 'mooli' in India. Large, white root vegetable with a crisp juicy flesh and a mild, refreshing taste, extensively used in Japan, also in China, India and Korea. It is believed to aid digestion, especially rich, oily foods, and in Japan is grated, shredded or pickled and eaten as a condiment or used as a garnish. In China it is sliced thinly and eaten raw, pickled or salted. Also cut in various ways and stir-fired, braised, boiled or steamed. The leaves can also be stir-fried as a vegetable.

daiquiri Rum cocktail from Cuba made with white rum, fresh lime juice and sugar syrup shaken together over ice and strained. A frozen daiquiri is made with crushed ice and often fruit (such as peaches and strawberries) whisked in a blender and served unstrained.

dal *see* DHAL.

damier | FRENCH | Rum infused sponge gâteau decorated with a checkerboard pattern on top.

damper | AUSTRALIAN | Type of unleavened bush bread traditionally made with plain flour, water and a little salt, baked in the hot coals of a camp fire. Modern versions are made with self-raising flour and milk, and sometimes butter.

damson plum (*Prunus damascena*) Small, oval, purplish-blue plum with a bitter, greenish-yellow flesh, highly valued for preserves, pies and homemade wine.

Danablu cheese *see* DANISH BLUE.

Danbo | DANISH | Semisoft, pressed cow's-milk cheese. It has a smooth, whitish cream interior with a number of small holes and a thin, natural rind, usually waxed. Often made with caraway seeds. Mild-tasting table cheese usually served with fruit.

dandelion leaves (*Taraxacum officinale*) Known as 'pissenlit' in France. Long, dark green, strongly indented leaves with a bitter, peppery taste. Rich in iron and vitamin A. Young leaves are served raw in the mixed green winter salad of Provence called 'mesclun'. They also appear in a salad with hot diced bacon; also cooked like spinach. Dandelion leaves are picked before the plant has flowered. Older leaves are too bitter. In cultivation, about a week before cutting, the plant is covered to exclude light. This blanches the leaves, making them paler, less bitter-tasting and more palatable. The roots are dried and used in a coffee-like beverage.

dang myun | KOREAN | Pale grey, long noodles made from sweet potato starch. They have a chewy texture and readily soak up other flavours. Traditionally added to the classic chap chae, a stir-fried dish of sliced beef and vegetables, with garlic, chili, soy sauce, sugar and sesame oil.

Danish Blue | DANISH | Sharp-tasting, semisoft, blue vein cow's-milk cheese with a creamy white interior and a dense network of blue veins. Widely available and reliable. Served as a snack, in salads, with fruit and after meals.

Danish pastry | DANISH | Flaky pastry made with yeast-dough layered with butter and containing a variety of fillings.

Danish salami | DANISH | Smoked, mildly spicy salami made from pork or a mixture of meats, seasoned with garlic and pepper.

dariole | FRENCH | Small, high-sided, cylindrical mold used to make small pastries, puddings and individual babas. Also the name given to the preparation cooked in a dariole mold.

Darjeeling tea High quality Indian black tea from the province of Darjeeling, in the foothills of the Himalayas.

darne | FRENCH | Thick slice of a large fish cut across the bone.

dartois | FRENCH | Puff pastry rectangles layered with pastry cream filling as a dessert; or filled with meat or fish and served as a hot hors d'oeuvre.

dasheen *see* TARO.

dashi | JAPANESE | All-purpose stock made from dried kelp (kombu) and flakes of dried bonito. Used as a soup.

date (*Phoenix dactylifera*) Fresh dates are becoming more widely available in fruit shops around summer and, although sweet, they have a winey taste and are excellent sliced and added to chicken and other cold meat salads; also stuffed with cream cheese or blue vein cheese and other fillings. They are also eaten fresh and used in various sweet dishes. Dried dates are sweeter and richer than the fresh; also eaten as a snack or used in cakes, puddings, rice dishes, curries or stuffed with a sweet filling for confectionery. Dried dates will store airtight up to six months in a cool dry place. They can be plumped up and made more succulent by steaming for 15 minutes or soaking in wine. *see also* RED DATE.

daube | FRENCH | Marinated meat and vegetables cooked slowly for a long time in red wine, herbs and spices in a heavy, covered casserole, or daubière.

daun salam | INDONESIAN | (*Eugenia polyantha*) Aromatic leaf similar to but larger than curry leaves. Used in Indonesian and Malaysian curries.

Dauphin | FRENCH | Soft, crescent-shaped cow's-milk cheese with parsley, tarragon, pepper and cloves, and dusted with paprika. Strong, spicy taste. Used as a snack or cocktail cheese.

dauphine potatoes *see* POMMES DAUPHINE.

Davidson's plum | AUSTRALIAN | (*Davidsonia pruriens*) Blue-black fruit, resembling a plum, from a small rainforest tree. The juicy, purple flesh has a sharp, acid taste and is mostly made into jams, jellies and sauces. Also available frozen whole.

daun pandan The Indonesian and Malaysian name for 'pandanus leaf'.

decant To gently pour liquid from one container to another, allowing the sediment to remain.

deep-fry To cook in hot oil or fat that is deep enough for the food to be completely submerged.

deglaze To add a small amount of liquid such as wine or stock to the pan juices, in which meat or poultry have been cooked, in order to make a base for a sauce or gravy.

dégorge / disgorge (1) To sprinkle certain vegetables such as eggplant and cucumber with salt to eliminate the bitter and excess juices. **(2)** To soak meat, poultry or fish in cold water to draw out strong tastes or coagulated blood.

dégraisser To remove excess fat from a stock, sauce or dish.

dégustation | FRENCH | A tasting or sampling. Some restaurants offer a set price menu with a number of entrée-sized dishes and a sampling of desserts.

Delicious apple *see* GOLDEN DELICIOUS APPLE *and* RED DELICIOUS APPLE.

demerara sugar Coarse-textured, dry brown sugar mixed with a little molasses. Traditionally used to sweeten coffee.

demi-deuil | FRENCH | A dish that contains both black and white ingredients.

demi-glace Concentrated beef-based sauce, lightened with consommé or white stock and spiked with Madeira or sherry. Used as a base for other sauces.

demi-sec | FRENCH | Translates to 'half dry'. Usually refers to champagne and other sparkling wines that are quite sweet.

demi-tasse | FRENCH | Translates to 'half cup'. Refers to an after-dinner coffee served in a small cup.

Denominazione di Origine Controllata (DOC) | ITALIAN | Italian legal system used to protect the regional names of certain wines and food. DOC wines are produced from specific grape varieties grown in a designated area and processed and aged following set methods in order to meet prescribed standards.

Derby | ENGLISH | Firm, pressed cow's-milk cheese with moist, slightly flaky, interior and pale yellow rind. Similar to a mild cheddar. Sage Derby is flecked with chopped sage leaves mixed with the curd. Served as a snack and on sandwiches.

Des Moines squash *see* ACORN SQUASH.

desiccated coconut The dry shredded flesh of the coconut.

Desiree potato *see* POTATO.

dessert Sweet dishes served at the end of the meal, or just before cheese and fruit.

desert lime | AUSTRALIAN | (*Eremocitrus glauca*) Small, rounded, yellow fruit obtained from a large, spiny shrub, related to the citrus group. It has a sharp, tangy taste and is popular in bush food restaurants. Used in a variety of sauces, chutneys and marmalade; also used in desserts, ice cream and whole as a garnish with seafood and poultry. Available frozen whole.

detendre | FRENCH | To dilute or soften to a thinner consistency.

devein To remove the dark intestinal vein along the back of certain crustaceans, such as prawns. A shallow cut is made with the tip of a sharp knife and the vein easily lifted out.

devil's tongue (*Amorphophallus konjac*) Root of a yam-like plant used to make a translucent loaf (konnyaku) and various types of noodles used in Japanese cooking. See konnyaku and shirataki.

devilled Dish or sauce that is highly seasoned with a hot spicy ingredient such as mustard, cayenne, Tabasco or Worcestershire sauce. Popular in English cooking.

devils on horseback | ENGLISH | Hot hors d'oeuvre made by wrapping stoned prunes in thin slices of bacon, then grilling.

devon Fairly salty, bland-tasting, soft-textured cooked sausage made from beef and pork.

Devonshire cream *see* CLOTTED CREAM.

dextrose Form of glucose found naturally in many sweets.

dhal / dal | INDIAN | Generic name for dried pulses, including lentils, beans, split peas and chickpeas. It is also the name of a spicy dish, made with lentils or other pulses, that often accompanies curries.

diable | FRENCH | Round pottery cooking dish with a single long handle on the base and lid. 'À la diable' refers to a dish served with a piquant devilled sauce.

dice To cut into small cubes.

dieppoise (à la) | FRENCH | Fish cooked in the Dieppe style; usually with white wine sauce, mussels, shrimp and mushrooms.

dietary fiber The cellulose of plants which is not completely digested in the human digestive system. It increases the bulk in the diet and assists in bowel movement, helping to prevent constipation. Prime sources are cereals, wholemeal flour, pulses, nuts, fruit and vegetables.

digestive General term for spirits or liqueurs served after dinner. Called 'digestif ' in French and 'digestivo' in Italian.

Dijon mustard | FRENCH | Mild mustard paste, made from black and brown mustard seeds, verjuice and white wine. Main centre for production is Dijon, France. Used as a condiment for meat and charcuterie and as a coating for poultry, pork and some oily fish before cooking.

dijonnaise (à la) | FRENCH | Dijon style; usually with mustard.

dill (*Anethum graveolens*) Small annual herb with fine thread-like leaves similar to fennel, but smaller. Both leaves and seeds used. Often associated with Russian and Scandinavian cooking where the leaves are used for curing raw fish, particularly salmon in the style of gravlax. Chopped dill is used in tartar sauce and other sauces for fish; also salads, egg dishes, vegetables and coleslaw. The seeds are used for pickling cucumbers and gherkins. Dill has a reputation for relieving indigestion.

dilute To add liquid to a mixture to make thinner or reduce its strength.

dim sim | CHINESE | Small dumplings made of thin sheets of noodle dough, filled with a variety of mixtures, and steamed or deep-fried.

dim sum | CHINESE | Translates to 'touch the heart'. A variety of small steamed or fried appetisers and dishes, served with tea as a snack at any time of the day. Dim sum served at brunch on Sundays is called 'yum cha' which means 'to drink tea'.

dinner Principal meal of the day, usually eaten in the evening.

diot | FRENCH | Small vegetable and pork sausage gently cooked in white wine. Speciality of the Savoy.

dip Light, savory cream or sauce used for dipping a selection of raw vegetables, bread or crackers. Popular at drink parties as they can be eaten while standing and do not require a plate.

diplomat pudding Molded dessert made with layers of sponge fingers soaked in Kirsch, candied and dried fruit, and Bavarian cream. It is chilled and unmolded and served with fruit or custard sauce.

diplomat sauce | FRENCH | Rich white sauce made with fish stock, roux, cream and brandy, which might include truffles and lobster meat or butter. Served with delicate white fish.

dirty rice | AMERICAN | Traditional Cajun dish of rice cooked with chicken livers and gizzards, minced pork, various spices and chopped vegetables.

disjoint To cut and separate at the joint, as with poultry.

distillation Process of separating a liquid by heating so that it vaporizes. When cooled, the vapor condenses into a more concentrated form and in the case of liquor has a higher alcoholic content.

distilled water Water purified by boiling and distillation.

ditalini | ITALIAN | Also known as 'tubetti'. Short small tubes of pasta, used in minestrone.

Dobos torte | HUNGARIAN | Many-tiered layer-cake spread with chocolate cream and coated with a crisp caramel glaze.

dodine | FRENCH | Braised, stuffed boned poultry, usually duck, served with a sauce made from the poultry carcass, vegetables, wine, cooking juices, the chopped liver of the bird and cream.

Dolcelatte | ITALIAN | Translates to 'sweet milk' and refers to a creamy, delicate Gorgonzola.

dolmas | GREEK | Also known as 'dolmades'. Vine leaves stuffed with cooked rice and minced lamb, rolled into small cylinders and braised in a light lemon or tomato sauce.

donburi | JAPANESE | Translates to 'bowl'. Rice dish served in a large bowl with various different types of topping. Also refers to the bowl, which often has a lid in which the food is cooked or served.

donguri udon | JAPANESE | White noodles made from wheat flour and 10 per cent acorn flour.

dorer | FRENCH | To brush with beaten eggs and bake until golden.

dorine | FRENCH | Small tartlet filled with chestnut purée and pastry cream, sprinkled with toasted almonds and glazed with apricot jam.

double-boiler Two pots of different sizes which are designed to fit together with a single lid which tops both pans. The lower pan holds hot, simmering water and gives a gentle all-round heat to the food in the top pan. Used to cook or keep sauces, custards and chocolate at a gentle heat without spoiling.

dough Basic mixture of flour, water and a little salt that is kneaded to become elastic and pliable enough to be rolled out with a rolling pin. At this stage pasta and noodles can be made. The addition of various other ingredients forms a more specialized product: for example when butter is added it becomes pastry dough; the addition of yeast makes a basic bread dough.

doughnut Small, ring-shaped cake made from leavened bread dough that is cooked in hot fat then coated with sugar. A round doughnut filled with jam is sometimes called a 'jelly doughnut'.

douillon | FRENCH | Whole pear or apple wrapped and cooked in pastry. Specialty of Normandy.

dragée | FRENCH | Sweet, usually sugar-coated, almond traditionally eaten at christenings and weddings.

dragon's eyes *see* LONGAN.

dragon's teeth *see* BIRD'S NEST.

dragon's well tea *see* LUNG CHING.

Drambuie | SCOTTISH | Liqueur made from Scotch whisky infused with heather honey and herbs.

dredge To coat food with a generous sprinkling of flour before cooking.

Dresden stollen *see* STOLLEN.

dried fruit Once only a few standard dried fruits were available in packets, now more and more interesting varieties are appearing loose in fruit markets, or in mysterious shapes and sizes in see-through drawers in Asian grocers. Dried fruit have full flavour, a high concentration of sugar and are a good source of vitamins and minerals. Stored airtight they will keep well for six months to a year depending on the fruit. Most can be eaten as a snack and are often chopped and included in breakfast cereal and muesli bars. They are used in many baked goods, desserts, confectionery, conserves, stuffings and sauces. Dried fruit can be reconstituted or plumped up by soaking in boiling water for 30 minutes or in cold water, tea or alcohol overnight.

drippings Melted fat and residue left in the pan after meat and poultry have been cooked. Used during cooking for basting and as the base for sauces.

drumstick Lower portion of the leg of poultry, such as chicken and turkey.

Dry Jack *see* JACK CHEESE.

Du Barry | FRENCH | Dish that contains cauliflower.

Dublin Bay prawns *see* SCAMPI.

Dubonnet | FRENCH | Vermouth-style aperitif with quinine and herbs.

duchesse | FRENCH | (1) Petits fours made with meringue containing ground almonds that are sandwiched together in pairs with butter cream. (2) A variety of pear.

duchesse (à la) | FRENCH | Dish served or garnished with mashed potatoes mixed with egg yolk and butter, that is often piped into rosettes and baked until golden.

duck Domestic water bird with a high proportion of fat to flesh. Duck is commonly roasted and is pricked all over to release the fat during cooking. It is often served with a tart fruit sauce to offset the fatty taste; duck served with orange segments and sauce (duck à l'orange) is a classic example. Ducks have been domesticated in China for 2000 years and are used extensively in cooking, particularly in braised dishes and the famous Peking duck, served with its specially prepared reddish-brown crispy skin. Duck eggs, also widely used in China, are often salted or preserved and called 'century eggs' or 'ancient eggs'. *see also* MAGRET.

dukkah | EGYPTIAN | Egyptian specialty comprising a coarse, dry mixture of sesame seeds, coriander seeds, hazelnuts, cumin, salt and black pepper. All the ingredients are roasted separately and lightly crushed together. Variations might include pre-cooked dried chickpeas, cinnamon, thyme, mint or oregano. The mixture is usually eaten with bread dipped in olive oil.

dulse (*Rhodymenia palmata*) Purplish-red, edible seaweed, traditionally used in the United Kingdom as a cooked vegetable eaten with dried fish; also dry-roasted and crushed and used in soups. Washed, dried and rolled it was used like a chewing tobacco in Ireland. It is available in health-food shops. Washing and soaking for a few minutes reduces its saltiness. Finely sliced it can be used uncooked in a salad or added to soups and stews.

dumpling (1) Small ball of dough dropped into simmering soup or stew. It can also enclose other food and is baked, boiled or deep-fried. **(2)** Small sweet pastry filled with fruit, poached in a sweet sauce and served as a dessert.

Dundee cake | SCOTTISH | Rich fruitcake topped with blanched almonds.

Dunlop | SCOTTISH | Firm, uncooked pressed cow's-milk cheese with moist interior and thin, cloth-wrapped or waxed rind. Served as a snack and good for melting.

durian (*Durio zibethinus*) This huge oval fruit with spiny thick skin is becoming more widely available in fruit shops and Asian grocers. The creamy sweet flesh has a bad reputation for its offensive smell, especially when overripe, but in taste the durian is strong and fruity. It is ready to eat when the skin yellows. It is slit open and segmented with a very sharp knife. Durian is usually eaten fresh; also cooked with rice, made into cakes and fruit jelly or used in ice cream. The large shiny seeds may be roasted and eaten like chestnuts.

durum wheat (*Triticum durum*) Hard, amber wheat with high gluten content. It is the endosperm that is ground to make the perfect flour for commercially made pasta products and semolina.

dust To coat food with a light sprinkling of powdery ingredients such as flour or icing sugar.

Dutch cocoa powder *see* COCOA POWDER.

duxelles Mixture of finely chopped mushrooms, onions and shallots sautéed in butter. Used as a stuffing, garnish and as a base for a sauce.

Earl Grey tea Black tea infused with oil of bergamot.

eau de vie | FRENCH | Translates to 'water of life'. Fruit brandy often aged in glass and therefore clear.

Eccles cake | ENGLISH | Small, round pastry made from flaky pastry filled with currants mixed candied fruit peel, and spices.

éclair | FRENCH | Finger-shaped bun of choux pastry filled with pastry cream or whipped cream and iced with chocolate or coffee icing.

Edam | DUTCH | Semihard, uncooked, pressed cow's-milk cheese with a light yellow, smooth interior and bright red, waxy coating over a very thin rind. Served as a snack and at the end of a meal; also used in cooking.

eel Freshwater and saltwater snake-like fish, sold fresh or smoked. Fresh eel is skinned before cooking and usually cut into convenient lengths. It can be steamed, poached, baked or grilled. The Japanese braise sea eel fillets (anago) in a mixture of equal parts of soy sauce, sake, mirin and sugar to use as a sushi topping. *see also* ANAGO. Smoked eel is served as an appetizer with rye bread and lemon or horseradish. *see also* ELVERS.

eel pie | ENGLISH | Classic pie made with a mixture of cooked eel, lemon, parsley, shallots, dry sherry and hard-boiled eggs, covered with a puff pastry crust and baked in the oven.

egg brick *see* JAPANESE OMELETTE.

egg fruit *see* CANISTEL.

egg noodles | ASIA | Made from wheat flour and egg, the most common variety of egg noodles look like thin spaghetti. They are yellowish and are sold fresh or dried. Used in stir-fried dishes and soups; also deep-fried. *see also* HOKKIEN NOODLES.

egg rolls | CHINESE | Small snack made from paper-thin egg wrappers folded and rolled around a savory filling, then deep-fried or steamed.

egg tomato *see* TOMATO.

egg wash Mixture of beaten egg yolks and a little water or milk, used to brush pastry and bread before baking to glaze.

eggah | MIDDLE EASTERN | Type of firm, round omelette that usually has the ingredients mixed with the eggs and cooked either slowly on top of the stove or in the oven. It can be eaten hot or cold, cut in small squares or wedges.

eggflower soup | CHINESE | Also known as 'eggdrop soup'. Commonly prepared soup consisting of seasoned chicken stock with beaten eggs slowly poured in and stirred to form thin threads.

eggnog Hot or cold drink made by beating egg yolk and sugar then mixing with milk, sometimes with the addition of brandy or rum.

eggplant (*Solanum melongena*) Also known as 'aubergine' in Europe and 'brinjal' in India. The eggplant varieties most often seen are shiny, deep- purple with tight skin, and are either large and bulbous or long and thin. Most fresh modern varieties of eggplants grown in Australia do not have bitter juices, but large overripe types are usually sliced, sprinkled with salt and left for about 30 minutes. The salt leeches out the bitterness and excess moisture. The slices are rinsed and dried before cooking. The smaller, thin, purple variety known as **Japanese eggplant** or **Asian eggplant**, used extensively in Asian cooking, do not require salting. Other varieties include small, round eggplants in shades of green, yellow and white, sometimes streaked with green or purple. The tiny **green pea eggplant** (*Solanum torvum*) is sold in bunches and used in Thai cooking, especially in chili sauce and to garnish green curries and salads. The extremely versatile eggplant is cooked in a large variety of dishes in many different cuisines. It is an important ingredient in the Middle Eastern baba ghanoush, moussaka from Greece, and the Provençal mixed vegetable stew, ratatouille. It is grilled, baked, stuffed, stewed and sautéed on its own or with other ingredients.

eggs Apart from its nutritional value and perfect packaging, the inexpensive and versatile egg is an indispensable ingredient in many kitchens of the world. It can be made into a satisfying breakfast, snack or light lunch; turn basic dough into pastry, pasta or noodles; bind sauces, forcemeats and mayonnaise; create custards, mousses, meringues and soufflés and go into many cakes and biscuits. As a cooking aid, eggs are used in many liaisons: to clarify stock, to coat food for frying and to glaze pastry. The eggs of many birds can be eaten and used in cooking if fresh. For most cooking purposes, freshly laid free-range chicken eggs are best. Eggs should be stored unwashed in the refrigerator in their carton with the pointed end downwards. Eggs will cook better at room temperature. When broken onto a plate a fresh egg will have a well-rounded yolk positioned in the center and the white thick, not runny.

eggs Benedict Rich breakfast or brunch dish consisting of poached eggs and slices of ham on toast or toasted English muffins with a topping of hollandaise sauce.

eggs foo yong | CHINESE | Omelette made with shredded chicken, meat or seafood and vegetables, served with a soy sauce and sherry sauce.

eggs, salted | CHINESE | Fresh duck eggs preserved in brine. The egg whites become salty and the yolks firm and bright orange. They are hard-boiled and served with snacks or used in pastries. Also used in steamed dishes or with plain rice. In Thailand salted eggs are pounded with chilies, garlic, shallots, shrimp paste, fish sauce and lime juice to make a dipping sauce for steamed fish.

ekiben | JAPANESE | Take-away food packed in lacquer boxes (bento) sold at most country railway stations in Japan.

elbow macaroni *see* GREMITI.

elderberry (*Sambucus* spp.) Shiny, purplish-black berries with a juicy tart flesh. Used mostly to produce homemade wine, jellies, pies and herbal medicines.

elvers Tiny immature eels. They are transparent and no more than 10 cm long. They are caught mostly in France (pibales) and are fried briefly in hot oil until they turn white. Served hot with salt and pepper.

émincer | FRENCH | To cut in thin flat slices or rounds. Usually refers to meat and poultry, also vegetables.

Emmental / Emmenthal / Emmenthaler | SWISS | Semifirm cow's-milk cheese with an ivory interior with large, shiny holes, and a yellow-brown rind. The flavour is mellow, sweet and nutty. Good table cheese; also excellent in cooking and for grating. Swiss Emmental has 'Switzerland' stamped in red on the outside of the rind. Also made in Savoy, France.

empanada | SPANISH | Savoury pie or individual turnover.

emperor (*Lethrinus nebulosus*) Also known as 'spangled emperor'. Large, greyish reef fish with bluish markings on the snout. It is common in northern Australian waters and is available whole or filleted. The flesh is white, moist and flaky and is excellent for eating. It can be poached, baked, grilled, barbecued or pan-fried. Four similar species of emperor, often marketed as sweetlips, are highly regarded eating fish and can be cooked in the same way. *see also* RED EMPEROR.

emu | AUSTRALIAN | (*Dromaius novaehollandiae*) This large flightless bird was highly sought after by Aborigines for its delicate, gamey flesh and large green eggs. The emu is now farmed and the fresh tender meat, low in fat, is available as fillets or steaks. It is pan-fried, roasted and barbecued and is best when cooked slightly rare. Smoked emu and emu prosciutto are available in gourmet specialty shops. The emu egg is the equivalent to 7–10 chicken eggs. Used for making emu egg pavlova and large omelettes. It is recommended that the egg be separated and let stand overnight to reduce the strong game taste.

emulsify To mix two or more liquids, such as egg yolks and olive oil, until they form a smooth and stable mixture (emulsion), such as in mayonnaise and hollandaise sauce.

en papillote | FRENCH | Cooked in oiled paper wrapping or foil.

enchilada | MEXICAN | Tortilla dipped in sauce (usually tomato) and quickly fried. It is then rolled around an elaborate filling, topped with cheese and baked. Served hot with the sauce.

endive *see* CURLY ENDIVE.

English muffin | ENGLISH | Round flat roll made with yeast dough. It is split in half, toasted and buttered.

English perch *see* REDFIN PERCH.

English spinach *see* SPINACH.

enoki / enokitake mushrooms (*Flammulina velutipes*) Tiny button mushrooms on long, slender stems that grow in clusters. They have a delicate taste. Available fresh. Choose those that are white and crisp. Cut away the base of the stems and discard. They require very little cooking and are used raw in salads, to garnish light soups or added to cooked dishes at the very last moment.

ensalada | SPANISH | Salad.

entrecôte | FRENCH | Translates to 'between two ribs'. Tender cut of beef rib steak.

entrée | FRENCH | In Australia an entrée is usually a dish served before the main course. In a full French menu it is served between the fish and the roast. In America the entrée is usually the main course of a meal.

entremets | FRENCH | Translates to 'between dishes'. Traditionally referred to side dishes served with or after the main course. Now refers to dessert.

Epoisses | FRENCH | Also known as 'Epoisses de Bourgogne'. Name-controlled soft cow's-milk cheese with smooth buttery interior that is ivory to yellow depending on age. The thin, edible rind is washed with sage and marc brandy. May also be include with pepper, fennel and cloves. It is eaten as a snack or at the end of a meal. Made in factories and some farms in most parts of Burgundy.

eryngo | VIETNAMESE | (*Erynigium foetidum*) Pungent perennial herb with oblong toothed leaves that have a strong coriander-like taste. Used mostly in cooking.

escabèche | SPANISH | Method of preserving small headless fish (usually sardines) which are first fried in olive oil then marinated in a cooked marinade consisting of vinegar, carrots, onions, herbs and spices for 24 hours or more. It is served cold as an appetizer. Poultry and game birds are also sometimes prepared in this way.

escalope | FRENCH | Thin slice of meat, often veal, that is sometimes pounded flat, then lightly sautéed. Called 'scaloppine' in Italian.

escargot | FRENCH | Snail.

escargot à la bourguignon | FRENCH | Snails prepared with butter, parsley and garlic.

escarole *see* BATAVIAN ENDIVE.

eschallots *see* SHALLOTS.

Escoffier, Auguste (1846-1935) Famous French chef and culinary writer.

espagnole (à l') | FRENCH | Spanish style. Dishes cooked with tomatoes, capsicum, onions and garlic, usually in oil.

espagnole sauce *see* BROWN SAUCE.

espresso | ITALIAN | Strong dark coffee made by forcing steam under pressure through finely ground coffee.

Esrom | DANISH | Semisoft cow's-milk cheese with yellow, buttery interior with tiny holes and thin, orange rind that has been rubbed with brine. Usually wrapped in foil and stamped with the name 'Esrom'. Served as a snack and at the end of a meal; also melts well.

essence Flavoring agent extracted from plants by distillation or infusion. Examples include almond essence, vanilla essence and essence of orange.

essential oil Strong oil that is extracted from different parts of plants usually by distillation. Used mainly in the perfume and pharmaceutical industries; also in certain foods. Examples include citrus oil, mustard seed oil and peppermint oil.

estouffade | FRENCH | Beef stew with onions, garlic and carrots cooked very slowly in a little wine.

étouffée | FRENCH | Translates to 'smothered'. (1) Refers to a method of cooking in a tightly covered pan with very little liquid. (2) Cajun dish of crawfish, onions, garlic, green capsicum, celery and spices cooked in a brown roux and a little stock. Served over steamed white rice.

etuyer | FRENCH | To cook slowly in a covered pot, using no liquid, but plenty of fat, usually butter.

Explorateur | FRENCH | Brand name of a French triple cream cheese made in Ile-de-France and considered one of the best.

Exton potato *see* POTATO.

fabada | SPANISH | Bean stew cooked slowly with ham, chorizo, blood sausage and salt pork, with garlic, chili and saffron.

Fabriano salami | ITALIAN | Salame di Fabriano. Thick salami made from a mixture of lean pork, fat and young beef.

fagara *see* SZECHWAN PEPPER.

faggot Small, ball-shaped dumpling made with minced pork, liver, breadcrumbs, onion and seasoning wrapped in pig's caul.

fagioli | ITALIAN | Beans. Usually refers to haricot, borlotti and small kidney beans.

fahrenheit Temperature scale with 32°F (0°C) freezing point, and 212°F (100°C) boiling point of water.

falafel | MIDDLE EASTERN | Egyptian specialty made with dried, soaked and minced white beans, onions, herbs and spices rolled into small rissoles and deep-fried. Served as an appetizer or filling for pita bread. In Israel they are made with ground chickpeas.

falette | FRENCH | Mutton breast rolled with a herby vegetable stuffing and cooked slowly in the oven with carrots, onions, white wine and stock. Served sliced with haricot beans.

fanchonnette / fanchette | FRENCH | Small puff-pastry tart filled with pastry cream and decorated with piped meringue.

far breton | FRENCH | Sweet flan made from a rich egg batter containing pitted soaked prunes. Served warm or cold.

farce | FRENCH | Forcemeat or stuffing.

farci | FRENCH | Mixture of finely chopped ham, garlic, vegetables, herbs and eggs that is wrapped in cabbage leaves and cooked in stock.

farcir | FRENCH | To stuff.

farfalle | ITALIAN | Pasta shaped like butterflies or bow ties. 'Farfallini' are small and 'farfallone' large versions.

farina Flour or meal made from cereal grains (usually wheat) with the bran and most of the germ removed. When cooked, it makes a protein-rich, but bland-tasting breakfast cereal.

farinaceous Ingredients and products containing flour or a high degree of starch, such as cereals, pasta, pulses and potatoes.

farmer cheese *see* COTTAGE CHEESE.

farmhouse cheese Cheese made by hand on the same farm where the milk is produced. Artisan or specialist cheese is made by hand using milk from different sources, but usually collected from a specific region. For example all handmade cheeses on King Island are made from milk collected daily from a number of dairy farms on the island and are artisan or specialist cheeses rather than farmhouse.

fasting Abstaining from all, or some kinds of food, for religious or political reasons.

fats and oils Fats are a natural part of many foods and are essential to good health. They provide energy, strengthen cells and capillaries and lubricate the skin and hair. All forms of fat are made up of a combination of **fatty acids** that are divided into two main groups that have considerable relevance to health: they are saturated and unsaturated fatty acids. **Saturated fats** predominate in animal fats, dairy products and eggs and, in lower concentrations, in margarine. Coconut and palm oil, although vegetable in origin, are mainly saturated. Saturated fats contribute to obesity, certain types of cancer and can raise the cholesterol level in the blood, leading to heart disease. **Unsaturated fats**, derived from plants, are usually liquid at room temperature in the form of oils. They are further divided into **mono-unsaturated** and polyunsaturated. Mono-unsaturated fats found in olive oil, canola oil and macadamia nut oil have a beneficial effect on blood cholesterol levels by reducing the harmful low-density lipoprotein (LDL) cholesterol while raising the beneficial high-density lipoprotein (HDL) cholesterol. **Polyunsaturated fats**, such as safflower oil, sunflower oil and corn oil, and most margarines made from plants, are beneficial when used to replace saturated fats.

fava | ITALIAN | Broad beans.

fedelini | ITALIAN | Very fine spaghetti just a little thicker than capelli d'angelo (angel's hair).

feijoa (*Feijoa sellowiana*) Aromatic, oval fruit with a thin, waxy, green skin and creamy or yellow flesh surrounding a jelly-like center containing a few small seeds. Available between late autumn and early winter. When fully ripe it is peeled and eaten fresh, used in fruit salads or preserved in syrup. The fruit is rich in vitamin C.

feijoada | SOUTH AMERICAN | National dish of Brazil. It consists of dried beef, smoked tongue, various types of sausage, pig's trotters, tails and ears cooked with black beans, onion, garlic and chili. Traditionally the meats are served on a large plate with the smoked tongue always in the middle. The beans are served separately in a bowl. The whole meal is accompanied by side dishes of rice, toasted manioc meal, shredded kale, spices, chili sauce, and sliced oranges.

Felino salami | ITALIAN | Salame di Felino. Regarded as one of the finest Italian salamis and the most expensive. Made from a high proportion of lean pork and white wine, whole peppercorns and a small amount of garlic. It has a delicate taste and because it is lightly cured does not keep very well.

fennel (*Foeniculum vulgare*) Perennial herb native of southern Europe and now wild throughout the world. Both the leaves and seed have a pleasant anise taste and have long been used as a fish herb. Chopped leaves are also added to cooked vegetables. Seeds sprinkled into bread dough, cakes, pumpkin soup, borscht or cottage cheese.

fennel, bulb (*Foeniculum vulgare* var. *dulce*) Called 'finocchio' in Italy. White, aromatic, fleshy bulb with a sweet, aniseed taste and a crisp, refreshing texture. Fennel is sliced and used raw in a salad with vinaigrette, added to a mixed salad or braised and served as an accompaniment to seafood dishes. In southern Italy pieces of raw fennel are served with cheese at the end of a meal to aid digestion and to refresh the palate.

fenugreek (*Trigonella feonum-graecum*) Annual herb cultivated in Europe, Asia, India and North Africa for its strong-smelling yellowish-brown seed. Used as a component in some curries and chutneys; also used in North African and Egyptian cooking. In India the leaves are used as a vegetable.

fermented black beans *see* BLACK BEANS, SALTED.

feta | GREEK | Crumbly sheep's-milk cheese that is cut into large slices and pickled in brine. It has a very salty taste and may be rinsed before use. Served as a snack with olives, bread and wine; also used in Greek cooking or cut into cubes in mixed salads.

fettuccelle | ITALIAN | Slightly wider version of fettuccine.

fettuccine | ITALIAN | Long, flat ribbons of pasta about 5 mm (1/4in) wide.

feuilleté | FRENCH | Puff pastry filled with a savory mixture, often cut into triangles or finger shapes and served hot as an appetizer.

fiadone | FRENCH | Corsican flan made from eggs, cheese, sugar and lemon peel, sometimes spiked with brandy.

fibre *see* DIETARY FIBRE.

ficelle | FRENCH | Translates to 'string'. Often refers to a small, thin baguette. Ficelle picarde is a thin crêpe rolled around a slice of ham, creamed mushrooms and cheese, topped with creamy cheese sauce and browned in the oven.

fiddlehead fern The tightly curled, immature frond of some species of ferns. Not all species are edible and many contain toxic compounds especially when they begin to open. The edible varieties are cooked and eaten like asparagus, used raw in salads or added to soups. Preserved fiddleheads can be found in Japanese grocers.

fideos | SPANISH | Thin vermicelli.

fig (*Ficus carica*) Fresh figs vary from pale or dark green to red, purple and black and are available mostly during the summer months and early autumn. All have thin tender skins, a sweet succulent flesh and are a good source of vitamins A and B, potassium, calcium and phosphorus. Figs are highly perishable, particularly in damp or humid weather, and should be eaten as soon as possible or stored briefly in the refrigerator. They are served on their own or as an antipasto with prosciutto or salami; also with cheese and nuts of all kinds and as a dessert served with cream or mascarpone cheese. Figs are also made into jam, biscuits, cakes and poached. Dried figs are considerably sweeter with the sugar content increasing by over 30 per cent. They are used in many types of baked goods, desserts, mousses and ice-cream.

figatelli | FRENCH | Spicy, long, thin pig's-liver sausage from Corsica.

filbert *see* HAZELNUT.

file (*Sassafras albidium*) Powdered leaves of a sassafras tree used as a spice and thickening agent for soups and sauces; an essential ingredient of New Orleans gumbo and other Creole dishes. Usually added just before serving.

filet mignon | FRENCH | Tender piece of beef cut from the pointed end of the fillet.

fillet Tender under-part of the sirloin and rump of beef, veal, pork or lamb. It is a choice cut and cooks quickly. The whole fillet can be roasted, or cut into steaks and pan-fried or grilled; also sliced and used in stir-fried dishes.

filleting Removing the bone, usually of fish or meat.

filo Also spelled 'phylo' and 'phyllo'. Very thin pastry dough used for baklava, strudel and many other sweet and savory pastries.

filter To strain liquid through a fine sieve, filter paper or cheesecloth.

financier | FRENCH | Oval or rectangular, crunchy sponge cake made with ground almonds and meringue.

financière sauce | FRENCH | Madeira sauce with mushrooms and truffles.

fines herbes | FRENCH | Delicate herb mixture of equal parts of fresh chervil, chives, parsley and tarragon. Traditionally used with omelettes, grilled fish, white sauces, flans and poultry.

finnan haddie | SCOTTISH | Split, salted and lightly smoked haddock. It is simmered in milk and butter with onion rings and peppercorns. Served as a breakfast dish and for high tea.

finnocchiona *see* FIORENTINA SALAMI.

fino | SPANISH | Type of pale, dry sherry, usually drunk as an aperitif.

finocchio *see* FENNEL, BULB.

Fiore Sardo *see* SARDO.

fiorentina salami | ITALIAN | Salame fiorentina. Large, moderately spicy salami made from large pieces of lean pork and fat.

fish Fish is a highly nutritious food and the perfect choice for the heath-conscious and the home cook. It is an excellent source of protein, low in calories, cholesterol and saturated fat and a great source of vitamins and minerals. It is also the most significant source of omega-3 fatty acids, known to have protective benefits against coronary heart disease, cancer and inflammatory conditions. The enormous variety of fresh fish sold in Australian fish markets is mostly of excellent quality. Whole fish should have clear, bright protruding eyes and clear red gills. The flesh should be firm and spring back when pressed. All fish should have only a very faint smell of the sea. If the fish is in fillets or steaks, the flesh should be bright, almost translucent, firm and springy. Fish can be cooked in almost any way, but is at its best when cooked simply and the delicate flesh has just begun to turn from transparent to opaque. Some very fresh fish can be eaten raw in sashimi or sushi; or marinated in citrus juice until the flesh turns opaque (ceviche). *see individual entries for details.*

fish farming *see* AQUACULTURE.

fish maw | CHINESE | Dried stomach lining of certain kinds of fish. It is soaked in warm water until soft. The bland taste and honeycomb texture readily absorb other tastes. Used in soups and slow-cooked dishes.

five spice powder Also known as 'Chinese five spices'. Fragrant pungent mixture of freshly ground dried spices that consists of star anise, Szechwan pepper, cloves, fennel seeds, cinnamon or the stronger cassia. Used sparingly to season meat and poultry in Chinese and Vietnamese cooking; also mixed with salt as a dipping condiment.

flageolet | FRENCH | (*Phaseolus vulgaris*) Small, pale green kidney bean, avail- able dried. After soaking they are gently simmered for 45 minutes. Traditionally served with roast lamb.

flake *see* SHARK.

flamande (à la) Flemish style. Usually refers to a dish served with stuffed cabbage leaves, carrots, turnips, potatoes and sometimes bacon and slices of sausages.

flambé | FRENCH | Flamed. To sprinkle with brandy or similar spirit and ignite. Usually the spirit is warmed first, then lit as it is poured over the dish.

flamiche | FRENCH | Savory vegetable tart, usually filled with leeks or cheese.

flammenküche | FRENCH | Thin-crusted tart, similar to a rectangular pizza, topped with fried onions, cream and bacon. Specialty of Alsace.

flamri / flamery | FRENCH | Baked semolina pudding served cold with a purée of red fruit.

flan Open sweet or savory tart.

fleur de courgette | FRENCH | Zucchini flower.

fleur de sel | FRENCH | Grainy, unrefined, greyish-white sea salt harvested from the top surface of the evaporating beds of natural saltpans from the island of Re and Noirmoutier and parts of Brittany in France. With its sweet taste and faint floral perfume, it is considered the world's best salt: it is also the most expensive.

fleurons | FRENCH | Small pieces of leftover pastry cut into decorative shapes and used to garnish pies, or baked or fried as a garnish for sauced seafood dishes.

floating islands Cold egg-custard topped with spoonfuls of poached meringue and decorated with caramel, crystallized violets or crushed praline.

florentine Flat, round biscuit made with butter, honey, sugar and candied fruit, coated with a thin layer of chocolate after cooling.

florentine (à la) | FRENCH | Dishes containing spinach.

flounder, greenback (*Rhombosolea tapirina*) An almost diamond-shaped, flat fish rarely more than 35 cm long. Its white succulent flesh is very good eating, especially when cooked whole, dusted with plain flour and pan-fried. Fillets are also available.

flour Finely ground cereal grains such as wheat, corn, rye, chickpea and rice. Used throughout the world to make breads, pasta, noodles and a multitude of baked goods.

flowery orange pekoe *see* PEKOE TEA.

flummery | ENGLISH | Cold gelatin pudding made with puréed fruit and beaten egg whites, with fortified wine and spices.

flûte | FRENCH | Very thin baguette.

flying fish roe Delicate, small grains of fish eggs tinged red, orange and golden. Used on canapés and added to seafood salads and fish dishes.

focaccia | ITALIAN | Flat, dimpled bread made from leavened dough that is brushed with olive oil and oven-baked. It can be plain or made with a variety of ingredients such as herbs, cheese, olives, sun-dried tomatoes or ham either worked into the dough or used as a topping.

foie gras | FRENCH | Translates to 'fat liver'. Enlarged liver of a fattened goose or duck that has been force-fed.

fold in To gently blend a light frothy mixture (such as beaten egg whites) with a heavier one (such as whipped cream) by lifting and turning the mixture with a rubber spatula while rotating the bowl slightly.

fond de cuisine | FRENCH | Basic kitchen stock. Fond de poisson is fish stock; fond de volaille is chicken stock.

fondant | FRENCH | Translates to 'melting'. Smooth, cooked sugar paste containing glucose, used for icing cakes and to fill chocolates and sweets.

fondre | FRENCH | To cook vegetables under cover in a little butter or oil until they are reduced to a pulp.

fondue | FRENCH | Dish cooked over a spirit burner at the table. Diners spear small pieces of food on a long handled fork and dip into the hot liquid. Originally a classic Swiss dish of Gruyère cheese melted in white wine with Kirsch and seasonings, eaten by dipping into it a piece of bread. Fondue bourguignonne is a variation in which cubes of good quality raw beef are dipped into very hot oil, then dipped into a selection of sauces. Chocolate fondue consists of a pot of melted chocolate into which pieces of fruit or cake are dipped.

fonduta | ITALIAN | Piedmontese version of cheese fondue made with melted fontina cheese, butter and egg yolks. It is served in a bowl covered with very thin slices of raw white truffles. Sometimes the cheese is poured over rice or slabs of polenta.

Fontainebleau | FRENCH | Fresh, unripened cow's-milk cheese beaten with whipped cream. Sold wrapped in cheesecloth and pre-packaged. Served as a dessert, often with fresh fruit and sugar.

Fontina dal Val d'Aosta | ITALIAN | Name-controlled semifirm, pressed cow's- milk cheese with pale, golden interior with tiny holes and soft, brown rind. It is a highly esteemed cheese eaten as a snack or at the end of a meal; also excellent melting cheese and basis for fonduta, a Piedmontese cheese sauce topped with sliced white truffles. Other Fontinas are made elsewhere, but authentic Fontina dal Val d'Aosta is made in the Piedmont region and bears a purple stencil of a mountain peak with the name printed across it in white writing.

fool | ENGLISH | Chilled dessert of strained cooked puréed fruit gently folded with whipped cream; usually made with fresh ripe gooseberries, red currants, raspberries, blackberries, rhubarb or apples.

forcemeat Seasoned mixture of raw or cooked, finely minced meat, fish, poultry or vegetables which may be bound with eggs, breadcrumbs, mashed potatoes, rice, water, milk or cream. Used in the making of sausage-meats, quenelles, terrines, stuffing and for garnishing.

forestière (à la) | FRENCH | Garnish of wild mushrooms, bacon and potatoes.

fortified wine Wine to which a grape spirit such as brandy has been added to stop fermentation and to raise the alcohol content. It also acts as a preservative. Examples include port, sherry, Marsala and Madeira.

fouace | FRENCH | Also known as 'fouasse' or 'fougasse'. Type of brioche with added candied fruits or orange-flower water.

fougasse *see* FOUACE.

Fourme | FRENCH | Any of the various cow's-milk blue vein cheeses from mountainous regions in central France that are often flavoured with parsley.

Fourme d'Ambert | FRENCH | Name-controlled pressed blue vein cow's-milk cheese with creamy, ivory interior with liberal blue veining and grey-brown crust. Pronounced strong fruity taste. Used as a table cheese, as a snack and at the end of a meal with fruit. The best examples are made in dairies around the town of Ambert in the Auvergne. Fourme de Montbrison is an identical cheese.

Fourme de Montbrison *see* FOURME D'AMBERT.

framboise Clear French brandy made from raspberries.

française (à la) | FRENCH | Classic accompaniment to roasts, consisting of asparagus tips, braised lettuce and cauliflower florets topped with hollandaise sauce.

Frangelico Hazelnut-flavoured liqueur.

frangipane | FRENCH | **(1)** Almond custard filling used in the preparation of various desserts and pastries. **(2)** Name given to a panada made with seasoned milk, butter, flour and egg yolks used to bind delicate poultry and fish forcemeat.

frankfurt / frankfurter Small, slender, pre-cooked sausage made with spiced minced beef and pork or veal and lightly smoked. Usually heated before eating. When served sandwiched in an individual slender roll and topped with mustard or tomato sauce it becomes a 'hot dog'.

frappé | FRENCH | Cold after-dinner drink made by pouring a liqueur over finely crushed ice.

Frascati | ITALIAN | Light, dry white wine sold in a flat, flask-shaped bottle. From the hills around Rome. There is also a semisweet version.

french fries | AMERICAN | Called 'pommes frites' in France and often 'chips' in Australia and the United Kingdom. Potatoes cut into strips and deep-fried until lightly browned.

friand | FRENCH | Small, oval, almond cakes. In France a friand is also a sausage roll.

fricadelle Fried meatballs made of minced meat, usually served with a sauce.

fricandeau | FRENCH | (1) Choice cut of veal wrapped in bacon and braised and served thinly sliced with vegetables such as spinach. (2) Meatballs made of minced pork, liver, kidneys and herbs wrapped in pig's caul and baked. (3) Braised fish steaks or fillets.

fricassee | FRENCH | White stew of chicken, white meat, fish or vegetables, cooked in white stock or wine sauce and thickened with cream and egg yolks.

fricelli | ITALIAN | Short lengths of hand-rolled pasta.

frijoles refritos *see* REFRIED BEANS.

frisée (*Chichorium endivia*) These are the tender, pale yellowish-green, curly leaves taken from the center of curly endive. Used to add a touch of bitterness to mixed green salads such as mesclun.

fritelle | FRENCH | Corsican fritter made with leavened dough, egg yolks and herbs containing sausage or cheese. A sweet version is made with chestnut flour.

friton | FRENCH | Coarse pork rillettes which includes organ meats.

fritot | FRENCH | Small fritters made from pieces of cooked marinated food such as fish, poultry or organ meats, dipped in batter and fried just before serving.

frittata | ITALIAN | Savory round omelette that has various fillings mixed with the beaten eggs. The frittata is cooked in olive oil over a moderate heat, left flat and turned over half way through cooking like a thick pancake.

fritter Batter or piece of food coated in batter that is deep-fried or sautéed.

fritto misto | ITALIAN | Assortment of fried food.

frogs legs Skinned hind legs of certain species of frogs that are immersed in cold water for several hours to whiten and swell the flesh. They are usually dipped in seasoned flour and grilled or sautéed briefly in butter or oil often with onions and shallots. Frogs legs are usually bought frozen or canned.

fromage | FRENCH | Cheese.

fromage blanc | FRENCH | Fresh, unsalted, low-fat cheese with a soft, delicate texture and a short storage life.

fromage de tête *see* BRAWN.

fromage frais | FRENCH | Fresh cheese with the addition of salt, made from all types of milk. Usually moist, soft and creamy and has a short storage life.

fromagerie | FRENCH | Shop or environmentally controlled section of a large food store, that specializes in the sale of cheese.

fructose Also known as 'fruit sugar'. Natural sweetener found mostly in fruit and honey. Available in granulated and syrup form, it is sweeter than sugar, but contains about half the kilojoules. It can be used by diabetics. Used mostly in cold foods and to sweeten beverages.

fruit butter Smooth, thick and creamy spread made from a sweetened purée of fresh fruit, often with the addition of spices. Used as a spread but also to fill pastries and layer cakes.

fruit confit Whole fruit preserved in sugar.

fruit curd Smooth, creamy spread usually made from lemons (or limes) sugar, butter and egg yolks. Used as a spread, but also as a topping or pastry filling.

fruit paste Thick, jelly-like product made from strained fruit pulp, sugar and pectin. It is poured into molds or trays and, when set cut into cubes or rectangles, is rather like Turkish Delight. The pieces are coated with caster sugar and kept in an airtight container.

fruit salad plant *see* MONSTERA.

fruits de mer | FRENCH | Serving of assorted seafood.

frumenty Very old, porridge-style dish from the Middle Ages. Made from wheat grains soaked in water in a warm oven for days until the grains swelled and burst, forming a thick jelly-like mass, sweetened with honey and served with hot milk.

fry To cook meat, fish and vegetables in direct contact with hot oil, fat or butter, either deep or shallow.

fu | JAPANESE | Light cake of wheat gluten that is toasted, steamed and dried. It is available in packets in a variety of sizes, and shapes. Used in soups and stews, or as a soup garnish. *see also* SEITAN.

fudge Semisoft caramel confection with various flavorings such as chocolate, nuts and candied fruit. Usually cut into small squares when set.

fugu | JAPANESE | Also known as 'puffer fish' or 'blow fish'. Poisonous fish with lethal toxic substances present in the ovaries and liver. It is considered a delicacy in Japan (especially the fish's testes) and is only safe to eat if those organs are immediately removed in the initial stage of cleaning. Restaurant preparation of fugu is very strictly controlled.

Fuji apple Red eating apple from Japan with a crisp texture and sweet taste. Also makes good pies and tarts.

fumé | FRENCH | Smoked.

fumet | FRENCH | Concentrated stock made with fish, poultry or game. Used as a basis of sauces and to enhance other stocks.

fungi Singular is 'fungus'. Class of plants which includes molds, yeasts, truffles and mushrooms. In cooking the term usually refers to edible mushrooms which may be cultivated or harvested from the wild. Fungi used in Asian cooking include white fungus and wood ear fungus. *see also* MUSHROOMS.

furikake | JAPANESE | Type of seasoning made chiefly from flakes of toasted seaweed with variations such as ground sesame seeds, salt, ground dried fish or fried bonito flakes. It is sold in shaker-type bottles and is usually sprinkled over rice and noodles.

fusilli | ITALIAN | Twisted spaghetti in varying lengths.

futo-maki *see* SUSHI.

fuzzy melon (*Benincasa hispida*) Also known as 'Chinese zucchini' or 'summer melon'. Cylindrical, green marrow covered with fine, hair-like fuzz. Must be peeled before use. It has a bland taste but readily absorbs others and may be steamed, braised, stir-fried or simmered in soups.

gado-gado | INDONESIAN | Cooked vegetable salad with a peanut sauce. The vegetables, which might include cabbage, potatoes, carrots, green beans and bean sprouts, are blanched and arranged on a plate with slices of cucumber and wedges of hard-boiled egg. The peanut sauce is poured over them.

gai choy (*Brassica juncea*) Also known as 'Chinese mustard greens' or 'Chinese cabbage'. Leafy, green vegetable with a small heart and firm broad leaves which overlap towards the base. Raw leaves have a strong mustard, almost wasabi-like taste. Wash thoroughly before use. When young the whole of the plant can be steamed or blanched. Also stir-fried and used in soups and some stews. There are a number of varieties of gai choy available and some are sold preserved in salt in cans or plastic packs. *see also* PICKLED MUSTARD GREENS.

gai larn (*Brassica alboglabra*) Also known as 'Chinese broccoli' or 'Chinese kale'. Leafy, green vegetable with dark green, rather coarse leaves that have a bluish-green sheen and become tender when steamed or blanched in salted water. Traditionally served with oyster sauce. Rich in vitamins A and C, calcium and iron. Also stir-fried or used in soups or noodle dishes.

Gala apple New Zealand variety of apple with golden skin streaked with red, and a firm, juicy flesh and sweet taste. Used mainly as an eating apple. Keeps well.

galangal, greater (*Alpinia galanga*) Pale yellow rhizome with pink skin and knobs, related to ginger but with a milder taste. Commonly used fresh in Thai and Malaysian cookery, especially in soups and pastes. Fresh galangal is becoming more widely available. In dried and powdered form, it is often sold as laos powder. Another form is lesser galangal which has orange flesh.

galantine | FRENCH | Boned meat or poultry that is stuffed, rolled and formed into a desirable shape. It is cooked in a gelatinous stock, then glazed with aspic and served cold; cut in slices as an entrée.

galette | FRENCH | Flat, round pastry, cake, biscuit or tart with various fillings and toppings. The traditional puff-pastry, galette des rois, sometimes filled with almond custard cream, is a Twelfth Night celebration cake.

Galliano | ITALIAN | Golden yellow liqueur infused with herbs and spices and packaged in a tall fluted bottle.

game In gastronomy, wild animals or birds killed for food. Game birds include pheasant, goose, wild duck, quail, guinea fowl, emu and ostrich. Animals include rabbit, hare, members of the deer family (venison), buffalo, kangaroo and crocodile. *See also* CAPE BARREN GOOSE, CROCODILE, EMU, GOOSE, GUINEA FOWL, HARE, KANGAROO, PHEASANT, QUAIL, RABBIT *and* VENISON.

Gammelost | NORWEGIAN | Semisoft cow's-milk cheese with ivory interior with irregular blue veins and brownish rind. Cheese darkens with age. Very strong pronounced taste. Used as a table cheese. Not widely available outside Norway.

gammon Hind leg of a side of bacon that is cut from the carcass after brining.

ganache | FRENCH | Rich mixture of chocolate, butter and double cream used as a filling for cakes or confectionery and to decorate desserts.

Gaperon | FRENCH | Pressed, uncooked cheese made from skimmed cow's-milk or buttermilk with garlic and cracked peppercorns and shaped like a ball with a flattened bottom. Used as a table cheese.

garam masala | INDIAN | Blend of dried spices used in Indian cooking; usually includes coriander seeds, cumin seeds, black peppercorns, cardamom seeds, cinnamon sticks, whole cloves and grated nutmeg. For extra fragrance the seeds are left whole, roasted slightly, then ground together. The mixture is usually added towards the end of cooking.

garbanzo *see* CHICKPEAS.

garbure | FRENCH | Rich stew or very thick soup that includes cabbage, dried beans, potatoes and other vegetables and preserved goose, flavored with garlic, herbs and seasoning.

garde-manger | FRENCH | Cold larder. Department set aside for preparation and storage of perishable foods both raw and cooked. Also in large kitchens where all cold items found on the menu are prepared and decorated, for example, hors d'oeuvres, cold sauces, salads and some desserts.

garfish (*Hyporhamphus* spp.) There are a number of different species of garfish. They are generally small with slender silvery bodies and a characteristic protruding lower jaw that varies in length according to species. They have a fine white flesh with a delicate taste and are usually grilled, pan-fried or deep-fried whole. Butterfly fillets are sometimes available.

gargouillau | FRENCH | Dessert made with sliced pears set in a thick pancake mixture and baked in a shallow dish.

garland chrysanthemum *see* CHRYSANTHEMUM LEAVES.

garlic (*Allium sativum*) Ancient and highly esteemed bulb belonging to the onion family. Each bulb consists of separate sections called 'cloves'. Garlic has been used as a food and medicine for 5000 years and is a classic ingredient in many cuisines. By stimulating the gastric juices, it acts both as an appetizer and a digestive. There are several varieties differing in size of bulb, pungency and skin. Garlic is usually used fresh and the cloves broken off when needed. Once detached the cloves dry out. Store in a cool, dry place, but not in the refrigerator. Garlic complements nearly all savory dishes, especially those of the cuisines of Asia and the Mediterranean regions. It is essential to aïoli, the garlic-rich mayonnaise of Provence, and bagna cauda, the northern Italian hot dip for raw vegetables.

garnish In classic cooking, 'a garnish' refers to one or more food items served with the main ingredient of a dish to give it a particular character and often providing the decoration. A garnish may also be a small edible trimming such as a herb sprig, caviar or sliced truffles added to a dish to enhance its appearance or taste.

gastronome Person who appreciates good food, however simple or elaborate, prepared by skilled cooks.

gastronomy The science of gourmet food and drinks.

gâteau | FRENCH | Word widely used for various kinds of decorated cakes.

gaudes | FRENCH | Thick, cornmeal porridge served hot with milk or cream, and sometimes with bacon added; also served cold and sliced as a dessert, sweetened with sugar or honey.

gayette | FRENCH | Small, flat sausage made with pork liver and fat with herbs and garlic. Served hot or cold as a hors d'oeuvre.

gazpacho | SPANISH | Chilled, uncooked soup of cucumber, tomato, onions, red capsicums, bread, olive oil and garlic. Sometimes served with croutons.

gefilte fish | JEWISH | Translates to 'stuffed fish'. Traditionally a mixture of ground fish, celery, onions, eggs and other ingredients stuffed back into the fish skin for cooking. Nowadays the mixture is formed into balls and simmered in a fish stock. Usually served cold in its own jellied stock, accompanied with pickles or horseradish.

gelatin Clear setting agent derived from the bones of animals and fish, or from red seaweeds (agar-agar). Available ground as a powder, or in sheets and soaked in cold water before using. Used for glazing or decorating cold savory dishes and for making jellies and desserts.

gelato | ITALIAN | Smooth, firm ice-cream made with egg yolks, cream and sugar and many flavorings such as coffee, chocolate, pistachio nuts, hazelnuts and candied fruit.

gemelli | ITALIAN | From the word 'gemello' which translates to 'double' or 'twin'. Two short strands of pasta twisted together.

gemfish (*Rexea solandri*) Also known as 'hake'. Long, narrow fish with firm, pale pink flesh, sold mostly in thick fillets. They can be grilled, poached, braised or pan-fried.

Genoa cake Almond sponge cake.

Genoa salami | ITALIAN | Salame genovese. Moderately spicy salami made with pork and beef, large fat pieces and whole peppercorns.

Genoese sponge Moist and light sponge cake in which the eggs are whisked together with the sugar over a gentle heat until thickened.

Genoise *see* GENOESE SPONGE.

geranium leaves (*Pelargonium* spp.) Fresh leaves of certain scented geraniums (rose, lemon, nutmeg, apple, peppermint and coconut) are used to impart fragrance to jellies, jams, ice cream, pickles or fruit cups. The well-defined leaves are sometimes used as a template for sprinkling icing sugar over cakes.

Germiny | FRENCH | Soup made with sorrel softened in butter, then cooked in stock and thickened with egg yolks and cream just before serving.

Géromé | FRENCH | Soft cow's-milk cheese with smooth, ivory-yellow interior and mottled, reddish rind. Sometimes with added caraway. Served as a table cheese as a snack or at the end of a meal.

ghee | INDIAN | Clarified butter made from cow's milk, popular in North Indian cooking. Ghee can be heated to a much higher temperature than butter without burning. It is sold in cans. *see also* CLARIFIED BUTTER.

gherkin Small cucumber with slightly prickly skin. Mainly pickled unripe in vinegar and used as a condiment.

giant crab (*Pseudocarcinus gigas*) Very large, red crab with cream markings and huge powerful claws. The giant crab is often seen live in tanks in Chinese restaurants and is particularly suited to Asian-style cooking. *see also* CRABS.

giant garlic *see* ROCAMBOLE.

giant perch *see* BARRAMUNDI.

gibassier | FRENCH | Round yeast cake in the shape of a crown, with lemon or orange zest, aniseed or orange-flower water. Specialty of Provence.

giblets The offal parts of poultry, including heart, kidneys and liver, also small external parts such as feet, wing tips, neck and head. Used mainly in soup, stock, sauces, stuffings and terrines. Chicken feet are a popular yum cha dish.

gigot | FRENCH | Leg of lamb or mutton.

gimblette | FRENCH | Ring-shaped biscuit made of flour, eggs, almonds and citrus zest. It is immersed in boiling water, dried and baked.

gin Spirit distilled from grain, usually malted barley, rye or corn; with various aromatics, particularly juniper berries and coriander seeds.

ginger (*Zingiber officinale*) Perennial herb native to southern Asia, but now cultivated throughout the tropics. The fresh, gnarled, pale beige root has a pungent, spicy taste and is an essential ingredient in many Asian dishes. Dried ginger root in powdered form is used in English-speaking countries for bakery goods, particularly gingerbread and ginger snaps, preserves, sweets and drinks; also used in some curry powders. *see also* SHOGA.

ginger juice Sometimes used in Chinese dishes. To extract place peeled ginger in garlic press and squeeze liquid into small bowl.

ginger, candied Ginger simmered in sugar syrup and preserved in syrup coated in sugar. It is eaten as a sweet or cut into small pieces and used in rich spice cakes.

gingerbread Tea-time cake with ginger and treacle. Sometimes baked in the shape of a man with currants for eyes and other features such as buttons. In England and Scotland the cakes are called 'gingerbread men' or 'husbands' and were common in medieval times; today they come in both genders are often called 'gingerbread people' (to be more politically correct). French gingerbread (pain d'epicé) is made with flour, strong honey and spices and made into loaves or cut into hearts and various other shapes. Specialty of Dijon.

gingersnap Thin, crunchy biscuit made with molasses, powdered ginger, flour and butter.

ginkgo nut (*Ginkgo biloba*) Small, pale, creamy nuts obtained from the ancient maidenhair tree, native to China. The nuts are edible and have long been used in Chinese medicine. The hard shell and skin must be removed before use and they are usually sold pre-shelled in Asian grocers. When cooked they turn an attractive green and are included in many Japanese and Chinese dishes. Used in soups, vegetarian dishes and stuffing for poultry; may be steamed, grilled or stir-fried.

ginseng (*Panax schinseng*) Also known as 'Chinese ginseng' or 'Korean ginseng'. Distinctive, man-shaped root, especially valued in Chinese medicine as a universal panacea and aphrodisiac. American ginseng (*Panax quin- quefolium*) was used by the American Indians and today is cultivated mainly in temperate regions of the United States and Canada where it is dried and exported to Hong Kong.

girolle *see* CHANTERELLE.

gizzard Digestive pouch in birds.

gjetost | NORWEGIAN | Firm, golden-brown cheese made from goat's milk or a mixture of cow's and goat's milk that is cooked until caramelized. It has a mild, sweet taste and is served at breakfast, as a snack or sandwich cheese.

glacé | FRENCH | Iced, crystallized or glazed.

glacé fruit *see* CANDIED FRUIT.

glass noodles *see* BEAN THREAD NOODLES.

glasswort *see* SALICORNE.

glaze (1) To brush a reduced meat sauce over meat and poultry during cooking to give a shiny appearance. **(2)** To place custard or buttered sauces under the grill to produce a golden surface. **(3)** To brush pastry products with beaten egg, milk or sugar to make them glossy during baking. **(4)** To coat fruit tarts and desserts with jelly or jam to create a decorative glossy coating and prevent drying out.

globe artichoke *see* ARTICHOKE, GLOBE.

Gloucester | ENGLISH | Hard, pressed cow's-milk cheese. Single Gloucester is made with skimmed milk and aged for up to nine months. Double Gloucester is made from whole milk and aged for six to nine months. It has a firm, pale orange interior and the best varieties are cloth-wrapped. Served as a snack or sandwich cheese; also good for melting.

glucose Also known as 'grape sugar'. Natural form of sugar found in grape juice, honey, corn and certain other vegetables.

gluten A protein in wheat and some other grains that, when moistened, gives elasticity to a dough.

gluten-free Food that is free of the gluten protein, suitable for those with a gluten intolerance.

glutinous rice *see* RICE *and* RICE FLOUR.

gnocchi | ITALIAN | Small dumplings made of choux pastry, semolina flour or potato. They are made into different shapes such as elongated shells, little clouds, ovals, cylinders or flat discs and are usually poached in simmering water. The best-known gnocchi are those from northern Italy made with potatoes and a little flour. Served as a first course, in soup or as an accompaniment to a main meal.

gnocchi pasta | ITALIAN | Short, cloud-shaped pasta shells.

Goa bean *see* WINGED BEAN.

goat's-milk cheese *see* CHÈVRE (FROMAGE DE).

goatfish *see* RED MULLET.

gobo *see* BURDOCK.

godiveau | FRENCH | Very fine forcemeat made of lean veal and fat pounded to a paste with egg whites and finely chopped shallots and passed through a fine sieve. Used to make quenelles, a hot mousse or to fill small pastry cases served as a hot hors d'oeuvre.

Golden Delicious apple Medium-yellow apple with a soft, juicy flesh and a mild, sweet taste. One of the major varieties of eating apples; also used for pies and tarts.

golden needles *see* LILY BUDS.

golden nugget pumpkin *see* PUMPKIN.

golden syrup Also known as 'light treacle'. Highly refined, clear, golden syrup with a thick, honey-like consistency. Used as a table syrup for ice cream and pancake topping; also popular in cooking and baked goods because it does not crystallize.

golden tomato *see* TOMATO.

golden trout *see* TROUT.

goma | JAPANESE | Sesame seeds. Goma-abura is sesame-seed oil.

gomo shio | JAPANESE | Roasted sesame seed salt is used as a table condiment in Japan and popular in macrobiotics. Sea salt and black sesame seeds are roasted separately, slightly ground, and combined. The proportion is usually one part salt to four parts sesame seeds.

gooksu | KOREAN | Translates to 'noodle' and usually refers to white noodles made of wheat flour, water and egg. They are sold dried and are either flat or round.

goose In northern Europe this large migratory bird is traditionally served for Christmas dinner. It is much larger than a duck and has a similar gamey taste. They are usually sold between three and five months old when they are between 3–5 kg. Older birds have darker meat with a stronger taste. In England it is stuffed with sage, onions and breadcrumbs, slowly roasted and served with apple sauce. Although geese have a high proportion of fat to flesh, the fat can be rendered and used as an excellent cooking medium, especially for frying potatoes. In France geese are mainly reared for fois gras and making confit (goose cooked and preserved in its own fat). Goose fat is available in some specialty and butcher shops. *see also* MAGRET *and* CAPE BARON GOOSE.

goose barnacles *see* PERCEBES.

gooseberry (*Ribes grossularia*) Largish, round berry which varies when ripe from yellow, green, amber and red. Usually available during summer. The smooth-skinned varieties can be eaten raw or made into preserves or many desserts, including the old-fashioned gooseberry fool; in France, also used in a sauce traditionally served with fish.

Gorgonzola | ITALIAN | Blue vein cow's-milk cheese with soft, creamy-white interior streaked generously with greenish-blue veins. The thin, natural, reddish-grey rind is scraped and washed. The flavour is strong, tangy and rich. Served at the end of a richly flavoured meal; also used as a snack, in salads or with aperitifs.

Gouda | DUTCH | Firm cow's-milk cheese with pale yellow, creamy, smooth interior with small holes scattered evenly throughout. The rind is coated in red or yellow wax, or left natural for local consumption. It tastes mildly nutty, strong and sharp when aged. Used as a snack or sandwich cheese; also good for grating.

gougère | FRENCH | Cheesey choux pastry; usually with Gruyère, Comte or Emmental.

goulash | HUNGARIAN | Beef stew with paprika, onions and tomatoes, to which cubed potatoes are added in final stages.

gourd, dried Creamy, ribbon-like strips made from the dried skin of a Japanese gourd (kanpyo), sold in cellophane packs in specialty shops. They are washed and soaked in cold water until soft and boiled for about 10 minutes until translucent. Used as a sushi filling or as a sushi tie; also used in soups and vegetarian dishes.

goyère | FRENCH | Maroilles cheese tart. Specialty of northern France.

grains of paradise (*Amomum melegueta*) Also known as 'melegueta pepper'. Aromatic beige berries obtained from an African perennial plant and once used as an adulterant to black pepper, now used in beer, vinegar, cordials and an aromatic wine called 'hippocras'.

gramolata Granular water ice made from sweetened fruit syrup.

Grana Padano | ITALIAN | Very hard cow's-milk cheese with a golden, rough, grainy texture. Very similar to Parmesan, but may be aged for less time and the milk used is from a less tightly defined area than that of Parmesan. Taste often milder than Parmesan, but this cheese is considerably less costly. Best used as a grating cheese.

granadilla *see* PASSIONFRUIT.

Grand Marnier | FRENCH | Orange liqueur with a cognac spirit base.

grand veneur sauce | FRENCH | Rich brown sauce made with game stock, red currant jelly and cream. Served with game, especially venison.

granita | ITALIAN | Granité in French. Grainy water ice made from lightly sweetened fruit syrup or coffee. It is served at the end of a meal or as a refreshment.

Granny Smith apple Known universally as an excellent cooking and eating apple. It is one of the best for apple sauce and its keeping quality is exceptionally good.

grape (*Vitis vinifera*) Among the oldest cultivated plants on record. It is highly valued for the fresh fruit itself, for winemaking and for drying into raisins, currants and sultanas. Table grapes are sold in bunches, and may vary from pale green, mauve, dark red, purple and black, depending on variety. Grapes do not ripen any further once they are cut from the vine. They should be plump and firm, and in neat, tight bunches. Apart from eating as a fresh fruit, in fruit salads and as a garnish with cheese, they can be used in aspic, jams, pies, sauces, juices and many desserts.

grape leaves (*Vitis vinifera*) Also known as 'vine leaves'. Leaves from the grape vine are used throughout the Middle East and Greece as an edible wrapping for food such as dolmas/dolmades. They are usually sold preserved in brine and these should be rinsed before using. If using freshly picked grape leaves, blanch first in boiling water to soften them enough for wrapping.

grapefruit (*Citrus paradisi*) Large, round citrus fruit usually with pale yellow, thin skin and very juicy flesh which may be pale yellow or pinkish-red. Those with pink-tinted flesh are generally sweeter and can be eaten without the addition of sugar. Grapefruit is a good source of vitamin C, is low in kilojoules and is popular served in halves for breakfast, as an appetizer or sprinkled with brown sugar and grilled for dessert. Also used for fruit salads, marmalade, juices and ices.

grapeseed oil Nutty, mild-tasting oil extracted from grape seeds. Used for sautéing and in vinaigrettes.

grappa | ITALIAN | Harsh-tasting marc brandy made from the remains of grapes after pressing.

grass jelly | SOUTH-EAST ASIAN | Dark brown, jelly-like product sold in cans in Asian grocers. Used in drinks and desserts.

grass mushrooms *see* STRAW MUSHROOMS.

grasshopper After-dinner cocktail made with equal parts of white crème de cacao, green crème de menthe and cream.

gratin | FRENCH | Dish browned quickly under the grill or in the oven; often sprinkled with breadcrumbs and grated cheese.

gratinée | FRENCH | Traditional onion soup topped with crusty bread and cheese and browned under a grill or very hot oven.

Gratte-Paille | FRENCH | High fat cow's-milk cheese with soft, double cream interior and whitish, velvety rind. Served as a dessert cheese.

gravlax | SWEDISH | Traditional method of curing raw salmon in a mixture of salt, sugar and dill. The salmon is sliced paper-thin and eaten with bread as part of a smörgasbord, often with a mustard sauce.

gravy Sauce that has been thickened with flour that has been browned in the meat juices after roasting and diluted by adding stock, wine or water.

gravy beef Boneless meat taken from the shin of beef. Used in slow-cooked dishes such as casseroles and curries.

great northern beans (*Phaseolus vulgaris*) White, medium-sized dried beans, similar to cannellini beans, but rounder. Soak overnight before cooking for about 45 minutes.

grecque (à la) | FRENCH | Mediterranean-style dish cooked in a seasoned mixture of oil, lemon juice and water. Often refers to cold vegetables, particularly mushrooms.

green bean vermicelli *see* BEAN THREAD NOODLES.

green curry paste | THAI | Popular paste used in the famous Thai green curry chicken; also used with duck and fish. It is made from shallots, garlic, fresh coriander root stem and leaves, lemon grass, fresh galangal, black peppers, coriander seeds, cumin seeds, nutmeg, fresh green chilies, shrimp paste, grated zest of kaffir lime, pounded together to form a smooth paste. Pre-made green curry paste is available in tubs.

green horseradish *see* WASABI.

green onions (*Allium fistulosum*) Called 'scallions' in America and often referred to as 'shallots' in Australia. Slender white bulbs with straight sides and bright green hollow tube-like leaves. Sold in bunches. They have a mild onion taste and are widely used in Asian dishes. Both the white bottoms and green tops are used. Sometimes called 'spring onions', but these are small versions of the common onion with a small white bulb and long green tops. *see also* SPRING ONIONS *and* SHALLOTS.

green perilla *see* SHISO.

green prawns Raw prawns still in their shells. *see also* PRAWNS.

green tea (*Camellia sinensis*) Unfermented leaves of the tea plant that are steamed immediately after harvesting, rolled and then dried, retaining much of their green shade and providing a pale green brew. It has a high caffeine content. Milk and sugar are not added. About 20 per cent of all tea produced is green. It is drunk throughout most of Asia, particularly in Japan. The special powdered green tea made from the young tips and buds, called **matcha**, is central to the traditional tea ceremony. **Sencha** is a quality tea, made from young tender leaves and is usually served at tea time and to guests. **Bancha**, made from the stems and twigs of the tea bush is the most commonly drunk green tea in Japan. It has a milder caffeine content and is drunk throughout the day.

greenback flounder *see* FLOUNDER, GREENBACK.

greenlip abalone *see* ABALONE.

greenlip mussels *see* MUSSELS.

gremiti | ITALIAN | Short, curved tubular pasta, also known as 'elbow macaroni'.

gremolata | ITALIAN | Blend of finely chopped parsley, finely chopped garlic and grated lemon zest. Traditional topping for osso buco.

Grenache Red wine-producing grape used for making rosé in southern France and Spain. It has a soft fruity taste.

grenadin | FRENCH | Small slice of veal wrapped in bacon and grilled, slowly shallow fried or braised.

grenadine Red sugar syrup made from pomegranates or other red fruits. Used as a long refreshing drink with ice water or to sweeten certain food and drinks.

grey sea salt *see* CELTIC SEA SALT.

gribiche sauce | FRENCH | Cold mayonnaise made from pounded hard-boiled egg yolks, oil and vinegar, capers, herbs and chopped egg white. Served with cold fish.

griddle Flat, heavy, metal plate with a long handle used to cook food over direct heat such as pancakes, griddle cakes and flat, unleavened breads.

grill To cook meat, fish, poultry or vegetables by placing it upon or under a high heat, normally produced by a grill or salamander, and searing the outside.

grissini | ITALIAN | Crisp, thin breadsticks.

grits | AMERICAN | Cornmeal porridge eaten at breakfast.

gros sel | FRENCH | Coarse salt.

ground rice *see* RICE FLOUR.

groundnut *see* PEANUT.

gruel Thin, porridge-like dish made by boiling ground oatmeal or barley in milk or water.

Gruyère | SWISS | Name-controlled firm cow's-milk cheese with smooth, ivory-yellow interior with small holes and natural, brushed rind. Used as a table cheese, as a snack, in sandwiches and at the end of meal; also melts well in fondues, gratins and quiches. A type of Gruyère is made in France.

see also COMTE.

Gruyère de Comte *see* COMTE.

guacamole | MEXICAN | Dip or filling made from mashed ripe avocado, finely chopped chilies, minced onions and lime or lemon juice; sometimes chopped tomato is added.

guajillo chili | MEXICAN | Long, smooth, light red chili, usually sold dried and then it is a deep red. It is fairly mild and used in salsas, soups and stews.

guar gum Partially soluble gum obtained from the bark of certain leguminous plants. Used in commercial food processing as a stabilizer and thickener in ice creams, sauces and chutneys, etc.

guava (*Psidium guajava*) Small, round, tropical fruit with thin, waxy, green skin that turns yellow when ripe. It has a creamy yellow to pink flesh, is highly aromatic and tastes like a mixture of pineapple and strawberries. It is an excellent source of vitamin C. Although it can be peeled and eaten raw, the guava is mostly used to make drinks, jellies, preserves, sauces and a fruit paste.

guinea fowl Small domestic bird originally from Africa. It has a lean, dry dark flesh with a slight gamey taste. To keep the flesh moist and tender, guinea fowl is usually barded with fat and well basted if roasted. It is also casseroled or braised.

gum tragacanth (*Astragalus gummifer*) Partially soluble gum used commercially to stabilize, emulsify and thicken foods such as sauces, confectionery, ice-cream and preserves.

gumbo | AMERICAN-CREOLE | Thick soup or stew made of fish, chicken, seafood and vegetables of various combinations to which okra and/or file powder is added as a thickening agent. Also another name for okra.

gunkan-maki *see* SUSHI.

gunpowder tea | CHINESE | Tiny rolled balls of high-grade green tea. The brew is a light yellow-green with a refreshing sharp taste.

gur *see* JAGGERY.

gurnards A distinctive group of fish with cylindrical, reddish bodies and large, bone-cased heads belonging to the Triglidae family. They are found mostly in European waters and are often poached or used in soups and bouillabaisse. The butterfly gurnard (*Lepidotrigla vanessa*) found in Australian waters can be used in all gurnard recipes. The lean, white flesh is firm with a delicate taste.

gyoza | JAPANESE | Steamed or deep-fried dumpling made with won ton wrappers folded over a minced savory filling.

gyulai | HUNGARIAN | Smoked, slender salami made from pork or a mixture of meats, seasoned with red capsicum.

habanero chili | MEXICAN | Also known as 'Scotch bonnet'. A variety of *Capsicum chinense* shaped like a lantern that ripens from green to bright orange. Considered one of the hottest chilies. Used in Mexican, Caribbean and Latin American cooking in stews and sauces; also in fresh salsas, chutneys and marinades, or pickled.

hachis | FRENCH | Minced or finely chopped meat or fish.

haddock (*Melanogrammus aegle finus*) Small member of the cod family, caught in the Atlantic Ocean and sold fresh or smoked in the British Isles and the United States. Lightly smoked haddock is called 'finnan haddie' in Scotland. *see also* FINNAN HADDIE.

haggis | SCOTTISH | Traditional dish consisting of cleaned sheep's stomach filled with a seasoned mixture of sheep's heart, lungs and liver combined with oatmeal, onions, herbs and fat. It is simmered for three to four hours in stock. Served on New Year's Eve and on national celebrations.

hake *see* GEMFISH.

halicot | FRENCH | Mutton stew.

Haloumi | MIDDLE EASTERN | Semifirm sheep's-milk cheese. Sold pre-packaged in small blocks usually in a small amount of brine. Served as a snack, often with pita bread.

halva | MIDDLE EASTERN | Rich, crispy confection made with ground sesame seeds and sugar or honey.

halwa | INDIAN | Fudge-like confection made from milk, coconut milk, sugar, fruit or nuts and infused with spices or rosewater. After the mixture is cooked, it is cooled in a flat tin, then cut into squares or diamond shapes to serve.

ham Upper part of the hind leg of a pig that is cured in various ways and then smoked and hung to dry. After smoking the ham is partially or fully cooked. It is ready to eat on the bone, boned or in slices. Raw hams such as the Italian prosciutto and French Bayonne ham are salted and air-dried for 6–18 months. They are usually sliced very thinly and served raw as an appetizer.

hamburger | AMERICAN | Fried, round and flattened minced meat rissole served in a round bread roll with salad and tomato sauce. Variations might include mayonnaise, cheese, beetroot, bacon or egg.

hanging To age meat by suspending for a period of time in a cool place to make the flesh more tender and succulent.

hangiri | JAPANESE | Round, rice-cooling, wooden tub used for dressing and cooling rice for sushi. Available at Japanese grocers. *see also* SUSHI.

hard ball stage Stage when a sampling of hot sugar syrup forms a hard but pliable ball when dropped into cold water.

hard crack stage Stage when a sampling of hot sugar syrup hardens to brittle threads when dropped into cold water.

hard sauce *see* BRANDY BUTTER.

hare (*Lepus capensis*) Large relative of the rabbit, with a darker flesh. Young hares are roasted and sautéed, older specimens are made into pies, casseroles and jugged.

haricot beans (*Phaseolus vulgaris*) Also known as 'navy beans'. Small, oval, dried white beans. After soaking overnight, they are simmered for about 45 minutes. Used in stews and casseroles and form part of the French regional dish, cassoulet. Also used in commercial baked beans.

harira | MOROCCAN | This thick national soup has many variations and contains pulses such as lentils, chickpeas and haricot beans, onions and tomatoes, chopped coriander and parsley, saffron, turmeric or paprika. It is sometimes made with cubes of meat and bones. Served only after sunset during the holy month of Ramadan.

harissa | NORTH AFRICAN | Fiery red paste made from pounded chilies, garlic, coriander, cumin and caraway seeds and dried mint mixed with olive oil. Used as a condiment, particularly with couscous, soups and Moroccan chicken.

harusame | JAPANESE | Translates to 'spring rain'. Thin dried cellophane noodles made from potato starch, sold in small short packets. Soak briefly in hot water to soften before using in salads. Take care when cooking as they may collapse. Deep-fried, they instantly puff up and become white.

hash | AMERICAN | Mixture of minced or diced left-over cooked meat or vegetables, crispy browned on both sides in a frying pan.

hash browns | AMERICAN | Crispy, brown potato cakes made with coarsely grated cooked potatoes and fried in hot oil.

haute cuisine | FRENCH | Gourmet cooking.

Havarti | DANISH | Semifirm cow's-milk cheese with a pale interior with numerous small holes and a thin, washed rind, sometimes waxed. It is mild, becoming sharper with age.

hazelnut (*Corylus avellana*) Also known as 'filbert'. Small, round, pale brown nut enclosed in a hard, brown shell with a pointed tip. An excellent source of vitamin E and high in mono-unsaturated fat (82 per cent). After shelling, the brown skin is removed by placing the hazelnuts in a medium oven for about 10 minutes, then rubbing with a clean tea towel. They have a very sweet taste and are used in all sorts of confectionery, desserts, cakes and biscuits; also used in sauces and stuffings for poultry.

hazelnut oil Expensive, strong mono-unsaturated oil, pressed from hazelnuts. Used in pastries and baked goods; also used in salad dressing and sauces.

head cheese *see* BRAWN.

hearts of palm Heart or tender young shoot cut from certain species of palm trees. It is obtained only by felling and completely destroying the tree. Available in cans. Used in salads and cooked dishes.

herb Aromatic leaves of various plants used mostly on cooking to enhancefood, to stimulate the appetite or to aid digestion.

herbes de Provence | FRENCH | Blend of mixed dried herbs of equal parts rosemary, thyme, marjoram, basil, fennel and oregano, sometimes with a little sage or mint added.

herring Large family of saltwater fish with a high fat content, most often sold salted, smoked or pickled rather than fresh. *see also* BISMARCK HERRING, BLOATERS, KIPPERS *and* ROLLMOP.

hibachi | JAPANESE | Small charcoal stove or grill that can be used on the table.

high tea | SCOTTISH | A light evening meal when the main meal of the day is eaten at midday. It usually consists of a cooked meat or fish dish and hot scones, cakes or biscuits. Tea is drunk with the meal.

hijiki / hiziki | JAPANESE | (*Cystophyllum fusiforme*) Short black strands of dried seaweed that look like tea leaves. It has a strong, fishy taste and is an excellent source of iron and calcium. Rinse in a fine-mesh strainer under cold running water. Soaking will remove some of the strong taste if required. It will expand considerably in cooking and is usually simmered in combination with other foods or sautéed in sesame oil as a side dish.

hock Lower portion of the pig's leg just above the trotter. It is often sold cured and smoked. Used in slow-cooked soups and stews.

hog plum *see* AMBARELLA.

hogget Meat from sheep that is between one and two years old. *see also* LAMB.

hoisin sauce | CHINESE | Thick, slightly sweet and spicy, brownish-red sauce made from fermented soya beans, flour, sugar, vinegar, spices, garlic and chili. Used in cooking pork and duck; also in marinades for poultry.

Hokkien noodles | CHINESE / MALAYSIAN | Thick, yellow, egg noodles sold fresh in plastic bags from the refrigerator in Asian food stores, health-food shops and supermarkets. Before adding to a stir-fried dish, they are covered with boiling water for one minute, then drained.

hollandaise sauce | FRENCH | Creamy sauce of butter, egg yolks, lemon juice and seasoning. Served with poached fish, steamed vegetables and egg dishes.

homard | FRENCH | Lobster.

hominy | AMERICAN | Dried corn kernels from which the bran and germ have been removed by soaking in a lye bath. When ground it is called hominy grits.

honey Thick, sweet liquid processed by bees from nectar obtained from flowers and stored in specially prepared cells in the bee hive. It consists mainly of a mixture of unrefined sugars (glucose and fructose) and is an important sweetener. Honey takes its taste from the type of flowers from which it is collected. Common honey-producing plants are acacia, clover, rosemary, linden or lime, leatherwood, thyme, eucalyptus and heather.

honeydew melon (*Cucumis melo* var. *inodorus*) Smooth-skinned, medium-sized melon with a bright yellow or pale yellow rind surrounding a pale green, sweet flesh. Eaten as a snack or entrée or used in fruit salads and desserts; also used as a garnish with cold meat or seafood platters. *see also* MELONS.

hongroise (à la) | FRENCH | Hungary-style. Usually dishes which contain paprika and cream.

hor fun noodles *see* RICE NOODLES.

horehound (*Marrubium vulgare*) Bitter perennial herb of the mint family. Leaves and flowering tops are used in for beverages and confectionery and as a traditional cough medicine.

horehound candy | AMERICAN | Popular medicinal candy used as a remedy for coughs.

horiatiki | GREEK | Translates to 'village salad'. Popular salad consisting of sliced cucumber, onion, green capsicum, tomatoes, black olives, topped with cubes of feta and dressed with olive oil.

horn of plenty *see* TROMPETTE DE LA MORT.

hors d'oeuvre | FRENCH | Small savory appetizers served before the first course or with drinks.

horseradish (*Armoracia rusticana*) Hot, spicy, fleshy root obtained from a perennial plant of the mustard family. Used as a condiment mainly in the form of a sauce as a complement to roast beef, corned meats, smoked fish and oysters.

hoso-maki *see* SUSHI.

hot pot The English version of hot pot is a layered stew of meat or fish and vegetables cooked slowly in a covered casserole in the oven. **Lancashire hot pot** contains mutton, onions and potatoes, and might include kidneys and oysters. A **Chinese hot pot** is a form of communal table cooking where a combination of vegetables and meat, poultry or fish are cooked in a seasoned broth; the best-known being the **Mongolian hot pot** which usually includes lamb or mutton.

hotchpotch Traditionally a Flemish stew containing oxtail and vegetables. Also refers to a soup or stew that contains many ingredients.

hotdog | AMERICAN | Fast food consisting of a frankfurt sandwiched in a thin roll, spread with mustard or tomato sauce.

huckleberry *see* BILBERRY.

huevos rancheros | MEXICAN | Translates to 'ranch-style eggs'. Fried eggs served on small tortillas and topped with tomato and chili salsa.

huile | FRENCH | Oil.

huître | FRENCH | Oyster.

humble pie | ENGLISH | Traditionally an inexpensive pie made with the innards of a deer, usually eaten by the servants, while the gentry were served the choicer cuts of venison.

hummus | MIDDLE EASTERN | Creamy dip made from puréed chickpeas, olive oil, lemon juice, garlic and sesame seed paste (tahini). Served with pita bread.

hundred-year egg *see* EGGS, PRESERVED.

Hungarian salami | HUNGARIAN | Large, fine-textured salami made from finely minced pork, or a mixture of meats, seasoned with paprika, pepper, garlic and white wine. White Hungarian salami has a white skin and is milder in taste.

Hungarian wax chili Also known as 'yellow banana chili'. It is a large, pale yellow chili about 15 cm long, with a mild heat and slightly sweet taste. Used in salsas, salads, stews or stuffed.

hure de porc | FRENCH | Type of brawn or head cheese made from the fleshy meat of the head of the pig, including the tongue and set in gelatin.

hush puppy | AMERICAN | Small, deep-fried balls made with cornmeal and flour mixed with butter, eggs, milk, chopped onions and cajun spices. Traditionally served with fried catfish.

hydrogenate Hardening process used in the manufacture of margarine to turn unsaturated vegetable oils from their normal liquid state into a semisolid spreadable form. This process also renders such fats more saturated to various degrees and produces substances known as 'trans fatty acids', believed to have the same potential as saturated fats for raising blood cholesterol levels. Soft spreadable margarines are lightly hydrogenated and contain less saturated fats.

hydroponic tomato *see* TOMATO.

hymettus | GREEK | Dark brown aromatic honey tasting of thyme, savory and marjoram.

hyssop (*Hyssopus officinalis*) Bitter, aromatic herb of the mint family used in small quantities in green salads, kidney recipes, with fatty fish and game; also to flavour a sugar syrup for fruit and liqueurs.

ice cream Frozen dessert of milk, cream, custard or syrup, sweetened with sugar and infused with fruit purées or juices, chocolate, coffee, liqueur, nuts, green tea or honey.

ice cream soda Drink made with scoops of ice-cream and syrup, topped with soda water.

iceberg lettuce Large, ball-shaped lettuce with dense heart of pale, crunchy leaves surrounded by darker, coarse leaves that are usually discarded. It has a neutral sweet taste and forms the basis of many salads.

icing Sweet, spreadable, decorative coating used on cakes, pastries and biscuits.

Idaho potato *see* POTATO.

Idiazabal | SPANISH | From Basque country and Navarre. Name-controlled raw sheep's-milk cheese that is usually smoked. It has a firm, pale yellow interior with many tiny holes, and an orange to brown natural rind. Used as a table cheese, appetizer or snack; when aged suitable for grating.

idli | INDIAN | Little round cakes, made from urad flour paste, that are steamed and served hot accompanied by a chutney.

ikan | INDONESIAN | Fish. Ikan goreng is fried fish; ikan kecap is fish in soy sauce; krupuk ikan is a type of fish wafer; ikan bali is fish Balinese style, and ikan bilis are dried tiny sprats or anchovies.

imitation crab sticks *see* SURIMI.

imitation vanilla extract *see* VANILLA.

impératrice (à l') | FRENCH | Rice pudding dessert made with candied fruit and cream, sometimes with added rum.

impériale (à l') | FRENCH | Various dishes garnished with extravagant ingredients such as cockscombs, lobster tails, fois gras and truffles.

inari-zushi *see* SUSHI.

Indian fig *see* PRICKLY PEAR.

Indian five spices *see* PANCH PHORA.

Indian tonic water *see* QUININE TONIC WATER.

indienne (à l') | FRENCH | Dish cooked in an Indian style, usually with curry paste or powder.

infuse To steep or soak an aromatic item to extract flavor, such as vanilla beans in hot milk or herbs in boiling water.

infusion Aromatic liquid or tea resulting from steeping herbs in boiling water.

insalata | ITALIAN | Translates to 'salad'. Insalata mista is a mixed salad; insalata verde, green salad; insalata di frutta, fruit salad; insalata caprese is sliced bocconcini topped with a slice of tomato and fresh basil, sprinkled with olive oil.

iodine Trace element essential to the thyroid gland. Found in iodized table salt, saltwater fish and seafood, seaweed and vegetables grown in soils containing iodine.

Irish coffee Hot black coffee served in a tall glass with a good measure of Irish whiskey and sometimes sugar. Double cream is slowly poured on top so that it floats; it is not stirred.

Irish moss (*Chondrus crispus*) Also known as 'carrageen/carragheen'. Small dried seaweed with thin black fronds. Commercially it is used as a basis for ice cream, pastries, cough mixtures and toothpaste. In cooking it is mainly used as a gelatin or thickening agent in the same was as agar-agar.

Irish stew | IRISH | This national dish consists of alternate layers of lamb, potatoes and onions with just enough water to cover, simmered on a low heat until cooked.

iron Mineral needed for red blood cell formation and muscle protein. Found in liver, red meats, egg yolks, sardines, pulses and some green vegetables such as spinach.

isinglass Old-time gelling agent extracted from the air bladder of the sturgeon.

isoflavones Compounds found in soya beans and other legumes that have oestrogen-like qualities.

Italian meringue Made by beating hot sugar syrup into stiffly beaten eggwhites, constantly until the mixture cools; usually piped as a topping on pies and other desserts then baked in the oven. *see also* MERINGUE.

Italian tomato *see* TOMATO.

italienne (à l') | FRENCH | Italian style. Often refers to dishes with a sauce containing ham, mushrooms and herbs.

jaboticaba (*Myrciaria* sp.) Also known as 'Brazilian tree grape'. Small, round, berry-like fruit with a tough, black skin and translucent pink flesh with a sweet taste. Usually sold in punnets, mainly in summer. Eaten as a fresh fruit, in fruit salads or made into jelly.

Jack | AMERICAN | Also known as 'Monterey Jack'. Semisoft pressed cow's-milk cheese with a moist, springy interior and thin, natural rind. Dry Jack is an aged Jack cheese with a sharp, nutty taste, used as a table and grating cheese. Originated near Monterey, California in the 1890s.

jackfruit (*Artocarpus heterophyllus*) Large, barrel-shaped, tropical fruit with knobbly, yellow-green skin and soft, yellow flesh containing large, white seeds. Immature fruit can be used as a vegetable or included in curries. Ripe jackfruit has an exotic sweet taste and can be eaten fresh or coated in batter and deep-fried.

jaggery | INDIAN | Light brown, unrefined lump sugar made from the juice of sugarcane, or from certain types of palm trees and then it is called 'gur'. *see also* PALM SUGAR.

jalapeño chili | MEXICAN | Named after the town Jalapa, in eastern Mexico. It is dark green, ripening to red, with thick skin and a rounded end. Used fresh in a variety of sauces, also stuffed and roasted; also pickled and canned. A dried smoked version of red jalapeños is called 'chipotle'.

jalebi | INDIAN | Golden coils of deep-fried batter, lightly coated with an aromatic sugar syrup.

jalousie | FRENCH | Translates to 'venetian blind'. Classic, small puff pastry filled with almond paste and topped with slatted pastry lid.

jam Sweet, jelly-like spread made mostly of one or more fruits cooked in a sugar syrup until soft and almost shapeless. Other ingredients may include chili, ginger and flowers such as rose petals or violets. Used to spread on toast, bread and biscuits, or as a filling or glaze for pastries and desserts.

Jamaica pepper *see* ALLSPICE.

Jamaican hot chili Bright red, hot chili related to the habanero, but a little smaller and rather distorted in shape. Used in stews, curries and condiments in Caribbean cooking.

jambalaya | AMERICAN | Creole dish derived from the Spanish paella, containing highly spiced rice, ham, chicken, shellfish and tomato and other vegetables, seasoned with cayenne pepper.

jambon | FRENCH | Ham. Also refers to a leg of fresh pork. Jambon blanc is unsmoked or slightly smoked ham used in cooking.

jambonneau | FRENCH | Cured ham or pork knuckle.

jamon | SPANISH | Cured ham, usually served raw in very thin slices. Variations include ibérico, made mostly from black Iberian pig, and serrano, or 'mountain ham'.

Jap pumpkin *see* PUMPKIN.

Japanese breadcrumbs *see* PANKO.

Japanese citron *see* CITRON.

Japanese eggplant *see* EGGPLANT.

Japanese medlar *see* LOQUAT.

Japanese omelette | JAPANESE | Tamago-yaki. Sometimes called 'egg brick'. Slightly sweetened egg mixture containing dashi, soy and saki or mirin that is cooked in a rectangular omelette pan and repeatedly folded to form a neat block. When cool it is cut into slices and served as an appetiser or as a topping for sushi.

Japanese omelette pan | JAPANESE | Tamago-yaki nabe. Rectangular frying pan, about 2 cm deep. The shape makes it easier to fold the omelette repeatedly, until it forms a solid mass. It is then cut into neat strips.

Japanese pepper *see* SANSHO.

Japanese pickles *see* TSUKEMONO.

Japanese rice *see* KOSHIHIKARI.

Japanese shishito *see* SHISHITO.

jardinière (à la) | FRENCH | Preparation or garnish of fresh cooked vegetables.

Jarlsberg | NORWEGIAN | Semifirm cow's-milk cheese with smooth, ivory interior, large holes and thick natural rind, coated with bright yellow wax. Mild and nutty. Used mainly for sandwiches and snacks; also in cooking.

jasmine rice | THAI | Aromatic long-grain white rice with a distinctive aroma. Served as an accompaniment to sauced dishes, or in pilaf or salad.

jelly (1) Clear, firm gel made with the juice of cooked fruit that is strained through a jelly bag or layers of cheesecloth, then boiled with equal parts of sugar. **(2)** Jelly-like dessert set with gelatin or agar-agar in a mold.

jelly fish (*Rhopilema esculenta*) Soft, gelatinous marine animal available in dried or salted form in Asian grocers. Popular in cold Chinese dishes for its crunchy texture. It is soaked for several hours and quickly blanched in boiling water before use. It is usually shredded and used in cold vegetable salads tossed with vinegar and soy dressing.

jerky / jerked beef Thin strips of very lean beef that have been salted and dried. Sold in sealed packs. Used by backpackers and bushwalkers as a lightweight food that can be eaten without cooking.

Jeroboam Bottle of champagne equivalent to four standard bottles.

Jerusalem artichoke *see* ARTICHOKE, JERUSALEM.

jésuite | FRENCH | Small, triangular-shaped puff pastry filled with almond paste and iced.

jesus | FRENCH | Plump, smoked pork sausage with a wooden hook tied in the casing at one end so that it can be hung up and smoked.

jewfish (*Argyrosomus hololepidotus*) Also commonly called 'mulloway'. Large, elongated, silvery fish sold whole, in fillets, steaks or cutlets. It has white to pale pink flesh with a large flake, and a mild, oily taste. It can be pan fried, baked, barbecued or grilled.

jícama (*Pachyrrhizus tuberosus*) Also known as 'yam bean'. Flattened, top-shaped tuber with thin, light brown skin and crispy, white flesh. Peeled and grated or thinly sliced, it is eaten raw as a snack or in salads, sometimes sprinkled with lime juice and chili powder. Also baked or lightly boiled. A popular vegetable in Mexico, also used in South-East Asia and often used instead of water chestnuts.

jigger Measure of alcoholic spirit, equivalent to 30 ml or 1.5 ounces. Also known as a 'shot'.

John dory (*Zeus faber*) Silvery, smooth fish with a distinctive dark spot in its side, and firm, white flesh that has an excellent texture and delicate taste. It can be bought whole or in fillets. John dory has no scales, is virtually boneless and can be gently pan-fried, grilled, barbecued, poached or baked..

joint Usually refers to a cut of meat used for roasting; also to cut up meat or poultry into large pieces at the joint.

Jonathan apple Bright red apple with a crisp, juicy flesh and sweet taste. Excellent eating apple, but also suitable for pies and sauce.

Josephine pear Medium-sized roundish pear with pale-green skin and fragrant juicy flesh. It is one of the best eating pears; also suitable for cooking. *see also* PEAR.

jugged hare | ENGLISH | Hare braised in a red wine and herb mixture in which it has been marinated overnight. Vegetables are included and traditionally the dish is thickened with the hare's blood at the last minute.

jujube *see* RED DATE.

julep | AMERICAN | Alcoholic drink made with bourbon and mint.

julienne | FRENCH | To cut into very thin sticks; mostly root vegetables such as carrots, also citrus rinds and sometimes meat and poultry.

juniper berry (*Juniperus communis*) Dark, purplish-black, round berry with a distinct aromatic, tart taste best known for providing the characteristic taste to gin; also used in other spirits and beer. Crushed berries are added to marinades and stuffings for game dishes and strong pâtés and terrines; in Germany they are added to sauerkraut and coleslaw.

junket Very simple, semifirm dessert made with warm sweetened milk and rennet.

jus | FRENCH | Natural, unthickened pan juices. Jus rôti are pan juices from a roast, and jus lié are roast pan juices thickened with cornflour or arrowroot.

kadaif | GREEK / TURKISH | Baked pastry made with very thin threads of dough wrapped around finely chopped sweetened nuts. Immediately after cook- ing it is saturated with a sweet heavy syrup.

kaeng | THAI | Curry dish cooked with coconut milk.

kaffir lime (*Citrus hystrix*) Called 'makrut' in Thailand. A variety of lime with a dark green, knobbly rind which is grated and used in many dishes. The distinctive aromatic leaves are widely used in Thai and Malay dishes. The characteristic twin-leaf distinguishes this from other limes. Finely shredded leaves are added to soups, fish dishes and curries. Available in small plastic bags at the fruit market, often in the herb section.

Kahlúa | MEXICAN | Coffee-flavoured liqueur.

kahwa | MIDDLE EASTERN | Turkish coffee made with freshly roasted and powdered coffee beans brought to the boil in a small amount of water with sugar (if any) added at the same time.

Kakadu plum | AUSTRALIAN | (*Terminalia ferdinandiana*) This small, yellowish green fruit that looks like an elongated green olive has exceptionally high levels of vitamin C and is considered the highest source in the world. Available frozen whole. Served pickled in vinegar as a nibble, or to accompany cold meat or fish. Also available as a light sweet jelly.

kakavia | GREEK | Fish soup with tomato paste and sometimes thickened with potatoes.

kalamata olive | GREEK | Oval, black variety of olive treated with brine and cured in oil and red wine vinegar.

kale (*Brassica oleracea* var. *acephala*) Decorative member of the cabbage family with textured, frilled leaves that do not form a head. The blue-green leaves have variations of cream, blue or purple. They should be crisp and fresh and show no signs of yellowing. Small amounts of young, tender leaves can be used raw in salads; also cooked like spinach or braised.

kaltschale | GERMAN | Cold mixed fruit salad dessert that has been steeped in wine and covered with purée of red berry fruits.

kamaboko | JAPANESE | Smooth, jelly-like fish paste formed in a round loaf and usually pink or green. Available frozen from Japanese grocers. It is thawed, sliced thinly and added to soups and simmered dishes. *see also* SURIMI.

kangaroo | AUSTRALIAN | (*Macropus* spp.) All parts of the kangaroo are eaten and are sold in various cuts including the tail. The meat is very lean, tender and delicate and should be rubbed with olive oil and cooked quickly at a high temperature and served rare to medium. It will toughen if over-cooked.

kanpyo *see* GOURD, DRIED.

kari | INDIAN | Tamil word (language spoken in Southern India) from which the word 'curry' is derived. *see also* CURRY.

kasha | RUSSIAN | Small pancakes made from buckwheat granules. Served with soup. In Poland, kasha is a semifirm sweet dish made from boiling barley in milk and butter to which beaten eggs are added.

kasseler | GERMAN | Cured and smoked loin of pork. **Kasseler rippen** is roasted kasseler traditionally served on a bed of sauerkraut accompanied by mashed potatoes. **Kasseler leberwurst** is a sausage of diced, lean pork and pork liver.

kasseri | GREEK | Firm-pressed sheep's-milk cheese with cream interior and thin, natural rind. Mild, savory taste. Served as an appetizer or snack.

katsoubushi *see* BONITO FLAKES.

kebab | MIDDLE EASTERN | Small pieces of meat, seafood or vegetables threaded on a skewer and grilled or barbecued.

kecap / ketjap manis | INDONESIAN | Soy sauce sweetened with palm sugar and usually less salty than most soy sauces.

kedgeree | ENGLISH | Traditional breakfast dish of Indian origin. Consists of smoked fish (usually haddock) boiled rice and hard-boiled eggs.

kefir | RUSSIAN | Yoghurt-like, cultured milk product made with fermented, slightly alcoholic milk.

kefta | GREEK | Flattened meatballs with chopped onions and spices, and shallow fried.

kelp (*Laminaria* spp.) Long, flat seaweed that is usually dried and sold as kombu. *see* KOMBU.

kencur | INDONESIAN / MALAYSIAN | (*Kaempferia galanga*) Also called 'aromatic ginger'. A small aromatic rhizome with a slightly bitter taste. Used mainly in spicy pastes. It has a distinctive taste and there is no substitute. Sold dried in slices or powdered form, also sometimes frozen.

kennebec potato *see* POTATO.

ketchup (1) Thick spicy sauce made with pulped fruit and vegetables (usually tomatoes) mixed with vinegar, sugar, salt and spices. Used as an accompaniment for meat and many other foods **(2)** American term for tomato sauce.

kewra water | INDIAN | (*Pandanus fascicularis*) Perfumed water or essence obtained from the male flower of a variety of screwpine. Used to impart a flowery fragrance to a variety of sweet dishes.

kheer | INDIAN | Creamy rice pudding with spices and a few drops of kewra water or rosewater.

khoshaf | MIDDLE EASTERN | Classic dried fruit salad of apricots, prunes, raisins, pistachio nuts and almonds that are soaked in cold water with rosewater and orange blossom water and sugar.

kibbeh | MIDDLE EASTERN | Mixture of fine cracked wheat (burghul), grated onion and finely minced lamb pounded to a paste and rolled into small thin fingers or biscuit shapes. Eaten raw with lettuce leaves or shallow-fried, grilled or baked.

kidney An edible internal organ of veal, lamb, pork and beef. The kidneys from young animals are the most tender. Before cooking, the transparent membrane is removed and the white central part and blood vessels cut out. If they have a strong smell kidneys are usually washed in acidulated water or soaked. Kidneys can be sautéed, braised, grilled or roasted and should not be over-cooked. They are also used in casseroles and the classic steak-and-kidney pie.

kidney beans (*Phaseolus vulgaris*) Medium-sized, kidney-shaped beans. *see also* BLACK KIDNEY BEANS *and* RED KIDNEY BEANS.

kiev | RUSSIAN | Breast of chicken rolled around a stuffing of herb and garlic butter and sealed. It is coated with egg and breadcrumbs and then deep-fried.

kilojoule Metric unit of energy value of food. One kilojoule equals 4.2 calories.

kimchi / kimchee | KOREAN | Strong-tasting hot pickle made from fermented vegetables, usually Chinese cabbage, highly seasoned with salt, chili and garlic.

kimpira gobo | JAPANESE | Vegetable side dish consisting of julienned burdock (gobo) sautéed and glazed with sugar, soy sauce, sake and chili powder. Julienned carrots are sometimes mixed with the burdock.

King Edward potato *see* POTATO.

kingfish *see* YELLOWTAIL KINGFISH.

Kipfler potato *see* POTATO.

kippers | SCOTTISH | Split, salted and cold-smoked herrings. Grilled kippers are served as a traditional breakfast dish. Kipper paste is served on thinly sliced toast.

Kir Aperitif made with blackcurrant liqueur and usually dry white wine, but sometimes red wine.

Kir Royal Kir made with champagne.

Kirsch White brandy liqueur distilled from cherries, including the stones. Widely used in pastries and desserts.

kiss Miniature meringue petit fours. When joined together with butter cream or thickened cream they become the French baiser.

kissel | RUSSIAN | Dessert of puréed red fruit thickened with either cornflour or potato starch. Served hot or chilled.

kiwano *see* AFRICAN HORNED CUCUMBER.

Kiwi fruit (*Actinidia chinensis*) Also known as 'Chinese gooseberry'. This small, brown, hairy fruit originated in China, but has been grown so successfully and marketed in New Zealand that it has become known as 'Kiwi fruit'. It has a bright green, sweet and slightly acid flesh and a mass of tiny black seeds. Rich in vitamin C. A smooth-skinned variety known as 'Kiwi Gold' has golden flesh. Used in fruit salads, desserts or with cheese. It is a popular garnish, especially with chocolate dishes and is the standard decoration for the pavlova. Kiwi fruit is also a good meat tenderizer.

kizami kombu *see* KOMBU.

knackwurst | GERMAN | Pre-cooked, thickish sausage made from finely minced beef and pork, and flavoured with garlic, cumin and parsley. Heated in water or grilled before serving.

knaidlach | JEWISH | Small, round balls made with matzo meal bound with egg, fat and seasonings. Used as a soup garnish during Passover.

knead To repeatedly work bread or pastry dough with the heel of the hand to evenly incorporate the ingredients until the dough is smooth and elastic.

knock back To knead or punch the air from risen dough so that it reverts to its former volume.

Kobe beef | JAPAN | World famous, high quality beef produced from pampered cattle raised in Kobe, Japan. The cattle are fed on beer and grain and are given a daily hand massage. The beef is evenly marbled with fat and extremely tender. It is also very expensive.

koeksister | GERMAN | Fried, snail-shaped pastry.

kofta | MIDDLE EASTERN | Small balls made of finely minced beef or lamb, fish or vegetables combined with aromatic spices and gently fried or simmered in a spicy sauce. Also minced meatballs in Indian dishes.

kohlrabi (*Brassica oleracea* var. *gonglyoides*) Round tuberous stem that can be either purple or cream. The white flesh has a turnip-like taste. Choose small specimens, cut off the shoots and steam or boil whole in its skin. It can then be sliced and added to salads, mashed or used in stir-fried dishes.

koikuchi shoyu *see* SHOYU.

konafa / kounafa | MIDDLE EASTERN | Baked pastry made with strands of dough filled with finely chopped nuts and saturated with a sweet syrup.

konbu / kombu | JAPANESE | (*Laminaria* spp.) Blackish-brown variety of edible seaweed sold in folded, dried, leathery strips. Kombu is rich in iodine, calcium and vitamin C. A very high content of monosodium glutamate is naturally present in kombu, making it an important flavor enhancer. Kombu should not be washed; the white powder on the surface is tasty and it is usually wiped lightly with a damp cloth. It is the basis for dashi, the Japanese-style stock used for soup and noodles; also finely shredded or cut into small pieces and deep-fried or simmered as a vegetable; also made into teas, pickles, condiments, snacks and confectionery. A very good pre-shredded green version labelled 'kizami kombu' is available in speciality shops. Used for fresh pickles, soups and as a garnish.

konnyaku | JAPANESE | Translucent brick made from the starch of tubers of the devil's tongue plant (*Amorphophallus konjac*). Available in plastic packs from the fridge of Japanese speciality stores. Used mainly for its chewy texture and simmered whole in one-pot dishes. A thinly sliced white noodle form sold in sausage-like plastic packs is known as 'shirataki'. *see also* SHIRATAKI.

korma | INDIAN | Mild curry dish, usually of lamb or mutton braised in a small amount of liquid and masala paste with cashew nuts, saffron and yoghurt.

kosher | JEWISH | Foods produced, prepared and served according to Jewish religious dietary laws.

koshihikari | JAPANESE | Short-grained, pearly rice that, when steamed, produces moist plump grains that cling together and can be easily picked up with chopsticks; also suited to Japanese sushi. Available from Japanese grocers.

kouing-aman | FRENCH | Large, flat, sweet, buttery pastry from Brittany.

koulibiac *see* COULIBIAC.

krachai *see* CHINESE KEYS.

kransky Spicy, European-style sausage made from pork or beef (sometimes both) and smoked. It is usually simmered in water before serving.

krapfen | GERMAN | Doughnut, usually filled with jam or almond paste.

kreplach | JEWISH | Ravioli-type dumpling filled with minced meat, prunes or cheese. Used as a soup garnish.

kringle | DANISH | Large pretzel-shaped pastry made with a yeast dough flavoured with cardamom. Traditionally served at Christmas.

krupuk emping | INDONESIAN | Wafer-like cracker made from the flattened kernel of the melinjo nut. They are quickly fried in hot oil, sprinkled with salt and served as a snack or accompaniment to a meal. *see also* PRAWN CRACKERS.

krupuk udang | INDONESIAN | Large, crispy cracker made from dried shrimp and tapioca flour. When fried in hot oil they expand and puff up. Served at most meals as a type of bread or garnish; eaten as a snack.

kueh teow *see* RICE NOODLES.

kugelhopf Light yeast-cake of Austrian origin and popular in Central Europe. It contains raisins and sometimes candied fruit and is cooked in a high- sided fluted ring mold (kugelhopf mold).

kulich | RUSSIAN | Tall, cylindrical yeast-cake containing crystallized fruit with saffron, cardamom, mace and vanilla. Traditionally served at Easter with paskha, a cream cheese dessert.

kumara *see* SWEET POTATO.

Kuminost *see* NÖKKELOST.

kümmel | GERMAN | Clear liqueur distilled from grain, sometimes potatoes, with caraway seeds.

kumquat *see* CUMQUAT.

kvass | RUSSIAN | Mildly alcoholic beer made from rye, barley and malt.

Labna/Labneh | MIDDLE EASTERN | Cream cheese made from salted yoghurt. Often served at breakfast.

labskaus | GERMAN | Stew-like dish originally cooked aboard ships, containing onions and potatoes with fish, beef or both with anchovies or herrings. May be served with a poached egg and pickled beetroot.

lacquered food | CHINESE | Term to describe food such as duck or pork that has been marinated and glazed with a sweet and savory sauce, roasted and basted several times. Served hot or cold.

lactose Natural sugar present in milk.

ladle Large, bowl-shaped serving spoon with a long handle used to serve liquids.

lager | GERMAN | Light-bodied, highly carbonated beer.

lait | FRENCH | Milk.

laksa | MALAYSIAN | Large, aromatic, coconut-milk soup containing prawns and round noodles, with shrimp paste, lemon grass, chilies and various other seasonings. There are many different versions: they might include chicken and fish or exclude the coconut milk.

lamb Meat of a young sheep less than a year old that has not developed its permanent teeth. Meat from an older animal (one to two years) is referred to as 'hogget' and over two years as 'mutton'. Milk-fed lamb, killed before being weaned, is the most tender and has the mildest flavour.

lamb's lettuce *see* CORN SALAD.

Lambrusco | ITALIAN | From Emiglia Romagna. Semisparkling dry red wine. There is also Lambrusco Bianco (white) and a semisweet version.

lamington | AUSTRALIAN | Small square sponge cake coated with chocolate icing and dipped in desiccated coconut.

Lancashire | ENGLISH | Firm, uncooked, pressed cow's-milk cheese with crumbly, white interior and natural, cloth-covered rind. Mild, but tangy and nutty. Served as a snack; also excellent melting cheese.

Lancashire hot pot | ENGLISH | Layered stew of lamb, onions and potatoes, which might include kidneys, mushrooms and oysters.

landaise (à la) | FRENCH | From Landes region in south-western France. Dishes that include or are garnished with ham, goose fat, mushrooms and garlic.

langouste | FRENCH | Spiny lobster. Type of saltwater lobster that does not have claws. Used extensively in Mediterranean cooking.

langoustine | FRENCH | Saltwater crustacean, related to the scampi and resembling a cross between a large prawn and a crayfish. *see also* SCAMPI.

Langres | FRENCH | Raw cow's-milk cheese with soft, creamy, pale yellow interior and washed, rust rind. Strong, spicy aroma and taste. Served at the end of a meal with full-bodied wine. Named after village in Champagne.

langue-de-chat | FRENCH | (Cat's tongue) Thin, narrow biscuit usually served with desserts.

languedocienne (à la) | FRENCH | Dishes that include or are garnished with tomatoes, eggplant and wild mushrooms.

laos *see* GALANGAL, GREATER.

lap cheong | CHINESE | Thin, dry pork sausage with a sweet, salty taste. Steamed or simmered for about 15 minutes, sliced and used in fried rice or stir-fried dishes.

lapsang souchong Chinese black tea with a strong smoky taste.

larb / larp | THAI | Aromatic salad consisting of finely chopped, cooked chicken or minced beef tossed in a dressing of lime juice, fish sauce, sliced shallots, red chilies, lemon grass, mint and toasted ground rice. A popular dish from northern Thailand and Laos.

lard (1) Thin strip of pork fat inserted with a special needle or wrapped around lean meat, poultry or game to help retain moisture during cooking and improve taste. **(2)** White cooking fat or dripping obtained by melting down pork fat.

larding needle Special needle for inserting or threading thin strips of pork fat (lardons) into meat or poultry.

lardo | ITALIAN | Extremely fatty bacon made from cured pork belly. Used only for cooking.

lardon / lardoon Long, thin strips of pork fat used to lard lean meats.

lardy cake | ENGLISH | White yeast-cake rich in fat and studded with currants.

lasagne | ITALIAN | **(1)** Pasta cut into wide flat sheets. **(2)** Dish with alternate layers of flat pasta, meat, seafood or tomato sauce and béchamel sauce, topped with cheese and baked in the oven.

lasagnette | ITALIAN | Broad, flat ribbons of pasta with ruffled edges.

lassi | INDIAN | Iced frothy drink made with yoghurt and water. It may be variously served with salt, pepper, sugar, kewra water, lemon juice, mint or spices.

latke | JEWISH | Small fried pancake made from grated raw potato and eggs, sometimes with caraway seeds.

lavender (*Lavandula* spp.) Fragrant evergreen shrubs of which several species are native to Europe. Well known for their flowers which are used in perfumery and cosmetics. Fresh lavender flowers are used in jelly, ice cream and to infuse vinegar and honey; also used to make a fragrant, herb- scented sugar for sweetening cakes, biscuits, puddings and ice cream; also sprinkled on custards, shortbreads and sponge cake.

laver *see* NORI.

leatherjacket (*Pseudomonacanthus* spp.) Generally they have a characteristic barbed spine on the back of the head and tough leathery or velvet skin. They are usually sold as fillets or whole gutted without their skin and head. The tender flesh is white, with very few bones and good taste. They are pan-fried, grilled or barbecued.

leaven To raise and lighten dough by adding an agent such as yeast or baking powder.

lebkuchen | GERMAN | Small spiced honey cakes traditionally served at Christmas.

leek (*Allium porum*) Closely related to the onion, this long, white, cylindrical bulb with broad, flattish leaves has been around since ancient Egyptian and Romans times. During the growing period, the thickened stems are blanched by hilling soil around them, therefore leeks need thorough washing before use. Cut off the green tops and trim the roots; the leek is slit lengthways and either washed under cold running water or soaked. Leeks can be cooked whole as a vegetable or sliced and used in soups, stews, flans, risotto and sauces. They are an essential ingredient in the Scottish cock-a-leekie soup and leek-and-potato soup which turns into the famous vichyssoise when served chilled. Tender baby leeks (sometimes available) are cooked and eaten like asparagus.

lees Sediment left in the bottom of a wine cask or vat.

legumes Large edible seeds belonging to the large pea family such as peas, beans and lentils. Dried legumes are known as 'pulses'. *see also* PULSES.

Leicester | ENGLISH | Hard, uncooked cow's-milk cheese with a flaky, dark orange interior and natural, cloth-covered rind. Served as a snack or light meal; also good for melting.

Leiden *see* LEYDEN.

lemon (*Citrus limon*) Rich in vitamin C, this bright yellow fruit is an invaluable ingredient for most cooks. A liberal dash of lemon juice enhances the taste of fish, poultry, veal and many vegetables. Lemon juice contains citric acid and is often used to prevent cut fruit and vegetables from browning when exposed to air. Its acidity also enhances the taste of other fruits. Also used in salad dressings, soups, drinks and marinades. The rind or juice, or both, are used in many sweet dishes, such as custards, tarts, pies, biscuits, mousses, ices and countless other desserts. Lemon wedges are always served with deep-fried food and many seafood dishes. Preserved whole lemons are used in the Middle East to add salty tartness to stews and salads.

lemon balm (*Melissa officinalis*) Lemon-scented leaves from perennial plant belonging to the mint family and native to southern Europe. Used mainly as a herbal tea and for summer drinks; also young leaves added to salads and fruit dishes. In Holland the leaves are used in pickled herrings.

lemon curd | ENGLISH | Tangy spread and pastry filling made with butter, caster sugar, eggs and lemon juice.

lemon grass (*Cymbopogon citratus*) Aromatic perennial grass native to tropical regions. The tender inner white part at the base of the plant is a popular ingredient in South-East Asian cooking; usually sliced finely or pounded and mixed with other ingredients to make a paste. Sold fresh in long stalks.

lemon myrtle | AUSTRALIAN | (*Backhousia citriodora*) Strong lemon-and-lime- flavoured leaves obtained from a native rainforest tree. Fresh and dried leaves are widely used in modern Australian cuisine, especially with seafood, white meats and oriental dishes; also used in tea, desserts, cakes and soups. Available fresh, dried whole or dried and then finely chopped; also lemon myrtle fettuccine.

lemon verbena (*Aloysia triphylla*) Lemon-scented leaves from fragrant shrub native to South America and introduced to Europe by the Spanish in the 17th century. Used mostly in herbal teas; also to flavour sugar and sweet dishes and to garnish iced drinks, teas and finger bowls.

lentilles de Puy | FRENCH | Superior, dark green lentils from the village of Puy, in the Auvergne.

lentils (*Lens esculenta*) Lentils come in several shapes and shades, but the most common are green (or brown) lentils when whole. Red lentils are slightly smaller; the orange fades to yellow with cooking. The much smaller, dark green lentilles de Puy are considered to have the best taste. Lentils are always sold dried and are available whole, split or ground to flour. Lentils do not require soaking, but are washed thoroughly before cooking which can take 20–30 minutes depending on type and age. Used as a vegetable side dish, in salads, soups, stews and the Indian dhal.

lettuce (*Lactuca sativa*) Valued for their crisp salad leaves, several varieties of lettuce are available. The best-known are the round hard-headed **iceberg**, the elongated **cos (romaine)** and the loose-headed red or green varieties of **mignonette**, **butter lettuce**, **oakleaf** and **coral**. **Radicchio**, a variety of red-leafed chicory, is also used as a salad vegetable. Although lettuce can be braised or used in soups or to wrap food, it is mainly used fresh in salads. After a good wash it needs to be completely dry to effectively take on the dressing. *see also individual entries.*

Leyde *see* LEYDEN.

Leyden / Leiden / Leyde | DUTCH | Also known as 'Liedse Kaas'. Semihard, pressed cow's-milk cheese with caraway and/or cumin seeds. Slightly granular, pale yellow to pale brownish interior and thin washed rind. Used for lunches and snacks and at the end of a meal.

liaison Binding or thickening agent used in sauces, soups or stews. Examples include egg yolks, cornflour, roux or cream.

licorice *see* LIQUORICE.

Liederkranz | AMERICAN | Semisoft cow's-milk cheese with creamy, ivory interior and washed, orange crust. Strong with slight salty taste. Served as a snack with breads and beer. Factory produced cheese in Van Wert, Ohio.

Liedse Kaas *see* LEYDEN.

lilly pilly *see* RIBERRY.

lily buds (*Hemerocallis* species) Also known as 'tiger lily buds' and 'golden needles'. Dried golden-yellow unopened flowers of a type of day lily commonly used in Chinese cooking. They have a distinctive earthy taste and are soaked for about 20 minutes before cooking.

lima beans (*Phaseolus limensis*) Large, flattish, dried white beans. After soaking overnight they are simmered gently for about 45 minutes. Used in salads, soups and stews.

Limburger Semisoft, cow's-milk cheese with smooth, pale yellow interior and thin, light brown edible rind. Highly developed aroma and strong taste. Served as a snack with breads and with beer. Originally and still made in Belgium, but now predominantly made in Germany.

lime (*Citrus aurantifolia*) Like the lemon, the lime is used as a seasoning and garnishing fruit, rather than one for eating. The bittersweet taste adds interest to many mixed drinks, desserts, preserves and cooked dishes. There are two main types used: the commonly available and most often used **Tahitian lime**, and the harder to find, knobbly skinned **kaffir lime** (*C. hystrix*), valued for its aromatic zest and fresh leaves used in Asian cooking, particularly in Thai food. *see also* KAFFIR LIME.

lime flowers (*Tilia* x *europea*) Also known as 'linden'. Fragrant, yellow flowers from deciduous tree widely grown in Europe. Flowers are picked in early summer and dried in a warm airy place. The dried flowers are made into a herbal tea used as a digestive and calming tonic. Warm lime tea is also used for soaking dried fruits. (Not to be confused with the citrus lime.)

linden *see* LIME FLOWERS.

ling (*Genypterus* spp.) This long, slender, eel-like fish is a member of the cod family. They are normally sold as large, skinless fillets. The most common is the pink ling which has a moist, firm, white flesh, very few bones and a mild, delicate taste. Suitable for grilling, pan-frying, baking or using in a curry dish.

linguine | ITALIAN | Thin pasta ribbons.

lipids General description for natural fats and oils. They contain essential fatty acids and are the principal source of energy provided by food.

Liptauer | HUNGARIAN | Sheep's-milk cheese spread, with variations such as paprika, onion, garlic and herbs.

liqueur Strong, sweetish alcoholic drink usually made from spirit and incorporating some taste such as herbs or fruit and sugar. Usually served after a meal.

liquorice / licorice (*Glycyrrhiza glabra*) Sweet, anise root obtained from perennial plant belonging to the pea family. Mainly cultivated in the Mediterranean regions, Russia and parts of the United States. A thick juice is extracted from the soft, fibrous roots and is used as an ingredient in cough lozenges, syrups and elixirs; also made into black pliable confectionery known as liquorice sticks.

litre Metric liquid measure equal to 13/4 pints or 41/3 cups.

Livarot | FRENCH | Name-controlled semisoft cow's-milk cheese with smooth, ivory-yellow interior and washed, brownish-red rind, traditionally encircled with five thin strips of red raffia. Very strong aroma and taste. Served at the end of a meal with full-bodied wine. From the Calvados region of Normandy, still produced on farms.

liver Large internal organ of domestic animals, game and poultry. It is highly nutritious, rich in iron, protein, vitamins A and B12, but is also high in cholesterol.

liverwurst | GERMAN | Soft, spreadable sausage made from pork liver, various other meats, milk and herbs. Used as a spread on bread or crackers.

lobscouse | ENGLISH | Layered stew of mutton and vegetables with the addition of barley or dried hard biscuits known as ships' biscuits. From Liverpool, England.

lobster (*Jasus* spp.) Also known as 'rock lobsters'. Commercial rock lobsters include the southern (*J. edwardsii*), the larger eastern (*J. verreauxi*) and the western (*Panulirus cygnus*) which is mostly exported to South-East Asia. Uncooked lobsters vary from creamy yellow, green, orange, to purple, turning bright orange to red when cooked. Live lobsters should be killed in the freezer (but not frozen) before use. To cook place in a large pot with cold water, bring to the boil and simmer for about 8 minutes per 500 grams of the lobster's weight. A well-cooked lobster should have a tightly curled tail.

loganberry (*Rubus* sp.) Oblong, deep red berry resembling a large raspberry, believed to be a cross between the blackberry and raspberry. A bitter- sweet fruit that can be eaten fresh or used for tarts, puddings, preserves and jams.

loin Roasting joint of lamb, pork or veal that is the front part of the hind- quarter and includes some of the ribs.

lollipop Boiled sugar confection mounted on a stick which is held in the hand.

lolly | AUSTRALIAN | Sweet, sugar confection such as fruit gums, liquorice, boiled sweets, caramels, toffees and fudge.

long-life milk Ultra heat-treated or UHT for short. Pasteurized and homogenized milk that has undergone heating to 135°C for three or four seconds, then rapidly cooled. It will keep for several months unopened at room temperature. Once opened it should be refrigerated and used fairly quickly.

longan (*Euphoria longana*) Also known as 'dragon's eyes' in China. Small, round, brownish-yellow fruit, related to the lychee and similar in appearance, but smaller and with a smoother skin. The flesh is translucent white with a sweet, musky taste. Available dried, or fresh in late summer and autumn. Eaten raw like lychees or poached gently in syrup.

longaniza | SPANISH | General term for an oven-cured pork sausage used in cooking.

Longchamp soup | FRENCH | Thick soup containing braised sorrel, purée of fresh green peas and vermicelli.

longtail tuna *see* TUNA.

loquat (*Eriobotrya japonica*) Also known as 'Japanese medlar'. Small, oval fruit with a slightly downy, yellow-orange skin and pale yellow flesh with a fragrant, slightly tart taste. They are harvested when fully ripe and are available in spring and early summer. Eaten fresh or used in fruit salads, stews and purées or made into jams or preserves.

lorraine (à la) | FRENCH | In the style of Lorraine, often includes smoked bacon and Gruyère cheese, such as quiche lorraine.

lotus (*Nelumbo nucifera*) Every part of this beautiful water lily has long been used as a food in Asian cooking. The large floating leaves are eaten raw or cooked as well as used to wrap food for steaming. Young shoots and stems are cooked as a vegetable or used in soups. Young seeds are eaten raw as a snack; when dried they can be roasted and used in cooking like nuts; also sweetened with sugar and used in desserts and pastry fillings. The better-known segmented lotus root, which is now becoming more readily available in Asian greengrocers, has a reddish-brown skin and crunchy flesh. It must be peeled before use and is usually sliced to reveal an attractive pattern of holes. Drop immediately into acidulated water to prevent browning. As a vegetable it is stir-fried or braised; also used in soups and stews. Also candied and used in sweet dishes.

loup de mer au fenouil *see* BASS.

lovage (*Levisticum officinale*) Strong-growing perennial plant that looks and tastes like a large celery with a peppery tang. Tender young leaves are added to green salads. The stems are cooked and eaten as a vegetable or candied as for angelica. Young stalks can be eaten like celery. Both the dried seed and dried root are used in bread and biscuits in some Mediterranean countries.

lox Type of delicately salted, smoked salmon. Popular with New York's Jewish population and traditionally served on bagels with cream cheese.

lumache | ITALIAN | Short pasta shaped like large snail shells. Used for stuffing.

lumpfish (*Cyclopterus lumpus*) Grey-green fish caught mainly in the North Sea and the Baltic for its tiny eggs which are dyed black or red and sold as a caviar substitute. They are used as a cheap alternative for garnishing canapés and hors d'oeuvres.

lung ching Also known as 'dragon's well'. High quality green tea from China.

lychee / litchi / lichee (*Litchi chinensis*) Small, round fruit with a red, knobbly skin, translucent, pearly-white flesh and a single shiny brown seed. Fresh lychees are available in summer and should be bought when fully mature as they do not ripen further after being picked. The brittle skin is easily peeled and the sweet juicy pulp can be eaten immediately. Also used in fruit salads or gently poached in syrup or wine. Dried lychees, sold in Asian grocers, have a sweet, smoky taste and are eaten as a snack, like nuts.

lyonnaise (à la) | FRENCH | In the style of Lyon; often garnished with glazed onions.

Lyonnaise sauce | FRENCH | Classic sauce based on finely chopped onions cooked in butter, vinegar and/or white wine, pan juices or demi-glace. Served mostly with meat.

MSG *see* MONOSODIUM GLUTAMATE.

macadamia nut | AUSTRALIAN | (*Macadamia integrifolia*) Also known as 'Queensland nut'. Regarded by some as the most delicious nut in the world, the macadamia has long been a food source for local Aborigines in eastern Australia. It is the only indigenous plant grown commercially as a world food crop. The small, round, creamy white kernel is protected by an extremely hard shell which is difficult to crack. Nuts are usually shelled commercially and sold pre-shelled, either roasted or raw. These are stored airtight in a cool place, such as the refrigerator. Macadamias are rich in mono-unsaturated fat, the good fat considered to be beneficial in lower- ing cholesterol and reducing the risk of heart disease. Macadamias are added to stuffings, stir-fries, soups, salads and curries; also eaten as a snack and used in biscuits, cakes, ice-cream, desserts and confectionery.

macadamia nut oil Pale, golden oil high in mono-unsaturated fat. Used for its mild, nutty taste in cooking and salad dressing.

Macaire | FRENCH | Flat potato cake made from mashed baked potatoes mixed with butter, then fried until golden brown.

macaroni | ITALIAN | Generic name for short lengths of tubular pasta. Available in various sizes. The Italian name is 'maccheroni'.

macaroon Small soft biscuit of almonds, egg whites and sugar.

maccheroni *see* MACARONI.

mace (*Myristica fragrans*) Bright red, lacy skin covering (aril) of the nutmeg that turns brownish-orange when dried. Taste is similar to nutmeg but more delicate. Available whole (called 'blades') or ground. Blades are used in sauce suprême for fish; also in pickles, chutneys and vinegar. Ground mace is used in cheese dishes, creamed spinach, cakes, puddings and curry paste.

macédoine | FRENCH | Diced mixed fruit or vegetables that may be cooked or raw. A fruit macédoine is often soaked in a sugar syrup or liqueur and served chilled as a dessert. A vegetable macédoine is made up of small pieces of vegetables that are cooked separately and bound with butter or mayonnaise, or decoratively set in aspic.

macerate To soak dried or fresh fruit in syrup, liqueur, brandy or wine.

mâche *see* CORN SALAD.

mackerel Related to the tuna and bonito, they are torpedo-shaped fish often with oily flesh. Good eating fish are the large **Spanish mackerel** (*Scomberomorus commerson*) and the smaller **spotted mackerel** (*Scomberomorus munroi*), available as whole fish or fillets. They can be marinated in citrus juice before cooling to moderate the rich taste and oiliness, and may be baked, pan-fried or grilled. The sleek, smaller **blue mackerel**, also known as 'slimy mackerel' (*Scomber australasicus*), has a dry flesh with a milder taste. Its fillets are salted and marinated in vinegar, dashi, sugar and mirin and used in pressed sushi known as 'battera'. Mackerel is also available smoked and salted.

Madeira Fine, fortified wine made from grapes grown on the Portuguese-owned island of Madeira in the Atlantic Ocean.

madeleine | FRENCH | Small, elongated, shell-shaped tea cake cooked in a special shallow-grooved mold.

madrilène (à la) In the style of Madrid. Usually refers to a poultry consommé with peeled chopped tomatoes; served hot or chilled as a light jelly.

mafalda | ITALIAN | Broad, flat ribbons of pasta with rippled edges.

magnesium Mineral found mainly in wholegrain cereals, soy beans and nuts. Important for the health of the nervous system.

magnum Bottle size equivalent to two standard wine/champagne bottles.

magret | FRENCH | Boned breast of fattened duck or goose with the skin and fat attached. It is grilled until the flesh is slightly underdone and the skin crispy. Also used for confits.

mahlab | MIDDLE EASTERN | Ground black cherry kernels used in breads and pastries.

Mahon | SPANISH | From Minorca. Name-controlled semifirm to firm cow's-milk cheese with smooth, pale interior with many tiny holes, and a golden-brown rind. It has a sharp salty taste and is served as an appetizer or snack sprinkled with olive oil, black pepper and tarragon.

maid of honour | ENGLISH | Small, round tart with a filling of ground almonds, cheese and lemon.

Maille | FRENCH | Famous brand name of a range of mustards and vinegars.

maison (à la) | FRENCH | Speciality of the restaurant, or a dish that is created by the restaurant's chef.

maître d'hôtel | FRENCH | (1) Headwaiter. (2) butter containing parsley and lemon. Served with grilled meat or fish.

maize Corn.

maki-zushi *see* SUSHI.

makisu | JAPANESE | Small, flexible bamboo mat used for firmly and evenly rolling nori, sushi rice and fillings to make maki-zushi. *see also* SUSHI.

makrut *see* KAFFIR LIME.

Malabar spinach *see* BASELLA.

Maldon sea salt | ENGLISH | Fine, white flakes of sea salt, hand-harvested by traditional techniques in Maldon in Essex, United Kingdom. Used at the table and at the end of cooking.

malic acid Acid found in apples.

malt Germinating cereal, usually barley, that is dried, roasted and then powdered, or made into a mash and used in the first step of beer production. The length of time the malt is roasted determines the shade and sweetness of beer. The powdered form is used to activate yeast and as a mild, natural sweetener.

malt vinegar *see* VINEGAR.

maltaise sauce | FRENCH | Hollandaise sauce with the juice and blanched, shredded zest of the blood orange. Served with poached fish or cooked green vegetables such as asparagus, spinach and green beans.

maltose Also known as 'malt sugar'. **(1)** Cereal starch which is converted to sugar by the malting process. **(2)** Semihard, sweet syrup called 'maltose' is sold packaged in tubs in Asian grocers. It is made from rice syrup and maltose and used as a natural sweetener in sauces and to brush duck before roasting; also as an ice-cream topping. Stand the tub in hot water to soften the contents and make spooning out easier.

Manchego | SPANISH | Name-controlled semifirm, pressed sheep's-milk cheese with a pale, yellowish interior, sometimes with small holes and thin, pale yellow rind with a crosshatch pattern. Often served as an appetizer in wafer-thin triangular slices; also melts well. Originally from the plains of La Mancha.

manchette | FRENCH | Paper frill used to decorate the projecting bones of rack of lamb, ham or other joints.

manchon | FRENCH | Tubular petit four made of almond paste and filled with butter cream.

mandarin (*Citrus reticulata*) Also known as 'tangerine'. Small, easy to peel relative of the orange, with a very sweet juice. It is usually eaten fresh as a snack or segmented and used in fruit salad; also used for pies, tarts, marmalade and candied fruit. Dried mandarin peel is first soaked and then used in Chinese soups, meat and duck dishes.

mandoline Vegetable slicer with sharp, adjustable blades held in a flat frame.

mangetout *see* sNOW PEAS.

manglak *see* BASIL, HOARY.

mango (*Mangifera indica*) Highly aromatic, round or oval fruit with bright orange-yellow or reddish skin when fully ripe. The light orange succulent flesh is deliciously sweet and an excellent source of vitamin A. Firm mangoes will ripen at room temperature. To eat out of hand, cut the unpeeled mango through lengthways on both sides of the large flat seed. With a sharp knife score halves into cubes or diamonds without cutting the skin, then bend back the mango sections. The cubes will rise and separate which makes eating easier. Mangoes are a popular fruit salad ingredient and can be made into many sweet dishes such as mousse, ice cream, pies, tarts, soufflés, purées and sauces. Green or under-ripe mangoes are used in chutneys, pickles, curries and many Asian dishes. *see also* AMCHUR.

mangosteen (*Garcinia mangostana*) Small, round tropical fruit with a deep purple, leathery rind surrounding segments of white, translucent flesh with a refreshing, sweet, tangy taste. The mangosteen is harvested when ripe and should be eaten soon after. Eaten raw or used in fruit salads.

mangrove crab *see* MUD CRAB.

Manhattan | AMERICAN | Cocktail of whisky and sweet or dry vermouth.

manicotti | ITALIAN | Large pasta tubes, often stuffed with a meat or cheese filling and baked with a sauce.

manioc *see* CASSAVA.

mannitol White sweetener used in commercial food products for seasoning, thickening and stabilizing.

manqué | FRENCH | Parisian sponge cake.

manzanilla | SPANISH | Very light and dry sherry. Served chilled as an aperitif; also to accompany shellfish.

maple syrup | AMERICAN | Reddish-brown syrup obtained from the sap of certain North American and Canadian maple trees (*Acer* spp.). Used mainly as a table syrup to sweeten pancakes, waffles, desserts and ice cream.

maraîchère (à la) | FRENCH | Usually refers to a dish that includes various fresh vegetables.

Maraschino | ITALIAN | Clear liqueur made chiefly from cherries. Used for desserts.

Maraschino cherry Pitted sour cherries preserved in sugar syrup and glazed with sugar. Used in baked goods and to decorate desserts and cocktails.

marc | FRENCH | Spirit distilled from the left-over pressings of grapes for wine.

marcassin | FRENCH | Young wild boar.

marchand de vin | FRENCH | Sauce made from reduced red wine, meat stock and chopped shallots, with butter, lemon juice, finely chopped parsley and seasoning. It is chilled until firm and cut into rounds to accompany grilled steak.

Marengo | FRENCH | Braised dish of chicken or veal cooked with white wine, tomatoes, garlic, mushrooms and parsley. Created by Napoleon's chef after the defeat of the Austrians in the Battle of Marengo (1800).

margarine Table-spread mostly made with polyunsaturated vegetable oils. It may contain a single oil or a blend of oils. Once purified and deodorized, the oils are hydrogenated (or hardened) in order to make a firm, spread-able, butter-like substance. This process produces trans fatty acids which have the same potential as saturated fats in raising blood cholesterol levels.

margarita Cocktail of tequila, triple sec and lime juice, served in a glass rimmed with salt.

Marguery sauce | FRENCH | White sauce made with reduced fish stock, egg yolks, butter and seasoning. Served with fillets of sole. Developed and named after French chef, Nicolas Marguery, who in the late 19th century owned the exclusive Parisian restaurant, Marguery.

marigold (*Calendula officinalis*) Young leaves of the annual calendula are sprinkled in salads and stews. The fresh orange and yellow petals are pulled from the flowers and tossed through salads; also used to give golden tones to rice, soups, cheese, butter and milk dishes. Not to be confused with African marigolds which have an unpleasant scent.

marinade Seasoned liquid in which meat, fish or vegetables are soaked to enhance flavor or to tenderize before cooking.

marinara sauce | ITALIAN | Highly seasoned pasta sauce made with tomatoes, onions, garlic, olive oil and a mixture of freshly caught local seafood.

marinate To steep, usually meat or fish, in a prepared marinade before cooking or serving to both flavor and tenderize.

marinière (à la) Preparation for cooking shellfish, often mussels (moules à la marinière) using white wine, butter, shallots, garlic, black pepper and parsley.

marjoram (*Origanum hortensis*) Also known as 'sweet marjoram' or 'knotted marjoram'. Small perennial herb with small, grey-green leaves and tiny, whitish flowers in a knot-like cluster. The leaves fresh or fried are used for seasoning a number of dishes and are said to aid digestion. Used with many meats and in sausages, terrines and in poultry stuffings; also has a special affinity with tomatoes. Together with dried sage and thyme, marjoram is one of the traditional mixed herbs.

marlin (*Tetrapturus audax*) Important game fish with a large, elongated body and long, spear-like snout. It has a reddish flesh similar to swordfish in texture and is sold as steaks or cutlets.

marmalade Jam made from citrus fruits, including the peel. The main gelling substance (pectin) is in the pips and pith which are often tied in muslin and included in the cooking process. The Seville orange is the main citrus used in marmalade.

marmite | FRENCH | Deep earthenware or metal casserole with two handles used for lengthy cooking.

Marmite Brand name of a yeast extract spread similar to Vegemite.

Maroilles | FRENCH | Name-controlled soft cow's-milk cheese with a creamy and yielding, pale yellow interior and washed, pale red rind. Very strong aroma and taste. Served at the end of a meal with full-bodied red wine or beer.

marquise | FRENCH | Mousse-like dessert.

marron (*Cherax tenuimanus*) Large freshwater crayfish found in permanent rivers and streams in the south-west of Western Australia. Farmed commercially in Australia and some overseas countries. Marron is sold live or cooked.

marrons glacés | FRENCH | Candied or glazed chestnuts.

marrow Members of the genus *Curcurbita*, often referred to as 'curcurbits'. They grow on vigorous trailing vines and include **pumpkins**, **cucumbers**, **squash**, **gourds**, **choko**s, **vegetable marrow** and the **Chinese bitter melon**. Zucchinis are actually immature vegetable marrows. The **scalloped button squash** or **pattipan** is also known as 'summer squash', named after the season when it is most available. All marrows are at their best when small and with the flesh delicate and tender. **Golden nugget** and **butternut pumpkins** are the best-known members of the winter squash group. They are ideal for lengthy storage and are chosen for their firm flesh and hard, blemish-free skins. *see also* cUCUMBER, BOTTLE GOURD, CHOKO, CHINESE BITTER MELON, ZUCCHINI, PUMPKIN *and* SQUASH.

marrow bone Soft, fatty substance found in the center of long bones.

Marsala | ITALIAN | Rich, brown fortified wine made in Sicily. Sweet Marsala is served as a dessert wine and is an ingredient of zabaglione. Dry Marsala is served lightly chilled as an aperitif and is used in cooking veal and poultry dishes.

marsh samphire *see* SALICORNE.

marshmallow | AMERICAN | Soft sweet made with meringue and gelatin, usually pink or white. Sometimes toasted on skewers or used in cooking.

martini | AMERICAN | Cocktail made of gin and dry vermouth and garnished either with a green olive or a twist of lemon. When served with a cocktail onion the martini becomes a Gibson.

marudaizu | JAPANESE | High quality (and more costly) soy sauce made in the traditional manner using whole soy beans. *see also* SHOYU.

maryland | AMERICAN | A piece of chicken, either the thigh or drumstick.

marzipan Thick, sweet paste made from ground almonds, sugar and eggwhites. Used in a variety of confections or rolled into thin sheets to cover fruit-cakes. As a pliable mixture marzipan can be modeled into decorative shapes, traditionally small fruits and animals.

masa | MEXICAN | Corn dough used to make tortillas and tamales. **Masa harina** is a type of corn flour for making masa. It is not the same as cornflour.

masala | INDIAN | Traditional mixture of whole spices ground in a precise combination according to a particular dish. To produce a wet masala, liquid, such as water, lime juice or coconut milk, are added during the grinding process.

masaman curry paste | THAI | Also known as 'Muslim curry paste'. Spicy curry paste with an Indian influence originating with Muslim settlers in southern Thailand. It consists of garlic, shallots, black peppercorns, dried red chilies, coriander seeds, cumin seeds, nutmeg, cloves, cardamom pods, lemon grass and shrimp paste pounded together to form a smooth paste. Used mostly with beef. Available in tubs in Asian grocers.

mascarpone | ITALIAN | High-fat dairy product made from the heavy cream of cow's-milk set to drain through a finely woven cloth. It is soft, smooth and pale ivory with a sweet, rich, cream-like taste. Used fresh in savory and sweet dishes, especially good with berries and other fruit. Main ingredient in tiramisu, a dessert from northern Italy.

mascarpone di bufala | ITALIAN | High-fat dairy product made from water buffalo cream. Produced in small quantities in Campania.

mask To coat or cover food with a sauce.

mastic Translucent resin obtained from the bark of certain species of *Acacia*. Used commercially in chewing gum, liquorice and other confectionery.

Mataro *see* MOURVEDRE.

matcha | JAPANESE | High quality, powdered green tea, made from young tips and buds, and central to the Japanese tea ceremony.

matchstick Puff pastry with many thin layers; usually a cream-filled rectangle which may be filled with jam. Known as 'mille-feuille' in France.

mate | SOUTH AMERICAN | Also known as 'yerba mate'. Caffeine-rich tea made from the dried leaves and shoots of a South American holly (*Ilex paraguayensis*).

matelote | FRENCH | Rich freshwater fish stew made with red or white wine.

matignon | FRENCH | Garnish of mixed vegetables stewed in butter and flavoured with Madeira or sherry.

matsutake | JAPANESE | (*Tricholoma matsutake*) Also known as 'pine mushroom'. Highly sought-after and very expensive, dark brown mushroom with a nutty taste and pine-like aroma. Occasionally imported fresh; also sold in cans. They are only very lightly cooked.

matzo | JEWISH | Unleavened, cracker-like bread made of flour and water, traditionally eaten during Passover. Also at this time the ground meal of matzo is used as a flour substitute to thicken sauces and in baked goods. Matzo balls (knaidlach) are used as a soup garnish.

mayonnaise Cold, emulsified sauce made with egg yolks, oil and lemon juice or vinegar, salt and pepper. Various additives might include mustard, anchovies, horseradish and wasabi.

Maytag Blue | AMERICAN | Renowned blue vein cheese handmade from unpasteurized cow's milk. After being seeded with the spores of *Penicillium roqueforti* the cheese is matured for six months in damp cellars. Farm-produced in Newton, Iowa.

mead | ENGLISH | Alcoholic drink made from honey and herbs.

meal The edible part of any grain, pulse or nut, ground to a coarse powder.

meatballs Small seasoned balls of minced meat.

mechoui | NORTH AFRICAN | Seasoned whole animal, usually lamb, that is roasted on a spit over an open fire.

medallion Round thick slice of meat, poultry or fish.

mee krob | THAI | Popular dish made with crisp, fried vermicelli tossed with various stir-fried ingredients that might include finely chopped pork, chicken, prawns, bean curd and eggs, seasoned with garlic, shallots, palm sugar, vinegar or lime juice and fish sauce. The dish is sprinkled with chopped red chilies, coriander leaves and sliced pickled garlic and served immediately before the noodles soften.

melagueta pepper *see* GRAINS OF PARADISE.

Melba sauce Sweet sauce made from raspberry purée or redcurrant jelly and sugar. Served with peach Melba and other desserts.

Melba toast Very thin slices of bread slowly toasted in an oven until crisp.

melinjo nut (*Gnetum gnemon*) Kernel of a small oval fruit used mostly in Indonesia to make krupuk emping or melinjo wafers.

melons (*Cucumis* spp.) Many different varieties of dessert melons are grown and eaten throughout the world for their refreshing, tangy flesh. Since earliest times the juice of melons and melon seeds have been used in herbal medicine. There are three main types eaten and loved: the **rockmelon** or **cantaloupe**, as it is sometimes called, the pale **honeydew**, a variety of winter melon, and the brilliant pink **watermelon**. Melons are harvested when fully ripe and rarely sweeten further, although they do soften. Choose sweet-smelling specimens that give slightly when pressed at the stem end. Melons contain vitamins A and C and are low in kilojoules; served as a snack, breakfast fruit, entrée, and used in fruit salads and many sweet dishes. *see also* HONEYDEW, ROCKMELON *and* WATERMELON.

mendicants | FRENCH | Traditional Christmas mixture of dried figs, almonds, hazelnuts and raisins whose colors suggest the robes of four Roman Catholic mendicant orders.

menthe | FRENCH | Mint.

menu List of food or dishes to be served at a meal, arranged in specific courses.

mère de vinaigre *see* MOTHER OF VINEGAR.

merguez | NORTH AFRICAN | Thin red sausage made from beef and mutton seasoned with red pepper. Pan-fried or grilled and served with steamed couscous and harissa.

meringue Combination of stiffly beaten eggwhites and sugar. There are three types. **Hard meringue** can be used in the first stage for making floating islands or baked in the oven for making shells and individual meringues of various shapes. **Italian meringue** is made by beating hot sugar syrup into the whisked eggwhites. Used mainly as a topping for pies, in soufflés and cream fillings. **Cooked meringue** is first whisked over a gentle heat and then baked in the oven. Used mainly for piping individual meringues and meringue baskets.

Merlot Red wine-producing grape widely grown in France, Italy, California and Australia. Merlot is used both alone and in blends, especially with Cabernet Sauvignon, to provide softness. It matures quickly and can be drunk when quite young.

mescal Clear Mexican liquor distilled from the century plant (*Agave tequilana*). Produced by the same method as tequila, has a similar taste, and is usually drunk straight. Mescal is often sold with a bloated agave worm in the bottle.

mesclun | FRENCH | A mixture of slightly bitter salad greens which might include endive, mâche, mizuna, dandelion, rocket, oak leaf lettuce, radicchio and sorrel.

Methuselah Bottle of champagne equivalent to eight standard bottles.

mets | FRENCH | Any dish or preparation served at the table.

mettwurst | GERMAN | Spreadable meat sausage made of pork and seasoned with coriander.

meunière (à la) | FRENCH | In the style of the miller's wife. Fish that is lightly floured, fried in butter and served with lemon, butter and parsley.

meurette | FRENCH | Dish cooked in a red wine sauce.

mexicaine (à la) | FRENCH | Meat dish served with stuffed mushrooms accompanied by tomato sauce containing finely sliced red capsicum.

Mexican chocolate | MEXICAN | Solid tablets of granular sweet chocolate with almonds and cinnamon. Mainly used as a hot drink and in making chocolate mole sauce for savory dishes, particularly mole poblano, a rich turkey stew.

mezzaluna | ITALIAN | Translates to 'half moon'. Curved knife with a handle at each end. Chops in a rocking motion and is used for chopping onions, garlic, nuts and herbs.

mezze | MIDDLE EASTERN | Selection of appetizers or hors d'oeuvres, usually served cold.

microwave oven An electric oven designed to cook with electromagnetic waves of radiant energy.

mie de pain | FRENCH | Fresh white breadcrumbs.

mignon | FRENCH | Small fillet.

mignonette | FRENCH | Coarsely ground peppercorns, usually white.

mignonette lettuce (*Lactuca sativa*) Small, round, loosely formed lettuce, often with dark reddish leaves. Popular in a mixed green salad.

mijoter | FRENCH | To simmer in a sauce at a low temperature for a lengthy period.

milanaise (à la) | FRENCH | In the style of Milan. Food coated in egg and breadcrumbs, mixed with Parmesan cheese then fried in butter.

Milano salami | ITALIAN | Salame milanese. Also known as 'cresponi'. Mass-produced, moderately spicy salami made of finely minced pork, fat and beef, seasoned with garlic, white wine and pepper and speckled with small pieces of fat.

milk This important component of the Western diet is mostly supplied by cows, although goat's, buffalo's and sheep's milk are also used, especially for making different cheeses. In some regions of the world the milk of camels, mares, yaks and llamas is also used. All milk contains lactose, which is a natural sugar. **Fresh milk** is pasteurized and available skimmed, low-fat and (whole) full cream. **Homogenized milk** has been processed so that the fat, which normally settles on the surface, is broken into small particles and is evenly distributed throughout. **Evaporated milk** has about 40 per cent of the water removed. It is pasteurized and homogenized and sold in the can, and will keep indefinitely if unopened. **Condensed milk** is heavily sweetened, evaporated milk, also canned. **Powdered** or **dried milk** is made from low-fat or full cream milk from which almost all the moisture has been removed; often used in baking. **Long-life milk** (**UHT**) is pasteurized and homogenized milk that has been further heat treated and packaged. Unopened it will keep at room temperature for up to six months. Once opened it should be refrigerated and used fairly quickly.

mill Small implement used to grind food stuffs such as pepper or coffee to a powder.

mille-feuille | FRENCH | Puff pastry with many thin layers, usually a cream-filled rectangle which may be filled with jam. Sometimes called 'matchstick'.

millet (*Panicum milaceum*) Cereal grass widely used for birdseed. It is a staple of the grain in parts of Africa and Asia where it is cooked and eaten in the same way as rice, or ground into flour to make flattish breads.

milt Also known as 'soft roe'. Reproduction glands and sperm of a male fish. It is usually prepared by gently washing the delicate membrane and poaching in court-bouillon, or coating it in flour, frying in butter and serving with lemon; also used in sauces.

Mimolette | FRENCH | Firm, pressed cow's-milk cheese with orange interior and hard natural rind, both organically dyed with annatto. Bland, mild, nutty taste. Served as a snack or at the end of a meal.

mimosa Garnish of chopped hard-boiled egg yolks, often sprinkled over salads.

mince To cut or chop into very small pieces using a knife or food processor.

mince pie | ENGLISH | Small individual pies filled with a mixture of finely chopped dried fruits, suet and spices, and spiked with brandy. Traditionally served at Christmas.

miner's lettuce *see* PURSLANE, WINTER.

mineral water Flat or sparkling bottled water taken from natural springs.

minerals Elements required in small amounts for regulation of the body's metabolism, cell manufacture and the maintenance of teeth and bones. The major elements are calcium, phosphorus, iron, potassium and sodium. Minerals required in small quantities are known as trace elements.

minestrone | ITALIAN | Thick, mixed vegetable soup containing pasta and dried beans. Served with grated Parmesan cheese.

mint (*Mentha* spp.) Refreshing, sweet-smelling leaves of certain mint plants. Used for centuries both for culinary and medicinal purposes. There are many different varieties and species; those most useful in the kitchen are apple mint, spearmint and bowles or winter mint. Traditionally used in mint sauce or mint jelly with roast lamb; also used with new potatoes, green peas and other vegetables. Fresh leaves are also added to some green and Thai salads. *see also* NATIVE MINT.

mint julep | AMERICAN | Refreshing alcoholic drink made with bourbon and mint, packed with ice and chilled long enough for a frost to form on the outside of the glass. Traditionally served in a silver mug or tall glass.

mint sauce | ENGLISH | Traditional accompaniment to roast lamb made with finely chopped mint leaves moistened with a little sweetened boiling water and vinegar. Served at room temperature.

mint tea | MOROCCAN | Refreshing infusion of green tea and fresh mint leaves, sweetened in the teapot. A popular beverage in Morocco where it is traditionally made in a richly engraved silver pot and poured into ornamental glasses.

minute steak Thin piece of steak quickly grilled or fried in butter.

Mirabeau | FRENCH | Dish garnished with anchovies, pitted olives, tarragon and anchovy butter.

mirabelle (*Prunus institia*) Small, round, yellow plum that is stewed or made into preserves. Also used to make a clear fruit brandy.

mirepoix | FRENCH | Mixture of finely diced onions, carrots, celery, and sometimes bacon or raw ham, cooked in butter. Usually used to boost soups, sauces, stews and braises.

mirin | JAPANESE | Sweet rice wine with a low alcohol content, used in cooking and for glazing foods.

mirror dory *see* silver dory.

mise en place | FRENCH | Traditional term for all the preparations carried out in a restaurant prior to service.

miso | JAPANESE | Fermented paste of soya beans, salt and either rice or barley. Many varieties and brands are available, from the strong tasting brown and red, to the mild-tasting white. Used in soups, sauces, dressings for vegetables and to season meat or fish.

misticanza | ITALIAN | This Italian version of the French mesclun is a mixture of several varieties of both wild and cultivated salad leaves, including different lettuces, endive, radicchio, rocket, corn salad and herbs. Usually simply dressed with olive oil and vinegar and served just after the main meal to refresh the palate.

mitonner | FRENCH | To simmer for a long time. Originally to simmer bread in soup.

mizuna | JAPANESE | (*Brassica rapa* subsp. *nipposinica*) Leafy green vegetable with finely dissected leaves on thin white stalks. It has a distinct mustard taste and is either eaten in a salad or lightly cooked.

mizutaki | JAPANESE | One-pot dish consisting of chicken pieces simmered in kombu infused water with different kinds of vegetables, and sometimes tofu. The dish is cooked and served at the table with condiments such as finely chopped green onions, radish, lemon and ponzu sauce for dipping. Udon noodles are sometimes added to the remaining broth and eaten as a final course.

mocha (1) Variety of Arabian coffee. **(2)** Coffee dish or drink.

mochi *see* RICE CAKE.

mode de (à la) | FRENCH | In the style of.

modern Australian cuisine | AUSTRALIAN | Distinctive style of cooking that reflects a diversity of culture, using the best and freshest of local ingredients and treating them in a Mediterranean, European or Asian way. The emphasis is on a lighter cooking style, using oil instead of butter and often includes exotic Asian tasted. With the increasing convenience of bush foods, contemporary chefs are also developing uniquely Australian dishes.

moisten To add or cover with liquid.

molasses Thick, brown syrup obtained from sugar during refining process. There are two main types: the light, mild molasses that is used as a table syrup as a topping for pancakes, ice cream and waffles; the stronger dark molasses is used in baked goods such as rich fruit cakes and gingerbread.

mole | MEXICAN | Smooth, rich sauce made with chili and spices.

mole poblano | MEXICAN | Famous festive dish of simmered or roasted turkey served with a chili sauce with onions, tomatoes, garlic, crushed almonds, tortilla pieces, spices and plain bitter chocolate.

molluscs Soft-bodied shellfish which include the single-shelled (univalves) gastropods such as the abalone and periwinkle and two-shelled (bivalves) types which include clams, mussels, oysters and scallops. All molluscs should be bought raw and alive in the shell. The shells should be tightly closed; if open they should shut strongly when tapped. They will open when cooked.

see also ABALONE, CLAMS, COCKLES, MUSSELS, OYSTERS, PIPIS, PERIWINKLES *and* SCALLOPS.

monastery-style cheese European cheese with monastic origins where specialized techniques for ripening cheese were perfected by monks. They are usually made from washed curd and have a surface-ripened washed rind; often with a strong aroma and a full-bodied taste. Good examples from France include Pont-l'Eveque, Maroilles, Epoisses and the famous Munster created by monks in the 7th century.

Mondseer | AUSTRIAN | Monastery-type, semisoft cow's-milk cheese with golden interior with some small holes and reddish-yellow, washed rind. It has a full taste and is often served as a snack with beer.

Mongolian hot pot | CHINESE | Communal one-pot dish placed on a spirit burner on the table where guests cook slices of raw meat and vegetables in simmering stock, then dip the food into a selection of condiments.

monkfish (*Lophius piscatorius*) Also known as 'angler fish'. Deep sea fish caught in the Atlantic Ocean and popular in Europe. The large flattish head is usually removed and the firm, moist, white flesh is pan-fried, grilled or baked; also used in soups and casseroles.

monosodium glutamate Flavor enhancer used in some Asian cuisines. Also known as 'MSG'.

mono-unsaturated fats Essential fatty acids high in HDL (high-density lipoproteins) known to help reduce blood cholesterol levels. Oils high in mono-unsaturated fats are macadamia, olive, canola and peanut (in that order).

monstera (*Monstera deliciosa*) Also known as 'fruit salad plant'. Widely grown as an indoor plant for its large, decorative leaves. The elongated, dull green fruit has many geometric segments which are ready to be eaten when they start to separate and fall off. The scented, white, soft flesh has a pineapple-like taste, but must be fully ripe, otherwise it will cause irritation to both the mouth and throat. The monstera can be placed in a paper bag and ripened at room temperature. It is eaten on its own or used in fruit salads or creamy desserts.

mont-blanc | FRENCH | Dessert made of chestnut purée formed into the shape of a mountain and topped with whipped cream. Sometimes it is mounted on a base of baked meringue.

mont dore | FRENCH | Mashed potatoes blended with egg yolks, cream and grated cheese, piled into a dome shape and baked until golden.

montagne, de la | FRENCH | From the mountains.

Montasio | ITALIAN | Name-controlled partially skimmed cow's-milk cheese with firm, whitish interior with small holes throughout and greyish, natural brushed rind. Used as a table cheese; also in cooking.

monter | FRENCH | To emulsify sauce. Monter au beurre is to finish a sauce with butter.

Monterey Jack *see* JACK.

Montmorency | FRENCH | Dish made with or garnished with sour cherries.

Montrachet | FRENCH | Unripened goat's-milk cheese with white, moist interior and very thin, natural rind, sold in small containers or as ashcoated logs. Used when fresh as a snack; also in canapés.

mooli / muli | INDIAN | (*Raphanus sativus*) Large white radish. *see also* DAIKON.

moon bok *see* BOK CHOY.

Morbier | FRENCH | Semisoft, pressed cow's-milk cheese with shiny, ivory interior with thin, horizontal layer of ash through the middle, and a natural, brushed rind. Served as a snack or at the end of a meal; also melts well.

morcilla | SPANISH | Smoked black sausage made from pig's blood and fat, seasoned with spices and onions.

Morello cherry *see* CHERRY.

morels (*Morchella* spp.) Wild mushroom with a spongy, elongated cone- shaped cap, with a honeycomb pattern, in shades of light brown to dark olive-brown. An almost black variety (*M. elata*) grows wild in some pine forests and small quantities occasionally appear in produce markets a couple of times a year. They are usually snapped up very quickly by the restaurant industry. Fresh morels are also imported. Morels are considered one of the finest edible mushrooms and appear in many French specialty dishes. They need to be thoroughly rinsed before cooking and are often split down the centre in order to remove the grit. Dried morels of excellent quality are available in specialty shops. The dried variety have a rich, smoky taste and aroma. They are soaked in warm water for about 30 minutes. The strained soaking liquid can be used in soups or stock.

mornay sauce Rich, creamy sauce enriched with egg yolks and cheese. Used to coat food to be browned under the grill or oven.

mortadella | ITALIAN | Large, lightly smoked pork sausage studded with cubes of white fat and sometimes pistachios or green olives. Served thinly sliced as an antipasto or in a sandwich. Also known as 'bologna'.

morue | FRENCH | Salted, dried cod. *see also* BACCALÀ, BRANDADE *and* COD, SALTED.

morwong (*Nemadactylus macropterus*) Also known as 'jackass fish' and some-times marketed as 'seabream'. Silvery grey fish with thick lips, a dark broad collar band, and a long ray protruding from the pectoral fin. Occurs in southern Australian waters and also in New Zealand where it is called 'terakihi'. It is sold whole or filleted, has a fine-textured white flesh, and is a good eating fish suitable for pan-frying, grilling and baking.

moscovite (à la) | FRENCH | Elaborate preparation of a cold buffet dish in which the centerpiece is set in aspic and surrounded by a display of garnishes which may also be coated with aspic.

mostaccioli | ITALIAN | Medium-sized pasta tubes cut on the diagonal.

mostarda | ITALIAN | Mustard.

mostarda di frutta | ITALIAN | Also known as 'Mostarda di Cremona'. Fruit mustard made of an assortment of candied fruits preserved in sugar syrup and mustard-seed oil. Sold decoratively displayed in glass jars. Served as an accompaniment to cold boiled meat, sausages and roasts.

mother of vinegar Called 'mère de vinaigre' in France. Jelly-like substance produced by a bacterial organism which promotes the fermentation in wine and cider turning it into vinegar. *see also* VINEGAR.

moule | FRENCH | Mussel. Also a mold.

moules à la marinière | FRENCH | Mussels steamed in dry white wine with shallots, garlic, butter (or olive oil), black pepper and parsley. *see also* MUSSELS.

mountain pepper | AUSTRALIAN | (*Tasmannia lanceolata*) Both the leaves and berries of this small native tree have a peppery, chili taste. Used as a spicy seasoning for a wide range of dishes.

Mourvedre Red wine-producing grape grown in parts of southern France and Spain, where it is called 'Mataro'. In Australia it is usually used in blends, often with Shiraz and/or Grenache, providing an earthy blackberry taste.

moussaka | GREECE | Dish made with layers of minced lamb, sliced eggplants, onions and tomatoes, often with a cream sauce, then baked.

mousse | FRENCH | Light, airy preparation usually containing egg whites, cream and sometimes gelatin, often set in a mold and served cold. It may be either savory, based on fish, poultry, meat or vegetables, or sweet, made with fruit purée, chocolate or coffee.

mousseline | FRENCH | (1) Thick sauce or mousse-like preparation that is lightened with whipped cream or egg whites prior to serving. (2) Also refers to baked goods that have a light, airy texture.

moutarde | FRENCH | Mustard.

mozzarella | ITALIAN | Fresh, pliable cow's-milk cheese made by the stretched-curd method known as 'pasta filata'. It has a white, smooth interior and is sold in various ball-shaped sizes, usually kept in salted brine. Bocconcini 'little mouthfuls' are tiny balls of fresh mozzarella; served as a snack and in salads. Supermarket mozzarella is used mainly in cooking, especially on pizza and in the preparation of lasagne. *see also* BOCCONCINI.

mozzarella di bufala | ITALIAN | Fresh, creamy-white water buffalo's-milk cheese made in Campania, around Naples in southern Italy. It is considered the best mozzarella. Served fresh as a table cheese.

mozzarella di bufala affumicato | ITALIAN | Buffalo mozzarella smoked with hickory and chestnut chips. Served fresh as a table cheese.

mud crab (*Scylla serrata*) Also known as 'mangrove crab'. Large, dark green crab with large, powerful claws, found in muddy estuaries and mangroves in subtropical and tropical coastal waters. Because dead mud crabs deteriorate quickly, they are usually sold live with their large claws tied. The white meat is rich, sweet and succulent – the best tasting is found in the claws. *see also* CRAB.

muesli | SWISS | Breakfast mixture of rolled oats and other grains, dried fruit and nuts. Usually served with milk and sometimes sugar or honey.

muffin (1) English muffins are round, flat rolls made of yeast dough that are split in half, toasted and buttered. **(2)** American muffins are made with baking powder and baked in deep individual muffins tins.

mulato | MEXICAN | Long, dried, dark brown chili, mild and smoky. Often used for making mole.

mulberry (*Morus nigra*) Oblong, reddish-black berry that is very juicy and bittersweet when ripe. There is also a red and a white, seedless variety. Eaten fresh with cream or used for pies, jams, preserves, sauces and mulberry wine. Mulberry leaves are used for rearing silkworms.

mulled wine Warmed red wine, with spices, citrus peel and sugar or honey.

mullet Several species of this group of fish occur, the most commercially important being the **sea mullet** (*Mugil cephalus*) caught mainly for its roe which is sold salted and either smoked or dried. Its flesh is reasonably cheap and is used in the fish-and-chip trade. The slender, **yellow-eye mullet** (*Aldrichetta forsteri*) is also widely available either whole or in fillets. The flesh is moist, pink and oily and is best when filleted and grilled, baked or barbecued.

mulligatawny | ANGLO-INDIAN | Peppery chicken (or beef) and vegetable soup, seasoned with curry leaves with coconut milk stirred in at the end of cooking. Translated from a Tamil word which means 'pepper water'.

mulloway *see* JEWFISH.

mung beans (*Vigna radiata*) Small dried beans that can be green or black with yellow flesh. Widely used for sprouting and used in salads and stir-fried dishes. Ground mung beans are used to make bean thread noodles.

Munster | FRENCH | Name-controlled soft cow's-milk cheese with a supple, creamy white to pale yellow interior and reddish-orange, washed rind. Strong aroma and full-bodied monastery-style taste. Served mainly at the end of a meal, often with fruit. From the Alsace region.

muntries | AUSTRALIAN | (*Kunzea pomifera*) These small, pinkish-green berries that grow in clusters on a small, prostrate shrub were eaten by Aborigines and used by early settlers to make pies. They have a spicy apple-like taste and can be used in sweet and savory dishes. Available frozen whole. Muntries chutney is sold at specialty shops.

Murazzano | ITALIAN | Name-controlled, fresh sheep's-milk cheese with a pale yellow, semisoft interior and golden edible crust.

Murray perch *see* GOLDEN PERCH.

musaman curry paste *see* MASAMAN CURRY PASTE.

Muscat Type of white or black grape. Used as a table grape and for making sweet fortified wines and table wines.

muscatels Large, dried black grapes often sold in clusters on the stem. Used in cooking and served with cheese at the end of a meal.

muscovado sugar Dark brown, unrefined sugar rich in molasses.

muscovy duck (*Cairina moschata*) Type of domestic duck used extensively in cooking.

mushrooms There are about 2000 varieties of edible mushrooms throughout the world. Mushrooms are rich in minerals, iron and vitamin B12 and contain almost no sodium, sugar or fat. Sizes and shapes vary considerably, but the most common **cultivated mushrooms** are field and button varieties (*Agaricus* spp.). More exotic mushrooms, such as **chestnut**, **enoki**, **nameko**, **oyster**, **shimeji**, **shiitake** and **Swiss brown mushrooms**, are now cultivated in Australia and are becoming more widely available. A number of highly prized wild mushrooms, such as **ceps**, **slippery Jacks**, **morels**, **chanterelles** and **truffles**, have a symbiotic association with the roots of certain species of trees. They are known as 'mycorrhizal fungi'. For this reason no one has yet succeeded in cultivating these mushrooms commercially, so they remain rare and expensive. These are usually snapped up by providores and sold to the very best restaurants. **Slippery Jack** (*Boletus luteus*), a black variety of **morel** (*Morchella elata*) and the **saf- fron milk cap** (*Lactarius deliciousus*) have a symbiotic relationship with pine roots. Occasionally small quantities of these highly sought-after mushrooms appear fresh in produce markets. Generally mushrooms that are fully opened and show the gills will have a stronger taste, and are tastier, more digestible and nutritious the less they are cooked. Several of the European and Asian mushrooms are available in dried form or canned. *see also* MUSHROOMS, COMMON CULTIVATED; MUSHROOMS, DRIED; MUSHROOMS, FIELD.

mushrooms, common cultivated (*Agaricus bisporus*) These familiar, white mushrooms are graded commercially according to their stage of development. **Button mushrooms** are small with caps still joined to the stems. These are mild-tasting, often served raw whole with dips, as a garnish or sliced into salads; also used whole in soups or casseroles. **Cup mushrooms** are partially opened with the pale brown gills showing. They are sautéed as a vegetable or used in casseroles, soups and pies; also stuffed, baked or grilled and served whole. The fully open or **flat mushrooms** have a stronger taste and are good for grilling and use in sauces.

mushrooms, dried A wide selection of dried mushrooms are found in gourmet and Asian food shops. **Shiitake** (*Lentinus edodes*) or Chinese black mushrooms are the most commonly used in Asian cooking. They have a much stronger taste than fresh mushrooms and are often preferred in braised, simmered and stir-fried dishes. The large, thick ones with light skins and well-cracked caps are best. Dried **morels** (*Morchella* spp.) and dried **porcini** or **ceps** (*Boletus edulis*) are popular in European cuisines. Dried mushrooms are softened in warm water for about 30 minutes before using. The stems are often discarded. The strained soaking water may also be used for soups, sauces and risotto. Dried mushrooms keep indefinitely stored in an airtight container.

mushrooms, field (*Agaricus campestris*) These large, flat mushrooms with dark brown gills are related to the common cultivated mushrooms and are available throughout the year. They have a strong pronounced taste and produce a rich dark juice when cooked.

muskmelon *see* ROCKMELON.

Muslim curry pate *see* MASAMAN CURRY PASTE.

muslin Loosely woven cotton fabric used to wrap food and for straining liquids. Small muslin bags containing herbs and spices, tied with string, used during cooking are easily removed.

mussels (*Mytilus edulis*) Oval-shaped bivalve molluscs usually with dark brown or black, thin hard shells. Live mussels should have tightly closed, intact shells when purchased. They need to be thoroughly washed and scrubbed under cold running water and the fibrous beard removed. The classic way to cook mussels (moules à la marinière) is to steam them quickly in a large pan with finely chopped onion, garlic, olive oil, dry white wine, black peppercorns and parsley. The covered pot is vigorously shaken a few times and the mussels removed as they steam open (discard any which stay closed after cooking). They can be served in their shells with the liquid strained, or removed and used in pasta sauces, salads, risotto and soups. They can also be baked or barbecued in their shells.

must Grape juice before it has been converted to alcohol.

mustard leaves (*Brassica* spp.) Tender young leaves used as a salad ingredient and as a seasoning or garnishing herb.

mustard oil Edible oil made from mustard seeds extracted by the cold press method. It does not have a pronounced mustard taste, but when heated takes on a strong aroma. Widely used in Indian cooking and pickles.

mustard pickles | ENGLISH | Also known as 'piccalilli'. Deep yellow relish made from individual cauliflower florets, chopped tomatoes, onions, cucumbers, capers, vinegar, sugar, salt, turmeric and mustard powder. Traditionally served with cold meats or bread and cheese.

mustard sauce | ENGLISH | Hot sauce made from butter, flour, milk, cream, vinegar and English mustard powder, salt and pepper. Served with poached fish.

mustard seed (*Brassica* spp.) Three main species of **Brassica** are grown for a condiment made from their pungent seeds. The **yellow** or **white mustard** (*B. alba*), which taste bitter, go into white sauce, cheese dishes and savory spreads; also used in pickles, as a preservative, an emulsifier in mayonnaise and in prepared pastes; **black mustard seeds** (*B. nigra*), which are spicy and piquant, are made into prepared pastes; brown or **Indian mustard seeds** (*B. juncea*) are dry-fried whole before being ground for use in curries. As a condiment mustard is sold in three main forms: as whole seeds, as a dry powder and as made-up pastes that may contain other spices, citrus, sugar, vinegar or wine.

mustard, American Sold in the form of a mild, sweet paste made mainly from white mustard seeds and turmeric.

mustard, English Often sold as a powder consisting of a mixture of brown and white mustard with turmeric added; usually mixed with water before use. Also sold ready mixed in jars. It has a hot sharp taste and is traditionally used with roast beef.

mustard, French Sold in the form of a mild paste. The main center for production is Dijon and it is often sold as Dijon mustard; made from black and brown mustard seeds, verjuice and white wine.

mustard, German Sold in the form of a strong, slightly sweet smooth paste. Traditionally used with frankfurt-type sausages and cheese.

mustard, Meaux Sold in the form of coarse paste made from crushed mustard seeds of various colors and vinegar.

mutton The meat of sheep older than 30 months.

myrtle (*Myrtus communis*) Aromatic shrub with strongly fragrant leaves used in rich stews, roasts, charcuterie and certain liqueurs.

Myzithra | GREEK | Fresh sheep's-milk cheese used as a table cheese with fruit; dried version used for grating.

naan / nann | INDIAN | Elongated, triangular-shaped, flat leavened bread made of plain white flour and a little yeast. Traditionally baked on the side wall of a tandoori oven.

nacho | MEXICAN | Appetizer made with corn tortillas or chips topped with beans, tomatoes, chilies and cheese, and baked in an oven until the cheese melts.

naeng myum | KOREAN | Slender noodles made from buckwheat flour and potato starch. Most often served at room temperature or chilled in large bowls of soup.

nage | FRENCH | Aromatic poaching liquid in which large shellfish are cooked.

nam pla | THAI | Fish sauce widely used in Thai cooking.

nam prik | THAI | Hot chili sauce of various ingredients that might include garlic, lemon grass, fresh red chilies, coriander root, dried shrimp paste, palm sugar, fish sauce, lime juice. It is blended to a smooth paste. Served as a condiment with a variety of dishes and as a dip for raw vegetables.

name control A means by which France, Italy, Switzerland and Spain are able to ensure that their best and most traditional wines, cheeses and other foods are protected by law from being copied or misrepresented. *see also* APPELLATION D'ORIGINE CONTRÔLÉE (AOC) *and* DENOMINAZIONE DI ORIGINE CONTROLLATA (DOC).

nameko | JAPANESE | (*Pholiota nameko*) Small button mushroom with a slippery, orange cap and rich, earthy taste. They are cultivated in Australia and occasionally available fresh. Also sold in cans.

nannygai *see* REDFISH; REDFISH, BIGHT.

nantais | FRENCH | Large, flat cake or small, round biscuits made with ground almonds and decorated with candied fruit.

nantais (à la) | FRENCH | Dish prepared in white wine sauce enriched with butter.

Nantua sauce | FRENCH | Rich, béchamel-based sauce made with cream and crayfish butter, flavored with brandy and cayenne. The sauce may also contain crayfish tails or truffles. Served with seafood or egg dishes, also as filling for vol-au-vent or barquettes.

napoletano salami | ITALIAN | Salame napoletano. Moderately hot salami from Naples. It has a chewy texture and is made from pork, or a mixture of meats, and seasoned with both red and black pepper.

nashi pear (*Pyrus pyrifolia*) Also known as 'Asian pear'. Round, apple-shaped pear with yellow skin and crisp, juicy flesh with the taste of a pear. Best eaten raw, either by itself or served with cheese or in fruit salad.

nasi goreng | INDONESIAN | Classic fried rice dish that may contain pork, chicken, prawns, onions, garlic, shrimp paste and chili, garnished with strips of plain omelette. If fried noodles are used instead of rice the dish becomes babmi goreng.

nasi kuning | INDONESIAN | Yellow rice dish served on festive occasions. White rice is cooked by the absorption method in thick coconut milk combined with ground turmeric and other seasonings such as lemon grass, pandan leaf or curry leaves.

nasturtium (*Tropaeolum majus*) Annual herb from Peru with round, flat leaves and red, orange and yellow flowers. Both the leaves and flowers are eaten and the unripened seedpods are pickled and used like capers. Leaves have a peppery, cress-like taste and can be stuffed and cooked like vine leaves. Both the torn leaves and whole or plucked flowers are an excellent ingredient in a mixed green salad. Flowers make a fine, peppery vinegar.

natto | JAPANESE | Fermented soy beans used as a condiment and for flavoring.

navarin | FRENCH | Lamb or mutton stew containing potatoes and onions and various other vegetables.

navel orange (*Citrus sinensis*) One of the best eating oranges, available from autumn through to spring. The navel is so named for the raised, umbilical-like end which contains a baby orange. It has a thick, easy to peel skin and a sweet, juicy flesh that contains very few seeds. Eaten fresh; also included in both sweet and savory recipes.

navette | FRENCH | Small boat-shaped pastry.

navy beans *see* HARICOT BEANS.

Neapolitan ice cream Oblong block of ice-cream consisting of a layer each of chocolate, strawberry and vanilla; usually served in slices.

napolitana sauce | ITALIAN | Basic pasta sauce made with peeled, fresh or canned plum tomatoes, olive oil, garlic and basil leaves.

Nebuchadnezzar Very large bottle of champagne containing the equivalent of 20 standard bottles.

nectarine (*Prunus persica* var. *nectarina*) This round stone fruit is very closely related to the peach, but does not have a furry skin and does not need peeling. The flesh varies depending upon variety and may be white, yellow or deep golden. Although similar in taste, the flesh is slightly firmer than that of the peach. It can be eaten fresh, in fruit salads, soaked in wine, stewed or poached, used in pies, puréed or made into jam or preserves.

neenish tart Small, individual round tart filled with cream and each half decorated with chocolate and white icing.

nègre en chemise | FRENCH | Rich chocolate mousse set in tall, round mold and decorated with piped whipped cream.

negroni Cocktail made with equal parts of gin, sweet vermouth and Campari. Served in a tall glass over ice and garnished with a slice of orange. Soda water is an option.

neroli Orange blossom oil used in perfumery, confectionery and some liqueurs.

Nesselrode Various dishes and pastries containing chestnut purée. Nesselrode pudding contains custard cream, puréed chestnuts, candied fruit, currants, raisins and whipped cream, flavored with Maraschino and set in a mold and frozen.

Neufchâtel | FRENCH | Name-controlled soft cow's-milk cheese with a smooth, ivory interior and white, velvety rind, mottled with red. Sold in various shapes and sizes including square, rectangular, cylindrical and small hearts. Mild, pleasant taste. Used as a snack or dessert. Named after village in Normandy where it is made. Widely copied elsewhere.

New Mexican chili Mild, large dried red chili used to make red chili sauces.

new potato *see* POTATO.

New Zealand spinach *see* WARRIGAL GREENS.

New Zealand yam *see* YAM.

Newburg | AMERICAN | Classic dish of lobster served in a rich, creamy sauce with sherry and the coral and liver of the lobster. Originally from the famous Delmonico restaurant in New York.

niacin B vitamin needed for the release of energy from food, especially carbohydrates. Found in wheat bran, liver, oily fish, nuts and pulses.

niçoise (à la) | FRENCH | Various Mediterranean-style dishes from the region around Nice, usually containing black olives, garlic, anchovies, tomatoes and green beans; salade niçoise for example.

Nicola potato *see* POTATO.

nigella (*Nigella sativa*) Sweet, aromatic seeds obtained from perennial plant of the ranunculus (buttercup) family. Sometimes used instead of pepper; also used as a seasoning in North African and Indian cooking, particularly in couscous and panch phora.

nigiri-zushi *see* SUSHI.

nivernaise (à la) | FRENCH | Roast meat or duck served with carrots cut into oval balls, and small onions.

noble rot *see* BOTRYTIS CINEREA.

Nocino | ITALIAN | Aromatic, dark brown, bittersweet liqueur made from unripe, green walnuts steeped in spirit.

noisette | FRENCH | (1) Hazelnut. (2) Small, round slice of tender meat (usually lamb). (3) Potatoes scooped into balls and lightly browned in butter.

noix | FRENCH | (1) General term for a nut, also walnut. (2) Term for cut of veal.

Nökkelost | NORWEGIAN | Also known as 'Kuminost'. Semifirm cow's-milk cheese with smooth, pale yellow interior usually spiced with cumin, car- away and cloves distributed evenly throughout the cheese; thin natural rind, coated with red wax. Spicy taste. Used in sandwiches and snacks; also in cooking.

nonpareille | FRENCH | (1) Name used for hundreds-and-thousands. (2) Small variety of caper pickled in vinegar from France.

Nonya | MALAYSIAN | Also known as 'Straits Chinese cooking'. Regionally specific cuisine evolved from the intermarriage of immigrant Chinese workers and Malay women on the Malaysian peninsula, mostly around Malacca. It combines elements of hot and pungent Malaysian spices with the Chinese Hokkien style of cooking. Dishes include the aromatic coconut milk and noodle soup laksa; otak-otak (steamed, spicy fishcakes wrapped in banana leaves); sweet, soupy dishes served for dessert and many varieties of kuch (small cakes or confectionery).

noodles Many types of starches are used in the making of noodles, such as wheat, rice flour, buckwheat, yam, soya bean, potato flour and mung bean (used for bean thread noodles). They form an important part in the diet of the people throughout Asia and are cooked in a variety of ways and with all sorts of textures and tastes. Cooking time varies according to type, thickness and whether fresh, dried or instant. Be careful not to over-cook as noodles should be served al dente. Fresh noodles of all types are available in Asian food stores. They should be kept in the refrigerator and used within a week. Dried noodles are readily available and will keep indefinitely. *see also* BEAN THREAD NOODLES, DANG MYUN, DEVIL'S TONGUE, DONGURI UDON, EGG NOODLES, GOOKSU, HARUSAME, HOKKIEN NOODLES, KONNYAKU, NAENG MYUM, RAMEN, RICE NOODLES, RICE VERMICELLI, SEVIAN, SHANGHAI NOODLES, SHIRATAKI, SOBA, SOMEN, UDON *and* WHEAT NOODLES.

nopales / nopalitos | MEXICAN | (*Opuntia vulgaris*) Also known as 'cactus leaves'. Tender, young, oval leaves of the prickly pear cactus. The spines are removed and they are usually diced or cut into strips. Used in a variety of Mexican dishes.

nori | JAPANESE | (*Porphyra* spp.) Type of edible seaweed sold in paper-thin strips. It does not need to be washed or soaked before using. To bring out the distinctive taste and increase its digestibility, nori is lightly toasted on the shiny side for about 30 seconds over a gas flame until the sheet changes to dark green. Used mainly for sushi rolls or crumbled and sprinkled over soups, noodles or rice. **Ogo nori** is very fine strands of nori in colors of bright green, purple and white (bleached), and is sold in vacuum-sealed packs in the refrigerator section of Japanese specialty shops. After rinsing it is used in salads, side dishes and as a garnish.

nori-maki *see* SUSHI.

normande sauce | FRENCH | Rich, creamy sauce made with fish stock, minced onion, herbs, cider or white wine, roux, egg yolks and cream. Served with fish, vegetables and egg dishes.

Normandy Celebrated region of northern France noted for its dairy products and seafood dishes. Apples grow abundantly here and provide the raw ingredients for cider, pastries and the apple brandy, Calvados.

northern bluefin tuna *see* TUNA.

Norway lobster *see* SCAMPI.

nougat | FRENCH | Confection made of egg whites, honey and almonds or other nuts.

nouvelle cuisine | FRENCH | New, health-conscious style of cooking that originated in France in the early 1970s. Fats, starches, sugar and salt are used with discretion. Fish and young, fresh vegetables feature prominently with the emphasis on shorter cooking times. Light sauces are made by reducing the cooking liquid and are served under or around the food, not poured over it. The portions are usually small; simple elegance, harmony and imagination are the keys to presentation.

nuoc cham | VIETNAMESE | Dipping sauce containing nuoc nam (fish sauce), rice vinegar, garlic, chilies, thinly sliced shallots, lime juice and sugar.

nuoc nam | VIETNAMESE | Fish sauce made from small, salted fish. Used as a flavouring in cooking.

nutmeg (*Myristica fragrans*) Hard, dried seed of tropical tree native to Indonesia. It has a sweet, spicy taste and is best finely grated when required. It is sprinkled over hot and cold milk drinks, puddings, eggnog and soups; also used in fish dishes, pumpkin pie, spinach, potato purée and cheese dishes; often included in garam masala and curry paste.

nuts Any edible kernel or seed enclosed in a hard or brittle shell. Nuts are nearly always eaten when ripe and, because of their high fat content and risk of rancidity, keep much longer stored in their shells. Shelled nuts, which come in various forms, do not keep as well and should be stored air- tight in a cool place or refrigerator. Since the earliest times, nuts have been an important source of food and oil and today are universal in their application: from simply being eaten as a snack or dessert, to being included in a wide variety of savory and sweet dishes and baked goods. Roasting or toasting before use will enhance their character, taste, fragrance and crunchiness. *see also* ALMOND, BRAZIL, CANDLENUT, CASHEW, CHESTNUT, COCONUT, GINKGO, HAZELNUT, MACADAMIA, PEANUT, PECAN, PINE, PISTACHIO *and* WALNUT.

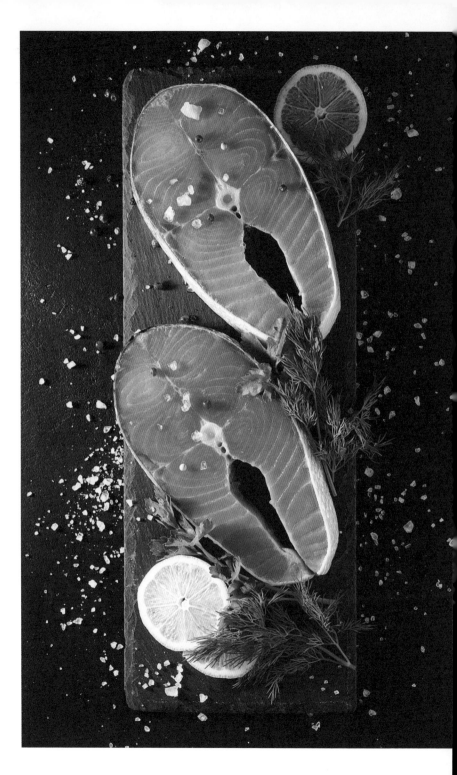

oakleaf lettuce (*Lactuca sativa*) Decorative, loosely formed lettuce with crispy, lobed leaves in both red and green varieties. Used on its own or in mixed green salads.

oatcake | ENGLISH | Round cake made of oatmeal, baking soda, water and fat, once cooked on the griddle, but now usually baked in the oven.

oats (*Avena sativa*) Highly nutritious cereal grain, usually ground into oat- meal of various grades. Used to make porridge and muesli, puddings and baked goods; also used in stuffings and as a thickener in soup and stews. Rolled oats are hulled grains that have been steamed and flattened between rollers which makes for quicker cooking.

ocean perch (*Helicolenus barathri*) Also known as 'red gurnard perch'. An inshore and deep water fish found in southern Australian waters. It grows to about 40 cm long and has reddish brown bands on its body. It has a mild-tasting, white, firm flesh and can be pan-fried, baked, poached or grilled. Usually sold in fillets.

ocean trout (*Oncorhynchus mykiss*) This is the name given to the sea-going rainbow trout once it changes its color and becomes a much larger fish. It is sold whole, as fillets or cutlets and is usually slowly cooked in a court-bouillon.

octopus (*Octopus* spp.) An oval-shaped cephalopod with eight arms, similar in taste to squid, but needs tenderizing before it is cooked. This is often done prior to selling. Pre-tenderized fresh octopus is recognized by its tightly curled arms. Small octopuses are quickly stir-fried, chargrilled or barbecued; larger specimens are stewed for several hours.

oenology Science of the study of wine.

oeufs à la neige | FRENCH | Translates to 'snow eggs' and refers to floating islands.

offal Also known as 'variety meats'. Edible internal parts of an animal, such as brains, kidneys, tripe or liver, that are removed before the carcass is dissected. Also refers to some extremities of an animal, such as chickens' feet or pigs' trotters.

ogo nori *see* NORI.

oils Essential in much of the world's cuisines, fruit, seed and nut oils are highly regarded for their intrinsic flavors, nutritious benefits and for giving balance and satisfaction to a meal. Oils are used in sautéing, pan-frying, deep-frying and basting, as well as in making mayonnaise, vinaigrette and dips. An oil is extracted by pressure and is classified as either refined or unrefined. **Unrefined oils** are cold-pressed, filtered and bottled. They are rich in cooler and retain the natural aroma and taste of the ingredient from which they are extracted. **Refined oils** are those that have been extracted with the use of heat and undergo further refinements such as bleaching, deodorizing and chilling. They are usually light-colored, have a bland flavor, a high smoke point and increased shelf life. *see also* ALMOND OIL, CANOLA OIL, CHILI OIL, COCONUT OIL, COPHA, CORN OIL, FATS AND OILS, GRAPESEED OIL, MACADAMIA NUT OIL, MARGARINE, MONO-UNSATURATED FATS, OLIVE OIL, PEANUT OIL, PISTACHIO OIL, RAPESEED OIL, SESAME SEED OIL, SOYA BEAN OIL *and* WALNUT OIL.

oils, seasoned A number of vegetable oils and some olive oils are infused with herbs and spices to give extra aroma and flavor to vinaigrettes and marinades; also used on pastas or for basting grilled seafood and meats. Garlic, black pepper, chilies, fennel, thyme, mint, rosemary and lemon grass make good seasoned oils. Because they can easily go rancid they should always be refrigerated.

oily fish Category of strongly flavored fish such as anchovies, bonito, herrings, mackerel, sardines, trout and tuna. They are best when grilled, baked or braised; also good for smoking. Some very fresh, oily fish, such as tuna, are eaten raw in sashimi and sushi.

Oka | CANADIAN | Semisoft, uncooked cow's-milk cheese with creamy, yellow interior and brown, washed rind. Fairly strong, monastery-type aroma and taste. Usually served at the end of a meal. It is made by the Trappist monks in the town of Oka, near Montreal, Canada.

okra (*Abelmoschus esculentus*) Also known as 'lady's fingers' and 'gumbo'. Green, tapered, ribbed seed pods obtained from a tropical member of the hibiscus family. Okra is best when very young. It is a good source of vitamins A and C, fiber, calcium and iron. It has a rather glutinous texture when cooked, giving body to soup and stews, and is particularly popular in Creole and Cajun gumbos. Also widely used in the Middle East, Greece, India and South-East Asia. In certain dishes when the glutinous texture is not desirable, whole okra are soaked in lemon juice for about 30 minutes, then rinsed to get rid of any trace of sliminess.

old-fashioned | AMERICAN | Cocktail containing bourbon, Angostura bitters and a twist of orange peel. Served in a short, heavy-based tumbler (old-fashioned glass).

olive (*Olea europaea*) Cultivated for centuries in Mediterranean countries originally for the oil extracted from the fruit; the olive itself is bitter and inedible until it is processed. Green olives are harvested while still immature and, after a preliminary steeping in a lye solution which helps to remove the bitter flavor, they are preserved in brine. They are sold in a variety of forms, including those already pitted or stuffed with foods such as pimiento, almonds or anchovy. The green **Spanish Manzanilla** is easy to pit and is the variety most often stuffed. **Black olives** are the ripe fruit and are usually salt-cured or preserved in brine, and often packed in olive oil. Black olives are sometimes sold flavored with aromatics such as garlic, herbs, orange or lemon zest and chilies.

olive oil Largely mono-unsaturated oil, long used in Mediterranean countries in cooking, as a flavoring agent and for medicinal purposes, and becoming increasing popular all over the world for its delicious, natural taste and positive health benefits. It also aids digestion and stimulates the appetite. Olive oils vary according to the region they come from, the techniques used for picking and pressing, and the varieties of olives used. **Cold-pressed** means the olives have been pressed without any heat treatment, filtered and bottled. **Extra virgin olive oil** from the first cold pressing is the best and the most expensive. It is clear, often green with a good, strong, olive flavor. **Virgin olive oil** is pressed in the same way, but has a slightly higher level of acidity and is not quite good enough to be called extra virgin. Subsequent pressings produce oil of a progressively lesser quality, a higher degree of acidity and little taste. **Pure olive oil** is a heat treated refined oil blended with virgin oil to add flavor. **Light olive oil** is refined oil that has been further filtered and is lighter in both color and flavor. Pure olive oil and light olive oil can be heated to high temperatures without burning or smoking and are suitable for sautéing and cooking. Extra virgin olive oil is ideal for salad dressing and for flavoring all types of fish and shellfish, on pasta and in marinades. Olive oil should always be stored in a cool place away from direct heat and sunlight.

olla | SPANISH | Traditional earthenware pot used for slow-cooked dishes. Also a name for stews cooked in it.

olla podrida | SPANISH | Traditional stew made with several types of meat and poultry, vegetables and chickpeas, simmered in a large pot for a long period. The broth is served first as a soup, followed by the meat and vegetables as a main course.

oloroso | SPANISH | Type of sweet, full-bodied sherry usually served after dinner.

omega-3 fatty acids Type of fatty acids found in fish, such as salmon, trout, mackerel, tuna and shellfish, and small amounts in canola-based products, for example, linseed, walnut and wheatgerm oil. They are known to reduce harmful cholesterol (LDL) levels in the bloodstream and are particularly beneficial to the heart, circulation, brain growth and development. Low salt, canned salmon, herrings and sardines are also rich in omega-3 fatty acids. *see also* CHOLESTEROL.

omega-6 fatty acids Type of polyunsaturated fats found in safflower oil, sunflower oil and corn oil, also margarines made from plants such as sunflowers. A diet high in omega-6 fatty acids cancels out many of the beneficial effects of omega-3 fatty acids.

omelette The classic French omelette is beaten eggs with a dash of water and seasoning, cooked quickly in butter in a frying pan and served plain or with various fillings that are usually added before folding the omelette in half. **Spanish omelette** is made with potatoes and onions, left flat and cooked on both sides like a thick pancake. The Italian **frittata** is also left flat, with the ingredients mixed with the eggs. **Eggah** is a Middle Eastern version. **Chinese omelettes**, known as 'eggs foo yong', are served with a savory soy and sherry sauce. The **Japanese omelette** (tomago-yaki) is cooked in a rectangular omelette pan and repeatedly folded to form a neat block.

omelette pan, Japanese *see* JAPANESE OMELETTE PAN.

onion (*Allium cepa*) The universal dry onion has been cultivated for food since very early times and can be traced to ancient Egypt. Onion varieties differ in shape, size, texture, color and intensity of flavor. The **brown onion**, the staple in most kitchens, has a strong flavor and is most often used in cooking. The red **Spanish onion** which has a mild, sometimes sweet taste is used raw in salads, as a garnish and makes good fried onions. The **white onion**, which has a sharp medium flavor, is used in salads and cooking. A larger, **yellow skinned variety** is mild and sweet and used raw in salads. Small, early harvested, dry onions are used for pickling, left whole in casseroles or braised in butter or stock.

oolong tea (*Camellia sinensis*) Partially fermented tea that combines the color, flavor and aroma of black and green teas. It has rather large leaves and is sometimes scented with jasmine, gardenia or orange blossoms. Oolong produced in Taiwan is labeled 'Formosa oolong'.

orange (*Citrus sinensis*) Long recognized for its high vitamin C content, the orange is probably the best-known citrus fruit, enjoyed throughout the world as a breakfast juice. There are two main varieties of sweet, eating oranges: the seedless, thick-skinned navel which is available from autumn to spring; and the round, thin-skinned Valencia, a spring/summer variety popular for juicing. Sweet oranges are eaten as a fresh fruit and used in hundreds of sweet and savory dishes and to make marmalade. Blood oranges have a sweet, reddish flesh, perfect for fruit and savory salads. The best known of the bitter-tasting oranges is the Seville which is unsuitable for eating raw and is used mainly for marmalades or flavoring meat, fish and game; its peel is also candied or dried and used for flavoring. *see also* BERGAMOT ORANGE, BLOOD ORANGE, NAVEL ORANGE, SEVILLE ORANGE *and* VALENCIA ORANGE.

orange blossom (*Citrus aurantium*) Fragrant flower of the bitter orange from which the essential oil, neroli is obtained. Used mainly in perfumery, aromatherapy and for flavoring foods. A diluted version, orange flower water, is used in confectionery (such as Turkish delight), pastries and desserts, particularly in Middle Eastern cooking.

orange pekoe *see* PEKOE TEA.

orecchiette | ITALIAN | Small pasta shaped like an ear. Orecchiette mixti are a mixture of plain, spinach and chili flavored, ear-shaped pasta. Orecchiotte are a giant version suitable for stuffing.

oregano (*Origanum vulgare*) Also known as 'wild marjoram'. Perennial herb with dark green, oval leaves, closely related to marjoram but with a slightly more pungent taste. Fresh or dried, the leaves are used in many Mediterranean-inspired dishes. In Italy it is used in pizza toppings and pasta sauces; also good with most tomato dishes.

oreillettes | FRENCH | Thin, crisp, rectangular fritters made of sweetened dough, sometimes knotted, and flavored with rum, orange zest or orange flower water.

oreo (*Pseudocyttus maculatus*) Also known as 'smooth oreo'. Dark bluish, smooth-skinned fish with very large eyes, trawled at great depths. It has a mild taste and is sold whole or in skinned fillets. It can be gently pan-fried, grilled, barbecued, poached or baked.

orientale (à l') | FRENCH | Name for dishes inspired by the cooking of Turkey and the Balkans, usually containing eggplants, tomatoes, red capsicums, garlic and sometimes saffron.

orly (à l') | FRENCH | Orly style. Deep-fried fish coated with batter. Usually served with tomato sauce.

Orvieto | ITALIAN | Fruity, dry white wine in a flask-shaped bottle, from Umbria.

orzo | ITALIAN | Small, rice-shaped pasta, mostly used in soups; also used as a rice substitute.

Osietra caviar *see* CAVIAR.

Ossau-Iraty | FRENCH | Name-controlled sheep's-milk cheese with a lightly pressed, firm interior and brownish, brushed rind. Served as a snack, on canapés, in salads and at the end of a meal. Often sold under the name 'Ossau-Iraty Brebis Pyrénées'.

osso buco | ITALIAN | Classic stew of veal knuckle braised in white wine with tomatoes, garlic and onion. Traditionally garnished with gremolata and served with risotto alla milanese.

Oswego tea *see* BERGAMOT.

Otaheite apple *see* AMBARELLA.

ouzo | GREEK | Aniseed-flavored, clear spirit that turns cloudy when water is added.

oxtail The tail of beef or veal cut into small pieces. Usually slowly cooked for a long time in soups and stews.

oyster Saltwater mollusc with two irregular-shaped valves. There are many edible varieties through the world, both natural and cultivated. Oysters are usually sold under the names of the different places from where they are grown and harvested. Oysters are high in omega 3, calcium, niacin and iron. *see also*

oyster blade Cut of beef that comes from the best part of the animal's shoulder blade.

oyster mushrooms (*Pleurotus ostreatus*) Also known as 'pleurotte' and 'abalone mushrooms'. Flattish, fan-shaped mushrooms in pale shades of cream, pink or grey. Available fresh. They have a sharp taste raw, but when cooked take on a more subtle taste. Used in simple cream sauces with pasta, in omelettes and lightly flavored stir-fried dishes.

oyster plant *see* SALSIFY.

oyster sauce | CHINESE | Thick, dark brown seasoning made of oysters, soy sauce, salt and spices. Used in stir-fried dishes, as a diluted sauce with steamed green vegetables and as a table condiment.

oysters czarina Oysters served on the half shell, each topped with caviar.

oysters florentine Oysters served on the half shell, each with a layer of buttered spinach coated with mornay sauce, sprinkled with grated cheese and either grilled or baked.

oysters kilpatrick Oysters served on the half shell, each topped with finely chopped bacon, seasoned with Worcestershire sauce and grilled.

oysters mornay Oysters served on the half shell, each covered with a mornay sauce, sprinkled with grated cheese, and browned under the grill or oven.

oysters Rockefeller Oysters served on the half shell, each coated with a cooked mixture of chopped spinach, butter, breadcrumbs, seasoning and Pernod and either grilled or baked.

paan | INDIAN | Translates to 'leaf'. An aid to digestion, and breath freshener chewed between or after meals. Ingredients vary from a betel leaf wrapped around a betel nut and fastened with a clove, to a blend of spices, lime paste, coconut, and sometimes includes tobacco.

paan-daan | INDIAN | Metal container with many small compartments used for storing and serving paan ingredients.

Pacific oyster (*Crassostrea gigas*) Also known as 'Coffin Bay oyster' and 'Japanese oyster'. *see also* OYSTER.

Packham's Triumph pear Large, green pear that gradually turns a light greeny- golden when ripe. It has white, juicy flesh with good flavor and is a good eating pear served with cheese; also popular for preserving. *see also* PEAR.

pad Thai | THAI | Strong-tasting, stir-fried dish based on rice noodles, eggs, bean sprouts, prawns and preserved radish, with garlic, chili, crushed peanuts, dried shrimp, fish sauce, tomato sauce, lime juice and chopped coriander.

paella | SPANISH | Classic, saffron-flavored rice dish containing, variously, seafood, chicken, various vegetables, garlic and olive oil.

Paglia | ITALIAN | Generic name for a style of soft ripened cow's-milk cheese, similar to Brie and Camembert, sold under specific brand names such as Pagliola and Paglietta. Sold paper-wrapped in thin discs. Most originate in Piedmont, also made in parts of Lombardy.

paglia e fieno | ITALIAN | Translates to 'straw and hay', meaning a mixture of plain and spinach, ribbon pasta.

pain | FRENCH | Bread.

pain d'épice *see* GINGERBREAD.

pak choy *see* BOK CHOY.

pakora | INDIAN | Small, savory fritters made with slices of vegetables coated with chickpea batter and deep-fried. Served as a snack.

palm hearts *see* HEARTS OF PALM.

palm sugar Hard, dense sugar obtained from the sap of various palms. Usually sold in solid pieces in colors ranging from creamy-white to dark brown. Widely used in India and South-East Asian countries, usually to sweeten desserts or sweet-and-sour dishes.

palmier | FRENCH | Palm leaf-shaped pastry made from folded, sweet puff pastry.

pan-bagna | FRENCH | Bread roll split and brushed with olive oil and garlic and filled with anchovies, onions, black olives, tomatoes, capsicum and celery. Speciality of Nice.

panada | FRENCH | Thick paste used to bind and thicken forcemeats and quenelles; usually flour and butter based, but can also contain egg yolks, breadcrumbs, rice or potatoes. Also refers to a soup made from bread, milk, stock and butter.

pancake Thin, flat, round cake made from a batter of flour, eggs and milk, cooked quickly over high heat in a shallow pan.

pancetta | ITALIAN | Unsmoked bacon made of cured pork belly in sausage-like rolls. Sometimes thinly sliced and served raw as an antipasto, but usually cooked like bacon.

panch phora | INDIAN | Also known as 'Indian five spices'. Combination of five different aromatic seeds of equal quantities of black mustard, cumin and nigella, with half the quantity each of fenugreek and fennel seeds. These are left whole, mixed together and used to flavor cooking oil for certain Indian dishes.

pandan leaf *see* PANDANUS.

pandanus (*Pandanus amaryllifolius*) Also known as 'pandan leaf' and 'screw pine'. Long, stiff, bright green leaves used for flavoring and color. Pandanus has a distinctive sweet, nutty flavor and there is no substitute. Used in South-East Asian dishes in rice, sauces, sweets and as a food wrapping.

pandowdy | AMERICAN | Sliced apple and butter pudding flavored with spices and sweetened with molasses or brown sugar, topped with a pastry batter and baked.

pane | ITALIAN | (panini, plural) Bread. Panino is a bread roll.

panettone | ITALIAN | Large, light textured, spiced, yeast bread containing sultanas and candied citrus peel. It is baked in a tall cylindrical mold and sold in dome-shaped boxes. Traditionally given as a gift and eaten at Christmas. Originally a specialty of Milan.

panforte | ITALIAN | Very rich, flat, spiced cake made with dried fruit, toasted nuts, honey and spices and very little flour. Specialty of Sienna.

panipuri | INDIAN | Small, deep-fried puff of dough filled with tamarind water and eaten as a snack.

panir | INDIAN | Preparation of curds resembling a firm cream cheese, cut into cubes and added to vegetable dishes and puddings.

panisse | FRENCH | Thick, fried pancake made from chickpea flour, cut into rectangles when cold. Specialty of Provence.

panko | JAPANESE | Large, light, white breadcrumbs used for coating fried foods. Sold in packets in Japanese grocery shops.

pannequet | FRENCH | Rolled crêpe filled and spread with sweet or savory mixture, browned under the grill, or coated with breadcrumbs and fried.

panzanella | ITALIAN | Bread salad.

panzerotti | ITALIAN | Deep-fried pastries made with pizza dough and filled with mozzarella cheese, tomato sauce and sliced salami. Served as a snack or part of a hot antipasti.

papain Enzyme extracted from unripe pawpaw used as a basis for commercial meat tenderizers, usually sold in the form of a white powder. Papain is present in all parts of the pawpaw plant. The small black seeds, the juice or the unripe fruit can be used to tenderize meat. Alternatively a large piece of meat can be wrapped in lightly bruised pawpaw leaves for a few hours before roasting it.

papaya *see* PAWPAW.

papillote | FRENCH | Paper frill used to decorate the ends of bones such as rack of lamb and ham.

papillote, en | FRENCH | Fish, meat, poultry or vegetables cooked in oiled paper wrapping or foil.

pappadam / pappadum | INDIAN | Savory crisp, wafer-thin bread made from lentil flour. Pappadams are deep-fried in hot oil until they puff up more than double in size. Sold dried in packets in various sizes and flavors.

pappardelle | ITALIAN | Broad, flat pasta ribbons with rippled edges. Often used with rich meat sauces.

paprika (*Capsicum* spp.) Bright red, powdered spice made from a red, mild-tasting pepper native to Central America. Paprika has a mild, slightly sweet taste. The best variety comes from Hungary where it is a distinctive feature in Hungarian goulash; also used as a seasoning in delicately flavored foods such as crab, chicken, veal, cream sauces, dips and cheese dishes. Hot and smoked paprika is also available.

Paradise pear Miniature pear. Usually available in summer.

paratha | INDIAN | Unleavened, wheat-flour bread that contains ghee and, when rolled and folded and lightly fried, resembles a type of flaky pastry. Aloo paratha has a spicy potato filling and gobi paratha is filled with cauliflower.

parboil To pre-cook briefly in boiling water.

pare To peel or to cut off the skin from fruit or vegetables with a knife or vegetable peeler.

parfait | FRENCH | Frozen custard dessert made from egg yolks, sugar and whipped cream, with a fruit purée or sweet syrup. Also the name given to a dessert made in a tall, slender glass and consisting of layers of fruit, syrup, ice cream and whipped cream.

Paris ham Lightly smoked, full flavored, boneless leg ham molded into a block shape and sold sliced with the rind.

Paris-Brest | FRENCH | Classic, large, ring-shaped choux pastry filled with praline butter cream and topped with chopped almonds.

parisienne (à la) | FRENCH | Varied vegetable garnish which often includes herb potato balls.

parkin biscuits | SCOTTISH | Large biscuits made of oatmeal and golden syrup, with ground ginger and cinnamon.

Parma ham *see* PROSCIUTTO.

Parmentier | FRENCH | Dish with potatoes in some form.

Parmesan *see* PARMIGIANO-REGGIANO.

Parmigiano-Reggiano | ITALIAN | Also known as 'Parmesan'. Name-controlled partially skimmed cow's-milk cheese with very hard, granular, straw- colored interior and thick, brushed, oiled rind. Relatively low in fat, about 30 per cent. It must be two years old before it is sold, and only cheese from a strictly controlled area can be called 'Parmigiano-Reggiano' which is stamped around the sides of the rind. Freshly grated, used as a topping for pasta, soups and gratins; also shaved over salads or served as a table cheese.

parsley (*Petroselinum crispum*) Fresh-tasting, aromatic leaves of a biennial herb native to the Mediterranean region. Used in many savory dishes and almost universal in its application as a garnish. The most common varieties used are the curly-leafed form and the far more aromatic, flat-leafed variety. Parsley blends well with other herbs and forms part of the classic bouquet garni and fines herbes. Chopped, it is added to white sauce, stocks, marinades, soups and stews. Fried parsley is used as a garnish for fried food, especially fish. Finely chopped parsley is an essential ingredient of tabbouli, persillarde and gremolata.

parsnip (*Pastinaca sativa*) Tapering root vegetable shaped like a carrot with creamy-white skin and flesh. It is chopped into pieces and used in soups and stews; mashed as a vegetable; cut into chips and fried, baked or blanched; and thinly sliced in salads.

parson's nose | ENGLISH | Also known as 'the pope's nose'. Fleshy part of the stubby tail of poultry and game birds, consisting of the last two dorsal vertebrae.

paskha | RUSSIAN | Pyramid-shaped cream cheese dessert containing nuts, raisins and crystallized fruit. Served at Easter, often decorated with the letters XB which stand for 'Christ is risen'.

pasilla | MEXICAN | Also known as 'chili negro'. Dried, medium-hot, elongated, dark brown chili up to 15 cm long. It has a rich strong taste and is used in sauces or salsas and for making mole.

passata | ITALIAN | Rich tomato purée made from sieved ripe tomatoes.

passionfruit (*Passiflora edulis*) Also known as 'granadilla'. Small, egg-shaped or rounded tropical fruit with a tough, leathery, purple skin, that is at its best when slightly wrinkled. A good source of iron, calcium and phosphorus and contains a small amount of vitamins A and C. The aromatic, sweet juicy pulp is eaten straight from the shell with a teaspoon; also used in fruit salads and to flavor many sweet dishes such as bavarois, mousse, crème brûlée, soufflé and ice cream. It is a standard topping for pavlova and popular in jellies and preserves.

pasta | ITALIAN | Dough made from flour and water and sometimes eggs, formed into hundreds of varieties of shapes and sizes. The flour used for dried commercial pasta is made from water and milled durum wheat (Triticum durum) which produces an elastic dough that holds together well during kneading, drying and cooking. Commercial dried pasta is sometimes enriched with eggs, or colored and flavored with ingredients like spinach (con spinaci), squid ink (al nero) or wholemeal (tipo inte- grale). Fresh or homemade pasta is made with plain white flour and eggs and is also sometimes flavored. Cooking times vary according to the size, shape and thickness of the pasta; fresh pasta cooks much faster than dried varieties. In recipes, quantities of dried pasta will be less than those for fresh. Whether fresh or dried, all pasta is cooked 'al dente', so that it is tender, but with some resistance to the bite. When choosing what shape of pasta to use with what sauce, many are interchangeable, but generally long pasta such as fettuccine and spaghetti is best for a good olive oil based coating sauce; meaty or chunky sauces go well with short, sturdy pasta, such as fusilli and penne; use light seafood or buttery sauces with fine pasta, such as vermicelli or angel hair. Whatever sauce is used, its function is to flavor and thoroughly coat the pasta, without swamping it. In Italy the pasta dish is usually served as an entrée after the antipasto. Generally a pasta shape with the suffix 'ini' or 'ette' means a smaller or thinner version, and those with the suffix 'oni' or 'otte' means wider or bigger: for example, farfallini are tiny, butterfly-shaped farfalle, and farfalloni are larger. Any pasta followed with the word 'rigate' means that it is ridged or grooved. *see also individual entries.*

pasta all'uovo | ITALIAN | Dried or fresh pasta enriched with eggs.

pasta ascuitta | ITALIAN | Any dish of pasta served with a sauce.

pasta filata | ITALIAN | Stretched-curd cheese that is made by kneading the warm curd until it is pliable and smooth, then pulling and spinning it into long threads. It is then shaped or molded by hand into a ball-like form. The fresh, uncured mozzarella and the matured Caciocavallo and Provolone belong to this category and are often used in cooking.

pasta fresca | ITALIAN | Freshly made pasta, usually enriched with eggs. Available in specialty shops and food halls.

pasta nero | ITALIAN | Dried or fresh black pasta, colored and flavored with squid ink.

pasta verde | ITALIAN | Dried or fresh green pasta, colored and flavored with spinach.

pastasciutta | ITALIAN | Dried pasta.

pasteurization The process of heating milk, beer, wine and other liquids to a temperature sufficiently high to kill bacteria and to allow for longer keeping. Developed in the 1860s by the French chemist, Louis Pasteur.

pasticcio | ITALIAN | Pie or baked dish made with cooked, short pasta, meat or vegetables and a white cheese sauce. In some regions it is made with a pastry topping.

pastilla *see* BASTELA / BASTILLA.

pastille | FRENCH | Small, round confectionery made from sugar syrup and various flavorings.

pastina | ITALIAN | Generic term for all tiny pasta shapes usually served in soups. The biggest of these is used in minestrone, and mini versions are used in consommé and broth.

pastis | FRENCH | (1) Aniseed-flavored spirit that becomes cloudy when water is added. Two well-known brands are Pernod and Ricard. (2) Also the name for various flaky pastries made in the south-west of France.

pastrami Dry-cured and smoked cuts of lean beef that have first been rubbed with salt and a spicy paste which can include chili, garlic, cinnamon, cloves and crushed black peppercorns. It is sold cooked and is usually sliced thinly and used for rye sandwiches and snacks.

pastry Rich dough made from flour, some type of shortening and a little liquid. Used for a multitude of baked goods. *see also* ALLUMETTES, BARQUETTE, BOUCHÉE, BRIK, BUGNE, BUNUELO, CAROLINE, CHOU, CONVERSATION, CROISSANT, CROQUEMBOUCHE, DANISH

PASTRY, DARTOIS, DOUILLON, ÉCLAIR, FANCHONNETTE/ FANCHETTE, FEUILLETÉ, FILO/PHYLLO, FLEURONS, GALETTE, GOUGÈRE, JALOSIE, JÉSUITE, KOEKSISTER, KONAFA/ KOUNAFA, KOUING-AMAN, MATCHSTICK, MILLE-FEUILLE, NAVETTE, PALMIER, PARIS-BREST, PITHIVIERS, PROFITEROLES, PUFF PASTRY, PUITS D'AMOUR, RELIGIEUSE, RÉTÈS, STRUDEL, TALMOUSE, TURNOVER *and* VOL-AU-VENT.

pastry bag Cone-shaped bag with interchangeable nozzles used to pipe soft mixtures into decorative shapes and to form pastries, biscuits and small cakes.

pastry brush Small brush used for glazing baked goods with beaten egg or milk before they are cooked. Sturdier brushes are used for coating food with oil or butter and for greasing pans and baking dishes.

pastry wheel Small, sharp, roller wheel with a handle. Used to cut pastry into strips. Large plain ones are used for cutting pizza; those with serrated cutting edges are used for decorative purposes and for ravioli.

pasty *see* CORNISH PASTY.

pâté | FRENCH | (1) Meat or fish enclosed in pastry. (2) Cooked mixture of finely minced meat, liver, poultry or fish that is set in a mold and served cold as a spread if smooth, or sliced if coarse.

pâté de fois gras | FRENCH | Smooth-textured terrine made from finely pounded goose liver, that may be flavored with truffles, brandy, Madeira, port or sherry and various seasonings.

pâté de tête | FRENCH | Type of brawn traditionally made of the head of the pig. In France it is also called 'fromage de tête' which translates to 'head cheese'.

pâtisserie | FRENCH | (1) Place where pastries are made and sold. (2) Sweet or savory pastries baked in the oven.

pâtissier | FRENCH | Pastry cook.

patna rice | INDIAN | Long-grained variety of basmati rice.

pattipan squash *see* BUTTON SQUASH.

patty Small, flattened rissole made from finely chopped meat, fish or vegetables.

patty cake Small cake baked in a fluted paper case.

paupiette | FRENCH | Thin slice of meat or fish spread with a savoury mixture and rolled up before cooking.

pavé | FRENCH | Translates to 'paving-stone' or 'block'. (1) Usually refers to a square dessert made with sponge cake; also a square-shaped savory mousse coated with aspic and served cold. (2) Thick slice of boned beef or calf's liver.

pavlova | AUSTRALIAN / NEW ZEALAND | Dessert of crisp meringue with a soft center, filled with whipped cream and decorated with fresh fruit. Named after the Russian ballerina, Anna Pavlova.

pawpaw (*Carica papaya*) Also known as 'papaya'. Large, elongated tropical fruit with thick, golden yellow skin and either yellow, pink or orange flesh. The Hawaiian Solo variety has orange-red skin and pinkish orange flesh. When fully ripe the pawpaw is highly fragrant and soft to the touch. It is an excellent source of vitamins A and C and is a popular breakfast fruit. Also served raw as an entrée, in fruit salads or made into a sorbet. Slightly green fruit is used in Thai salads or cooked as a vegetable, used in curries or chutneys. Unripe pawpaw contains the enzyme papain, a natural meat tenderizer. This enzyme also prevents gelatin from setting, so fresh pawpaw cannot be used when making jelly. *see also* PAPAIN.

payasam | INDIAN | Semi-liquid, sweet, rice dessert containing nuts and raisins.

paysanne | FRENCH | Garnish of mixed vegetables cut into small squares.

pea eggplant *see* EGGPLANT.

pea shoots (*Pisum sativum*) The thin tendrils, growing tips and uppermost leaves of the pea plant. Sold in lidded punnets at fruit and vegetable markets. Used fresh in salads or very lightly stir-fried as a vegetable.

peach (*Prunus persica*) Round, stone fruit with soft, velvety skin and succulent, juicy flesh. The flesh color varies from white to deep golden depending upon variety. Peaches are high in vitamin A and C. They are usually classified as freestones and clingstones. The best peaches are those that are harvested when ripe. Although slightly under-ripe fruit may continue to ripen and gain flavor at room temperature, rock hard peaches will not improve. Peaches are usually peeled before eating either as a snack, dessert fruit or in compotes, fruit salads, mousses and ice cream. They can be poached, baked, grilled or made into pies, puddings, preserves or drinks. Tiny **immature peaches** that have been pickled and marinated in truffle-infused oil are sold in cans in gourmet specialty shops. Used as a savory garnish in salads and appetizers.

peach Melba Dessert consisting of poached peach halves and vanilla ice-cream served with a sauce made from raspberry purée and sugar (Melba sauce). Created by Escoffier in honor of Dame Nellie Melba, the famous Australian soprano.

peanut (*Arachin hypogaea*) Also known as 'groundnut', so-called because after pollination the peanut flower bends down and penetrates the ground where the tip develops into a soft, cream-brown shell containing two kernels. Peanuts are high in fat, protein and dietary fiber and are a good source of vitamin E and other vitamins. They keep much longer stored in their shells. They are easy to shell and make an ideal snack; also widely used in various sweet and savory recipes. Peanuts are also an important ingredient in South-East Asian cooking and widely used in satay sauce. **Peanut butter** is made from ground roasted nuts and vegetable oil.

peanut oil Light golden oil with a subtle, nutty flavor, widely used in stir-fried Asian dishes. Because it can be heated to a high temperature without burning, peanut oil is suitable for deep-frying.

pear (*Pyrus communis*) Cultivated and eaten since ancient times, there are now thousands of varieties of pears, but only a few of these are generally available in fruit markets. Most **European pears** have the familiar pear shape and, when ripe, a slightly grainy, juicy flesh, while the **nashi** or **Asian pear** (*Pyrus pyrifolia*) is shaped more like an apple and is crisp. Pears are an excellent source of dietary fiber as well as vitamins A and C. When ripe they are eaten raw as a snack or served with cheese or in fruit salad. Slightly unripe firm pears are best for cooking and are excellent when poached in wine or champagne, baked or used in pastries, pies, tarts, puddings and preserves. Peeled and cut pears should be brushed with lemon juice to prevent discoloration. Different varieties of pear appear in fruit markets from March through to July. *see also* BEURRE BOSC, CORELLA PEAR, JOSEPHINE PEAR, NASHI PEAR, PACKHAM'S TRIUMPH *and* WILLIAMS PEAR.

pearl barley *see* BARLEY.

pearl perch (*Glaucosoma* spp.) Three closely related saltwater fish are commonly referred to as 'pearl perch'. The **eastern pearl peach** (*G. scapulare*) is a silvery-grey, deep-bodied fish with large eyes and a pearly bone protruding from the gill cover. The similar **threadfin pearl perch** (*G. magnificum*) and the **northern pearl perch** (*G. buergeri*) are caught in northern Australian waters. All have a sweet, white flesh and are excellent table fish, suited to pan-frying, grilling, poaching or barbecuing.

pearl tapioca *see* TAPIOCA.

peas (*Pisum sativum*) Plump, sweet, green seeds shelled from their pod. They are an excellent source of fiber, vitamin C and B and iron. Shelled peas are boiled or used in soups, pasta sauces, risotto, curries and stir-fries. Some varieties, such as **snow peas** and **sugar peas**, are picked when the peas within the pods are very small. These edible pods are topped and tailed and the stringy spine removed before blanching whole for salads or using in stir-fried dishes. *see also* SNOW PEAS, SUGAR PEAS, CHICKPEAS *and* SPLIT PEAS.

pease pudding | ENGLISH | Traditional accompaniment to boiled beef made from cooked and puréed, dried, green split peas.

pecan (*Carya illinoensis*) Native to Northern America, the shelled pecan resembles the related walnut in structure and can be used similarly. It is a useful source of B group vitamins. Nuts keep much longer stored in their brittle, reddish brown shells. Used as a snack, in pecan pie, fruitcakes, biscuits, ice cream and in confectionery; also used in a variety of savory dishes such as stuffings for vegetables.

pecorino | ITALIAN | Generic name for all sheep's-milk cheese made in Italy. Derived from 'pecora', the word for sheep. The best known and oldest is **Pecorino Romano** first made near Rome. Other versions are **Pecorino Toscano** made in Tuscany and **Pecorino Sardo** from Sardinia. They generally have a strong flavor and when mature are used as a grating cheese, like Parmesan.

Pecorino Romano | ITALIAN | Name-controlled hard pressed, partially skimmed sheep's-milk cheese with a granular white, cream or pale yellow interior and yellow, natural rind that is rubbed with oil or sometimes blackened. Strong flavor and often quite salty. Used as a table cheese, or when aged for grating, like Parmesan.

Pecorino Sardo *see* SARDO.

pectin Natural gelling agent found in certain fruits such as oranges, lemons, apples and quinces.

Peking cabbage *see* CHINESE CABBAGE.

Peking duck | CHINESE | Classic preparation and presentation of roast duck. The skin is distinctly crispy and served with thin slices of duck meat which are wrapped in a pancake with shredded spring onions and plum-based sauce.

pekoe tea Quality classification given to small-leafed black tea that is graded and sorted by size and age. Flowery orange pekoe made from the downy terminal bud and growing tip is the top of the range, followed by orange pekoe, the grade for the leaves harvested below the buds, and then the shorter, elongated pekoe.

pelmeni / pelmieni | RUSSIAN | Type of dumpling made with ravioli dough filled with minced meat, chicken, vegetables or cream cheese, cooked in boiling salted water. They are served with sour cream or as a garnish for a clear soup.

penicillin Beneficial blue or green mold found on certain foods and used as an antibiotic and in the production of blue cheeses. The spores of *Penicillium roqueforti* are used in the production of Roquefort cheese.

penne | ITALIAN | Short, straight tubes of pasta cut on the diagonal; pennette are narrower.

peperonata | ITALIAN | Classic dish of sliced capsicums, onions, tomatoes and garlic cooked gently in olive oil, seasoned with wine or balsamic vinegar. Served hot or cold. Red capsicums retain their color best.

peperoncini | ITALIAN | Dried red chilies.

peperoni | ITALIAN | Capsicums.

pepino (*Solanum muricatum*) This elongated, melon-shaped fruit has yellow skin with purplish streaks and pale yellow flesh that is sweetly fragrant when ripe. It is peeled before eating fresh, added to fruit salads or served with cheese.

pepita Edible pumpkin seeds with the husks removed. Available raw, roasted, salted or plain.

pepper (*Piper nigrum*) Dried, berry-like fruit from a climbing vine native to tropical Asia. Both black and white peppers are derived from the same plant. **Black peppers** are picked before fully ripe, dried and left to turn black and wrinkled. They have a strong aromatic taste. **White peppers** are allowed to fully ripen before harvest when the dark outer husk is removed and they are dried, leaving a smooth, creamy, white kernel and a milder taste. White pepper is used in pale foods such as white sauces. Pepper is the world's most commonly used seasoning in practically all savory dishes. Ideally it should be purchased whole and freshly ground in a mill over food as required. **Green peppercorns** are unripe peppers sold pickled in vinegar or brine; used in fish terrines, salads and sauces.

pepper, grey Mixture of black and white pepper.

peppercorns, pink (*Schinus terebinthifolius*) Unripe berries obtained from pepper trees cultivated in Madagascar. Available dried or pickled in brine.

peppermint (*Mentha* x *piperita*) Dark green, oval leaves with a distinct pepper- mint smell. Used mostly in teas, cool drinks and some desserts. Oil of peppermint is used to flavor confectionery, chewing gum and some pharmaceutical products.

pepperoni | ITALIAN | Slender, air-dried salami, made from pork and beef, highly seasoned with ground red and black pepper. Sliced thinly as an antipasto or pizza topping; also used in cooked dishes.

pequín chili *see* BIRDS' EYE CHILI.

percebes | SPANISH | Goose barnacles. Dark grey barnacles, with finger-like projections, that grow in clusters anchored to rocks on the north-western coast of Spain and Portugal. They are collected at very low tide and boiled until tender. The thick skin is peeled back to reveal the sweet, pink, succulent flesh which is bitten off from the shell.

perciatelli | ITALIAN | Long strands of tubular pasta.

Périgord | FRENCH | Region in France noted for its black truffles, wild mushrooms, fois gras and confits of preserved duck and goose.

périgourdine (à la) | FRENCH | Dish served with a demi-glace sauce, enriched with a little foie gras and garnished with chopped truffles. Also a dish served with Périgueux sauce.

Périgueux sauce | FRENCH | Demi-glace sauce enriched with chopped truffles and flavored with Madeira. Served with beef, poultry and egg dishes; also as filling for vol-au-vent, timbales or barquettes.

perilla *see* SHISO.

periwinkle (*Turbo undulatus*) Small edible sea snails found along the coast on rocks and wharves. They are boiled in their shells until the pearly covering drops off, and are extracted with a small pick or pin. They can be dressed with a vinaigrette or pan-fried; also used in pasta sauces.

Pernod Aniseed-flavored spirit that becomes cloudy when water is added. Used as an aperitif.

perry Cider-like drink made from pears.

persil | FRENCH | Parsley, usually the flat-leaf variety.

persillade | FRENCH | Blend of finely chopped parsley, finely chopped shallots (or garlic) and grated zest of lemon; added to sautéed fish or veal in the final stages of cooking or sprinkled over food just before serving.

persillé | FRENCH | Term that describes certain blue vein cheeses with bluish-green mold.

persimmon (*Diospyros kaki*) Medium-sized, round fruit with a bright orange skin. There are two main types. The astringent type (sometimes seen in gardens) needs to be eaten when the flesh is overripe, soft and jelly-like, otherwise the tannic acid is unpleasant. The soft flesh has a delicious flavor and can be scooped out and eaten with a spoon or puréed and made into sauces, mousses, ice cream and other desserts. The non-astringent type is the persimmon most often seen in fruit markets, the most common being the cultivar Fuyu or Fuji. It is still firm when ripe and can be eaten like an apple. Persimmons are an excellent source of vitamin A and are available mostly in autumn.

pestle and mortar Heavy bowl made of earthenware, marble, stone or wood in which foods are ground to a powder or paste using the pestle, a short heavy grinding tool.

pesto | ITALIAN | Uncooked paste made from fresh basil, pine nuts, Parmesan cheese, olive oil and garlic. Used with pasta and in soups.

petit déjeuner | FRENCH | Breakfast.

petit four | FRENCH | Tiny cake, biscuit, pastry or sweet served with coffee after dinner.

petit pois | FRENCH | Small green pea.

petit-beurre | FRENCH | Small biscuit made with butter.

Petit-Suisse | FRENCH | Fresh cow's-milk cheese enriched with cream. It has a soft, white texture and is sold in small cylinders. Served as a dessert with fruit and a little sugar or honey; also mixed with fresh herbs to spread on canapés.

petite marmite | FRENCH | (1) Meat and vegetable broth cooked and served in its own pot, usually topped with croutons spread with marrow bone and sprinkled with grated cheese. (2) The name of the vessel in which it is cooked, being a smaller version of the casserole pot known as 'a marmite'.

Pézenas pie | FRENCH | Small sweet and spicy mutton and kidney pie. Speciality of the Languedoc region.

pfeffernüsse | GERMAN | Spice biscuits served at Christmas.

pheasant (*Phasianus* spp.) Long-tailed game bird originally from Asia, but naturalised in Europe and North America. Farmed in Australia and sold in specialist poultry and game shops. The male is larger than the female, but the female's flesh is finer, plumper and juicier. When young, pheasants may be roasted like chicken, but barding or a moist-cooking method is necessary for older birds.

Philadelphia Cream Cheese | AMERICAN | Brand name. *see* CREAM CHEESE.

pho bo | VIETNAMESE | Traditionally a breakfast noodle soup made with spicy beef stock, slices of beef and onions ladled over strips of fresh rice noodles. Served with accompaniments such as bean sprouts, mint sprigs, chopped coriander, sliced red chilies, lime or lemon wedges and fish sauce.

phosphorus Essential mineral present in most foods, needed for bone tissue and teeth.

phylo / phyllo *see* FILO.

piballes | FRENCH | Tiny eels. *see* ELVERS.

piccalilli *see* MUSTARD PICKLES.

pickled mustard greens or cabbage | CHINESE | Several varieties of whole mustard greens are preserved in salt and pickled in different ways. They are sold in cans, sealed plastic packs or straight from large tins. They are usually washed, dried and chopped before use as a side dish, stir-fried or in soups or noodle dishes. Red-in-summer is a red-rooted variety preserved in salt. Used mostly as an accompaniment to pork or in soup. A Szechwan variety is preserved in salt and chili.

pickled pork Pork preserved in brine to which a little saltpetre may be added.

pickles Condiment of fruit or vegetables that is preserved in spiced vinegar.

pickling spice Mixture of a number of different spices such as mustard seeds, cinnamon sticks, cloves, whole peppers, fennel seeds or chilies, added in various proportions to the vinegar when making pickles.

picodon | FRENCH | Generic name for a small disc of goat's-milk cheese produced in several regions. Derived from the word 'pico' (to prick or sting), the cheese is traditionally pricked with holes and soaked in white wine or brandy and aged in earthenware jars and known as **Picodon de Dieulefit**. Unmarinated picodons have a soft, creamy interior and less pronounced flavor.

Picodon de Dieulefit *see* PICODON.

Picon | SPANISH | Also known as 'Picos de Europa'. Name-controlled blue vein cow's-milk cheese (sometimes a mix of cow's, goat's and sheep's milk) with moist, semifirm interior streaked with bluish-purple veining. Rich, intense flavor. Served as a snack or at the end of a meal.

Picos de Europa *see* PICON.

pigeon pea (*Cajanus cajan*) Also known as 'Angola pea'. Legume native to Asia and commonly grown in India; also Africa and the Caribbean regions. Yellow to dark red seeds are used fresh in soups or salads, or dried in purées and curry sauces.

pigfish (*Bodianus unimaculatus*) Also known as 'wrasse'. Highly sought after and expensive reef-dwelling fish. It has a reddish, elongated body with a pointed snout and firm, white flesh.

pike (*Esox* spp.) Family of freshwater fish with long bodies, large strong jaws and countless small, sharp teeth, found in lakes and rivers in North America, Canada and Europe. Because of their voracious nature, they are a popular sporting fish and have been given such names as 'water wolf' and 'freshwater shark'. Pike is mostly eaten in France. The firm, white meat is relatively dry and is often puréed with cream to make quenelles and mousses, or served with a rich sauce or beurre blanc.

pikelet | ENGLISH | Type of small, thick pancake made from batter and cooked on both sides on a hot plate or griddle.

pikey bream *see* BREAM.

pilaf / pilau | MIDDLE EASTERN / INDIAN | Rice fried in oil or ghee then cooked in seasoned stock by the absorption method. Meat, poultry, vegetables and nuts are sometimes added.

pilchard (*Sardinops neopilchardus*) Small, slender, silvery fish found in Australian waters south of the Tropic of Capricorn, similar to the sardine (*Sardina pilchardus*) of European waters. Fresh pilchards are sold whole and should be gutted and cleaned before cooking. Butterfly fillets are sometimes available. Their oily flesh is best when fried, grilled or barbecued.

pilsner / pilsener A pale gold lager beer. Originated in Pilsen, Bohemia in 1842.

pimento *see* ALLSPICE.

pimiento | SPANISH | (*Capsicum annuum*) Capsicum. Also refers to canned or bottled capsicums pickled in salt and vinegar, which may also be spelled 'pimento'.

pinch Very small measurement of salt, pepper or spice held between the thumb and index finger.

pine bolete *see* SLIPPERY JACK.

pine mushroom *see* SAFFRON MILK CAP *and* MATSUTAKE.

pine nuts (*Pinus* spp.) Small, oblong, creamy kernels from the cones of some species of pine trees. They are always sold shelled and because of their high fat content should be stored airtight in the refrigerator. They are sprinkled on salads, added to rice and pasta dishes, sauces and soups; also used in sweets and baked goods. In Italy they are used to make pesto sauce.

pineapple (*Ananas comosum*) This large, rough-textured fruit with a small tuft of prickly leaves will not ripen further once it is picked, although it may soften and change color. A ripe pineapple will be slightly soft to the touch and have a full rich aroma. The skin and core are removed before use. It is eaten as a fresh fruit, in fruit salads, crushed to make juice or sorbets or used in many baked goods such as tarts, puddings and cakes. Also used in savory sauces and stir-fries or grilled and served with meats such as ham. Fresh pineapple contains an enzyme which prevents gelatin from setting, however canned or cooked pineapple can be used successfully.

Pink Eye potato *see* POTATO.

Pink Fir Apple potato *see* POTATO.

pink gin | ENGLISH | Cocktail invented by the Royal Navy, consisting of straight gin stained pink with a few dashes of Angostura bitters. Served with plain iced water.

Pink Lady apple Small to medium apple with red and yellow skin with generous pinkish-red blushing. It has a juicy, sweet taste and is mostly eaten raw.

pink ling *see* LING.

pink peppercorns *see* PEPPERCORNS, PINK.

pinto beans (*Phaseolus vulgaris*) Dried pink beans with reddish-brown specks. After soaking overnight, they are simmered for up to 60 minutes. Used in stews, chili con carne and other meat and bean dishes such as refried beans.

pipe To decorate by forcing a soft mixture such as icing or whipped cream through the nozzle of a pastry tube or piping bag. Also method for forming certain pastries or biscuits.

pipe | ITALIAN | Short pasta shaped like a snail shell.

piperade | FRENCH | Dish of tomatoes and capsicums, and sometimes onions, cooked in olive oil then mixed with scrambled eggs.

pipis (*Donax deltoides*) Small, wedge-shaped bivalve molluscs found in the wet sand along coastal beaches. They are a popular fishing bait, and are sold in the shell at fishmarkets. Like clams, they need to be soaked in cold water prior to cooking in order to disgorge any sandy residue inside the shell. Pipis are quickly steamed like mussels until the shells open. Shelled cooked pipis are used in salads, soups, rice and pasta dishes.

pippin Large group of dessert apples, for example Cox's Orange Pippin.

piquant(e) | FRENCH | Sharp or spicy-tasting.

piquante sauce | FRENCH | Spicy sauce made with shallots, white wine, vinegar and demi-glace, flavored with finely chopped gherkins, capers, parsley and various other herbs. Served with slices of beef, lamb and pork.

piri piri | PORTUGUESE | Hot red sauce made with small red chilies chopped and soaked in olive oil.

piroshki | RUSSIAN | Small pastries with savory fillings served with soup or as a hot entrée.

pissaladière | FRENCH | Flat, open tart, like a pizza, topped with onions, anchovies, black olives and capers. Specialty of Nice.

pissenlit *see* DANDELION LEAVES.

pistachio nut (*Pistacia vera*) Small, pale green kernel within a thin, pale shell that is partially open when mature. They are sold both in their shell or shelled; raw, blanched, roasted and salted. Used extensively in savory dishes such as in stuffings, pâtés, terrines and sauces; also eaten as a snack, used in pastries, cakes, desserts, ice-cream and soufflés.

pistachio oil Delicious and extremely expensive nut oil, imported from France. High in mono-unsaturated fats. Used in vinaigrettes, marinades and to drizzle over cooked vegetables.

pisto | SPANISH | Vegetable stew of capsicums, tomatoes, zucchinis and onions cooked together in olive oil and served as an accompaniment to roast meat.

pistou | FRENCH | Paste made of fresh basil, garlic and olive oil. Used as a condiment and in a vegetable soup of the same name. Specialty of Provence.

pit To remove the seeds from olives or cherries or other stoned fruits.

pita | MIDDLE EASTERN | Also known as 'pocket bread'. Round or oval, flat bread that, when cooked, forms a hollow into which various savory fillings are placed to make a sandwich; also served plain, cut into wedges with meals or dips.

pith Soft, white layer next to the outer rind of citrus fruit. It is somewhat bitter and usually avoided when using the rind.

pithiviers | FRENCH | Classic, large puff-pastry tart filled with almond cream.

pizza | ITALIAN | Flat yeast dough topped with savory ingredients such as tomato sauce, eggplant, capsicum, salami, herbs, olives, anchovies and cheese, then baked.

pizzaiola sauce | ITALIAN | Neapolitan sauce, richly flavored with garlic and herbs.

plaice (*Pleurinectes platessa*) Flatfish with orange spots found in the North Sea, English Channel and Atlantic Ocean. The Australian greenback flounder can be used as a substitute.

planter's punch *see* PUNCH.

plat du jour | FRENCH | Today's special.

pleurotte *see* OYSTER MUSHROOMS.

plombières | FRENCH | Classic ice cream of sweet custard cream, almond flavored milk, whipped cream, crystallized fruit and flavored with a liqueur such as Kirsch.

plum (*Prunus domestica*) These are countless varieties of plums grown mostly for their sweet, juicy, stone fruit. Available mostly during summer. They vary from yellow to green, ruby red to deep purple or black, often with a powdery bloom on the skin. They are usually eaten raw with or without the skin; also stewed or poached or cooked in pies and puddings, and sweet or savory sauces. Plums make excellent jams, jellies and chutney. Prunes are dried whole plums. *see also* PRUNE.

plum pudding | ENGLISH | Traditional Christmas pudding made with a variety of dried fruits, almond, spices and rum. Served flamed with brandy or rum and accompanied by brandy butter.

plum tomato *see* TOMATO.

plump To soak dried fruit such as prunes and raisins in liquid until soft and swollen.

poach To cook in a liquid, such as water, stock, syrup, milk or wine, which should be kept just under boiling point.

poblano chili | MEXICAN | Dark green, elongated, bell-shaped chili. Usually mild to medium hot with a rich flavor. Often roasted, and frequently stuffed with other ingredients; also used in sauces and stews.

pochouse / pauchouse | FRENCH | Famous Burgundy fish stew made from a selection of freshwater fish from the region, such as perch, pike, eel or carp, cooked with white wine, garlic and seasoning and thickened with a flour and butter paste (beurre manié).

pocket bread *see* PITA.

pogne / pognon | FRENCH | Rich brioche flavored with orange-flower water and filled with mixed crystallized fruits. Served hot or cold, often with raspberry coulis.

poi | POLYNESIAN | Cooked taro root that is pounded to a paste, mixed with water and fermented for several days.

point (à) | FRENCH | Cooked medium rare. Done to a turn.

poire | FRENCH | Pear.

Poire Williams | SWISS | Clear fruit brandy often made from Williams pears. Sometimes sold with a whole pear inside the bottle.

poireau | FRENCH | Leek.

poisson | FRENCH | Fish.

poisson cru | FRENCH | Raw fish soaked in lemon or lime juice.

poissoniere | FRENCH | Fish kettle.

poivrade | FRENCH | Peppery sauce made from a browned mirepoix, vinegar and white wine blended with a brown sauce, flavored with crushed black peppercorns and strained before serving. Served with beef or game.

poivre | FRENCH | Pepper.

pojarski | RUSSIAN | Savory mixture of finely chopped veal, chicken or fish, shaped like a cutlet, coated in flour or breadcrumbs and fried.

polenta | ITALIAN | Type of grainy yellow cornmeal. It is slowly cooked in salted water or stock to a porridge-like consistency. Plain boiled polenta can be enriched with butter and cheese or cooled and cut into squares, then fried, grilled or baked. Often served as a first course; also as a side dish to a main course or made into biscuits, cakes and sweet fritters. Staple of northern Italy.

pollack (*Pollachius virens*) Large member of the cod family found in North Atlantic waters.

pollo | ITALIAN / SPANISH | Chicken.

polonaise (à la) | FRENCH | Cooked vegetables garnished with chopped, hard- boiled egg yolks, parsley and breadcrumbs fried in butter.

polpette | ITALIAN | Meatballs.

polyunsaturated fats Essential fatty acids found in high concentration in grains, legumes, seeds and fish. Two types occur; **omega-3** in fish and shellfish and **omega-6** in oils such as safflower, sunflower, cottonseed and soya bean. Margarines made from plants such as sunflowers are mostly polyunsaturated. *see also* OMEGA-3 *and* OMEGA-6 FATTY ACIDS.

pomegranate (*Punica granatum*) Round fruit with thick, reddish brown or bright red skin, topped with a persistent crown-like calyx. The edible parts are the numerous seeds and their fleshy, pinky red outer coat. The bitter-tasting white pith is not eaten. The seeds are used in fruit salads, jellies, sauces and meat dishes in the Middle East. Pomegranate juice is used in drinks, sweet and savoury sauces, soups and makes a good jelly. The juice is extracted by warming the whole fruit, rolling it between the hands, making a small hole in the base and then leaving to drain.

pomelo (*Citrus grandis*) Also known as 'shaddock'. The largest of the citrus fruits, the pomelo can be bigger than a grapefruit, but has a thick soft rind and is often not as juicy. It is native to South-East Asia and is widely grown in tropical regions. Varieties can be acid or fairly sweet and the firm flesh either light yellow or pink. They are used as a fresh fruit or in recipes suitable for grapefruit. The thick peel is suitable for marmalade.

pommes à la boulangère | FRENCH | Dish of sliced sautéed potatoes layered with onions and baked covered with stock.

pommes à la lyonnaise | FRENCH | Potatoes sautéed with onion.

pommes Anna | FRENCH | Translates to 'Anna potatoes'. Refers to a dish of thinly sliced potatoes arranged in layers and sprinkled with butter and seasoning. It is covered and baked in a hot oven for about 30 minutes, then turned over and browned on the other side.

pommes dauphine | FRENCH | Mashed potatoes mixed with choux pastry, shaped into small balls and fried.

pommes de terre | FRENCH | Potatoes.

pommes duchesse | FRENCH | Creamy mashed potato mixed with egg yolk and nutmeg; often piped into decorative shapes and used as a garnish.

pommes frites | FRENCH | French fries.

pommes soufflées | FRENCH | Thin slices of large potatoes that after deep-frying are fried a second time until they inflate and turn golden brown.

pomodori insalata | ITALIAN | Green tomatoes sliced and used in a salad.

pomodoro | ITALIAN | Plural is 'pomodori'. Tomato.

pompe aux grattons | FRENCH | Type of tart or brioche containing cubes of bacon or crackling.

Pont-l'Évêque | FRENCH | Name-controlled semisoft cow's-milk cheese with ivory interior with a few small holes, and smooth golden rind with criss-cross impressions. Pronounced rich flavour and aroma. Served at the end of a meal with a full-bodied red wine.

Pontiac potato *see* POTATO.

ponzu sauce | JAPANESE | Dipping sauce consisting of soy sauce, lemon juice, mirin and/or sake. Served with grilled seafood or meat.

popcorn (*Zea mays everta*) Dried corn kernels that, when cooked in hot oil, burst and puff up due to the expansion of the natural moisture inside the hull. Served as a snack, either salted, or sweetened with caramelised sugar.

pope's nose *see* PARSON'S NOSE.

popover | AMERICAN | Moist, puffy and somewhat hollow muffin-like bread made with eggs, butter, flour and milk.

poppadam *see* PAPPADAM.

poppy seed (*Papaver somniferum*) Small blue-grey seed obtained from the opium poppy, used mainly as a topping for breads and other baked goods; also added to Indian curry powders, cream cheeses, mixed with cooked noodles and vegetable dishes. Also the source of poppy seed oil, used in France as a salad and cooking oil. Narcotic properties are absent from the seeds.

porcini | ITALIAN | (*Boletus edulis*) Translates to 'little piglets'. Called 'ceps' in France. Highly prized in Italian cooking, there are a number of different varieties of these creamy brown mushrooms with rounded caps and bulbous stalks. Dried porcini have an excellent flavor and are available at specialty food shops. They are soaked in warm water for about 30 minutes before use. The strained soaking liquid can also be used in sauces, stocks and soups.

pork The flesh of pigs bred for their meat.

porridge Thick mixture of any kind of cereal (usually oatmeal) cooked with water or milk; usually eaten hot at breakfast with milk and sugar.

port Sweet fortified wine, named after Portuguese city of Oporto. There are three main types, vintage, tawny and ruby.

Port-Salut | FRENCH | Factory-produced semisoft, uncooked cow's-milk cheese with a smooth, creamy texture and washed orange rind. Flavor mildly monastery-type with a slight tang. Served as a snack and at the end of a meal.

porterhouse steak Choice cut of beef taken from the rump end of the sirloin.

portugaise (à la) | FRENCH | Portuguese style. Usually referring to a dish containing tomatoes.

posole / pozole | MEXICAN | Thick, chunky soup containing pork, hominy, chilies, garlic and coriander. Chopped chilies, radishes, lettuce and onions are served separately and added to the soup according to individual taste.

posset Hot beverage consisting of hot milk mixed with ale or wine flavored with honey and spices. It is sometimes thickened with beaten egg.

pot roast Inexpensive whole or large pieces of meat, poultry or game that have been firstly seared and browned on all sides in oil and/or fat. It is then cooked in the oven in a tightly covered pot, containing a small amount of stock or wine.

pot-au-feu | FRENCH | Traditional dish of beef simmered with vegetables. Often served in two courses, as a rich broth followed by the meat and vegetables.

pot de crème | FRENCH | Individual classic custard dessert, traditionally flavoured with vanilla; also sometimes with chocolate and coffee.

potage | FRENCH | Soup.

potassium The predominant mineral found in all body cells. Combined with sodium it helps to regulate the functioning of the body cells. Rich sources are vegetables, nuts, molasses, fruit and pulses.

potato (*Solanum tuberosum*) Potatoes originated in the northern parts of South America and were grown by the Incas before explorers introduced them to North America and carried them back to Europe in the 16th century. Many kinds of potato have been developed and each potato- growing country has its own regional varieties. Potatoes are a rich source of complex carbohydrates, fiber, vitamin C and various other vitamins and minerals. As many new and heritage varieties come onto the market, choosing potatoes becomes quite a challenge as different varieties have different qualities and cooking methods. **Bintje**, oblong with creamy white skin and waxy, yellow flesh; can be boiled, roasted, deep-fried and is good for salads. **Bison,** round with smooth, bright red skin and firm, white flesh; a general purpose potato for boiling and roasting and particularly good for mashing and for salads. **Colican**, round with very white, smooth skin and white flesh; general purpose potato for deep- frying, baking, boiling and steaming; good for chips but may break-up during boiling. **Desiree**, oval with smooth, pink skin and yellow, slightly waxy flesh; good general purpose potato when boiled, steamed or roasted; excellent in salads, but not good mashed. **Exton**, round with white skin and flesh is boiled, steamed and roasted; very good mashed. **Kennebec** is a common variety with white skin and flesh, usually sold unwashed; deep-fried, roasted, boiled and steamed; excellent for chips. **King Edward**, oval with pale, dappled skin and white flesh, often sold in bags; roasted, deep-fried, boiled; good for mashing. **Kipfler (Golden Crescent)**, elongated with pale yellow skin and waxy flesh; boiled, steamed and roasted; good in salads. **New potatoes** (chats) are small young potatoes of any variety, with very thin skin and sweet flesh. They are small enough to cook whole either boiled, steamed or roasted; excellent for salads. **Nicola**, oval with cream skin and yellow, waxy flesh are best boiled and steamed; good for mashing and in salads. **Patrones**, round with yellow skin and slightly waxy flesh are best boiled, steamed and sautéed; good in salads, hash browns, but not for mashing. **Pink Eye (Pink Gourmet** or **Pink Lady)**, round with creamy skin, pink eyes and yellow, waxy flesh with outstanding flavor; excellent boiled and steamed and good for salads, but not for mashing. **Pink Fir Apple**, elongated with creamy pink skin and firm, yellow flesh; boiled, steamed or baked; excellent for salads. **Pontiac**, round with red skin and firm, white flesh; a good general purpose potato when boiled, steamed, baked in jacket and roasted; good mashed and for salads. **Purple Congo**, elongated with purple skin and floury flesh is good deep-fried or boiled; makes purple mash. **Russet Burbank (Idaho)**, oblong with rough, creamy skin and pale yellow flesh is best deep-fried and roasted; excellent chips. **Sebago**, oval with creamy skin and white flesh, usually sold unwashed; general purpose, boiled, steamed, baked, roasted, fried; excellent mashed and good for salads. **Sequoia**, oval with pale skin and white flesh, usually sold unwashed; general purpose and best boiled and mashed. **Spunta**, large, elongated with pale yellow skin and yellow flesh; roasted, deep-fried and baked and good for chips. **Toolangi delight**, round with purple skin and white flesh with good flavour. Boiled baked and roasted and excellent for mashing and potato salads; also good for making potato gnocchi.

potée | FRENCH | Traditional country style soup/stew of mixed meat and vegetables, usually containing pork, cabbage and potatoes. Served as a single course.

potted shrimps | ENGLISH | Very small or finely chopped shrimps cooked in butter, flavored with mace, nutmeg, cayenne pepper and salt. The mixture is spooned into small individual pots and sealed by pouring a thin layer of clarified butter over the top and refrigerating.

Pouilly-Fuissé | FRENCH | White wine made from the Chardonnay grape. From the Mâconnais.

poulet | FRENCH | Chicken.

Pouligny-Saint-Pierre | FRENCH | Name-controlled goat's-milk cheese shaped like a truncated elongated pyramid. It has a smooth, ivory-white interior and mottled, bluish rind. Sometimes matured between plane leaves. Pronounced piquant taste. Served as a snack or at the end of a meal. Farm-produced and named after a village in the Loire valley.

poultry General term for a domestic bird used for food, which might include chicken, duck, turkey, goose, quail and guinea fowl.

pound cake Loaf-shaped cake made with equal weights of butter, sugar, eggs and flour, and a flavoring such as vanilla, orange or lemon.

pousse-café | FRENCH | (1) General term for after-dinner drink served with coffee. (2) An American invention consisting of a rainbow of different liqueurs carefully poured into a slender liqueur glass so that they sit on top of one another without running together.

poussin | FRENCH | Very young, small chicken. *see* SPATCHCOCK.

pozole *see* POSOLE.

Prague ham Ready-cooked, usually double-smoked, boneless ham molded into a cylindrical shape and sold sliced.

prairie oyster A pick-me-up and alleged hangover cure consisting of one raw egg yolk (left whole), a small amount of Worcestershire sauce, tomato sauce, a dash of vinegar and salt and pepper. Usually consumed in one gulp.

praline Crisp confection made of caramelized almonds. When ground, the powder is used as an ingredient in pastries and sweets, or as a topping for ice cream and desserts.

prawn crackers | CHINESE | Small, wafer-thin crisps (often in multiple colors) that when dropped in hot oil expand and puff up to more than double the size. Eaten as a snack or served as an accompaniment to a meal. Larger crackers, known as 'krupuk udang' are popular in Indonesia and Malaysia.

prawns Also known as shrimp, they considerably in size from the small succulent school prawn (*Metapenaeus* spp.) to the large king prawn (*Melicertus* spp.) which can grow to 30 cm in length. Other common varieties include the tiger prawn, the tropical banana prawn, the redspot king prawn and Endeavour prawn (also known as the 'greasyback prawn'). When raw the body color can vary, but all prawns become bright orange when cooked. They are sold raw or cooked and most often in their shells. Uncooked (or green) prawns are best to use for stir-frying, barbecuing and grilling either peeled or in their shells. Pre-cooked prawns are eaten straight from their shells, peeled and tossed in a salad or added in the final stages of cooking.

pré-salé | FRENCH | Mutton or lamb that has been raised on coastal salt meadows and gained a salty flavour.

preserved egg | CHINESE | Also known as 'hundred-year egg', 'ancient egg', 'century egg' and 'thousand-year egg'. Eggs that have been coated with a paste of ashes, lime and salt and buried for 100 days. They are sold individually in Asian grocers and are washed and peeled before use. Usually eaten uncooked, served with soy sauce or minced ginger and vinegar.

preserved lemons | NORTH AFRICAN | Lemons that have been cut into quarters (but still joined at the stalk end) and well salted on the inside. They are packed in a wide-necked jar and, if necessary, covered with extra lemon juice. They are ready in about a month. Used in Moroccan tagines, chicken dishes and salads. Limes can also be used in this way.

preserves Whole fruit or large pieces of one kind of fruit cooked in a sweet syrup until clear, but so that the shape is still definable.

pressure cooker An airtight metal pot that cooks food quickly by steaming under pressure at a very high temperature.

presunto | PORTUGUESE | Cured ham, similar to Spanish jamon.

pretzel | GERMAN | Glazed, crisp biscuit shaped in a loose knot, ring or stick, usually sprinkled with coarse salt. Served with beer or pre-dinner drinks.

prick To make small holes in the surface of food by piercing with a fork or the point of a knife.

prickly pear (*Opuntia* spp.) Also known as 'Indian fig'. This barrel-shaped cactus fruit varies from green, yellow, orange to purplish-red. The succulent, sweet flesh, which also varies in color, is scattered with a few edible black seeds. The fruit is covered with fine bristles which makes testing it for ripeness in fruit shops enough to ruin your day. Wear rubber gloves and use tongs to hold the fruit. Cut a slice from the top and bottom and slice downwards to remove the peel. The raw fruit is usually served chilled, sliced and sprinkled with a little sugar and lemon or lime juice; also used for fruit salads and preserves.

prik | THAI | Chili. **Nam prik** is a hot chili sauce that includes dried shrimp, paste, garlic, lime juice and various other flavorings. **Prik yuak is** capsicum.

primavera, alla | ITALIAN | Dish served or garnished with a variety of young spring vegetables.

primeur | FRENCH | Early spring vegetables and fruits.

printanière (à la) | FRENCH | Dish served or garnished with a variety of spring vegetables, usually tossed in butter.

prix fixe | FRENCH | Fixed price menu.

profiteroles | FRENCH | Small choux pastry puffs filled with either a sweet or savory mixture. Savory profiteroles are usually served as hors d'oeuvres. Sweet profiteroles are filled with pastry cream, whipped cream or ice cream. The classic croquembouche is made with glazed and custard-filled profiteroles piled into a tall tower.

proof Standard measure of strength of alcohol in distilled spirits or other liquor.

prosciutto | ITALIAN | Translates to 'ham'. Prosciutto crudo is lightly salted and air dried, the most famous being prosciutto di Parma (Parma ham) and the rarer more expensive cured ham, prosciutto San Daniele. Served in wafer thin slices as an antipasto. Prosciutto cotto is cooked and often flavored with herbs and spices; eaten in sandwiches and snacks, also as an antipasto.

proteins Naturally occurring amino acids in varying combinations found in all animals and plants. As well as providing energy for the body, they play a vital role in building and repairing tissues.

prove To allow dough to rise after a leavening agent has been added, usually covered with a cloth and left in a warm place.

provençale (à la) | FRENCH | In the style of Provence. Usually a dish which includes garlic, tomatoes and olive oil.

Provolone | ITALIAN | Name-controlled cow's-milk cheese with a firm, waxy texture made by the pasta filata method and molded by hand into various shapes (pear, melon, salami, balls, etc.). It is bound with rope and hung to dry and ripen for three to six months or more, depending on size. Provolone aged a year or more is referred to as 'Provolone piccante'. Served as a table cheese when young; grated like Parmesan when aged.

Provolone piccante *see* PROVOLONE.

prune (*Prunus domestica*) A whole dried plum. Several varieties are dried but one of the best, d'Agen, which has a very sweet, purple-skinned fruit, is grown, dried and widely available in Australia. Prunes can be plumped up by soaking in cold water, or gently stewed and served at breakfast or as a dessert. Also used in cakes, puddings and stuffings and cooked with pork and game.

pudding | ENGLISH | Sweet or savory dishes that are boiled, steamed or baked, usually in a pudding basin. Typical dishes include steak-and-kidney pudding, bread-and-butter pudding, summer pudding and traditional Christmas pudding.

puff pastry Short pastry dough that is rolled and folded six to eight times with butter placed between layers. The dough puffs up when baked forming many flaky layers. Examples include croissants, vol-au-vent, pies and palmiers.

puits d'amour Small sweet pastry, similar to a vol-au-vent (without the lid), filled with pastry cream or jam.

pulque | MEXICAN | Stimulating alcoholic drink made from the fermented sap of the maguey plant (*Maguey americana*).

pulses Also known as 'legumes'. Generic name for the dried edible seeds of several members of the pea family, such as peas, beans and lentils. Low in cholesterol and fat, they are an excellent source of protein and dietary fiber. Pulses are readily available, inexpensive and will keep well for at least a year. Most are soaked before cooking to clean, tenderize and reduce cooking time. Split peas and lentils generally do not require soaking prior to cooking.

Cooking time varies according to type and age of pulses. Salt is not added as this hardens and splits the skins.

pumpernickel | GERMAN | Dark, heavy-textured bread with a pronounced taste. Made with rye flour and often colored and flavored with molasses.

pumpkin (*Cucurbita maxima*) Also known as 'winter squash'. Pumpkins have a very hard smooth rind, covering a firm, orange or yellow flesh. They range in size from the small bush types, such as **Golden Nugget**, to the large, squat **Queensland Blue. Butternut** is a popular cylindrical variety with sweet orange flesh and easy to peel yellow skin. The **Jap** pumpkin, with dark green skin and yellow markings, has bright orange flesh of an excellent flavor and smooth texture. Pumpkins are a valuable source of vitamin A. They are usually peeled and cut into sections before use, although small Golden Nuggets can be halved or left whole. They can be boiled, baked, mashed and used in stews, soups, scones and jam. Pumpkin pie is a traditional Thanksgiving dish in America. Edible pumpkin seeds (pepitas), are available raw, salted and roasted. *see also* PEPITA.

punch | ENGLISH | Mixed hot or cold drink made according to various recipes, containing alcoholic or non-alcoholic liquids such as wine, rum, fruit juice and tea. They are usually made to serve a number of people. **Planter's punch**, the most famous, is made with rum, lemon or lime juice, grenadine and a dash of Angostura bitters, garnished with an orange slice and maraschino cherry.

punnet Small square container, without a lid, in which soft fruits such as strawberries and raspberries are sold.

puntalette | ITALIAN | Tiny, grain-shaped pasta usually used in soups.

purée | FRENCH | Any food, but usually fruit or vegetables that have been mashed, processed in a blender or passed through a fine sieve until smooth.

puri | INDIAN | Deep-fried round bread made with wholemeal flour and ghee; traditionally served at breakfast or with curries.

Purple Congo potato *see* POTATO.

purslane, summer (*Portulaca oleracea*) Also known as 'pussley'. Fleshy-leafed herb that originated in India and now grows wild throughout warmer parts of the world. It was a popular pickled vegetable in Europe during the 16th century. The slightly nutty-tasting leaves are used raw in salads, lightly cooked like spinach, and pickled in vinegar and salt and used as a garnish or to flavor sauces.

purslane, winter (*Montia perfoliata*) Also known as 'miner's lettuce'. Fast-growing annual herb with fleshy, rounded leaves used raw in winter and early spring salads or cooked briefly like spinach.

pussley *see* PURSLANE, SUMMER.

puttanesca sauce | ITALIAN | Pasta sauce made with olive oil, garlic, anchovies, tomatoes, pitted black olives and capers. Served with spaghetti or vermi- celli and garnished with chopped parsley.

Pyengana Cheddar | AUSTRALIAN | One of Australia's oldest farmhouse cheeses, dating back to 1901 and still made by hand using traditional methods. It is a cloth-bound, pressed cow's-milk cheese with a rich, well-developed flavour, aged from six to nine months or longer, depending on the size of the barrels.

quadrettini | ITALIAN | Small flat squares of pasta.

quail Very small migratory bird that is farmed in Australia and widely available in poultry shops. They are roasted whole, or cut in half and grilled or pan-fried; also braised and casseroled or used in pies and pâtés. The small and thin-shelled eggs are used in salads, aspic dishes and hors d'oeuvres.

quandong | AUSTRALIAN | (*Santalum acuminatum*) Small, glossy, red fruit with a leathery skin and rather dry pulp that has a tart, fruity flavour. Fresh fruit is sometimes available, but it is mostly sold dried or frozen. They are usually stewed and made into jams, chutneys and sauces for beef or game.

Quark | GERMAN | White, unripened cheese very similar to cottage cheese. It has a delicate flavour and is relatively low in fat. Used in both sweet and savoury dishes. It is best eaten as soon as possible after making.

quatre-épices | FRENCH | Blend of four ground spices, usually pepper, nutmeg, dried ginger and cloves. Used for seasoning charcuterie, soups, stews, cakes, pies, etc.

quatre-quarts | FRENCH | Pound cake made with equal weights of eggs, flour, butter and sugar.

Queensland nut *see* MACADAMIA NUT.

quenelle | FRENCH | Oval dumpling made of finely minced seasoned fish, meat or poultry, bound with eggs or panada, and gently poached in water or stock. Served with a béchamel sauce as an entrée, or part of a main meal.

quesadilla | MEXICAN | Small turnovers made by stuffing flat rounds of tortilla dough with a variety of savoury fillings. They are fried in hot oil and served as an appetiser or entrée.

queso | SPANISH | Cheese. Often followed by place-names to identify local variations in manufacture. Also used in Spanish-speaking Latin American countries.

queso fresco | MEXICAN | Fresh cow's-milk cheese with soft, white, slightly salty curds pressed in round moulds. Served crumbled or diced with tacos and enchiladas.

quiche | FRENCH | Savoury custard tart, with various fillings of vegetables, ham, fish, poultry or herbs. The original quiche lorraine contains bacon and double cream. Served as a light lunch or entrée.

quince (*Cydonia oblonga*) Irregular pear-shaped or oblong fruit with a yellow, downy skin and firm, golden yellow flesh with a bitter, acid flavour and a distinct pleasant aroma. Its high pectin content makes it particularly good for setting jams, jellies and preserves; also poached in syrup or cooked with apples and pears to enhance their flavour. When cooked the color changes to a deep pink and the bitterness softens. Quince paste is a popular accompaniment for cheese or a roast.

quinine tonic water Also known as 'Indian tonic water'. Soda water containing a tiny amount of quinine, the anti-malarial drug. First used in the British colonies, Africa and India during the 19th century, where it was enjoyed mixed with gin. Gin and tonic (G&T) is still a very popular long drink.

quinoa | SOUTH AMERICAN | (*Chenopodium quinoa*) Protein-rich grain native to the Andes and a staple crop of the ancient Incas. Still grown in parts of Peru and Bolivia and gaining popularity elsewhere because it contains all eight essential amino acids. Boiled and used like rice. Available from health-food shops.

rabbit (*Oryctolagus cuniculus*) The European rabbit is widely naturalised in Australia and is considered a pest. For various reasons wild rabbits are not freely available and it is usually farmed rabbits with a light flesh that are sold fresh, skinned and dressed, in some butchers and speciality shops. Young rabbits can be prepared in the same way as chicken such as roasted, grilled or sautéed. Both young, older and wild rabbits are suitable for wine stews, pâtés and pies.

rack of lamb Cut of lamb that contains several ribs. Usually grilled or roasted in a whole piece.

raclette | SWISS | Semifirm, pressed cow's-milk cheese with pale ivory interior and brushed, natural rind. It has a strong aroma that intensifies when heated. Also made in France. Traditionally used in a dish called raclette, a Swiss speciality of melted cheese, served with boiled potatoes and pickles.

radicchio | ITALIAN | (*Chichorium intybus*) Variety of red-leafed chicory in a round head with tightly packed leaves. The variety di Treviso has elongated, purplish-red leaves with pronounced cream veins. Both types have a slightly bitter, peppery taste and are used in mixed green salads. Radicchio is also grilled with olive oil, stuffed and baked, or added to pasta sauces and risotto.

radish (*Raphanus sativus*) Most often seen as small red or white bulbs sold in bunches; there are also oblong and elongated varieties and the giant white radish known as 'daikon'. All radishes are best when young, firm and crunchy. Used mostly raw as a salad ingredient or appetiser. Remove the stringy root. *see also* DAIKON.

ragi flour | INDIAN | Flour made from millet. Often mixed with atta to make flat, unleavened breads.

ragoût | FRENCH | Rich, thick stew made from meat, poultry or fish, sometimes with vegetables, and often flavoured with wine, herbs and seasoning.

ragu | ITALIAN | Rich meat pasta sauce originating in Bologna and known in English-speaking countries as 'Bolognese sauce'. It contains minced beef, tomatoes, onions, celery, carrots, garlic, red wine, milk and seasonings and is served mainly with tagliatelle or spaghetti, garnished with grated Parmesan cheese.

rainbow chard *see* RUBY CHARD.

rainbow trout *see* TROUT.

raisin Dried grape. Eaten as a snack or used in cakes, desserts, pastries and chutneys.

raita / rayta | INDIAN | Yoghurt-based, salad-like side dish served as a cooling accompaniment to curries. Yoghurt, herbs and spices are mixed with various raw or cooked ingredients such as cucumber, baked eggplant, cubed spicy potatoes, tomatoes or sliced banana and grated coconut.

raki | TURKISH | An aniseed liqueur drunk with ice and water.

rambutan (*Nephelium lappaceum*) Oval, red fruit, similar to and closely related to the lychee, but with a covering of soft spines. The firm, pearly-white, juicy flesh is easily extracted from the single seed. Rambutans are sweet enough to eat fresh, in fruit salads or served with cheese; also cooked in Asian dishes.

ramekin Small, straight sided, ovenproof dish used for individual soufflées, custards or sweet or savoury mousses.

ramen | JAPANESE | Round, pale brown noodles made from wheat flour and egg, in fresh, instant and dried forms. Served in a bowl of broth with small pieces of meat and vegetables, and flavoured with soy sauce.

rancid Term that often refers to stale fats that have a strong, unpleasant smell.

rapeseed oil Now marketed as 'canola'. Largely mono-unsaturated oil and known to lower cholesterol. Canola is a good, mild-tasting cooking and salad oil. *see also* CANOLA OIL.

rare Underdone cooked meat, particularly beef or steak. The inside of the meat is pink with a hint of blood, and the outside brown.

ras el-hanout | NORTH AFRICAN | Blend of powdered spices used mainly in Tunisia and Morocco which may include cloves, cinnamon, peppercorns, ginger or nutmeg. The Tunisian mixture is perfumed with dried rosebuds. Used to season stews or broths which accompany couscous.

rascasse | FRENCH | (*Scorpanenea* spp.) Red scorpion fish caught in Mediterranean waters and considered an essential ingredient in authentic bouillabaisse. The related red rockcod (*Scorpaena cardinalis*), caught in eastern Australian waters, can be used as a substitute.

rasher Strip or slice of bacon.

raspberry (*Rubus idaeus*) Deep red, scented berry with a sweet, distinct flavour. A golden variety (Fallgold) is sometimes available. Raspberries are eaten fresh with cream or added to fruit salads or compotes; also used for many different desserts such as bavarois, flans, pancakes, sorbets, and ice- cream, as well as purées, cordial, jams and jellies. Raspberries are among the best fruits to freeze.

raspings Breadcrumbs obtained from oven-dried bread.

rastegai | RUSSIAN | Small, oval, fish pie. Served as an appetiser.

ratafia (1) Homemade liqueur made by infusing fruit or nuts in brandy. **(2)** Biscuit made with bitter and sweet almonds.

ratatouille | FRENCH | Mixed vegetable stew consisting of eggplant, onions, capsicums, tomatoes, garlic and herbs, gently simmered in olive oil. Served hot or cold as a side dish.

ravigote | FRENCH | Highly seasoned mayonnaise, vinaigrette or butter, flavoured with finely chopped capers, onions and herbs such as tarragon, parsley, chervil and chives. Traditionally served with calf's head, also with poultry, seafood and salad.

ravioli | ITALIAN | Small squares of stuffed pasta, often with crinkly edges. Usually served with a creamy cheese or tomato sauce.

Reblochon | FRENCH | Name-controlled soft-pressed cow's-milk cheese with a fine-textured, ivory interior and washed, velvety rind, produced on farms and dairies in the Savoie region of France. Served as a snack and at the end of a meal.

reconstitute To add water to dehydrated or condensed food to return it to its original shape or consistency.

red caviar *see* CAVIAR.

red cooking | CHINESE | Method of slowly cooking foods, such as chicken, in a soy sauce, rice wine and spice mixture and sometimes water, which imparts a deep red color to the finished dish.

red curry paste | THAI | Rich curry paste used with beef, lobster and prawns. Made from shallots, garlic, coriander root and seeds, fresh galangal, lemon grass, black peppers, cumin seeds, nutmeg, dried red chilies, shrimp paste and grated zest of kaffir lime pounded together to form a smooth paste. Pre-made red curry paste is sold in tubs in Asian grocers.

red date (*Ziziphus jujuba*) Also known as 'jujube' and 'Chinese date'. Small, dried, reddish fruit with a wrinkled skin and subtle, sweet flavour. Used in Chinese cooking, they are soaked for one to two hours before being added to soups and stews.

Red Delicious apple Medium to large, deep red apple with a sweet, juicy flesh and highly aromatic flavour, popular throughout the world as an excellent eating apple. Not good for cooking. Keeps moderately well.

red dory *see* SILVER DORY.

red emperor (*Lutjanus sebae*) Large, red, reef fish found in northern Australian waters. It is sold whole or filleted, and its sweet firm white flesh is excel- lent eating. It can be poached, baked, grilled, barbecued or pan-fried.

red gurnard perch *see* OCEAN PERCH.

red kidney beans (*Phaseolus vulgaris*) Dried, dark red, kidney-shaped beans with cream flesh and strong flavour. After soaking overnight, they are simmered for up to 60 minutes. Used in soups and stews, chili con carne and other Mexican bean dishes.

red mullet (*Upeneichthys vlamingii*) Also known as 'barbournia' and 'goatfish'. Red mullet is a highly valued eating fish in Europe and is called 'rouget-barbet' in France, where its full-flavoured liver is reserved for sauces. The Australian species is a relatively small fish with a deep-reddish body and a pair of long chin barbels that resemble a goat's whiskers. Found in south- ern Australian waters at great depths. Whole fish are baked, pan-fried or grilled. Fillets can be stir-fried with Asian flavours.

red pepper *see* CAPSICUM.

red perilla *see* SHISO.

red rockcod *see* ROCKCOD, RED.

red-in-snow *see* PICKLED MUSTARD GREENS.

redcurrant (*Ribes sativum*) Small, round, red or white berry, according to variety. It has a translucent flesh and is closely related to the blackcurrant, but can be eaten as a fresh fruit; also stewed or made into jam, jelly or sauces.

redfin perch (*Perca fluviatilis*) Also known as 'English perch'. An introduced freshwater fish from Europe now widespread in southern waterways in Australia. Sold whole or in fillets. Its closely grained, white flesh is sweet and mild-tasting. Whole fish are baked or pan-fried. Fillets can be steamed or stir-fried with Asian flavours.

redfish (*Centroberyx affinis*) Also known as 'nannygai'. Small, bright orange- red fish with a large black eye, found in south-eastern Australian waters. Usually sold skinned and filleted. The delicate, pale pink flesh is best suited to frying in a batter or coating.

redfish, Bight (*Centroberyx gerrardi*) Also known as 'red snapper'. This close relative of the redfish (*C. affinis*), also known as 'nannygai', is found in the Great Australian Bight and off the south-western West Australian coast. It is a large fish with a distinctive white line along its salmon-colored body. Mostly sold as fillets; best pan-fried in a batter or coating, or used in fishcakes.

reduce To boil a liquid to lessen by volume and concentrate the flavour.

refresh To plunge partially cooked fruit and vegetables into cold water to prevent further cooking and to help retain color.

refried beans | MEXICAN | Frijoles refritos. Cooked dried beans that have been mashed to a thick, smooth paste then fried in lard or olive oil. Served with tortillas or as a filling.

Rehoboam Bottle of champagne equivalent to six standard bottles or 4.5 litres.

religieuse | FRENCH | Classic pastry consisting of one large chou puff filled with coffee or chocolate pastry cream, and a smaller chou (also filled) placed on top and coated with chocolate or coffee icing to resemble a nun in her habit.

relish Highly spiced condiment of vegetables or fruit; served with rice dishes, curries and cold meats.

rémoulade | FRENCH | Classic sauce of mayonnaise, capers, mustard, finely chopped herbs and gherkins, and sometimes anchovies. Served chilled as an accompaniment to cold meat and seafood; also mixed with shredded or grated celeriac and served as a salad.

rendang | INDONESIAN | Very hot, beef curry originating in Sumatra. The beef is cooked in spicy curry paste and thick coconut milk over a high heat. It is stirred constantly until the curry sauce is very dry, a film of red oil has formed and the meat has turned dark brown.

render To remove fat by gently heating.

rennet Extract from the inner lining of the stomach of calves and lambs. Contains the enzyme rennin, which is used to make junket and cheese. Sold in tablet form.

rétès | HUNGARIAN | Type of strudel with various fillings such as cream cheese, cooked cherries or plums, grated walnuts and apple.

retsina | GREEK | White or rosé wine strongly flavoured with pine resin. Served cold.

rhubarb (*Rheum rhaponticum*) The long, red, fleshy stalks of the rhubarb are really a vegetable, but are usually cooked as a fruit or with other fruits in various desserts, pies, tarts, puddings and jams. Only the stalks are edible; the leaves contain oxalic acid and are poisonous. The stalks are cut into short lengths and usually stewed with sugar until tender.

ribbon Culinary term that refers to a beaten eggwhites and sugar mixture that forms a thick trail of ribbon-like patterns when the whisk is lifted.

riberry | AUSTRALIAN | (*Syzygium leuhmanii*) Also known as 'lilly pilly'. Small, red, pear-shaped fruits obtained from a native rainforest tree. They have a pleasant spicy flavour and make a good wine sauce to serve with red meats; also used in pies, cakes, ice-creams, jams and to flavour vinegar.

riboflavin Known as vitamin B2. Forms part of several enzymes involved in energy metabolism and necessary for healthy skin, hair and eyes. Most important sources are milk, liver, eggs, pulses and cereal.

rice (*Oryza sativa*) Starchy cereal grain obtained from an annual grass. There are about 2500 different varieties of rice, most of which are grown in Asia, providing a staple food for about half the world's population. It is usually sold by weight and is classified by its length. **Short- or medium- grain rice** is usually cooked by boiling and tends to be softer and starchier than the long-grain variety, but firm and clingy enough to be picked up with chopsticks or moulded into Japanese sushi; also used for making puddings and sweet dishes. **Long-grain rice**, such as basmati, is slender, has narrow pointed ends, a firm structure, is relatively dry and separates easily. It can be cooked by boiling, steaming or the pilaf method. Used for salads and served plain as an accompaniment to curries and sauced dishes. Both short and long-grain rice are available as regular white rice which is the polished wholegrain milled to remove the bran and greatly diminished in nutrients. **White glutinous rice** is a high starch, stickier version of short-grain rice, also known as 'sticky rice'. Widely used in Asia for desserts, sweets and stuffing. **Brown rice** is a natural unpolished rice than has been hulled, but retains its nutritious bran layer. It takes longer to cook than white rice. **Converted** or **par-boiled rice** is processed before milling to retain most of the nutrients. It is a long-grain, pale brown rice and takes slightly longer to cook than white rice, but less time than other brown rice. *see also* ARBORIO, BASMATI, BLACK RICE, CALROSE RICE, JASMINE RICE, KOSHIKIKARI, SUSHI *and* WILD RICE.

rice bran Brown outer layer of the rice grain. High in dietary fibre. Used in cakes, biscuits and breads.

rice cake | JAPANESE | Known as 'mochi' in Japan. Round or square cake made from crushed, steamed glutinous rice. Popular as a snack either plain or grilled with a sprinkling of soy sauce. Also used in soup.

rice flour Flour made from finely ground white or brown rice. Used to make rice noodles in many Asian desserts and as a thickening agent. Ground rice is a coarser form of rice flour. Used to make milk desserts, in shortbread and as a thickener and binder for forcemeats. Glutinous rice flour is used in pastries, sweet dishes and to thicken sauces.

rice noodles | ASIAN | Also known as 'hor fun' (Chinese) and 'kueh teow' (Malaysian). Noodles made from rice flour and available fresh in white sheets which are cut into ribbons in various thicknesses. Dried rice stick noodles are flat and narrow with a translucent appearance. They have little flavour of their own, but readily absorb the flavour of other ingredients. Fresh rice noodles are soaked in hot water and served in a soup, sauce or stock. Dried rice noodles and sticks must be soaked or parboiled before use in soups or stir-fried dishes.

rice papers | VIETNAMESE | Paper-thin sheets of dough made from rice flour and then dried until stiff. Before use, dampen with warm water to make the rice paper pliable. Used mainly for wrapping spring rolls.

rice syrup | CHINESE | Sweet liquid obtained from rice. Used sparingly in the cooking of savoury dishes and as a sweetener for baked goods and desserts.

rice vermicelli | ASIAN | Thin, dried white noodles made from rice flour and water. Sold in bundles tied with twine. Can be parboiled, steamed, simmered and deep-fried. When deep-fried they instantly puff up and become crisp.

rice vinegar | ASIAN | Mild-tasting, slightly sweet vinegar made from fermented rice. Widely used in Japan, Korea and China. A clear, pale red rice vinegar is used in Chinese sweet-and-sour sauces, in shark's fin soup or as a dipping sauce or salad dressing. The aromatic and richly flavoured black rice vinegar is used for pickled eggs, braised dishes and as a condiment. A good variety is Chenkiang from China. The slightly sweeter and mild-tasting Japanese white rice vinegar is used to season sushi rice and salads.

rice wine | CHINESE | Sweet, amber wine made from fermented glutinous rice. Usually served warm and consumed with a meal. Also widely used in cooking, in marinades and sauces. For general cooking dry sherry can be used as a substitute. Sake is a quite different Japanese version of rice wine.

ricer Kitchen utensil used to make food the size and shape of rice by pushing it through tiny holes. Used mostly for boiled potatoes and other cooked root vegetables.

ricotta | ITALIAN | Fresh dairy product made from sheep's-milk whey, or cow's-milk whey or a mixture of whey and whole milk. It has a white, crumbly texture and a creamy, delicate taste. Used mainly in cooking in sauces for pasta, to stuff cannelloni and ravioli, in desserts such as cheese- cake, and as a pancake filling; also on canapés and in salads.

ricotta salata | ITALIAN | Also known as 'ricotta-pecorina'. Fresh dairy product made from the whey produced as a by-product in the making of pecorino. Used mostly in desserts and pasta dishes.

rigate | ITALIAN | Describes any pasta that has ridges or grooves. These help the sauce cling to the pasta.

rigatoni | ITALIAN | Short and wide, ridged tubes of pasta.

rijsttafel | DUTCH | Translates to 'rice table'. Elaborate version of an Indonesian meal consisting of steamed white rice and numerous small, spicy dishes of meat, fish, eggs and vegetables with accompanying sauces and condiments.

rillettes | FRENCH | Type of coarse, potted spread made mostly from cooked and pounded seasoned pork, but also duck, rabbit, goose or fish. Served cold as an appetiser with crusty bread or toast, or on canapés. If sealed with fat, it will keep refrigerated for several weeks.

rillons | FRENCH | Salted pork belly, cut into chunks and baked very slowly until brown and crispy. The rillons are then packed into pots in their own fat and left to set. Served hot or cold with a salad.

ripieni / ripieno | ITALIAN | Stuffing, or food that is filled or stuffed.

risoni | ITALIAN | Small pasta, shaped like rice grains. Used in soups.

risotto | ITALIAN | Creamy rice dish made by continually stirring arborio rice while gradually adding stock as it cooks, then mixing in other ingredients such as cheese, shellfish, sausage, vegetables, herbs and sometimes saffron.

risotto alla milanese | ITALIAN | Classic risotto cooked in chicken stock and flavoured with grated Parmesan cheese and saffron. Traditionally served with osso buco.

rissole (1) Flattened, seasoned meatballs that are usually fried. **(2)** Turnover-like pastries with a sweet or savoury filling, usually deep-fried.

ristra | SPANISH | Decorative rope or wreath of dried food; usually made with chilies or heads of garlic.

roast (1) To cook a large piece of meat either on a spit over direct heat, or in an oven. **(2)** Also the name for the meal where roast meat is served.

Robert sauce | FRENCH | Brown sauce of white wine and demi-glace, flavoured with finely chopped and browned onion and mustard. Served with grilled pork and other meats.

Robiola di Roccaverano | ITALIAN | Name-controlled unripened goat's-milk (or combination of milks) cheese with a pure white, creamy texture.

Robiola Lombardia | ITALIAN | Semisoft cow's-milk cheese with ivory interior and brownish washed rind. Strong nutty flavour with slightly salty taste. Served at the end of a meal with a full-bodied wine.

Robiola Osella | ITALIAN | Brand name of a very good, factory-produced Robiola Piemonte.

Robiola Piemonte | ITALIAN | Generic name for a group of fresh cow's, sheep's or goat's-milk cheese (or a mixture of all three), usually with cream added. They have a white, creamy texture and sweet, mildly tangy flavour. Served at breakfast or lunch with fruit and pastries. *see also* MURAZZANO.

rocambole (*Allium scordoprasum*) Also known as 'Spanish garlic', 'giant garlic' or 'sand leek'. Mild-tasting type of garlic with large red bulbs and mauve flowers that also develop small edible bulblets. Used in place of onions and shallots.

rock cake | ENGLISH | Small, dome-shaped dry cake filled with a sprinkling of chopped dried fruit.

rock lobster *see* LOBSTER.

rock salt *see* SALT.

rockcod, red (*Scorpaena cardinalis*) This small to medium sized saltwater fish caught in south-eastern Australian waters has a dark reddish body with marbled patterns. It has a firm, white flesh and faint fatty flavour. It is steamed, grilled, baked or barbecued; also used in soups and fish stews. Can be used as a substitute for the scorpion fish (rascasse), a traditional ingredient in bouillabaisse.

rocket (*Eruca sativa*) Also known as 'arugula' and 'roquette'. Peppery- flavoured, young lobed leaves of a Mediterranean annual herb used in mixed green salads and included in the Provençal mixture known as 'mesclun'.

rockmelon (*Cucumin melo* var. *reticulatus*) Also known as 'cantaloupe' and forms part of the muskmelon group. Medium-sized, round melon with a netted patterned skin. When ripe it has a pale orange, highly scented, juicy flesh. It is halved and seeded before eating on its own or as a dessert fruit. As an antipasto it is served sliced with wafer-thin prosciutto or other cured meat. Also used in fruit salads and with seafood salads. *see also* MELONS.

rocky road Slab of chunky confection consisting of marshmallows, nuts and chocolate.

roe Eggs of fish and shellfish. Hard roe is female fish eggs, the preferred roe for culinary purposes. Soft roe is the sperm, or milt, of a male fish. *see also* CAVIAR, CORAL, FLYING FISH ROE, MILT, MULLET, SEA URCHIN ROE *and* TARAMASALATA.

roghan josh / rogan gosh | INDIAN | A rich Kashmiri speciality dish of lamb cooked in ghee with pounded aromatic spices and finely chopped ginger, coriander leaves and chilies. Ready-made roghan josh paste is sold in gourmet shops.

rohschinken | GERMAN | Cured, uncooked ham, similar to prosciutto.

rolled oats *see* OATs.

rollmop Herring fillet that is wrapped around a piece of pickled gherkin or onion and cured in spiced vinegar.

Rollot | FRENCH | Spicy, soft cow's-milk cheese with pale yellow, spreadable interior and washed ochre rind, in small rounds or heart shapes. Highly flavoured and usually served at the end of a meal.

romaine lettuce *see* COS LETTUCE.

Romandur | GERMAN | Also known as 'Romandurkase'. Soft, cow's-milk cheese with smooth, pale yellow interior with a few small holes and a thin, brownish, edible rind. Similar to Limburger, but cured for less time and contains less salt. Mild to strong flavour. Served as a snack with strongly flavoured breads and beer.

Romandurkase *see* ROMANDUR.

Romanoff / Romanov Fruit, often strawberries, soaked in Curaçao and topped with whipped cream.

romesco sauce | SPANISH | Classic sauce from Catalonia in Spain made with cooked tomatoes, roasted red capsicum, red chilies, garlic, almonds, lemon juice (or wine vinegar), olive oil and seasoning. Served with pan-fried, grilled or baked fish or shellfish.

Roncal | SPANISH | Name-controlled pressed sheep's-milk cheese with firm, pale yellow interior and natural, greyish rind. Rich nutty flavour. Served as a table cheese as a snack; also good for grating.

rondels Round slices.

Rondolet *see* KERVELLA CHEESE.

Roquefort | FRENCH | Name-controlled blue vein sheep's-milk cheese with smooth, ivory interior with green-blue veining and thin, natural rind. Strong, spicy flavour and aroma. Served at the end of a meal with full-bodied red wine or port; also used in salad dressings and on canapés. The cheese is exposed to a special mould, *Penicillium roqueforti*, and aged naturally in the limestone caves in the mountains of Cambelou, near the town of Roquefort-sur-Soulzon in France, where the humid currents of air encourage the development of the blue veins.

roquette *see* ROCKET.

rose buds | NORTH AFRICAN | (*Rosa* spp.) Dried rose buds are ground and used as a spice either alone or combined with other spices such as in the Tunisian mixture, ras el-hanout.

rose hips (*Rosa rugosa*) Red, berry-like fruit from the wild dog rose, especially rich in vitamin C. The green stems, seeds and whiskers are first removed. Used in teas, syrup and jams; also steeped in wine for use in game or meat sauces.

rose petal butter Rose petals are layered with fine salt in a crock, covered and allowed to mature. When required, the butter is wrapped in waxed paper and placed in the crock overnight to absorb rose flavour. Used in baked goods, rose petal sandwiches and in cooking carrots.

rose petal honey Equal quantities of clear honey and red rose petals are gently heated for 10 minutes in a double boiler, then strained. Used as a sweet- ener for herbal teas and yoghurt, toast and fresh, crusty bread.

rose petal jam Red rose petals simmered with sugar, a little water and lemon juice until just tender. Popular in the Middle East; served with coffee, small pastries or with thick cream.

rose petal sugar Dried rose petals are mixed with sugar and stored in an airtight container for a couple of weeks, and sifted before use. Used in icings, icecream, puddings and baklava.

rose petal syrup Equal quantities of fragrant red rose petals, sugar and water boiled for about 15 minutes, or until syrupy. Used on ice-cream, pancakes and puddings.

rose petals (*Rosa* spp.) Historically valued for jam, vinegar, tart fillings, confectionery and as a garnish, rose petals are used in many sweet dishes, particularly in the Middle East and France. Heavily scented, dark red roses work best, with the bitter white heel removed.

rose petals, crystallised Rose petals brushed with eggwhite and lightly coated with castor sugar, then placed on a wire rack in an open-door, barely warm oven until dry. Store between tissue paper in an airtight container. Used to decorate cakes, ice-creams, fruit salads and various desserts.

rosewater Natural flavouring made from the diluted essence of distilled rose petals. Used to flavour Indian and Middle Eastern confectionery such as Turkish delight. Also used in drinks, jellies, puddings, as well as some savoury dishes.

rosella (*Hibiscus sabdariffa*) Bright red fruit of a hibiscus plant. They are usually stewed with sugar and used for pies and pastries, for flavouring ice-cream, or in savoury sauces; also in jams and other preserves.

rosemary (*Rosmarinus officinalis*) Slightly bitter, linear leaves from small, shrubby perennial native to the Mediterranean region. Used fresh or dried, in moderation, to flavour meat, chicken, fish and various vegetable dishes. Sprigs removed before food is served. Seldom used in salads, but good for flavouring oil and vinegar.

Rossini Dishes that include fois gras, truffles and a demi-glace sauce, often flavoured with Madeira. Named after Italian operatic composer Gioacchino Rossini. The best-known dish is tournedos Rossini.

rösti | SWISS | Large potato cake made from partly cooked, coarsely grated pota- toes fried in butter on both sides until golden. Served hot, cut into wedges.

rotelle | ITALIAN | Small, round pasta shaped like a wheel. Rotelline are tiny wheels.

roti | INDIAN | Bread. *see also* CHAPATI, NAAN, PARATHA *and* PURI.

Rôti | FRENCH | Roast.

Rouge d'Anjou pear Small, crimson pear with a sweet, firm flesh. Available mostly in winter. Good eating or cooking pear.

rouget-barbet *see* RED MULLET.

rouille | FRENCH | Fiery, red mayonnaise-like sauce made by pounding together garlic, chilies and breadcrumbs, then blending with olive oil and a little fish stock. Usually served with fish dishes and soups such as bouil-labaisse. Speciality of Provence.

roulade | FRENCH | Thin slices of meat or fish rolled around a stuffing and tied. It is then baked or poached.

roux | FRENCH | Mixture of equal parts butter and flour cooked together and used as a basis of many sauces. A brown or long-cooked roux, usually made with lard, is an important ingredient in many Cajun dishes. Used as a thickener and flavouring agent.

royal icing Type of firm icing made from eggwhites and icing sugar. Often used to cover and decorate wedding cakes.

Royal Victorian Blue *see* TARAGO RIVER CHEESE COMPANY.

royale | FRENCH | Moulded savoury custard that, after cooking, is cut into small, decorative shapes and used as a garnish for consommés.

royale (à la) | FRENCH | Classic preparation, usually with truffles and a cream sauce.

ruby chard (*Beta vulgaris*) Also known as 'rainbow chard'. Variety of silverbeet with a bright red stalk and colored leaf veins. Prepared and used in the same way as silverbeet.

rujak / rudjak | INDONESIAN | Spicy fruit salad with a savoury dressing of chilies, shrimp paste, palm sugar, fish sauce and lemon juice.

rum baba *see* BABA.

rump steak Choice cut of beef taken from over the hip bone. It can be fried, grilled and barbecued; large pieces can be roasted.

rusk Crispy dry bread made by baking bread slices a second time until golden brown.

Russet Burbank potato *see* POTATO.

Russian salad | FRENCH | Cold mixed salad of cooked peas and diced potatoes, carrots and turnips tossed in mayonnaise.

Russian tarragon (*Artemisia dracunuloides*) *see* TARRAGON.

rutabaga *see* SWEDE.

rye (*Secale cereale*) Hard cereal grain used in making flour. Contains less gluten than wheat and produces a very heavy dark bread such as pum- pernickel. Usually blended with wheat flour to make a lighter ryebread and crispbread.

Saanen | SWISS | Very hard pressed cow's-milk cheese with granular, dark yellow interior with a few or no holes and a slightly rough, brownish rind. Strong Gruyère-like flavour. Long shelf life. Used as a grating cheese as a milder form of Parmesan; also shaved into thin slices as a snack or salad cheese.

sabayon *see* ZABAGLIONE.

sablé | FRENCH | Thin, short-bread biscuit, sometimes flavoured with cinnamon, ground almonds or citrus zest, cut with a pastry cutter or rolled into sausage shapes and sliced before baking.

Sabra Chocolate-orange liqueur made in Israel.

saccharin White crystalline powder or liquid used as an artificial sweetener; said to have a sweetening power 300 times stronger than sugar. Widely used in commercial foods, especially dietary products.

saccharometer Instrument for measuring the density of sugar in water.

Sachertorte | AUSTRIAN | Classic, rich chocolate cake with layers spread with apricot jam and coated with chocolate icing. Traditionally served with whipped cream.

saddle Tender cut of meat including two loins attached at the backbone. Usually roasted whole.

safflower oil Neutral-tasting, polyunsaturated vegetable oil used for cooking at high temperatures and as a salad dressing; also used in margarine.

saffron (*Crocus sativus*) Pungent, aromatic spice obtained from the orange, thread-like stigmas of the purple crocus flower. The hand-harvested stigmas are dried and used to flavour and color foods and as a dye. The best saffron comes from Spain. It is an expensive spice, but only a small amount is used at a time. Saffron threads are usually infused in hot liquid or crushed before use. Used in many Mediterranean and Oriental dishes, particularly rice and fish. It is an important ingredient in the saffron cakes of Cornwall, the French fish soup bouillabaisse, the Spanish paella and the Italian risotto milanese; it also enhances some sauces, milk puddings, breads and cakes.

saffron milk cap (*Lactarius deliciosus*) Also known as 'milky saffron'. Flat or funnel-shaped mushroom with an orange cap with darker concentric markings. Grows wild under pine trees and is occasionally available fresh. The flesh is hard and brittle with a mild tase. Needs to be well washed and grilled or cooked quickly. Sometimes called 'pine mushroom', but this name is more correctly applied to the Japanese matsutake.

sage (*Salvia officinalis*) Aromatic, grey-green leaves from perennial herb native to the Mediterranean region. Used to counteract the richness of fatty meats such as pork, goose and duck; also in sage and onion stuffing, to flavour sauces and some charcuterie. Italians use fresh sage with calf's liver, saltimbocca, osso buco and minestrone.

Sage Derby *see* DERBY.

sago (*Metroxylon sagu*) Starchy pith obtained from the inner trunk of various palm trees that is processed into a type of flour or granules of pearl sago. Used for baking, thickening soups and in puddings.

Saint-André | FRENCH | Brand of triple cream cheese.

Saint-Germain | FRENCH | Dish containing, or served with, fresh green peas.

Saint-Honoré, gâteau | FRENCH | Named after the patron saint of pastry cooks. Classic Parisian cake of choux puffs dipped in caramel and set in a ring upon a choux pastry base. The centre of the ring is filled with a firm pastry cream, stiffened with eggwhites, sprinkled with sugar and caramelised under a grill.

Saint-Marcellin | FRENCH | Soft cow's-milk cheese (once made of goat's milk) with creamy white interior and beige rind with blue mould. Sold as small discs often wrapped in chestnut leaves, dipped in wine or marc, and tied with raffia. Tangy, creamy flavour. Served as a table cheese.

Saint-Nectaire | FRENCH | Name-controlled semisoft, pressed cow's-milk cheese with pale yellow interior and reddish, natural rind. Mellow, earthy flavour and aroma. Served at the end of a meal.

Saint-Paulin | FRENCH | Soft, pressed cow's-milk cheese with a light yellow, springy interior and washed, smooth orange rind. Flavour and aroma mild, monastery-type. Served at the end of a meal.

Saint-Saviol | FRENCH | Mass-produced, soft goat's-milk cheese with creamy, spreadable interior and white, velvety rind with pinkish-brown pigmentation. Sharp flavour and intense goaty aroma. Served at the end of a meal.

Sainte-Maure de Touraine | FRENCH | Name-controlled goat's-milk cheese with moist, soft to firm, white to ivory interior and thin, bluish rind. Traditionally a piece of straw is inserted through the centre of the cheese. Strong flavour and pronounced goaty aroma. Served at the end of a meal.

saishimomi shoyu *see* SHOYU.

sake | JAPANESE | Clear alcoholic drink made from fermented rice. Served warm in small tumblers before a meal or during a meal. Also used extensively in Japanese cooking.

salad Combination of raw or cooked foods, usually with a savoury dressing. Most salads are served cold as an appetiser, entrée, between courses, as an accompaniment to a main meal or as a light meal in itself. *see also* AEMONA, CAESAR SALAD, CEVICHE, GADO-GADO, INSALATA, LARB, MESCLUN, MISTICANZA, RUSSIAN SALAD, SALADE DE CRUDITÉS, SALADE NIÇOISE, SALADE/SALADIER LYONNAIS, SALMAGUNDI, SUNOMONO *and* TABOULLEH.

salad burnett *see* BURNETT.

salade de crudités | FRENCH | Raw vegetable salad.

salade niçoise | FRENCH | Salad with many variations, such as tomatoes, green beans, anchovies, tuna, potatoes, black olives, hard-boiled eggs and capers.

salade / saladier lyonnais | FRENCH | Salad of diced sautéed chicken livers, sheep's trotters, hard-boiled eggs and herring, dressed in mustard vinaigrette.

salam leaf *see* DAUN SALAM.

salamander (1) Type of oven used in professional kitchens to quickly brown or glaze the tops of savoury or sweet dishes. **(2)** Long, rod-like instrument that is heated over a flame, then held over food such as créme brûlée, to quickly caramelise the surface layer of sugar.

salame di Fabriano *see* FABRIANO SALAMI.

salame di Felion *see* FELINO SALAMI.

salame fiorentina *see* FIORENTINA SALAMI.

salame genovese *see* GENOA SALAMI.

salame milanese *see* MILANO SALAMI.

salame napoletano *see* NAPOLETANO SALAMI.

salame sardo *see* SARDO SALAMI.

salami | ITALIAN | Generic name given to a number of highly seasoned cured sausages of different sizes that are ready to eat without any preparation other than slicing. Salami is usually composed of finely minced lean pork or a mixture of meats, pieces of fat and various seasonings. The texture and flavour varies according to the way the meat is minced, the proportion of fat, the seasoning, salting and period of drying. Salamis are generally dried by air-drying rather than smoking. Although originating in Italy, salami is also made throughout Europe, Denmark and other countries, including Australia. *see individual entries.*

salchichon | SPANISH | Type of salami made from finely chopped pork and fat, seasoned with whole white peppercorns. Sliced thinly and eaten as a tapas.

salicorne (*Salicornia europaea*) Also known as 'glasswort' or 'marsh samphire'. Marine plant common in salty marshes by the sea throughout Europe, where it is harvested in summer and cooked and eaten with melted butter like asparagus. It is also pickled in vinegar and is available in gourmet speciality shops. Used as a condiment with cold meats and fish.

Sally Lunn | ENGLISH | Light yeast cake of flour, eggs and cream, that is split in half while still warm and served with whipped cream. Reputed to have been made by a young pastrycook named Sally Lunn in Bath in the 18th century.

salmagundi | FRENCH | Elaborate mixed salad of various ingredients such as chopped or finely sliced cooked meats, fish, vegetables, anchovies, hard-boiled eggs and pickles decoratively arranged on a flat platter and sprinkled with a dressing.

Salmanazar Large bottle of champagne equivalent to 12 standard bottles or 9 litres.

salmis | FRENCH | Classic stew of game birds and mushrooms served with a sauce made from the pressed carcass and wine.

salmon *see* ATLANTIC SALMON.

salmonella Strain of bacteria which can cause food poisoning. Found in contaminated water, raw meat and poultry, cracked egg shells and on chopping boards.

salpicon | FRENCH | Various ingredients that are finely diced and bound with a sauce. Used for filling small pastry cases such as vol-au-vent and bouchées; also to make croquettes and rissoles or for stuffing.

salsa Translates to 'sauce' in both Italian and Spanish; also a term commonly used for Mexican sauces.

salsa agrodolce | ITALIAN | Sweet-and-sour sauce used to accompany various meat dishes.

salsa di pomodori | ITALIAN | Cooked tomato sauce.

salsa di pomodori crudo | ITALIAN | Fresh, uncooked sauce made with chopped, skinned and seeded tomatoes, finely chopped onion, olive oil, garlic and basil.

salsa verde Translates to 'green sauce' in both Italian and Spanish. The Italian version is a type of vinaigrette made with oil, lemon juice, finely chopped parsley, capers, garlic (sometimes anchovies) and seasoning. Used as condiment for meat and fish. The Spanish green sauce is made with chopped parsley, celery, garlic, bread, vinegar, olive oil and seasoning. Used as dressing for cold cooked vegetables and seafood. A basic Mexican green sauce used as a dip contains finely chopped tomatillos, onion, hot green chilies, garlic and coriander.

salsify (*Tragopogon porrifolius*) Also known as 'oyster plant'. Long, white root vegetable with a delicate taste of fresh oysters. Salsify needs to be well washed and peeled before cutting into slices and should be dropped into acidulated water to prevent browning. It has a soft, creamy texture when cooked; usually boiled or steamed and served as a vegetable; also grated and used raw in salads. **Black salsify** (*Scorzonera hispanica*), also known as 'scorzonera' is a close relative with black skin. It is used in much the same way.

salt White, odorless condiment made up of sodium chloride, used throughout the world as a food seasoning and preservative. Since ancient times salt has been produced in much the same way as it is today, either extracted from sea water or harvested from dried salt lakes. **Table salt** is refined salt with added magnesium carbonate to make it flow smoothly. **Sea salt** is the result of evaporation and is available in fine grains or large crystals. **Iodised salt** is a table salt with added iodine. **Kosher salt** is additive free and has coarse crystals. **Rock salt** refers to its larger crystals rather than where it comes from and as it is not as refined as other salts, it usually retains more valuable minerals and less impurities. Used for cooking or ground in a salt mill. **Seasoned salt** is table salt with ground herbs or spices such as celery salt and garlic salt. *see also* BLACK SALT, CELTIC SEA SALT, FLEUR DE SEL, MALDON SEA SALT *and* SICILIAN SEA SALT.

saltimbocca | ITALIAN | Classic dish of thin slices of veal topped with prosciutto and sage, either left flat or rolled up and cooked gently in white wine.

saltpetre (*Potassium nitrate*) Small white crystals used to preserve foods and add pink coloring, especially to meats such as ham, beef and tongue.

sambal | INDONESIAN / MALAYSIAN | Small, strong side dish or condiment served with rice and curry dishes.

sambal bajak / badjak | INDONESIAN | Blend of chilies, sugar and spices such as garlic, kaffir lime leaves, galangal and tamarind, used as an accompaniment to rice and curry dishes.

sambal oelek | INDONESIAN | Very hot seasoning made from ground red chilies and soy sauce.

sambuca | ITALIAN | Strong, aniseed-tasting liqueur distilled from witch elder, often served ignited with a coffee bean or two floating on top.

samosa | INDIAN | Small pastry turnovers filled with a spicy mixture of vegetables or meat and deep-fried. Served as a snack or appetizer.

samovar | RUSSIAN | Large, pot-bellied vessel, heated by a small spirit lamp, that provides boiling water for brewing tea.

Samsoe | DANISH | Mild-tasting, firm cow's-milk cheese with smooth, yellow interior with a few round holes and a washed, golden-yellow rind, sometimes wax-covered. Served as a table cheese with fruit and nuts.

San Daniele ham *see* PROSCIUTTO.

San Simon | SPANISH | Tangy, pressed cow's-milk cheese with semifirm, white interior and dark brown, natural rind, molded into torpedo shapes and smoked over hardwood. Served as a snack and appetizer.

sand crab *see* BLUE SWIMMER CRAB.

sand leek *see* ROCAMBOLE.

sandwich | ENGLISH | Two slices of loaf bread enclosing a savory filling. Named after John Montague, fourth Earl of Sandwich, who ordered this simple meal so as not to take a break from gambling tables for food. An open sandwich consists of one slice of bread with a topping. *see also* BOOK-MAKER SANDWICH *and* CLUB SANDWICH.

sangria | SPANISH | Chilled long drink made with red wine, fruit juices, soda or mineral water and pieces of fruit; sometimes a spirit or liqueur is added. Sangria blanco is made with white wine.

sangrita | MEXICAN | Non-alcoholic mixture of chilled tomato juice, orange juice and lime juice, seasoned with finely chopped onions and chilies or Tabasco sauce. Served in a tumbler and drunk with tequila served separately in a shot glass.

sansho | JAPANESE | (*Zanthoxylum piperitum*) Also known as 'Japanese pepper'. Ground peppery spice made from the dried seed pods of the prickly ash. Used as a seasoning, particularly with grilled eel and chicken to counteract fatty tastes and in red miso soup. It is one of the components of the seven-spice powder mixture.

sapodilla (*Manilkara zapota*) Oval fruit with a green skin that turns brown as it ripens. The sweet yellowish, translucent flesh must be soft and fully ripe before eating, otherwise the tannin content will set the mouth on edge. Peel and remove the seeds before adding to fruit salads or mashing as a pancake filling. The milky latex extracted from the trunk of the sapodilla tree has been used as a basis for chewing gum.

sapote (*Diospyros digyna*) Also known as 'black sapote' and 'chocolate pudding fruit'. Rounded, tomato-shaped tropical fruit with a green skin that turns dark green or brown when fully ripe. The sweet, pulpy flesh varies from red to dark brown. High in vitamin C, it can be eaten from the skin with a spoon, or puréed for sauces, mousses or ice creams.

Sapsago | SWISS | Low fat, skimmed cow's-milk cheese containing less than 10 per cent fat. It has a very hard, pale green interior and light green, rind- less exterior and is shaped into a small, flat-topped cone. Flavored with fenugreek and a local wild clover which give it an unusual taste and color. Used mostly as a grating cheese.

Saratoga chips | AMERICAN | Commercially made potato crisps.

sardine Small, slender, silvery fish belonging to the herring family. This is the fresh or canned sardine of European waters. The closely related Australian pilchard (*Sardinops neopilchardus*) is available fresh in fish markets. In Spain, Portugal and Provence a cold dish called 'escabèche' is made with fried sardines that are covered in a spicy, vinegar marinade for at least 24 hours. *see also* PILCHARD.

Sardo | SARDINIA | Also known as 'Fiore Sardo' and 'Pecorino Sardo'. Firm sheep's-milk cheese with a buff, natural rind that is frequently rubbed with oil. Used as a table cheese or, when aged, for grating like Parmesan.

sardo salami | ITALIAN | Also known as 'Salame sardo'. Hot, salty salami made with pork and red pepper. Made in Sardinia.

sashimi | JAPANESE | Dish of very fresh, raw fish or seafood, such as tuna, snapper or squid, sliced paper-thin and arranged attractively on a plate, garnished with shredded daikon and slices of pickled ginger. Served with a dipping sauce and wasabi.

satay | INDONESIAN / MALAYSIAN | Small pieces of meat, fish or poultry threaded on thin skewers and grilled or barbecued. Served with a spicy peanut sauce known as 'satay sauce'.

saturated fat Type of fat where the fatty acids hold their full complement of hydrogen molecules and is usually solid enough to hold its shape at room temperature. Found mostly in meats, dairy products and eggs. Some vegetable fats, such as coconut oil and palm oil, widely used in commercial food processing, are also high in saturated fats. Saturated fats raise blood cholesterol levels, which can be a contributing factor in heart disease.

sauce Seasoned liquid prepared to complement and enhance the taste of food it accompanies. The many different types of sauces range from a simple serving of unthickened pan juices (jus) to countless elaborate French classics derived from concentrated, slowly cooked stocks that might take days to prepare. It was the 19th-century French chef Antonin Carême who devised a system of classifying sauces under one of six groups known as 'mother sauces'. The mother sauces are again placed under two main families. One is the roux-based family which includes **brown sauce** (espagnole) made with a rich brown stock; **béchamel**, a white sauce made with milk; and **velouté**, a white sauce made with stock. The second family, comprising the emulsified group of sauces, includes **hollandaise**, made with butter and egg yolks; **mayonnaise**, made with olive oil and egg yolks; and **vinaigrette**, a combination of oil and vinegar. Countless variations have been developed using the mother sauces. *see individual dishes.*

saucisse | FRENCH | Small fresh sausage.

saucisson | FRENCH | Large, smoke-cured sausage such as salami.

sauerbraten | GERMAN | Traditional dish of beef marinated in spiced vinegar for two to three days, then pot-roasted gently in the marinade for several hours. Served with dumplings or boiled potatoes and red cabbage.

sauerkraut | GERMAN | Finely shredded cabbage layered with salt and allowed to ferment. Served as an accompaniment to meat dishes and also in combinations with other foods.

sausage Seasoned minced or chopped meat stuffed into a tube-shaped casing, then tied into links. Pork is the most common sausage meat, but veal, beef, lamb, game, poultry and offal are also used. All sausages contain varying amounts of fat, a binding agent, such as breadcrumbs or flour, and a wide range of seasonings. Most sausages are sold fresh and are cooked before eating. Dry sausages, such as the many different types of cured salami, are ready to eat without any preparation other than slicing.

sautée | FRENCH | To shallow-fry food quickly in a small amount of hot oil or fat such as butter.

sautée pan Round pan with a long handle with straight or slightly curved sides that are a little higher than the sides of a frying pan.

Sauternes | FRENCH | Naturally sweet, golden white wine made from over- ripe Semillon and Sauvignon Blanc grapes in the Sauternes district of Bordeaux. Served chilled usually at the end of a meal with desserts, fruits or blue cheese. The undisputed best Sauternes is the famous Chateau d' Yguem. *see also* BOTRYTIS CINEREA.

Sauvignon Blanc White wine grape widely cultivated in France and other wine- producing countries, including Australia. It produces classic dry white wines including Pouilly-Fume and Sancerre. In its over-ripe state it is one of the white grapes used in the sweet wine of Sauternes.

savarin | FRENCH | Rich yeast cake shaped like a ring, soaked in a sweet, rum infused syrup and filled with pastry cream or whipped cream.

saveloy Garlicky, cured pork sausage with red skin. Usually heated before eating.

savoiardi | ITALIAN | Light, sponge finger biscuits.

savory (*Satureia* spp.) There are two main forms of this aromatic herb: the annual **summer savory** has dark green spicy leaves with a hint of mint and thyme often known as the 'bean herb' and traditionally used for pulses, also good in egg dishes and with vegetable dishes; the perennial **winter savory** has a peppery, coarser taste and is used mostly in marinades and in herb bouquets for meat stews.

savoury (1) Small portion of food served as a hot appetizer or snack with drinks. **(2)** In classic English terms, savories were served at the end of a meal; for example Welsh rarebit and angels on horseback.

savoyarde (à la) | FRENCH | In the style of Savoy. Usually potato or egg dishes with Gruyère cheese.

sayur | INDONESIAN | Soup-like vegetable dish made with a coconut milk stock.

Sbrinz | SWISS | Very hard, pressed raw cow's-milk cheese aged for two years. It has a compact, granular, dark yellow interior and thick, brushed rind. Used mainly for grating; also shaved into thin slices as a table cheese.

scald (1) To bring milk to just below boiling point to retard souring. **(2)** To plunge food, such as tomatoes, into boiling water to make peeling easier.

scale (1) To remove scales from the skin of fish. **(2)** Utensil used to accurately weigh ingredients.

scallions | AMERICAN | Straight-sided spring onions, called 'shallots' in Australia and 'green onions' elsewhere. *see also* SHALLOTS.

scallop (*Pecten fumatus*). Bivalve mollusc with a strongly ridged, fan-shaped shell and plump, creamy white flesh with orange coral (roe) attached. Dry-shucked scallops sold on the half shell have the best taste. Scallops should be pan-fried or grilled very quickly and lightly. Cooked scallops are also added to salads. Raw they are used in braised dishes or added in the final stages to soups or fish stews.

scallop potato Round slice of boiled potato that has been dipped in batter and deep fried until golden brown and crisp outside. Sold in fish and chip shops.

scallop squash *see* BUTTON SQUASH.

scaloppine | ITALIAN | Thin slices of meat (usually veal) coated in seasoned flour and lightly browned in oil and/or butter.

scampi (*Metanephrops velutinus*) Large, prawn-like crustacean. Available fresh or frozen. 'Scampi' is a name assigned to similar crustaceans in the Northern Hemisphere which are also known as 'Norway lobsters', 'langoustines' and 'Dublin Bay prawns'. They have a fine, strong taste and are boiled, pan-fried, grilled, barbecued or braised.

scarole *see* BATAVIAN ENDIVE.

schmaltz | JEWISH | Rendered and clarified fat, usually made from chicken or goose fat.

schnapps Generic term for various distilled spirits made from grains or potatoes. *see also* AQUAVIT.

schnitzel | GERMAN | Thin slices of meat dipped in egg and breadcrumbs, then fried.

Schwarzwalder Kirschtorte *see* BLACK FOREST CAKE.

scone | SCOTTISH | Small, flour-based cakes cut into rounds and baked in the oven. Served with tea, split in half and spread with jam and/or cream.

score To make shallow cuts on the surface of foods, such as fish, meat and vegetables. Tomatoes are scored with a cross at the base before blanching to make peeling easier.

scorzonera *see* SALSIFY.

Scotch bonnet *see* HABANERO CHILI.

Scotch broth | SCOTTISH | Hearty soup made with lamb or mutton, barley and various vegetables.

Scotch egg | SCOTTISH | Peeled, hard-boiled egg coated in sausage meat, then dipped in egg and breadcrumbs and fried. Popular pub snack in the United Kingdom.

Scotch woodcock | SCOTTISH | Creamy scrambled eggs placed on toast that is spread with anchovy paste and garnished with anchovy fillets.

Scottish Dunlop *see* DUNLOP.

scrag Neck of lamb, used for stews, terrines or stock.

screw pine *see* PANDANUS.

screwdriver Alcoholic drink made with orange juice and vodka in a tall, ice-filled glass.

sea bream *see* MORWONG.

sea cucumber (*Holothuria scabra*) Also known as 'bêche de mer', 'sea slug' or 'trepang'. Black, cucumber-shaped marine animal usually sold dried and/or smoked. It is highly regarded in China both for cooking and supposed aphrodisiac qualities and is frequently served at banquets. It must be first soaked in several changes of water for at least 24 hours. Used in soups, steamed or braised dishes.

sea slug *see* SEA CUCUMBER.

sea urchin roe (*Heliocidaris* spp.) Spiny marine animal valued for its soft, orange-yellow roe commonly sold prepared in small, oblong, wooden boxes. It spoils quickly and should be eaten soon after purchase. It can be eaten raw on toast or made into a paste for pasta or seafood sauces; also used in omelettes or soufflés. In Japan the roe is used as a topping for sushi.

seal To brown meat or fish quickly in hot oil or butter to seal in the juices and to retain good flavor and color.

sear To brown meat, fish or poultry quickly over a high heat in a pan or hot plate to seal in the juices.

season To flavor food by adding salt and pepper, and other flavorings such as herbs and spices, oil and vinegar to taste.

seaweed Widely distributed class of plants (Algae) growing in the sea and utilized by coastal people for centuries for food, fertilizer, as a source of salt, for therapeutic purposes and for the production of agar-agar, soda and iodine. Seaweed is widely used in Japanese cuisine and constitutes about 10 per cent of the diet of the people. Most seaweed sold in Australia is dried and will keep for a very long time if stored tightly sealed to keep out moisture and sunlight. Washing and soaking requirements vary and are explained under individual entries. *see also* AGAR-AGAR, ARAME, DULSE, HIJIKI, IRISH MOSS, KOMBU, NORI *and* WAKAME.

Sebago potato *see* POTATO.

sec | FRENCH | Dry, often used to describe still wines with little or no residual sugar. When applied to champagne, sec refers to one of the sweeter varieties; brut is actually the driest.

sediment Natural, grainy deposit that many wines develop as they age in the bottle.

222

seitan Also known as 'wheat gluten', 'wheat meat' or 'vegetarian steak'. Whole-wheat product made from wheat gluten and used as a meat substitute in many macrobiotic and Japanese dishes, such as soups, noodles and one-pot dishes. High in protein. Available in the refrigerator section of health food stores and Japanese grocers. Fu is a similar product that is toasted, steamed and dried. *see also* FU.

sel | FRENCH | Salt. **Sel gris** is unbleached sea salt; **sel gros** is coarse salt; and **sel marin** is sea salt.

Selles-sur-Cher | FRENCH | Name-controlled soft goat's-milk cheese with a smooth, pure white interior and a soft, natural rind dusted with powdered charcoal and shaped like a flattened cone. Served as a snack or at the end of a meal.

Seltzer water | GERMAN | Naturally sparkling mineral water which takes its name from Niederselters, a village in the Weisbaden region of Germany.

semi de melone | ITALIAN | Tiny, flat pasta shaped like melon seeds. Used in soups.

semifreddo | ITALIAN | Translates to 'half-cold'. Chilled or partially frozen dessert, including some ice creams or mousses, often with a fruit filling.

Semillon Variety of white-wine grape. When harvested ripe it is used to make dry white wine, often blended with Sauvignon Blanc. When over-ripe and left on the vine to develop Botrytis cinerea, it is one of the white grapes used in the classic French dessert wine Sauternes. *see also* SAUTERNES.

semolina (*Triticum durum*) Granules made mainly from coarsely ground durum wheat flour. Used for making pasta, gnocchi, couscous, puddings, cakes and soups. Other types of semolina include rice semolina and polenta made from ground corn. *see also* POLENTA.

Septmoncel *see* BLEU DE HAUT-JURA.

Sequoia potato *see* POTATO.

sereh powder | INDONESIAN | Dried lemon grass powder sold in jars. *see also* LEMON GRASS.

serpolet *see* THYME, WILD.

serrano chili | MEXICAN | Small, tapered, bright green to red chili with a thick flesh and a hot, savory taste. Used fresh in salads, dips and salsa, or roasted in sauces; also pickled.

sesame oil Amber or dark brown oil noted for its stability and resistance to spoiling. Used as a seasoning in Chinese, Japanese and Middle Eastern cooking, mostly as a condiment or flavoring. It has a strong taste and should be used sparingly.

sesame seed (*Sesamum indicum*) Tiny, creamy-white, brown or black, oval-shaped seeds with a rich, nut-like taste from an annual herb native to the tropics. Valued highly in Middle Eastern and Asian countries as a staple food, sesame seeds are an excellent source of oil and are high in calcium and other nutrients. The seeds are usually toasted lightly before use. They are sprinkled on breads, rolls, cakes and biscuits; in cheese spreads, over salads and used in vegetables, casseroles, chutneys and health-food bars. Sesame seed paste (tahini) is extremely popular in the Middle East and is mixed with other ingredients to make various appetizers or mezze; also used in the rich confection halvah. The Chinese use a light brown sesame paste in various hot and cold dishes and biscuits. Black seeds are mixed with salt in Japan to make the condiment called 'goma shio'.

set To allow food to become firm enough to hold its shape. Usually applied to gelatin based dishes.

seven-spice mixture | JAPANESE | Also known as 'shichimi togarashi' or 'shichimi' for short. Combination of seven spices blended to suit individual tastes and usually includes two hot spices, such as dried red chili flakes and sansho pepper, and five aromatic spices, which might include hemp seeds, dried mandarin or citron peel, sesame seeds, poppy seeds, nori flakes or shiso seeds. The mixture is sprinkled over udon noodles, added to soups and used to season many dishes, especially yakitori.

sevian | INDIAN | Ultra fine strands of dried vermicelli sold in boxes. Associated with Muslim holy days and usually made into a sweet milk pudding (sevian kheer) that is garnished with finely beaten silver leaf.

seviche *see* CEVICHE.

Seville orange (*Citrus aurantium*) Very bitter orange unsuitable for eating raw, but very popular for marmalade, candied peel and orange liqueur. It is widely used in Mediterranean countries (it lines the streets of Seville in southern Spain) and is used in sauces and relishes. In France the zest and juice is made into bigarde sauce, a bitter orange sauce served with duck and game. An essential oil distilled from the flowers is used in orange blossom water. *see also* ORANGE BLOSSOM.

Sevruga caviar *see* CAVIAR.

shabu-shabu | JAPANESE | One-pot dish cooked at the table and made with thinly sliced beef and vegetables and sometimes tofu. The ingredients are first stirred into the simmering broth then dipped in sauces such as ponzu and sesame seed sauce. Noodles are sometimes added to the remaining broth which is eaten as a soup at the end of the meal.

shad (*Alosa* spp.) Generic name given to a number of migratory fish belonging to the herring family. They occur naturally in the Atlantic Ocean and Mediterranean waters. Shad has a fine, rich flesh, but contains a large number of small bones. Shad roe is considered a delicacy.

shaddock *see* POMELO.

shallot flakes Dried, golden-brown pieces of shallots sold in jars. Used as a flavoring and garnish, particularly in Malaysian cooking.

shallots (*Allium cepa* var. *ascalonium*) Also known as 'eschallots'. These small onions grow as a small bunch of bulbs and most often have a reddish-brown, thin, papery skin. They have a finely textured flesh and a mild onion taste. They are used in Asian and French cooking and are featured in classic sauces such as beurre blanc and marchand de vin. Also used in salads or for a delicate onion-like taste in stir-fried or braised dishes.

shamoji | JAPANESE | Rice paddle or flat wooden spoon used when making sushi to toss rice and help separate the grains.

Shanghai bok choy *see* BOK CHOY.

Shanghai noodles | CHINESE | Thick, pale noodles lightly dusted with flour and sold fresh in Asian food stores. They are boiled for four minutes until nearly done then quickly rinsed in cold water and drained before using in stir-fried dishes.

shank The front leg of lamb, beef, veal or pork. Used for stocks, soups and slowly cooked stews. Osso buco is made with veal shanks.

shark Also known as 'flake'. Numerous shark species are sold as boneless fillets. Both the gummy shark and the school shark are sold in large quantities for fish and chip shops. The boneless fillet is firm and flaky, suitable for coating in batter and deep-frying. It can also be stir-fried and braised with Asian flavors, grilled or baked.

shashlik / shashlyk | RUSSIAN | Cubes of marinated lamb threaded on a skewer and grilled. Served with buttery rice.

shellfish Category of aquatic animals with shells outside the body, usually divided into two general groups, crustaceans and molluscs. Crustaceans include prawns, crabs, lobsters and crayfish. Molluscs have a shell made up of one (univalves) or two pieces hinged together (bivalves). Univalves include abalone; bivalves oysters, mussels, clams and scallops. Squid, octopus and cuttlefish belong to a class of mollusc that do not have shells and are known as cephalopods. *see also* CRUSTACEANS, MOLLUSCS, CEPHALOPODS *and individual entries.*

shepherd's pie | ENGLISH | Also known as 'cottage pie'. Traditional pie made from cooked minced meat, usually lamb or beef, covered with onions and topped with mashed potato, then baked in the oven until browned.

sherbet Frozen mixture of water and sweetened fruit juices.

Sherry | SPANISH | Fortified wine, originating around the town of Jerez de la Frontera, and aged by the solera system of progressively blending older and younger wines.

shichimi togarashi *see* SEVEN-SPICE MIXTURE.

shiitake (*Lentinus edodes*) Also known as 'winter mushroom'. Rich brown mushrooms with curled-under edges. They have a strong taste and can be stir-fried, baked, grilled and stuffed. The stems are discarded because they are too woody to eat, but can be used for flavoring liquids. Available fresh in some fruit markets; also in dried form in Asian and health-food shops, sometimes labeled Chinese black mushrooms.

shimeji (*Tricholoma conglobatum*) Straw-colored, cultivated mushrooms which grow in short clumps and have small caps. Sometimes available fresh. They have a delicate sweet taste and readily soak up other flavors; also used raw in salads.

shinma / shinmai | JAPANESE | Highly desirable, freshly harvested rice. Being moist and tender it requires less water and a shorter cooking time.

shioyaki | JAPANESE | Method of preparing food, usually fish, which is rubbed with salt and left to stand for 30 minutes before grilling.

shirataki | JAPANESE | Translates to 'white waterfall'. Long, white, vermicelli-like noodles made from the root of a yam-like plant known as 'devil's tongue' (*Amorphophallus konjac*). They form part of sukiyaki. Available canned or in long plastic packs from Japanese speciality stores; also sold in brick form known as 'konnyaku'. *see also* KONNYAKU.

shiro shoyu *see* SHOYU.

shirred eggs Whole eggs baked in cream, sometimes topped with breadcrumbs, in individual ramekins.

shish kebab | MIDDLE EASTERN | Small pieces of meat, seafood or vegetables threaded on a skewer and grilled or barbecued.

shishito | JAPANESE | Mild-tasting green capsicum, but looks like a hot green chili. Usually barbecued on a skewer between chicken; also used in condiments.

shiso | JAPANESE | (*Perilla frutescens* var. *crispa*) Also known as 'perilla' and 'beefsteak plant'. Bright green or reddish nettle-like leaves from annual plant belonging to the mint family, grown mainly in Japan and China. Green shiso (aojiso) is used in various ways as an aromatic garnish with sushi and sashimi or chopped and added to hot rice. Rich in calcium and iron. Small packs of fresh green leaves can be found in Japanese specialty shops. Red shiso (akajiso) is used mostly to give color to pickles, especially umeboshi (picked plums). Shiso seeds are sometimes included in the Japanese seven-spice mixture.

shoga | JAPANESE | (*Zingiber officinale*) Ginger. Fresh ginger has many uses in Japanese cuisine and is often used with fish to mask the smell. Grated ginger is added to the dip for tempura. Thinly sliced pickled ginger, known as beni shoga is served as a digestive condiment with sushi.

shortbread | SCOTTISH | Rich, buttery biscuit traditionally cooked in a flat, round mold and cut into wedge-shaped biscuits. Popular at Christmas and New Year.

shortcake | AMERICAN | Classic dessert made from a cooked round biscuit dough that is sliced into two layers and filled and topped with sliced, fresh strawberries and whipped cream.

shortening A solid fat such as butter, margarine, lard and suet.

shoyu | JAPANESE | Soy sauce made with steamed soy beans and roasted cracked wheat that is inoculated with yeast and spores of mold. After incubation of three days the dry mash is mixed with a brine solution then left to mature. When ready, it is pressed, pasteurized and bottled. **Koikuchi shoyu** is the regular dark soy sauce of Japan. **Usukuchi shoyu**, lighter and saltier in taste, is often used in cooking. **Saishimoni shoyu** is twice-brewed and has a strong taste; used as a table condiment, especially with sushi and sashimi. **Marudaizu** is a high quality, traditional soy sauce made from whole beans. **Shiro shoyu** is a thin, pale soy sauce with a mild, salty, sweet flavour. *see also* TAMARI.

shred To cut food with a sharp knife, or grate or tear, into thin narrow strips.

shrimp paste *see* BLACHAN.

shrimp, dried | SOUTH-EAST ASIAN | Tiny sun-dried prawns. They are sold in air-tight containers or packets and are usually soaked before adding to soups, noodles and rice dishes; also ground to a fine powder and used as a seasoning.

Shropshire Blue | ENGLISH | Firm, blue vein cow's-milk cheese with bright orange interior with dense, blue veining and natural, wrinkled, brown rind. Rich, sharp taste. Served at the end of a meal.

shuck To open an oyster or scallop shells with an oyster knife or shucker.

shungiku *see* CHRYSANTHEMUM LEAVES.

Sichuan pepper *see* SZECHWAN PEPPER.

Sicilian sea salt | ITALIAN | Unrefined salt crystals harvested from the sea with a strong sea taste. Used in seafood dishes.

sidecar | AMERICAN | Cocktail of brandy, Cointreau and lemon juice, shaken with ice.

Sienna cake *see* PANFORTE.

sieve To strain liquid through the mesh of a sieve, strainer or muslin to remove solids.

sift To pass dry ingredients, such as flour and icing sugar, through the fine mesh of a sifter to remove any lumps.

silk squash *see* ANGLED LOOFAH.

silver bream *see* BREAM.

silver leaf *see* VARAK.

silver trevally *see* TREVALLY.

silver warehou *see* WAREHOU, BLUE.

silverbeet (*Beta vulgaris*) Also known as 'Swiss chard' in some Northern Hemisphere countries. Silverbeet has white, thick stems and large, dark green, crinkly leaves. Good source of vitamins A and C as well as iron. The stems are removed, but can be chopped and used in soups, stews or stir-fried. The leaves are thoroughly washed and cooked like spinach in a saucepan with no added water, with a tight-fitting lid until just tender; also used in soups, sauces, curries and stir-fries.

simmer To cook food in liquid just below the boil so that small bubbles are just breaking the surface.

simnel cake | ENGLISH | Rich, spicy fruitcake topped with a layer of almond paste and decorated with 12 balls of marzipan which are said to represent the Apostles, sometimes the number is reduced to 11 to exclude Judas. Traditionally baked on Mothering Sunday, the fourth Sunday in Lent.

Singapore sling Mixed alcoholic drink consisting of gin, cherry brandy and lemon juice shaken, then strained over ice in a tall glass, and topped with soda water. Originated in the famous Raffles Hotel, Singapore.

skate (*Raja* spp.) Ray-like saltwater fish with a flattened body and head. It is the flap-like pectoral fins that are used. The boneless flesh is soft, white and sweet. The thick skin is always removed before cooking and the flesh can be pan-fried, poached and baked.

skewer Thin metal or wooden stick with a pointed end used to pierce food and hold it in place during cooking.

skim To remove fat and scum from the surface of a liquid such as stock, with a spoon or skimmer.

skimmer Large, metal, perforated spoon with a long handle, used to lift food from cooking liquid and to skim floating matter from the surface of a liquid.

skipjack *see* TAILOR.

skordalia | GREEK | Sauce or dip made with mashed potatoes (or sometimes breadcrumbs and ground nuts), with garlic, lemon juice and olive oil. Traditionally served with a rich seafood broth; also served as a dip for raw vegetables, or as an accompaniment for grilled meat, fish and vegetables.

slimy mackerel *see* MACKEREL.

slippery Jack (*Boletus luteus*) Also known as 'pine bolete' and 'sticky bun'. Dark yellow or purplish-brown mushroom with an expanded cap with a glutinous coating. Grows wild in some pine plantations and sometimes available fresh in autumn. The sticky cap is usually peeled before use. It has a mild, pleasant taste and chewy texture. Used in soups, sauces, casseroles and risotto.

slivovitz Slightly bitter, clear plum brandy from the Balkan countries.

sloe (*Prunus spinosa*) Small, sour blue plum. Used in preserves and to flavor gin.

smelt Name for several species of small migratory fish found in European and North American waters. Usually gutted and cooked whole in the same way as whitebait.

smoke To cure or flavor food such as meat, fish or poultry by exposing to the smoke of an aromatic wood fire. Sometimes herbs such as sage, rosemary, juniper and bay leaves are added.

smoothie | AMERICAN | Cold smooth drink made in the blender with milk, yoghurt or ice-cream and various fruits; for example, banana smoothie.

smörgasbord | SWEDISH | Variety of hot and cold dishes served buffet-style, either as appetizers or to make up an entire meal.

smörrebröd | DANISH | Open-faced sandwiches, often made with pumpernickel bread and topped with a variety of foods.

snails (*Helix* spp.) Land-dwelling gastropods of several varieties widely cooked fresh in France in numerous ways. Often baked in the shell with a garlic and parsley butter.

snake bean (*Vigna sesquipedalis*) Also known as 'asparagus bean', 'yard-long bean' and 'Chinese long bean'. Very long and narrow, dark green bean. It is sliced into lengths and cooked like green beans, or quickly stir-fried in Asian dishes.

snapper (*Pagrus auratus*) Medium to large, saltwater fish which develops a large bulge on the top of the head as it grows older. Fishermen have given the snapper a number of different local names according to size and where it is caught. The small cockney and red bream (up to 700 g) are caught in estuaries; squire (up to 1.5 kg) are usually found offshore, and larger fish are known as snapper. The firm, white flesh is highly regarded and is sold whole, or in fillets or steaks. Whole fish can be baked, poached or barbecued; fillets and cutlets are pan-fried with a coating or chargrilled. Very fresh snapper can be used for sashimi.

snotty trevalla *see* WAREHOU, BLUE.

snow peas (*Pisum sativum*) Also known as 'mangetout' which translates to 'eat all' in French. Flat, edible pea pods eaten whole before the peas inside have fully developed. The stringy spine is removed by snapping off the top stem and tearing the string off to the tail. They need very little cooking and should be still crisp. Steamed or stir-fried; also blanched for salads, or as a garnish.

snowball Frozen dessert made from ice-cream and mousse, and various flavorings, set in a round mold.

snoweggs *see* FLOATING ISLAND.

Soave | ITALIAN | Light, dry white wine from Verona, Veneto.

soba | JAPANESE | Long, thin noodles made from buckwheat and plain flour. They are a light brownish and usually sold dried, although fresh soba are sometimes available. A green variety is made with the addition of green tea powder. Soba are served in soups or as part of a tempura dish. Chilled soba noodles (zaru soba) are traditionally served in a basket or slatted bamboo box, topped with a little nori and accompanied by a cold dipping sauce, wasabi and sliced spring onions.

sobresada | SPANISH | Large spreadable sausage made with pork, highly seasoned and colored with paprika and cayenne pepper. Used for spreading on bread and as a flavoring for other dishes.

socca | FRENCH | **(1)** Flour made from chickpeas and used for porridge, purées or tart fillings. **(2)** Type of crêpe made with chickpea flour, sold on the streets of Nice and eaten as a sweet snack.

soda water Water carbonated by the injection of carbon dioxide.

sodium bicarbonate *see* BICARBONATE OF SODA.

sodium chloride *see* SALT.

sodium nitrate *see* SALTPETRE.

sofrito / soffrito | SPANISH / ITALIAN | Cooked thick sauce of olive oil, finely chopped onions, garlic, tomatoes, celery and seasoning. Used as a base for soups, stews and sauces.

soft roe *see* MILT.

sole The best-known sole is the European or Dover sole fished in deep European waters as far north as Denmark. The small, oval, thick-skinned Australian species (*Synaptura nigra*) is sometimes available, usually sold skinned. Although there are a variety of ways to cook sole, many cooks will agree it is best grilled whole and served à la meunière.

somen | JAPANESE | Very fine, thin noodles made from hard wheat flour, usually sold dried. Traditionally served cold, accompanied by a dipping sauce.

sommelier | FRENCH | Person in charge of the selection and serving of wine in a restaurant.

sopaipilla | MEXICAN | Deep-fried pastry puffs. Served with soups and dips or, with syrup sprinkled with sugar and cinnamon, as a dessert.

soppresse | ITALIAN | Large, fine-textured, moderately hot salami made from pork and beef. From the Veneto.

sorbet Watery ice flavored with lemon or other fruit, wine or liqueur. Served between courses as a refreshment or as a dessert.

sorbitol Natural sweetener found in some fruit and seaweed. Used as an alternative to sugar and in diabetic foods such as jams.

sorghum (*Sorghum vulgare*) Cereal grass related to millet that is used as a staple food in hot countries, particularly Africa, but also China and India. Used mainly for porridges and flat breads. Sorghum syrup or sorghum molasses is extracted from the stems which are rich in sugars.

sorrel (*Rumex acetosa*) Bright green, crisp leaves from a perennial plant that grows in clumps. Young leaves have a sharp, lemony taste. Cooked as a vegetable, like spinach. When puréed, it is the basis for many sauces served with fish and eggs and for the classic French sorrel soup. Young leaves are used in green salads.

soubise | FRENCH | Dish prepared with or accompanied by a purée of cooked onions thickened with a béchamel sauce and enriched with cream.

soufflé | FRENCH | Light mixture of egg yolks, stiffly beaten egg whites and puréed ingredients, that puffs up when baked in a round, straight-sided dish. Served hot or cold as a savory dish or dessert. **Iced soufflés** are made with a mixture of ice-cream and mousse, variously flavored, and set in a soufflé dish with a tall collar wrapped around the outside of the dish so that the increased height is supported during freezing.

soufflé dish Round, straight-sided, ovenproof dish that enables the soufflé to rise evenly during cooking.

soup Clear, thick or chunky liquid food made with vegetables, seafood, meat or chicken cooked in a liquid, and served either strained, puréed or with ingredients left whole. Most soups are served hot as an appetizer at the beginning of a meal. Many substantial chunky soups, such as bouillabaisse or minestrone, are often main meals in themselves. Some summer soups, such as the Spanish gazpacho and the French vichyssoise, are served cold.

sour cream Thick cream with a 35 per cent fat content that has been soured by the addition of a harmless bacterial culture to give it a slightly tangy taste. Used in savory sauces and soups and as a topping for jacket potatoes.

sourdough bread Bread leavened with fermented dough.

soursop (*Annona muricata*) Related to the custard apple, this large, heart-shaped tropical fruit has green skin with rows of soft, fleshy spines. It is fully ripe when slightly soft to the touch. The toxic seeds must be removed. The white, pulpy flesh has a sweet acid taste and is usually poached with sugar and puréed for various cream desserts, jellies and drinks.

sous vide | FRENCH | System whereby raw or pre-cooked food is vacuum sealed in a heavy-duty plastic pouch in individual servings. The pouch is then chilled, ready to be cooked or reheated in the bag. The advantage is convenience, hygiene and the retention of natural flavors. Used mainly in the food service industry, but sous vide take-away gourmet food is becoming increasingly available in supermarkets.

soused Pickled in brine or vinegar.

southern bluefin tuna *see* TUNA.

southern bream *see* BREAM.

souvlaki | GREEK | Marinated cubes of lamb threaded on skewers and grilled or barbecued.

soy flour Fine flour made from soya beans. It has twice the protein content of wheat flour and is low in carbohydrates. Usually mixed with other flours for baked goods; also used to make sweets and snacks in Japan.

soy milk White, non-dairy drink made from ground soya beans. Used as a milk substitute and high protein, cholesterol-free drink. When curdled it is used to make tofu.

soy sauce Indispensable ingredient used in all types of Oriental cooking. Soy sauce is made from fermented soya beans and roasted grain. It comes in many types and grades, ranging from light to dark. **Light soy sauce** is thin, light-colored and saltier than dark soy sauce. Used in cooking and as a table condiment. **Dark soy sauce** (usually darkened with caramel) is richer and thicker than light soy sauce, but not as salty. Used in dishes that require stronger taste and color. **Heavy soy sauce** made with molasses is extremely thick and dark and is used mostly in Chinese dishes requiring rich, dark brown sauces. **Mushroom soy sauce** is infused with dried straw mushrooms. *see also* SHOYU *and* TAMARI.

soya bean oil Pale yellow, strongly flavored oil extracted from soya beans. Used to make margarine and, when refined, widely used as a good quality cooking oil.

soya bean paste *see* BEAN PASTE.

soya beans | ASIAN | (*Glycine max*) Small, very hard, oval beans in a variety of colors. They are the most nutritious of all beans and contain a large amount of protein and desirable oil, vitamins A and B, iron, calcium, potassium, magnesium and zinc. The whole soya bean is not easy to digest and a wide variety of naturally processed products have been developed, including tofu (bean curd), tempeh, miso, soy sauce, shoyu, tamari, soy flour, soy milk, soya bean oil and soya bean shoots. Because of their high protein content, soya beans are popular in vegetarian cooking. Dried soya beans are soaked overnight and simmered for an hour or more, until tender. Used in soups and casseroles. *see individual entries for details.*

spaetzle | GERMAN | Translates to 'little sparrow'. Tiny dumplings made from a soft dough that is passed through a special colander, directly into boiling water. Served sprinkled with toasted breadcrumbs with roasted meats.

spaghetti | ITALIAN | Long, solid strands of pasta of medium thickness.

Spalen | SWISS | Also known as 'Sparen'. Younger and smaller version of Sbrinz, a hard mountain cheese used mostly for grating. *see also* SBRINZ.

spanakopita | GREEK | Pie made of eggs, feta cheese, onions and spinach and filo pastry.

spangled emperor *see* EMPEROR.

Spanish garlic *see* ROCAMBOLE.

Spanish mackerel *see* MACKEREL.

Spanish omelette | SPANISH | Savory dish made with beaten eggs, diced potatoes and onions that have been cooked in olive oil. The omelette is also cooked in olive oil, left flat and turned over half way through cooking, like a thick pancake. May be eaten hot or cold.

Spanish salami | SPANISH | Moderately hot, fine-textured salami made from finely ground pork, or a mixture of meats, highly seasoned with spices and garlic.

spanner crab (*Ranina ranina*) Triangular-shaped, red crab with the legs, claws and body shells edged with fur. The spanner crab is usually sold whole and already cooked. The fine white meat is sweet, but may contain bits of shell and cartilage. It can be used in salads, pasta sauces and soups. *see also* CRAB.

Sparen *see* SPALEN.

spareribs Fatty, narrow cut of meat taken from the upper part of the pork belly with the lower portion of the ribs intact. Often marinated and barbecued.

spatchcock 'Poussin' in French. Very young, small chicken with delicately flavored flesh. It is roasted or barbecued whole or butterflied and flattened, then grilled.

spatlese | GERMAN | Sweet wines made from extra-ripe grapes picked after the normal harvest.

spatula Flat kitchen utensil, made of wood, metal or rubber, used for scraping the sides of bowls and pots, stirring, and for spreading soft icing on cakes.

spatzele *see* SPAETZLE.

spearmint *see* MINT.

speck Smoked pork that comes from the top side of the leg. It has a strong flavor and high proportion of fat to lean meat. It is sold in a slab or slices and served as an appetizer; also used in soups and stews. Speck blutwurst is a sausage consisting of solid pork fat, blood and pork.

spice Aromatic flavoring agent obtained from the bud, seed, fruit or bark of certain plants; for example cloves, cumin, nutmeg and cinnamon. Individual spices are treated under their separate entries.

spiedini | ITALIAN | Skewers on which food is threaded, then barbecued, grilled or baked.

spinach (*Spinacea oleracea*) Also called 'English spinach' where the name 'spinach' is often applied to silverbeet (*Beta vulgaris*). It is a dark green, leafy vegetable with triangular or arrow-shaped leaves that are rich in iron, vitamins and potassium. Spinach needs to be thoroughly washed and often the stems are removed before use. Young, fresh leaves may be eaten raw in salads or cooked very gently in a saucepan with a tight-fitting lid, with no added water; also used in soups, sauces, curries and stir-fries.

spiny lobster *see* LANGOUSTE.

spit Long, thin metal rod onto which a large piece of meat or whole animal is held and rotated while roasting over an open fire.

split peas (*Pisum sativum*) Dried variety of the common garden pea which is peeled and split in half. There are two types available, green and yellow. They do not need to be soaked, but may take up to 60 minutes to cook. Split peas do not keep their shape in cooking and are often used as a purée or a thickener in stews and soups, sometimes flavored with ham or bacon.

sponge cake Light, airy cake made from plain flour, sugar and egg yolks, with no raising agent. It is lightened by the addition of whisked egg whites.

spotted Dick | ENGLISH | Boiled pudding made with breadcrumbs, suet and currants or other dried fruit.

spotted mackerel *see* MACKEREL.

spring onions (*Allium cepa*) Immature onions with a small, white, satiny bulb and long, flattish leaves, usually tied in bunches. They have a mild onion taste. Eaten raw thinly sliced in salads, or used in stir-fried dishes or soups; also cooked whole.

spring roll | CHINESE / SOUTH-EAST ASIAN | Savory cooked mixture that is firmly rolled in a rice paper wrapper and deep-fried. They are usually quite small and served as a snack or appetizer. So named because it is a Chinese custom to eat spring rolls at the beginning of spring each year. The Vietnamese spring roll contains minced pork, vermicelli and shredded vegetables, with fish sauce and fresh herbs, and is fried until the rice paper turns a crispy brown. A larger version is served in an uncooked rice paper wrapper.

springerle | GERMAN | Aniseed-flavored, biscuit-like sweets that are served at Christmas. They are pressed in patterned molds with symbolic Christmas designs, before baking.

spritzer Long drink made with white wine and soda water.

sprouts Young, crispy shoots of various rapidly germinating beans, peas and seeds. As the seeds sprout, the starches stored within are released and converted to vitamins, minerals and proteins. Those most commonly sprouted are the mung bean and soya bean, but alfalfa, fenugreek, adzuki beans, lentils, chickpeas, mustard and cress all sprout well. They are sold loose (such as bean sprouts) in cellophane bags, but are more often packaged in plastic punnets, sometimes in combinations such as a salad mix. They are eaten fresh in salads, sandwiches and cold dishes, or lightly cooked in stir-fries, soups, omelettes and crêpes; also used as a garnish. *see also* ALFALFA SPROUTS *and* BEAN SPROUTS.

spud | ENGLISH | Slang term for potato.

spumante | ITALIAN | Sparkling wine. *see also* ASTI SPUMANTE.

spumoni | ITALIAN | Light, foamy ice cream made with a rum flavored layer of whipped cream in the center.

Spunta potato *see* POTATO.

squash flowers Yellow, trumpet-shaped flowers from members of the curcurbit family, particularly zucchini flowers. They are often stuffed, lightly battered and deep-fried; also used in salads, soups and as a garnish.

squash, summer (*Cucubita pepo*) Large group of curcurbits, often with highly ornamental fruits. The best-known summer squash are the zucchini and button squash (or pattipan). They grow very quickly and are picked immature when the skins are tender and the flesh soft. The smaller the better, in taste and texture. *see also* BUTTON SQUASH *and* ZUCCHINI.

squid (*Sepioteuthis australis*) Also known as 'southern calamari'. Tube-shaped cephalopod belonging to the same family as the octopus and cuttlefish. It has

10 tentacles and a long, thin, transparent spine (quill) down its back which is removed before use. The head and tentacles are pulled away from the body and the head cut from the tentacles just below the eyes. The ink can be extracted from the dark ink sac and used in dishes such as risotto, pasta and seafood dishes. The body and tentacles are washed thoroughly and the thin outer membrane peeled off. The squid can be stuffed and baked, or sliced into rings or small chunks and quickly sautéed or barbecued along with the chopped tentacles. Sometimes the chunks are scored with a diamond pattern to stop the squid curling and for fast, even cooking. Calamari rings are also coated with batter and very quickly deep-fried. Pearly white, raw calamari is often served in Japanese sushi. Whole dried squid is sold in Asian grocers. It is soaked overnight before use as a flavoring in soups, steamed dishes and stir-fries.

St. John's bread *see* CAROB.

stabilizer An additive used in the food industry to improve the texture and life of emulsified sauces, creams and ice-creams. Tartaric acid, pectin, lecithin, agar-agar and vegetable gums are commonly used stabilizers.

star anise *see* ANISE, STAR.

star apple (*Chrysophyllum cainito*) Slightly flattened, rounded tropical fruit with a thick, green or dark purplish-brown skin when ripe. The translucent white flesh, divided into eight segments, is soft and sweet. Halved it can be eaten with a spoon, added to fruit salads or made into a purée for ice cream or sorbets.

star fruit *see* CARAMBOLA.

starch Type of carbohydrate stored in plant foods such as vegetables, grains, pulses, nuts and fruits. Starch in the form of flour is used as a thickener. The main types are cornflour, arrowroot, tapioca and potato starch.

steak and kidney pudding | ENGLISH | Pie made in a pudding basin lined with suet pastry and filled with a mixture of cubed beef, lamb's kidneys, mushroom, onions, nutmeg and seasoning. It is steamed for up to five hours. Steak and kidney pie has a similar filling, but is made in a pie dish, topped with a puff pastry and baked in the oven for about an hour.

steak au poivre | FRENCH | Pepper steak. Thick slice of steak sprinkled with freshly ground black pepper before being sautéed in butter and served with a sauce made from pan juices, stock, wine and brandy. The sauce is sometimes flamed with Cognac with cream added. Whole green peppercorns are sometimes used.

steak tartare High quality minced beef served raw with egg yolk and seasoning; sometimes garnished with capers, chopped parsley and onions.

steam To cook fish, poultry, vegetables and some puddings in a perforated container or basket placed inside another vessel with boiling water or stock and covered. The food is cooked in the moist heat of steam and must not be in direct contact with the liquid. The aim is to retain the food's texture and taste, vitamins and minerals which may otherwise be lost in the cooking water.

steel Long and thin, cylindrical, grooved rod made of hard, high-carbon steel, used to maintain the sharp edge to knives.

234

stelline | ITALIAN | Tiny star-shaped pasta. Used in soups.

stew (1) To cook food in a little stock, water or sauce by gently simmering in a covered pot. The rich liquid is served with the food. **(2)** The name of a dish prepared in this way.

stick of butter | AMERICAN | Measurement of butter equal to ½ cup, 125 g, 4 oz or 8 tablespoons.

sticky bun *see* SLIPPERY JACK.

stifado | GREEK | Rich beef stew with tomatoes, onions, garlic, white wine and herbs.

Stilton | ENGLISH | Name-controlled blue vein cow's-milk cheese with moist and creamy, ivory interior uniformly mottled with greenish- blue veins and a natural, brownish rind. Considered one of the world's best cheeses. Served at the end of the meal with fruit and traditionally with vintage port.

stir-fry Fast cooking technique where bite-sized pieces of food are constantly stirred over a high heat with a little oil until crisp and slightly underdone. Mainly used in Oriental cooking and often in a wok.

stock Flavored liquid obtained from simmering meat, vegetables, poultry or fish in a pot of water with other seasonings and then straining. Used as a base for soup, braising, poaching and, when reduced, for sauces.

stollen | GERMAN | Dryish, yeast loaf filled with almonds, raisins, currants, candied citrus peel, decorated with glacé cherries. Traditionally eaten and exchanged as a gift at Christmas.

stout Very dark, bittersweet beer made with a high proportion of malt and hops, flavored with roasted barley. Guinness is the best- known stout.

Stracchino | ITALIAN | Also known as 'Crescenza' or 'Stracchino di Crescenza'. Soft, fresh cow's-milk cheese with white, satiny interior and white, velvety rind. Sold in small rectangular shapes. Rich, buttery taste. Served at breakfast and lunch with fruit and bread. Specialty of the Lombardy region.

strain To pour liquid through a fine sieve or cheesecloth in order to remove unwanted lumps.

Strasbourg sausage Medium-sized, mild-tasting sausage made from pork or beef (sometimes both), pepper, coriander and nutmeg.

strasbourgeoise (à la) | FRENCH | Dish which is served with ingredients typical of Strasbourg, including braised sauerkraut, fois gras, streaky bacon or slices of Strasbourg sausage.

straw mushrooms (*Volvariella volvacea*) Also known as 'grass mushrooms'. Small, pale yellow, conical mushrooms, so-called because of the rice paddy straw on which they are grown. Sold in cans. Used in steamed chicken and vegetable dishes.

straw potatoes Potatoes cut into very thin strips, then deep-fried.

strawberries Romanoff / Romanov Dessert of strawberries soaked in Curaçao and topped with whipped cream.

strawberry (*Fragaria virginiana*) Although available all year, strawberries are best in summer. The size and taste of strawberries vary according to the variety. They are an excellent source of vitamin C. Wash just before using. Fresh strawberries are served on their own with cream or ice cream and are used in a variety of ways in desserts, preserves and drinks.

strawberry tree *see* ARBUTUS BERRY.

Strega | ITALIAN | Bittersweet, bright yellow liqueur infused with herbs, barks and spices.

streusel | GERMAN | Translates to 'sprinkle' or 'strew'. Sugar-crumb topping made by rubbing together butter, flour, sugar and cinnamon until they look like breadcrumbs. It is spread evenly over cakes, breads and biscuits.

streuselkuchen | GERMAN | Yeast cake with a sugar-crumb topping. Traditionally served with coffee.

striped bass (*Morone saxatilis*) Large migratory fish found along the Atlantic coast of North America. Popular as a sporting fish and valued for its sweet, flaky white flesh.

Stroganoff / Stroganov, beef *see* BEEF STROGANOFF.

strudel | AUSTRIAN | Classic pastry made with very thin stretched dough spread with a filling such as apples and raisins, cherries or cream cheese, then rolled up, brushed with melted butter and baked until golden.

stud To insert flavoring such as pieces or garlic, almonds or cloves into food to give extra flavor during cooking; for example a raw onion studded with cloves or a roast studded with garlic.

stuffing | ENGLISH | Well-seasoned mixture of ingredients such as finely chopped onions, breadcrumbs, rice, egg yolks, mushrooms, herbs, etc, used to fill poultry, meat or vegetables. In France the term 'farce' is used and in America, 'dressing'. *see also* FORCEMEAT.

su | JAPANESE | Rice vinegar. Available at most oriental food stores.

succès | FRENCH | Round cake made with two layers of baked nut meringue, sandwiched with praline butter cream and topped with butter cream, decorated with nuts and marzipan.

succotash | AMERICAN-INDIAN | Dish of corn kernels and lima or kidney beans cooked in the same pot.

suckling pig Young piglet, usually roasted on a spit whole.

sucrose Natural sugar composed of glucose and fructose. It is obtained from sugarcane, sugar beets, maple sap and sorghum.

suet Solid white fat surrounding the kidneys of animals, usually beef or sheep. Traditionally used in English puddings, dumplings and stuffings.

sugar Sweet, crystalline substance obtained chiefly from the juice of the sugarcane (*Saccharum officinarium*) or sugar beet (*Beta vulgaris*). Sugar is named according to its source: for example beet sugar, cane sugar, maple sugar, date or palm sugar. Sugar is available in a variety of forms, differing mostly as to the degree of refinement. The highly refined **white sugar**, also known as '**granulated sugar**', consisting of almost pure sucrose, is the most common table and cooking sugar. A finer white sugar, **caster sugar**, is used to make cakes, pastries, biscuits and desserts, especially meringues and confectionery. **Icing sugar**, also known as '**confectioners' sugar**', is a finely ground or powdered white sugar used for icing cakes and in sweets where a grainy texture is undesirable. Icing sugar is also sometimes used to make meringues and for dusting on cakes and sweets such as Turkish delight. **Cube, loaf** or **lump sugar** is granulated sugar that is moistened and molded and cut into convenient cubes of various sizes, most often used to sweeten hot drinks; also used in champagne cocktails and rubbed on citrus skins for certain sweet dishes and sauces. **Brown sugar**, often specified in recipes for breads and cakes, is small crystals of white sugar that has been mixed with clarified molasses to give it a soft, moist texture in shades of light or dark brown. **Dark brown sugar** is the stronger in flavor. **Barbados sugar** is a moist, finely textured dark brown sugar that has been treated with dark molasses. **Raw sugar** has large crystals and is made from the residual syrup after the removal of molasses. **Demerara sugar** is a dry brown sugar with coarse crystals mixed with a little molasses and traditionally used to sweeten coffee. *see also* PALM SUGAR, YELLOW ROCK SUGAR, MOLASSES, MALTOSE, CORN SYRUP, GOLDEN SYRUP, MAPLE SYRUP *and* RICE SYRUP.

sugar beet (*Beta vulgaris*) Sugar-producing variety of the common garden beet. The sucrose obtained from the beet sugar is indistinguishable from cane sugar both in strength and quality, and is produced in huge quantities as a sweetener, second only to that of cane sugar. *see also* SUGAR.

sugarcane (*Saccharum officinarum*) Very tall perennial grass which accounts for over half the world's sugar supply. Sugarcane stalks are sometimes found in fruit markets. The stalk can be split lengthways and cut into thin strips and used as skewers for grilling prawns. The inner white flesh is shredded or finely sliced and used as a garnish in some Asian dishes; also eaten as a snack. *see also* SUGAR.

sugar peas (*Pisum sativum*) Also known as 'sugar snap peas'. A small version of the common garden pea and, like snow peas, the whole pod is eaten. They are topped and tailed and briefly cooked.

sugar snap peas *see* SUGAR PEAS.

sugar syrup Sweet syrup made by combining water and white sugar and simmering until the sugar is dissolved. It differs in density according to the amount of sugar used in relation to the volume of water. The syrup can be bottled and used in desserts, baked goods, fruit dishes, punches, confectionery, and cocktails.

sugocasa | ITALIAN | Ready-made thick sauce made from crushed tomatoes and sold in bottles. Used for pasta sauces, soups or stews.

sukiyaki | JAPANESE | Dish of thin slices of beef, chopped vegetables and sometimes noodles and bean curd, flavored with dashi and cooked at the table. The cooked food is dipped into beaten raw egg before eating.

sultana Dried, seedless, pale green grape. Eaten as a snack and used in various baked goods and chutney.

sumac | MIDDLE EASTERN | (*Rhus* spp.) Dark purplish-red berries with a sharp fruit taste, used dried or ground as a seasoning in meat and vegetable dishes; also in place of lemon juice with fish.

summer melon *see* FUZZY MELON.

summer pudding | ENGLISH | Cold dessert made by lining a pudding basin with slices of white bread and filled with a sweetened mixture of ripe berries such as raspberries, red currants and blackberries. The top is completely covered with more bread and the whole pudding is pressed down with a weight and refrigerated overnight. It is turned out on to a plate and served with whipped cream.

summer savory *see* SAVORY.

sun dory *see* SILVER DORY.

sundae | AMERICAN | Ice-cream dessert, topped with a sweet sauce, various nuts and fruit and decorated with whipped cream. Originally a family Sunday treat at the end of the 19th century.

sunomono | JAPANESE | Vinegared salad. The main ingredients are raw crisp vegetables, and sometimes cold cooked fish or shellfish, tossed in a thin dressing of rice vinegar, dashi, sugar and soy sauce. Served as an appetizer or side dish.

suprême | FRENCH | Boned and skinned breast of poultry or game birds, also fillets of fish.

suprême sauce | FRENCH | Smooth white sauce made with velouté sauce, chicken stock and mushrooms, thickened with cream. Served with poached or roast chicken.

suribachi | JAPANESE | Mortar-like mixing bowl with a ridged surface, used for grinding ingredients such as fish and sesame seeds to a fine paste.

surimi | JAPANESE | Traditionally fine fish paste made in a suribachi, thickened with starch and egg white, molded into various shapes and steamed or grilled. Commercial surimi is mixed with a flavor concentrate and artificial coloring and is cut into shapes for imitation lobster, crab sticks, shrimp and scallops. The process of skinning, deboning, rinsing and mincing is usually carried out on factory ships and the finished product frozen into blocks.

sushi | JAPANESE | The Japanese spelling is 'zushi', and when a type of sushi is preceded with a Japanese word, it should be spelled this way. Vinegared rice, combined with a multitude of toppings and fillings, served in bite- sized pieces and presented very fresh. Sushi is eaten at any time of the day as a snack, as an appetizer or as a full meal. There are a number of varieties of sushi made up of different ingredients and prepared in different ways. The best-known, **nigiri–zushi**, is a hand-molded oblong of rice smeared with wasabi and topped with a piece of raw fish or any of a number of other ingredients. Sometimes it is held together with a strip of nori. If there is a high wall of nori encircling the rice and holding together a soft topping, such as salmon roe or sea urchin roe, the sushi is called **gunkan-maki**. **Maki-zushi** (or **nori-maki**) is rice and other ingredients rolled up in nori and sliced into bite-sized rounds. A flexible bamboo rolling mat is used to make a tight roll. **Hoso-maki** is a thin roll and **futo-maki** a thicker version, often with a vegetarian filling. **Temaki-zushi**, or **California roll**, are hand- rolled maki, often cone-shaped with the filling poking out at the wide end. Deep-fried tofu pouches (aburage), stuffed with sushi rice and sprinkled with toasted sesame seeds are called **'inari–zushi'**. Sushi rice covered with a piece or rolled omelette and usually secured with a tiny belt of nori is called **'tamago–zushi'**. **Oshi-zushi** is pressed sushi rice with one or more types of fish. It requires a special rectangular wooden box which has a removable top and base. After pressing in one block, the sushi is then cut into finger-length pieces. **Battara-zushi** is pressed sushi with vinegared blue mackerel. **Scattered sushi**, **chirashi-zushi**, is sushi rice served in a large serving bowl with a variety of sliced fish, vegetables and omelette artfully arranged on top.

sushi rice | JAPANESE | Steamed short-grain rice that is poured into a wide wooden bowl (hangiri) or non-metallic tray and flavoured with a sweetened rice vinegar. It is folded and tossed with a rice paddle (shamoji) or flat wooden spoon, and fanned to cool quickly and bring out a pearly sheen to the grain.

sweat To cook gently in oil or butter without coloring until the ingredients soften.

swede (*Brassica napus*) Also known as 'rutabaga'. This round root vegetable with pale yellow skin and slightly sweet, firm flesh is believed to be a cross between the turnip and cabbage. It is mostly used in vegetable soups and casseroles, but can also be simmered and mashed; in this form it is a traditional accompaniment to haggis in Scotland. Also baked, caramelized or, when young, sliced thinly and marinated as a salad.

sweet cicely (*Myrrhis odorata*) Soft, fern-like herb with a taste slightly of aniseed and liquorice. Used finely chopped in salads and stews. Leaves have a sweetening effect on acid fruits and are cooked with tart fruits such as rhubarb, gooseberries and currants.

sweet peppers Usually in reference to capsicums.

sweet potato (*Ipomoea batatas*) Long, round, tuberous root obtained from a climbing plant belonging to the same genus as the ornamental morning glory. There are two main varieties: the white sweet potato with light brown skin and dry-textured white flesh; and the red sweet potato (also known by its Maori name 'kumara') with orange-brown skin and a much sweeter, moist, bright orange flesh. Both varieties are suitable for roasts, pies and soups. Kumaras are also good steamed and mashed, or in sweet dishes such as jams, puddings, cakes and desserts.

sweetbreads The thymus glands of a calf, lamb or pig. There are two glands, an elongated one in the throat and a larger, rounded gland near the stomach. Before cooking they are blanched, soaked in several changes of water and trimmed of their outer membrane. They may be prepared in various ways, such as frying, grilling, poaching and braising, as a main meal, appetizer, as a filling for vol-au-vents or used in pâté. Calves' sweetbreads are considered the best.

sweetlip emperor *see* EMPEROR.

sweetmeat *see* SWEETS.

sweets Small confectionery, such as boiled candies, caramels, toffees, crystallized fruit, sugared nuts and liquorice.

Swiss brown mushrooms (*Agaricus bisporus*) Form of the common cultivated mushroom, with a brown cap and stronger flavor.

Swiss chard *see* SILVERBEET.

Swiss Gruyère *see* GRUYÈRE.

Swiss Tilsit *see* TILSIT.

swordfish (*Xiphias gladius*) Very large ocean fish with a distinctive sword-like projection from the upper jaw. It is regarded as a good, but variable eating fish, and has a dense, fine-textured flesh that is most often sold in steaks. A marinade of oil and citrus juice helps keep it moist during cooking. Grilled, barbecued and pan-fried; also when very fresh used raw in sushi.

syllabub | ENGLISH | Creamy dessert made by beating together either brandy, Madeira, sherry or wine with caster sugar, lemon juice and cinnamon, then whisking in double cream until stiff peaks are formed. Served by itself or as a topping on fruit.

syrinki / sirniki | RUSSIAN | Sweet cheese fritters made with cottage cheese, flour, eggs, sugar and butter. Served hot with a bowl of sour cream.

Szechwan / Szechuan pepper | CHINESE | (*Zanthoxylum* spp.) Also known as 'Chinese pepper' and 'fagara'. Dried reddish-brown berries that have a sharp, spicy fragrance when roasted and ground. It is used extensively in Szechwan cooking and is one of the components of five-spice powder. An excellent seasoning is made with sea salt and Szechwan peppers coarsely ground together.

tabasco chili | MEXICAN | Very hot, small, red chili mostly used in the production of the famous McIlhenny Tabasco Sauce. The chili is also used in South-East Asian and Indian cooking.

Tabasco Sauce | AMERICAN | Brand name for the famous, biting-hot, peppery sauce originating in Louisiana and still made by the McIlhenny family. Made from tabasco chilies, it is extremely hot and only a few drops are needed to enliven a variety of savory dishes and some cocktails, such as Bloody Mary.

tabbouleh / tabbouli | MIDDLE EASTERN | Popular salad dish served as a cold entrée with a Lebanese meal. Made with bulgur (cracked wheat), chopped onions, finely chopped flat-leafed parsley, finely chopped mint, cubed tomatoes, lemon juice, olive oil, salt and pepper.

taco | MEXICAN | Crisp folded tortilla that can be filled with various mixtures of cooked minced meats, beans, tomatoes, lettuce, cheese and guacamole. Eaten as a snack or entrée.

taffy | AMERICAN | Soft, chewy toffee.

tagine / tajine | MIDDLE EASTERN | Traditional glazed terracotta cooking pot with a tall conical lid used throughout North Africa, particularly Morocco, for slowly cooking spicy mixtures of meat or seafood, vegetables and dried fruit. The tall lid enables the steam to circulate and helps cook the food. These stews are called tagines and are often served with couscous or plain boiled rice.

tagliatelle | ITALIAN | Long, flat ribbons of pasta slightly narrower than fettuccine.

tahini | MIDDLE EASTERN | Cream paste made from ground sesame seeds used in Greek and Middle Eastern dishes, particularly in rich creamy dips that are served as appetizers with Lebanese bread.

tailor (*Pomatomus saltatrix*) Also known as 'skipjack' and 'bluefish'. It is a medium-sized silvery fish with a large tail and big jaws. The slightly oily, soft flesh has a strong taste and is best if the fish is gutted and bled as soon as it is caught, and eaten very fresh. Available whole or as skinned fillets. It can be baked, grilled or barbecued; also smoked.

takuan | JAPANESE | Pickled daikon radish, often yellow.

Taleggio | ITALIAN | Name-controlled semisoft cow's-milk cheese with a pale yellow, creamy interior and salted, washed, pinkish-brown rind. Mild to strong yeasty taste and pronounced aroma. Served at the end of a meal with full-bodied red wine.

242

talmouse | FRENCH | Square savory pastry filled with a cheese-flavored choux dough topped with cheese and baked. Originating in the Middle Ages, several types of talmouse are made today. Mainly served as a hot hors d'oeuvres.

tamago | JAPANESE | Egg. Tamago-yaki is a thick omelette made with folded layers of egg mixture cooked in a rectangular Japanese omelette pan called tamago-yaki nabe.

tamago-zushi *see* SUSHI.

tamale | MEXICAN | Small parcel of food made with a filling of finely chopped meat or vegetables spread on corn dough and wrapped in softened corn husks, tied with string, then steamed.

tamale pie | MEXICAN | Pie made with cornmeal dough filled with ingredients that would otherwise be used in tamales. The pie is covered with dough and baked. *see also* TAMALE.

tamari | JAPANESE | Naturally fermented soy sauce that contains a low percentage of wheat. It has a mellow taste and is used both in cooking and as a dipping sauce.

tamarillo (*Cyphomandra betacea*) Also known as 'tree tomato'. Deep red, egg-shaped fruit with a smooth skin and sweet, acid flesh. When ripe it should be firm but not hard. Halved it can be eaten with a spoon, or peeled and used in fruit salads and sweet dishes, hams and chutneys; also served with cheese or made into a savory sauce to accompany smoked or rich meats.

tamarind (*Tamarindus indica*) Brown, acid-tasting pulp from the fruit of a large tropical tree. Often sold dried in slabs. To obtain liquid, soak a piece in hot water until soft, squeeze the pulp and strain before use. In India it is used in curries, jams, chutneys, salads and condiments. In Middle Eastern dishes small quantities are used to flavor stews and other dishes.

tandoor oven | INDIAN | Special kind of cylindrical clay or brick oven with a rounded top. Used to bake bread, chicken and other meats.

tandoori | INDIAN | Method of cooking in which food (often chicken) is coated with yoghurt and a bright seasoned paste containing onions, garlic, ginger, chili powder, turmeric, paprika and garam masala. The food is left to marinate overnight, then cooked quickly at a high temperature in a tandoor oven.

tandoori mix | INDIAN | Blend of hot and fragrant spices including cardamom, chilies, turmeric, saffron, ginger and garam masala. Usually mixed with yoghurt and used to marinate chicken or other meat before cooking in the tandoor oven.

tangelo (*Citrus tangelo*) This deep orange citrus fruit with a knob at the stem end is a cross between a grapefruit and a mandarin, and is almost as easy to peel as a mandarin. It has an acid, sweet flavor and is good for juicing, eating fresh or adding to fruit or savory salads.

tangerine *see* MANDARIN.

tannin Astringent substance found in tea, the bark of some trees and the skin, seeds and stems of grapes.

tansy (*Tanacetum vulgare*) Bitter-tasting, dark green leaves of perennial herb that was once used as a flavoring for sausages, meat pies, stuffings and a rich egg custard pudding also called 'tansy' and served at Easter.

tapas | SPANISH | Selection of hors d'oeuvres and appetizers. Served in bars and cafés with pre-dinner drinks.

tapenade | FRENCH | Thick paste of black olives, anchovies, capers, olive oil and lemon juice. Spread on toasted bread or served with crudités. Specialty of Provence.

tapioca (*Manihot utilissima*) Starch extracted from cassava roots. It is cooked then ground and sold in various forms. When finely ground (also known as 'cassava flour') it is used as a starch to thicken sauces and soups. Pearl tapioca is used in milk puddings and other desserts.

tarama | GREEK | Pale orange carp roe.

taramasalata | GREEK | Thick creamy paste made of carp or mullet roe, milk-soaked breadcrumbs, lemon juice, olive oil and seasonings. Served as a dip or hors d'oeuvre topping.

tarator sauce | MIDDLE EASTERN | Smooth creamy sauce made with breadcrumbs, ground pine nuts or almonds, olive oil, lemon juice or vinegar, crushed garlic and seasoning. Traditionally served separately in a bowl, as an accompaniment to baked fish.

taro (*Calocasia esculenta*) Also known as 'dasheen'. Tropical root vegetable with hairy brown skin and a starchy dry-textured flesh. In tropical countries it is a valuable staple, taking the place of the potato. The rough skin is peeled, then the flesh is sliced and either boiled, steamed, baked, sautéed or cut into chips and fried; also used as a thickener in soups. In Hawaii it is the main ingredient of poi. In Chinese dishes it is frequently cooked with duck or pork. The leaves are also edible and are called 'callaloo' in the Caribbean. *see also* POI *and* CALLALOO.

tarragon (*Artemisia dracunculus*) Aromatic linear leaves, with refreshing aniseed-like taste, from slender perennial herb native to parts of Asia and Europe and one of the important herbs in French cuisine. Used as an accompaniment to chicken and white meat dishes. Included in *fines herbes* mixture and classic sauces such as béarnaise; also good with eggs, mushrooms and carrots. Tarragon makes a first-rate vinegar. **Russian tarragon** (*A. dracunculoides*) has paler leaves and a coarser, bitter taste.

tart Open-faced pie or flan filled with various sweet or savory mixtures. A tartlet is a small individual tart.

tartare (à la) | FRENCH | Traditionally, minced raw beef served with egg yolk and seasoning. Also applied to a highly seasoned, raw fish dish that is often served as an appetizer.

tartare sauce Mayonnaise mixed with chopped onions, capers, gherkins, lemon juice and chives. Served mainly with grilled or fried fish.

tarte Tatin | FRENCH | Caramelized upside-down apple tart made famous by the Tatin sisters in their hotel restaurant in Lomotte-Beuvron, south of the River Loire. The bottom of the flan dish is thickly covered in butter and sugar, with wedges of apples arranged in concentric circles. The tart is covered with short crust pastry and baked. When cooked it is turned upside down so that the caramelized apple becomes the top.

tartufi | ITALIAN | Truffles.

tarwhine *see* BREAM.

Tasmanian Cheese *see* LACTOS.

Tasmanian trevally *see* WAREHOU, BLUE.

tasso | AMERICAN | Hot-tasting and highly seasoned smoked pork used in Cajun cooking as a flavoring in jambalayas and other dishes. Smoked ham with the addition of cayenne and other spices can be used as a substitute.

tat soi *see* BOK CHOY, ROSETTE.

tea Universal beverage made from the dried leaves of the plant *Camellia sinensis*. Both green and black teas are obtained from the same species and both contain caffeine and antioxidant properties. The difference is that the leaves of green tea are not fermented and are steamed as soon as they are picked, then rolled and dried. For black tea, the leaves are withered, rolled, fermented and dried. They turn black during the fermentation process and develop astringent tannins. Oolong tea is partially fermented, combining the color, taste and aroma of both black and green teas. *see also* ASSAM TEA, CEYLON TEA, CHAI, DARJEELING, EARL GREY, GREEN TEA, GUNPOWDER TEA, LAPSANG SOUCHONG, LUNG CHING, MATCHA, MATE, OOLONG *and* PEKOE.

temaki-zushi *see* SUSHI.

tempeh | INDONESIAN | Firm pressed bean curd product similar to tofu, but sturdier, and sometimes with whole beans visible. It will keep for several weeks.

tempura | JAPANESE | Deep-fried pieces of vegetables, fish, eel or prawns which are first lightly coated in a thin batter of egg, ice cold water and flour. Served as an appetizer, first course or as part of a meal, with a dipping sauce consisting of dashi, mirin and light soy sauce; grated daikon and ginger are served separately.

tentsuyu | JAPANESE | Clear dipping sauce of dashi, mirin and light soy sauce. Served warm with tempura.

teppan | JAPANESE | Metal hot plate on which teppanyaki is cooked.

teppanyaki | JAPANESE | Popular style of cooking in Japanese restaurants where diners sit around a large metal hot plate while the chef puts on a show of cooking and serving. All types of seafood, chicken, red meat and sliced vegetables are cooked teppanyaki style. The food is served hot with a piquant dipping sauce such as ponzu.

tequila | MEXICAN | Strong white spirit made from the pulp of mature agave plants (*Agave tequilana*). The extracted sugary liquid is fermented and the resultant brew distilled and aged in wood to provide tequila of varying strengths and smoothness. Straight tequila is drunk from a small shot glass with a lime wedge and a pinch of salt (separately). It also forms part of several cocktails such as margarita and sangrita.

terakihi *see* MORWONG.

teriyaki sauce | JAPANESE | Seasoned mixture of mirin (sweet rice wine), soy sauce, sake, sugar and ginger. Used as a marinade for pieces of beef and chicken that are also basted with the sauce while grilling to form a glaze. Food cooked in this way is also known as teriyaki.

terrine | FRENCH | Mixture of highly seasoned meats (usually chopped or ground) baked in an oblong container, lined with bacon, with a tight fitting lid. Served cold, sliced out of the container or turned out as a loaf and sliced. A terrine can also be made with poultry, seafood or vegetables. The container in which a terrine is cooked is also called a terrine.

testicles *see* ANIMELLES.

Tête-de-Moine | SWISS | Also called 'Bellela', named after the town where it is produced in small dairies. Pressed, uncooked cow's-milk cheese with firm, pale yellow interior and yellowish, natural, washed rind. Strong, spicy taste and pronounced aroma. Served as a snack or at the end of a meal.

Tetilla | SPANISH | Name-controlled semisoft, pressed cow's-milk cheese with a supple, white interior and greenish, natural rind, molded into squat rounded cone shapes. Mild, creamy taste. Served as a snack and appetizer.

Thai chili | THAI | Small, elongated chili ranging from green to red with medium heat and lots of seeds. Used chopped in many South-East Asian dishes, including Thai curry pastes; also sliced as a garnish on salads and noodle dishes.

thali | INDIAN | Traditional circular metal tray used for holding a number of small bowls containing different preparations of food that are served at the same time.

thermidor | FRENCH | Classic lobster dish. The tail is split lengthways, the cooked flesh is removed, chopped and mixed with a mustard cream sauce. It is spooned back into the shell, covered with the remainder of the sauce and sprinkled with grated Parmesan cheese, then browned in a hot oven.

thicken To add flour, egg yolks, roux or other thickening agents to give body to a liquid such as a sauce or soup.

Thousand Island dressing Salad dressing consisting of mayonnaise flavored with chili, finely chopped green olives, green capsicums, onions and hard-boiled eggs.

thousand-year egg *see* PRESERVED EGG.

thyme, caraway (*Thymus herba-barona*) Dark green, caraway-scented leaves of low-spreading perennial herb, Used to flavor beef, vegetables or in salads.

thyme, garden (*Thymus vulgaris*) Tiny but strongly aromatic leaves from low, shrubby plant native to the Mediterranean region. Used fresh or dried it has many uses as a seasoning and forms part of bouquet garni. Thyme aids digestion of fatty foods and is one of the major herbs used in charcuterie, a wide variety of meat dishes; also used with eggs, tomato dishes, green vegetables, lentils and all vegetable juices.

thyme, lemon (*Thymus* x *citriodorus*) Tiny, bright green, lemon-scented leaves. Used in same way as garden thyme; especially suited to chicken, fish and egg dishes.

thyme, wild (*Thymus serphyllum*) Called 'serpolet' in France. Shrubby herb that grows freely in the Mediterranean regions. Used lavishly in provençal cooking with trout, chicken, mutton and rabbit.

Tia Maria Jamaican rum-based liqueur with coffee and spices.

tian | FRENCH | Shallow, earthenware gratin dish from Provence. Also the name of vegetable gratins baked in such a dish.

tiger flathead *see* FLATHEAD.

tiger lily buds *see* LILY BUDS.

Tillamook | AMERICAN | Cheddar-style cheese produced in a cooperative dairy in Tillamook, Oregon. Considered a premium cheese.

tilleul | FRENCH | Linden tree. Linden or lime blossom herb tea.

Tilsit | SWISS | Also known as 'Swiss Tilsit'. Pressed cow's-milk cheese with semifirm, yellow interior scattered with small holes and yellow-brown rind. Served at the end of a meal and sometimes used in cooking. Originally from Holland, Tilsit is also made in all Scandinavian countries, northern Germany and central Europe, however the Swiss version is considered superior.

Tilsiter | GERMAN | Partially skimmed cow's-milk cheese with semifirm, pale yellow interior with numerous small holes and yellowish, washed rind. Medium to sharp monastery-type taste. Used for snacks and for cooking.

timbale | FRENCH | **(1)** Small, round mold with straight or sloping sides, sometimes fluted. **(2)** Mixture prepared in such a mold. **(3)** Round pastry shell filled with various dessert mixtures.

tipsy pudding | ENGLISH | Old-fashioned dessert of layers of sponge cake soaked in wine or brandy, then topped with custard or whipped cream.

tiramisu | ITALIAN | Translates to 'pick-me-up'. Popular dessert made with savoiardi biscuits (sponge fingers) saturated in strong coffee then layered in a serving bowl. A mixture of beaten egg yolks, sugar, mascarpone with Cognac or Marsala is folded with beaten egg whites, then poured into the serving dish and chilled for several hours. It is dusted with a bitter cocoa powder and grated chocolate before serving.

tisane | FRENCH | An infusion of herbs, flowers or spices steeped in boiling water to make a tea-like drink.

toad-in-the-hole | ENGLISH | Dish of small sausages arranged in a dish, covered with batter and baked in the oven until crisp and brown. Originally it was made with slices of left-over cooked meat and bacon.

toddy | ENGLISH | Alcoholic drink, usually hot, consisting of rum or whisky and hot water. Usually sweetened and served with a slice of lemon, and often with a small cinnamon stick, cloves or ground nutmeg added.

tofu | JAPANESE | Smooth, custard-like substance made from freshly pressed bean curd. Easily digested and highly nutritious, tofu has a bland taste but readily absorbs the flavors of the food it is cooked with. Fresh tofu is readily available and is sold covered in water in vacuum packs or plastic containers, labelled soft or firm. Firm tofu is cut and sliced in a variety of ways and can be boiled, steamed, stir-fried, baked, deep-fried, used in pickles or eaten raw. Soft tofu is used mainly in soups, salad dressings and smooth sauces. Fresh tofu is delicate, perishable and fragile and requires brief and gentle cooking. Store in the refrigerator, use quickly and change the water daily. Tofu is available in a number of other forms, including fermented, deep-fried puffs and sheets. Thin sheets or sheets of deep-fried tofu (aburage) are used for inari-zushi, other vegetarian dishes and pastries.

Tokay | HUNGARIAN | Sweet, amber white wine that is usually served slightly chilled at the end of a meal.

tom yum goong | THAI | Sour prawn soup. Popular dish consisting of prawns, lemon grass, Kaffir lime leaves, straw mushrooms, fish sauce, chilies, lime juice and coriander leaves.

toma | ITALIAN | Generic name for a style of soft ripened cow's-milk cheese, similar to Brie and Camembert, sold under specific brand names (Toma di Carmagnola, for example). Sold paper-wrapped in thick discs. Originated in Piedmont, but also made in parts of Lombardy.

tomalley The green liver of a lobster.

tomago-yaki *see* OMELETTE.

tomatillo (*Physalis ixocarpa*) Also known as 'Mexican green tomato'. Small green vegetable with a parchment-like covering, related to the cape gooseberry and the tomato. It has a distinctive taste and is an essential ingredient, for which there is no substitute, in many Mexican dishes, including salsa verde.

tomato (*Lycopersicum esculentum*) Originating in South and Central America, the tomato was taken to Europe by early explorers during the 16th century. Tomatoes are a good source of vitamins A, B and C, minerals and fibre. They are grilled, sautéed, baked, stuffed and made into sauces and soups; also widely used raw in salads, juices, on toast and as a garnish. As well as the well-known medium-sized, round, red tomato, there are a number of other varieties available. The large **beefsteak tomato** has an irregular, almost pumpkin-like shape, thick flesh and a good taste both raw and cooked. The bite-sized, round **cherry tomato** is sweet-tasting and popular in salads and canapés, also lightly sautéed in olive oil and served as a warm side dish. There are both red and yellow cherry tomatoes. The oblong **egg tomato**, also called 'plum', 'Italian', or 'Roma' tomato, holds its shape well during cooking and is good for casseroles, bottling, preserving, making sauces and sun-drying, and also in salads. This is the variety most often sold whole in cans. The round **golden** tomato is a mild-tasting, low-acid variety with a rather hollow center suitable for stuffing. The very first tomatoes were yellow—the Italian word for tomatoes, pomodoro, literally means 'golden apple'. Green tomato varieties and unripe tomatoes are popular in Italian salads or in chutneys. The **hydroponic tomato** is grown in artificial light without soil; the nutrients and water are fed directly to the plant's roots. It is available all year round and although it has the same nutritional value as a tomato grown in the ground, it is rather bland. This tomato often has its green calyx intact and unfortunately looks very much like the better-tasting and more expensive **vine-ripened tomato** which is allowed to fully ripen on the plant and is hand-picked. It is likely to have a far better taste than those mechanically harvested, artificially ripened and stored in a cool room. The small, teardrop-shaped **yellow pear tomato** is low in acid with a mild taste, popular in salads and as a garnish.

Many dishes are improved if the skins and seeds are removed. Score a small cross in the skin at the base of each tomato. Cover with boiling water for about half a minute, then refresh in cold water. The skins will slip off easily. Cut the tomatoes in half or quarters and remove the seeds with a knife or teaspoon.

tomato concassé Tomatoes skinned, seeded and coarsely chopped.

tomato coulis Liquid purée made from skinned, seeded and finely chopped tomatoes.

tomato paste Rich, concentrated paste made from tomatoes that have been cooked and reduced by about a fifth of their original weight. Used in sauces, stews, soups and casseroles.

tomato purée Thick, smooth liquid made from cooked tomatoes that have been strained or processed in a blender.

tomatoes, sun-dried These are halved tomatoes that are dried naturally in the sun or, more often, artificially. They are sold loose by the weight or packed in jars and covered with oil. Dried tomatoes are reconstituted by gently simmering in a little water until tender.

tomme | FRENCH | Also known as 'tome'. (1) Generic name for cheese which usually refers to various semisoft, cows'-milk cheeses made in the French Alps and which often take the name of the specific district. (2) Also the name given to a number of goat's- or sheep's-milk cheeses produced in south-eastern France.

tomme de chèvre | FRENCH | Goat's-milk cheese.

Tomme de Savoie | FRENCH | Semifirm, pressed, uncooked cow's-milk cheese with an ivory to pale-yellow interior and natural, greyish-brown rind. Mild monastery-type taste and slightly salty. Served as a snack and at the end of a meal.

tonguewurst Also known as 'tongue sausage'. Medium-sized sausage made from tongue, various other meats and often pig's blood.

tonic water *see* QUININE TONIC WATER.

tonnato sauce | ITALIAN | Mayonnaise-style sauce made with puréed tuna, anchovies, chopped capers, parsley and hard-boiled egg yolk, olive oil and lemon juice. Served with slices of cold, roast veal.

Toolangi Delight potato *see* POTATO.

torte / torten | GERMAN | Rich sponge cake, often multilayered and filled with whipped cream, jam, chocolate or fruit.

tortellini | ITALIAN | Small, ring-shaped, stuffed pasta.

tortilla | MEXICAN | (1) Thin, round, unleavened bread made from cornmeal, either eaten on its own, with a meal or as a wrapping for many fillings, usually dressed with a chili sauce. (2) In Spanish cooking a tortilla is a flat omelette, often filled with potatoes.

toss To turn and lift food, such as salad, to ensure it is evenly mixed and coated with seasoning or dressing.

tostada | MEXICAN | Medium-sized or small tortilla fried in oil until crisp. Served topped with various fillings.

tour de pâtisserie | FRENCH | Cold marble or metal slab used by professional pastrycooks to roll out and fold puff pastry.

tournedos | FRENCH | Centre portion of fillet of beef cut in thick rounds. Usually grilled or sautéed.

tournedos Rossini | FRENCH | Sautéed tournedos garnished with fois gras and truffles.

trans fatty acids *see* HYDROGENATE.

transparent noodles *see* BEAN THREAD NOODLES.

Trappiste | FRENCH | Generic term used for monastery-style, rind-washed cow's-milk cheeses made by monks of Trappist monasteries, particularly in France, but also in Belgium and Austria. They usually bear the name of the abbey from which they are made, preceded by the words 'Trappiste de' (Trappiste d'Echourgnac, for example).

trasi *see* BLACAN.

travailler | FRENCH | To work and thoroughly mix various ingredients for a long period.

treacle Thick, dark brown syrup which is a refined form of molasses. It is quite strong-tasting and is used in baked goods such as fruitcakes or gingerbread and in confectionery. A paler, more refined form is known as 'golden syrup'. *see also* GOLDEN SYRUP.

tree ear fungus *see* WOOD EAR FUNGUS.

tree tomato *see* TAMARILLO.

trepang *see* SEA CUCUMBER.

trevally (*Pseudocaranx dentex*) The silver trevally is the best-known in this group of deep-bodied saltwater fish. It is sold whole or in fillets and has a strongly flavored, firm, white flesh that is best when very fresh and small. Suitable for baking and pan-frying.

triangol | ITALIAN | Triangular stuffed pasta.

trifle | ENGLISH | Dessert of pieces of Madeira cake or sponge fingers, placed in a glass serving dish and moistened with sherry and brandy. This is topped with berries or preserves, custard and whipped cream and garnished with almonds, fruit or grated chocolate.

triglycerides Form of fat consisting of three fatty acids attached to a molecule of glycerol. High blood triglycerides is a risk factor for heart disease and stroke.

tripe Stomach lining of beef; also sheep and pork.

triple cream cheese Category of cow's-milk cheese with a high percentage of butter fat, for example the famous Brillat-Savarin from Normandy, France.

Triple Sec Sweet, clear, orange liqueur served after dinner; also used in pastries and desserts.

tripoux | FRENCH | Sheep's tripe.

triticale Highly nutritious grain which is a cross between wheat and rye. Used in breakfast cereals, soups, casseroles, cakes and pancakes.

trompette de la mort | FRENCH | Also known as 'black trumpet mushroom' and 'horn of plenty'. Very expensive, dark brown woodland mushroom with a strong flavor. Occasionally imported fresh from France.

Tronchon | SPANISH | Firm, pressed sheep's or goat's-milk cheese (or a combination of the two) with ivory interior with many small holes and pale-yellow, natural rind. Served as a snack or appetizer.

trotters Feet of pigs, cattle and sheep. Usually boiled or used in stocks for making meat jellies and sauces.

trout Three main species of trout have been introduced into Australia from the Northern Hemisphere. These salmon-like fish are popular sport fish and are also farmed commercially. The **rainbow trout**, **golden trout** and **brown trout** are freshwater fish and have delicate, white to pink flesh or golden flesh (golden trout) with a mild flavor. The closely related, highly regarded, **brook trout** is a deep-bodied, olive green fish with creamy mottling. All are best grilled, pan-fried or baked and are mostly cooked whole. The rainbow trout changes its color as it moves from fresh water out to sea where it grows into a much larger fish and becomes known as **ocean trout.** It is available as fillets or steaks with a salmon-like taste and texture best suited to poaching or baking. Whole trout is also available smoked. *see also* CORAL TROUT *and* OCEAN TROUT.

truffle, chocolate Confectionery made with chocolate, butter or cream, sugar and flavorings such as brandy, rum, coffee, nuts or spices. They are shaped into rough, truffle-shaped balls and rolled in cocoa powder. Usually served with coffee.

truffles (*Tuber* spp.) Small, knobbly, round fungus that grows underground near the roots of oak or beech trees in France and Italy. They are only located through their scent and are sniffed out by trained pigs or dogs. The two main varieties are the highly prized **black truffle** (*T. melanosporum*), mostly from the Perigord region of France, and the **white variety** (*T. magnatum*) from Italy's Piedmont region. Both are rare and expensive. Fresh truffles are sold from late autumn to midwinter and usually marketed locally. They should be used as soon as possible. The white truffle is rarely cooked and is usually shaved very thinly over fresh pasta, risotto, cheese or egg dishes. Black truffles feature in various classic French sauces, are used raw in salads or as a decorative garnish; also cooked with poultry or white meat. They are also delicious on their own heated briefly in butter or dry white wine. Canned or bottled truffles are sold in specialty food shops. A more economical way to enjoy the flavor of truffles is to use a few drops of truffle oil.

truss To prepare poultry by tying with twine so that it keeps its shape during cooking.

trussing needle Long stainless steel needle threaded with twine. Used to secure poultry or other food before cooking.

tsukemono | JAPANESE | Pickles. Considered an aid to digestion, pickled vegetables are served with every Japanese meal, including breakfast. There is a wide variety of commercially produced pickles available in vacuum packs and jars such as daikon, sliced ginger, sliced lotus root, umeboshi, cucumbers and many other vegetables. Some home-prepared pickles are usually not intended to be preserves and are consumed soon after preparation. Usually served in small individual dishes.

tsumamimono | JAPANESE | Nibbles or small pieces of food eaten with drinks; for example, rice crackers individually tied with a tiny band of nori. Sold in specialty grocers.

tuile | FRENCH | Translates to 'roof tile'. In cooking refers to delicate, almond-flavored biscuit that is curved over a rolling pin while cooling.

tulipe | FRENCH | Thin, tulip-shaped biscuit that is used as an edible dish for serving ice-cream or sorbet.

tulsi | INDIAN | (*Ocimum sanctum*) The native and sacred basil of India. Its narrow, reddish-purple leaves are used sparingly in salads, and the tiny black seeds are floated on cool, sweet drinks. *see also* BASIL, SACRED.

turmeric (*Curcuma domestica*) Bright orange root resembling ginger, only smaller. Used fresh in Thai, Indonesian and Malaysian dishes. When dried and ground to a powder used in curries and pickles, often added to rice dishes, fish kedgeree and devilled eggs. Usually sold in dry, powdered form, but can be found fresh in some Asian grocers.

tuna (*Thunnus* spp.) There are several commercially important species of tuna found in coastal Australian waters. The **southern bluefin** (*T. maccoyii*) is one of the most popular, renowned for its firm, pink-red flesh with a high oil content, and is often used raw in sashimi. It is farmed in sea pens off South Australia. The **yellowfin tuna** (*T. albacares*), the **albacore** (*T. alalunga*) and the **northern bluefin tuna** (*T. tonggol*) (internationally known as the 'longtail tuna') are also highly valued for food. Tuna is usually sold as steaks or cutlets. It is best quickly seared on a chargrill, barbecued or grilled on both sides and left rare in the middle. Very thin slices are eaten raw in sashimi accompanied by wasabi and soy sauce. *see also* ALBACORE.

tung hao *see* CHRYSANTHEMUM LEAVES.

turban | FRENCH | Food arranged in a circle, or a mixture of ingredients cooked in a ring mould.

turbot (*Scophthalmus maximus*) Highly valued marine flatfish found in Atlantic and Mediterranean waters.

tureen Large, deep container with a lid, used for serving soup or stew at the table.

turkey (*Meleagris gallopavo*) Large wild bird native to America that has been domesticated in Mexico since the time of the Aztecs. It was introduced to Europe by the Spanish conquistadors. Turkey is usually eaten on festive occasions, such as Christmas; in North America roast turkey is the traditional dish for Thanksgiving dinner. Turkeys are sold fresh or frozen whole, or in parts, such as the double breast on the bone, breast fillets and drumsticks. The flesh is lean, and moist cooking methods are used to prevent the flesh from drying out when roasted or barbecued. Turkey parts can also be braised or used in a casserole.

Turkish delight | MIDDLE EASTERN | Jellied sweet usually containing almonds or pistachio nuts. Often pink or green, cut into cubes and coated in icing sugar. Served with Turkish coffee.

turn To shape vegetables with a knife into barrel or olive shapes to ensure even cooking and an attractive appearance.

turnip (*Brassica rapa* subsp. *rapa*) White root vegetable that is usually round with a purplish skin, but may also be yellowish, pure white or green, and can be carrot-shaped. There are also baby turnips. The fresh green tops are cooked as a vegetable, like spinach. When young and small the roots are steamed or baked whole, or sliced and used raw in salads. Some chefs use a chopped turnip to give extra flavor to chicken stock.

turnover | ENGLISH | Pastry dough circles or squares that are covered with a sweet or savory filling and folded over to form a triangle or semicircle. Most are individual and either baked or fried.

turron | SPANISH | Nougat-like sweet made of toasted almonds, honey and egg whites, with various fillings such as ground coriander seeds, pine nuts, walnuts and cinnamon. Traditionally eaten at Christmas.

tutti-frutti | ITALIAN | Mixture of crystallized or fresh fruits cut into small pieces and used in cassata and various other icecream desserts.

tzatziki | GREEK | Cucumber and yoghurt salad seasoned with crushed garlic, chopped mint and salt and pepper; served cold as an accompaniment to fried fish and barbecued meats, also as a mezze.

tzimmes | JEWISH | Casserole of meat, sweetening and vegetables. A carrot tzimmes is traditionally served on the New Year, Rosh Hashana.

udo (*Aralia cordata*) Tender young stems and leaves of large perennial plant commonly cultivated in Japan. They have a delicate taste reminiscent of asparagus and can be eaten raw or blanched. Used in vinegared or cooked salads, in clear soups or with green vegetables.

udon | JAPANESE | Thick, round or squarish, long, white noodles made from wheat flour, sold in fresh, pre-cooked and dried forms. Used mostly in soups. Donguri udon contain 10 per cent acorn flour.

ugli (*Citrus* spp.) Large citrus fruit with a thick, yellowish-green skin and sweet, bright yellow flesh, said to be a cross between the grapefruit and tangerine, originating in Jamaica.

UHT milk *see* LONG-LIFE MILK.

umeboshi | JAPANESE | Small pickled plums packed in brine and preserved with reddish-purple shiso leaves to impart deep red color. They have a salty, tangy taste and have long been used as a start to the morning meal, eaten as a pickle with soft rice or steeped in morning green tea. Umeboshi customarily appears in the middle of rice in bento. In cooking it is used whole, chopped or puréed as a mild sour seasoning in many recipes.

uni | JAPANESE | Sea urchin roe used as a topping for sushi. *see also* SEA URCHIN.

unleavened Baked goods that contain no raising agent such as baking powder or yeast.

unmold To remove food from the container in which it was made; often ice cream, jellies, some cakes and savory mousses.

upside-down-cake Type of cake that, when baked, is inverted onto a plate so that the bottom becomes the top. *see also* TARTE TATIN.

urad flour | INDIAN | Type of flour made from the black gram (*Phaseolus mungo*) which is hulled, soaked and then ground into a paste. Used as a type of leaven to make round little cakes known as idlis and paper-thin pancakes. *see also* IDLI.

urap | INDONESIAN | Lightly cooked vegetables tossed with freshly grated coconut and spices. Served as a salad or accompaniment to a meal.

usuage *see* ABURAGE.

usukuchi shoyu *see* SHOYU.

vacherin | FRENCH | Elaborate cold dessert of flat meringue circles filled with ice-cream and placed in layers on a sweet pastry case. It is covered with whipped cream and decorated with crystallized fruits or flowers.

vacherin cheese Several cow's-milk cheeses with a soft, creamy texture and a washed rind. Produced in Switzerland and in the Savoy mountains in France. All are consumed young, usually at the end of a meal.

Vacherin du Haut-Doubs | FRENCH / SWISS | Also known as 'Vacherin Mont d'Or'. Soft cow's-milk cheese with a smooth, creamy-white, runny interior and velvety, pinkish rind encircled by a band of resinous bark, usually spruce. Served when young, usually as a dessert cheese eaten with a spoon.

Vacherin Fribourgeois | SWISS | Soft cow's-milk cheese with pale yellow interior with occasional tiny holes and smooth, light brown or pink, washed rind. Highly esteemed aromatic cheese served as a snack or at the end of a meal; also excellent melting cheese and basis for fondue fribourgeoise.

Vacherin Mont d'Or *see* VACHERIN DU HAUT-DOUBS.

vacuum seal The exclusion of air from a container so that the food within keeps longer.

Valençay | FRENCH | Soft goat's-milk cheese with ivory, smooth interior and velvety, white rind, usually dusted with charcoal and made in the shape of a small truncated pyramid. Strong, goaty flavor and aroma.

Valencia orange (*Citrus sinensis*) Available mostly in spring and summer. This thin-skinned, sweet and juicy orange is one of the best for juicing and for eating fresh. It is also a good addition to salads and savory dishes.

Valpolicella | ITALIAN | Light dry, red wine from Verona, Veneto.

vanilla (*Vanilla planifolia*) Aromatic, dark brown, slender pod from tropical climber of the orchid family. Used for ice cream, pastry, confectionery, cakes, desserts, sweets and chocolate; also to flavor mulled wine, sangria and hot chocolate. Vanilla is sold in pods, in powdered form and as an essence. Imitation vanilla extract is made from commercial synthesized vanillin. It has a strong smell and pronounced vanilla taste which is vastly inferior. Used commercially in bakery goods, confections and chocolate.

varak | INDIAN | Thin, silver leaf used as a decoration on both sweet and savory dishes. Sold in sheets in some Asian stores and cake decorating shops. It is tasteless, odorless and can be quite safely eaten.

varieniki / varenyky | RUSSIAN | Round dumpling made from basic noodle dough and filled with a mixture of cottage cheese, eggs and butter, and poached in salted water. Some versions are made with a fruit or chopped meat filling. Traditionally served with sour cream.

variety meats *see* OFFAL.

vatrouchki | RUSSIAN | Cottage cheese and egg tartlets, baked in the oven and served as an accompaniment to soup or as a first course.

veal The meat from a young calf. Mild-fed veal are slaughtered before they are weaned and produce a very pale, tender meat with no fat. Most veal sold is slaughtered up to nine months old and is pink to light red and has a stronger taste. The older the animal the darker the flesh. All cuts are tender, but the choice cuts are the fillet, which is sliced very thinly and used for scaloppine; the loin, which is usually roasted; and the rump which is sliced into steaks or left whole as a roast. The rib section can be cut into chops and cutlets or left together as a rack. The veal knuckle or shank are sawn into pieces for osso buco. Veal bones are often the preferred red meat by many cooks for making brown stock.

vegan Person who does not eat any meat or animal products, including butter, cheese, eggs and milk.

vegetable pear *see* CHOKO.

vegetarian Person who does not eat meat, poultry and sometimes fish, but may include cheese, eggs and milk in their diet.

vegetarian steak *see* SEITAN.

velouté sauce | FRENCH | Basic white sauce made from veal, chicken or fish stock, thickened with a white roux and used as a base for other sauces or soups.

venison Very lean, dark red meat of a deer or related species.

verjuice The unfermented juice of unripe grapes. Verjuice was a feature of the highly spiced sauces of the Middle Ages. It has a light acidity and is used in place of vinegar as a delicate flavoring for many dishes. Once opened it will keep in the refrigerator for about one month.

vermicelli | ITALIAN | Translates to 'little worms'. Very thin strands of pasta.

veronique (à la) | FRENCH | Dish garnished with peeled, white seedless grapes.

verte sauce | FRENCH | Green sauce made with mayonnaise and a purée of herbs such as parsley, tarragon, spinach or watercress. Served with cold poached fish.

vervain (*Verbena officinalis*) Strong-smelling herb used mainly in herbal teas as a digestive and sedative. Not to be confused with lemon verbena.

Vichy | FRENCH | (1) Sliced rounds of carrots cooked gently in a little water, butter and sugar until all the liquid is absorbed and the carrots are tender and glazed. (2) Brand of naturally sparkling mineral water, which some suggest is the correct water to use when cooking Vichy carrots.

vichyssoise | FRENCH | Creamy leek and potato soup, usually served cold.

Vietnamese mint | VIETNAMESE | (*Persicaria odorata*) Strong-tasting, aromatic leaves used as a garnish in salads and soups, also in spring rolls.

vinaigrette | FRENCH | Basic seasoned oil and vinegar dressing to which various flavorings such as spices, herbs, mustard, onions or garlic may be added.

vine leaves *see* GRAPE LEAVES.

vine-ripened tomato *see* TOMATO.

vinegar Acidic liquid usually made from the natural fermentation of wine, beer or cider. When exposed to air the alcohol is oxidized by bacterial activity and converts into a diluted solution of acetic acid. **White** and **red wine vinegars** are mainly used to make salad dressings, marinades and sauces. **Sherry vinegar** has a mellow, full-bodied flavor, often blended with a nut oil and used in salad dressings, or to deglaze the pan when cooking. **Champagne vinegar** is also available and can be used to dress white fish or poultry. **Balsamic vinegar** from Italy has a rich, sweet mellow taste and is widely used as a salad dressing or to deglaze the pan when cooking. The flavor is concentrated and it should be used in small amounts. The golden **cider vinegar** has a mild, fruity taste, often used with seafood and when making court bouillon. The sharp-tasting distilled **white vinegar**, based on distilled grain alcohol, is clear and used for pickling. **Malt vinegar**, which can be white or brown, is obtained from malted barley or cereals and is widely used for pickling. In England it is the vinegar regularly used with fish and chips and other seafood. **Rice vinegar**, made from fermented rice, is widely used in South-East Asia and is available in three types: white, red and black. Used in sweet-and-sour dishes, salad dressings, pickling and as a table condiment. The **Japanese white rice vinegar** is used to season sushi rice and salads. Other vinegars include the slightly sweet, **fruit vinegars**, such as raspberry vinegar, used in certain salad dressings and fresh fruit dishes. **Herb vinegars** are made by steeping fresh herbs, such as tarragon, ginger, vanilla, dill, basil or marjoram, in vinegar for about a month before use. Also available in specialty shops is **honey vinegar** imported from Italy. It has a mild, sweet-and-sour taste and can be used to sprinkle over delicate white fish and as a salad dressing. *see also* BALSAMIC VINEGAR, RICE VINEGAR *and* MOTHER OF VINEGAR.

et (*Viola odorata*) Scented, purple flower long cultivated for its perfume. Mainly used in crystallized form to decorate cakes, puddings and ice cream; also tossed raw in salads, such as mesclun.

Virginia ham Country-style, dark ham that has been dry-cured and seasoned. Traditionally smoked over hickory, and aged for up to 12 months.

vodka Clear spirit distilled from potatoes, grain and other ingredients. It is the national drink of Russia and is enjoyed internationally, either served straight icy-cold or as part of a mixed drink.

vol-au-vent | FRENCH | Small, round puff-pastry sheet with a lid, filled with a creamed savory mixture and served hot as an entrée or hors d'oeuvre.

vongole *see* CLAMS.

wafer Small, crisp biscuit that can be plain, rolled, molded or filled with cream; also shaped like a cone for holding ice-cream.

waffle Crisp, flat cake made from a thin batter and cooked in a special hinged waffle iron with the pattern of honeycomb on both sides. Waffles are usually served while still hot and crisp, often sprinkled with icing sugar and accompanied by a sweet syrup, ice-cream, jam or whipped cream. Savory waffles can be made with cheese, ham or vegetables.

wakame | JAPANESE | (*Undaria pinnatifida*) An edible seaweed sold dried in long curled strands. Wakame is extremely rich in calcium and contains large amounts of iron and vitamins A and C. It is soaked briefly in cold water, which makes it turn an attractive translucent green. Wakame is extremely delicate and cooks more quickly than most other seaweeds. It is widely used in miso soups and noodle dishes; also added to side dishes and salads. A salted, bright green, fresh version, labelled **nama wakame**, is available in specialty shops. It is rinsed before cooking and tossed gently in stir-fries, or added to soups, rice dishes or vinegared salads.

Waldorf salad | AMERICAN | Mixed salad of diced apples and celery, chopped walnuts and a thin mayonnaise. Named after the Waldorf Astoria Hotel in New York.

walnut (*Juglans regia*) Creamy-colored, wrinkly nut which is formed into two distinct halves. The pale brown skin does not need to be removed before eating. Walnuts are often eaten straight from the shell as a snack or after dinner. Shelled they are used extensively in every form of cooking in baked goods, desserts, confectionery and ice cream; also in soups, sauces, stuffings, salads and vegetarian dishes. Unripe walnuts (including the shell) are pickled in spiced vinegar and used as an accompaniment to cold meats; also added to casseroles.

walnut oil Expensive, amber oil with a distinct, fruity, walnut taste. It makes an excellent salad and vegetable dressing and is good for sautéing shellfish.

warehou, blue (*Seriolella brama*) Also known as 'snotty trevalla' and 'sea bream' (not to be confused with the morwong). The name 'warehou' originates in New Zealand. It is a blue-grey, medium-sized fish with a mild-tasting, fairly oily flesh with a large flake and few bones. The **silver warehou** (*Seriolella punctata*) has firm, pale-pink flesh, usually sold as skinned fillets. They can be grilled, pan-fried or deep-fried; also used in fishcakes, soups and salads.

warrigal greens | AUSTRALIAN | (*Tetragonia expansa*) Also known as 'New Zealand spinach'. The fleshy triangular leaves of this small native plant are cooked and eaten like spinach. Always blanch and refresh to remove intensely sour acids. Available fresh.

wasabi | JAPANESE | (*Wasabia japonica*) Thick, green root of aquatic plant cultivated extensively in Japan where it is freshly grated and mixed with soy sauce as a dip for sashimi or smeared between the rice and fish of sushi. Outside of Japan the best wasabi is sold as a paste in tubes. Powdered wasabi (a cheap substitute), which is mixed with water, is usually ground horseradish with green food coloring and some mustard added. Very occasionally fresh wasabi is available from specialty produce markets.

water bath Bowl of ingredients placed in a saucepan or baking dish containing hot water in order to cook the food with gentle heat. Used for cooking egg sauces or custards without curdling them; also useful for keeping sauces hot. *see also* BAIN-MARIE.

water biscuit Plain, crisp biscuit with little taste. Served with cheese and wine.

water caltrop (*Trapa bicornis*) Also known as 'water chestnut'. Cultivated mostly in China for its edible black seeds with two curving horns. The seeds must be boiled for at least one hour as they contain harmful substances when raw. *see also* WATER CHESTNUT.

water chestnut (*Eleocharis dulcis*) Dark brown, swollen tubers from aquatic plant commonly grown in China and in South-East Asia. They have papery layers enclosing a crunchy, white flesh with a sweet, nutty taste. Used chopped or sliced in stir-fried dishes for texture or as a garnish. Also used fresh as a snack or simmered in rock sugar as a preserve. Available in cans or fresh from Asian grocers. *see also* WATER CALTROP.

water chestnut flour | ASIAN | Flour made from ground, dried water chestnuts. Used as a thickener, binder and batter ingredient for foods before deep-frying.

water lily *see* LOTUS.

water spinach | ASIAN | (*Ipomoea aquatica*) Leafy, green vegetable with spear-shaped leaves and slender, cylindrical stems; both are used. It has a delicate flavor and as a spinach-type vegetable requires very little cooking; also stir-fried, used as an omelette filling or in soups.

watercress (*Nasturtium officinale*) Slightly bitter salad herb from aquatic plant of the mustard family. The small, dark green leaves have a sharp, peppery taste and are a good source of vitamin C and iron. They are added to salads, soups, cooked as a purée and used raw as a garnish; also used in traditional English watercress sandwiches and added at the last moment to Asian stir-fry dishes.

watermelon (*Citrullus vulgaris*) Huge, green melon with extremely juicy, bright pink flesh containing many dark brown seeds. Frequently eaten raw in slices as a thirst quencher; also cut into cubes or balls for fruit salads, or liquidized for drinks and iced desserts.

waterzooi | FLEMISH | Rich freshwater fish and eel stew cooked slowly in court bouillon with vegetables and herbs, enriched with butter and cream. There is also a chicken version.

Weisslackerkäse | GERMAN | Also known as 'Bierkäse' (beer). Semisoft, rind-washed cow's-milk cheese with a dense texture and shiny, thin rind. Pronounced, pungent taste. Served as a snack with ryebread and beer. Produced in factories, mostly in Bavaria.

weisswurst | GERMAN | Translates to 'white sausage'. Pale, delicate sausage with a veal-based stuffing bound with cream and eggs. Simmered gently in water and often served as a snack with mustard, ryebread and beer.

Welsh rarebit | ENGLISH | Savoury dish of melted cheddar cheese mixed with beer and English mustard, seasoned with a dash of Worcestershire sauce, then spooned onto toast, and browned under a grill.

Wensleydale | ENGLISH | Lightly pressed cow's-milk cheese with white, moist and crumbly interior and thin, natural rind that is cloth-wrapped in cylinders or plastic-wrapped in blocks. All-purpose table cheese. A blue version has a creamy interior with blue veins. Served at the end of a meal.

Westphalian ham | GERMAN | Salt-cured ham that is traditionally cold-smoked over juniper or other fragrant wood, then dried. Traditionally sliced very thinly and served raw with pickles and pumpernickel.

wheat (*Triticum vulgare*) Universal bread grain and the world's chief cereal crop. Whole-wheat is whole, unprocessed grains available in health-food shops, used like rice to accompany fish and meat, as a porridge or cooked to use in salads. Soaking overnight shortens the cooking time. Cracked wheat such as bulgur are wholegrains which are hulled and steamed before cracking, then dried.

wheat germ Embryo of the wheat grain where most of the vitamins and minerals are stored. Used raw or toasted in breakfast cereals, as a topping on cooked vegetables, to crumb fish or chicken, or in meat or nut loaves.

wheat gluten *see* SEITAN.

wheat meat *see* SEITAN.

wheat noodles | CHINESE | Noodles made from wheat flour, water and salt. They are smooth and white and sold mostly dried in bundles, but fresh wheat noodles are also available. They are usually boiled first until nearly done, then quickly rinsed in cold water and drained before using in stir fried dishes and soups.

whey Watery liquid that separates from the curd in cheese making.

whisk (1) To beat air into a mixture to increase its volume, such as cream, eggs and sauces. **(2)** Hand-held kitchen utensil, often made of stainless steel, consisting of a series of wires bent into loops joined and held together on a handle. They come in different designs and sizes to suit various purposes.

white fungus (*Tremella fuciformis*) Also known as 'coral fungus'. Cultivated fungus that resembles a creamy-white piece of frilled coral or sponge. It has a crunchy texture and mild flavour. Used in salads, soups and braised dishes. Also available dried.

white truffles *see* TRUFFLES.

whitebait (*Lovettia sealii*) Tiny silvery fish sold whole. They are cooked and eaten whole without removing the head or gutting. Often they are coated in flour and deep-fried, and served with lemon as an appetizer; also dipped in an egg batter and deep-fried in small clusters.

whiting (*Sillago* spp.) Various species of these small, elongated, round fish with a pointed snout are sold whole or in fillets. They have a white, fine textured flesh with a delicate taste and are regarded as excellent table fish. The fine bones can be removed when filleted. Whole fish may be grilled or pan-fried. The fillets can be fried in batter or coated with flour to help retain moisture.

Wiener schnitzel | GERMAN | Thin slices of veal dipped in egg and breadcrumbs and fried. Served with lemon wedges.

wild marjoram *see* OREGANO.

wild peach *see* QUANDONG.

wild rice | NATIVE AMERICAN | (*Zizania aquatica*) This is not technically a rice, but seeds from a tall aquatic grass native to North America. Since earliest times it has been the staple grain of the Anishinabe Indians who served it as an accompaniment to strong-tasting game. It has a distinct, nutty taste. The longest grains are the best quality. Wild rice must be cleaned in cold water before cooking, which takes about 25 minutes after it has been brought to the boil.

Williams pear Also known as 'Bartlett'. Large green pear that rather quickly turns yellow when ripe. It has a sweet, white, juicy flesh and is a good eating and cooking pear; also dries well and popular in preserves. An early autumn variety. *see also* PEAR.

winged bean (*Psophocarpus tetragonolobus*) Also known as 'Goa bean'. Four-sided, winged pod obtained from a tropical climbing plant. Although all parts of the plant are edible, the young pods are the most popular, especially in Asian cooking. They are blanched and used in salads or gently steamed or simmered.

winter cress *see* CRESS, GARDEN.

winter melon | CHINESE | (*Benincasa hispida*) Large, round, frosty green melon with a delicate white flesh that is treated like a young vegetable marrow. The melon is peeled, seeds discarded and chopped. Cooked briefly in stir-fry dishes or used in soup with pork, chicken or duck; for special occasions, the soup ingredients are steamed inside the scooped-out melon itself on which elaborate designs are often carved.

winter mint *see* MINT.

winter mushroom *see* SHIITAKE.

winter savory *see* SAVORY.

witchetty / witjuty grub | AUSTRALIAN | (*Cossidae* spp.) These delicacies of the desert are very rich in protein and are traditionally an important food in the diet of Aborigines, particularly women and children who dig them up from the shallow roots of the witchetty bush (*Acacia kempeana*). They are eaten raw or lightly cooked in ashes. When roasted they have a soft flesh, a crispy skin and are nutty in taste. Available mostly in cans or frozen.

witloof / witlof (*Chichorium intybus*) Called 'Belgian endive' in America and 'chicory' in the United Kingdom. Small, tightly pointed heart of white overlapping leaves with yellow or pale green tips. There is also a slightly more bitter variety with red frilly tips. Witloof is grown in a dark, climate-controlled situation to reduce bitterness and prevent greening. This growing technique is known as blanching and is also used for leeks to give a longer white area at the base. Witloof means 'white leaf'. To minimize bitterness do not expose witloof to unnecessary light prior to preparation. Used raw in a salad or braised in butter or baked.

wok Round cooking pan with curved sides and two loop handles on each side or with a single long handle. It comes in various sizes with a round or flat bottom and is an essential piece of equipment in Asian cooking, perfect for sautéing, stir-frying and deep-frying. By using a cover it can be used for braising, simmering and boiling, and with the addition of bamboo steamers and a high dome cover, the wok can be used as a steamer. The most common metal for woks is rolled steel, which transmits heat evenly, but they can also be made of cast iron, aluminium and stainless steel. A rolled steel wok should be seasoned before use. It is washed thoroughly with hot water and detergent, rinsed and dried. Place over a medium heat, then wipe the surface with a paper towel soaked with vegetable oil. Continue heating and wiping the surface with oil until the paper towel wipes clean. After this preliminary seasoning, clean the wok after each use with hot water and a soft scouring pad and dry thoroughly. Don't use an abrasive material as this will destroy the seasoned surface. In time the wok will turn black.

wonton wrappers | CHINESE | Square, thin sheets of dough available fresh or frozen. They are filled with a variety of savory mixtures and made into dumplings, then fried, steamed or used in soups. The wrappers or uncooked filled wontons may be frozen.

wong bok *see* CHINESE CABBAGE.

wood ear fungus (*Auricularia polytricha*) Also known as 'cloud ear', 'tree ear' or 'black fungus'. Dark brown or black, gelatinous fungus of frilled, irregular shapes. It has a delicate taste and is used mainly for its crunchy texture and dark color. Mainly sold in dried form in Asian food shops. When soaked they will expand considerably. Occasionally available fresh. Used in soups, braised, steamed and stir-fried dishes.

Woodburne *see* MEREDITH DAIRY.

Worcestershire sauce | ENGLISH | Commercial condiment used as a flavoring in soups, casseroles and stews. It is a dark brown, strong-tasting sauce containing powerful tastes such as anchovy essence, tamarind, soy sauce, malt vinegar, molasses, garlic and meat extract. Also used in various cocktails, including Bloody Mary.

wrasse *see* PIGFISH.

wurst | GERMAN | Sausage. *see* BRATWURST, KNACKWURST, LIVERWURST, METTWURST, WEISSWURST *and* ZUNGENWURST.

Xacuti | INDIAN | Very spicy curry which includes white poppy seeds, red chilies, and roasted grated coconut. Speciality of Goa.

Xato | SPANISH | Spicy winter salad with sliced witloof soaked in vinegar, oil, garlic, almonds and chilies. Speciality of Catalonia.

Xeres | SPANISH | The former name for Jerez de la Frontera, the capital of the sherry region. Vinaigre de Xeres is sherry wine vinegar.

yabby (*Cherax destructor*) Small Australian freshwater crayfish with two large claws and a tail similar to a miniature lobster. It is sold live and cooked. Live yabbies should be stunned in the freezer before cooking. To cook, place in a large pot with cold water, bring to the boil and simmer for a short time until the yabbies are red. They are also grilled, barbecued and baked. *see also* CRAYFISH.

yakimono | JAPANESE | Term used for grilling or pan-frying food. Sometimes the food is cut into bite-sized pieces, marinated then threaded onto skewers. Skewers are also used with whole fish and prawns to stop them curling as they are being cooked. Basting sauces are often used to achieve a crispy exterior. Yakitori and shioyaki are examples.

yakitori | JAPANESE | Bite-sized pieces of chicken, marinated in soy sauce, mirin and sake, threaded onto a skewer and grilled.

yam | THAI | Translates to 'mix with the hands' and refers to a tossed salad of raw or cooked vegetables. **Yam neua** is the popular Thai beef salad made with paper-thin slices of raw roast beef.

yam (*Dioscorea* spp.) About 10 distinct varieties of yam are cultivated in tropical regions of the world for their starchy tuberous roots. Yams have white, yellow, pink or purplish flesh covered with light grey to dark brown, thin skin which must be removed before cooking. They are used as a potato substitute and cooked in the same way as sweet potato. The one most often seen in local markets is elongated with thin, off-white, tightly adhering skin and white flesh with a dry, floury texture. The New Zealand yam (*Oxalis crenata*) has pink skin and resembles a small sweet potato.

yam bean *see* JÍCAMA.

yard-long bean *see* SNAKE BEAN.

yarrow (*Achillea millefolium*) Pungent, bitter herb with finely dissected leaves. Sometimes added to salads, but mostly used as a herbal tea.

yeast Living, microscopic organism used as a raising agent in various types of dough.

yellow banana chili *see* HUNGARIAN WAX CHILI.

yellow bean sauce *see* BEAN PASTE.

yellow garlic chives *see* CHIVES, GARLIC.

yellow pear tomato *see* TOMATO.

yellow rock sugar | CHINESE | Amber sugar sold in lumps or flat slabs. Used sparingly in glazes, sauces and braised dishes; also in desserts, pastries and confectionery.

yellow sapote *see* CANISTEL.

yellowbelly *see* GOLDEN PERCH.

yellowfin bream *see* BREAM.

yellowfin tuna *see* TUNA.

yellowtail kingfish (*Seriola lalandi*) Also known as 'kingfish'. Smaller fish are the best for eating and can be grilled or baked. The flesh is pink, slightly oily and is sometimes used in making sushi and sashimi.

yerba mate *see* MATE.

yoghurt Semisolid milk product that has been fermented by the addition of friendly bacteria (*Streptococcus thermophilus* and *Lactobacillusbul- garicus*). *Lactobacillus acidophilos* is commonly used to make yoghurt more easily digestible.

yokan | JAPANESE | Jelly-like confection made of sugar, agar-agar and azuki beans. Served with Japanese tea.

Yorkshire pudding | ENGLISH | Batter made of eggs, plain flour and milk that is poured into the hot pan drippings of a cooked roast and baked until puffy, crisp and brown. Served immediately with the roast.

yosenabe | JAPANESE | One-pot dish of many kinds of fish cooked with vegetables in a flavored stock.

youngberry (*Rubus* sp.) Dark red, juicy berry which is a cross between the dewberry and the loganberry. Used in summer pudding, pies, tarts and jams.

yum cha | CHINESE | Traditional Sunday morning brunch in which a large variety of small, sweet and savory foods (dim sum) are served from trolleys that are pushed between the tables. Yum cha, which means 'to drink tea', is served with pots of hot Chinese tea.

yuzu *see* CITRON.

zabaglione | ITALIAN | Warm, foamy dessert made by whisking egg yolks, sugar and Marsala in a basin over simmering water until the mixture becomes thick and frothy. Served on its own in glasses or poured over a dessert. In France it is called 'sabayon'.

zahtar / za'atar | MIDDLE EASTERN | Traditional blend of dried thyme, sesame seeds, sumac and salt. Used to coat poultry before roasting or in marinades.

zakuski | RUSSIAN | Selection of small, hot or cold appetizers served before a meal, usually accompanied by vodka.

zampone | ITALIAN | The forefoot of the pig, boned and stuffed with minced pork and seasoning, then boiled for two to three hours. Traditionally sliced into thick rings and served with lentils, haricot beans or mashed potatoes. Also used as an ingredient of bollito misto. Specialty of Modena.

zaru | JAPANESE | Small slatted bamboo tray or basket used for straining food and for serving cold soba noodles.

zarzuela | SPANISH | Translates to 'operetta'. Catalan stew of many kinds of shellfish and firm white fish cooked with olive oil, tomatoes, finely chopped ham, onions, crushed almonds, garlic and saffron, often seasoned with a dash of anis at the end of cooking.

zeilook | MOROCCAN | Spicy salad made with roasted cubes of eggplant and chopped tomatoes, tossed with a dressing of olive oil, garlic and lemon juice, seasoned with paprika, cumin, salt, chili, chopped coriander leaf and parsley.

zest The outer rind of citrus fruits.

zingara (à la) | FRENCH | Gypsy style. Usually a rich tomato sauce seasoned with paprika and garnished with strips of ham, tongue and truffles. Served with meat, poultry and eggs.

ziti | ITALIAN | Wide tubular spaghetti.

zitoni | ITALIAN | Also known as 'cannaroni'. The widest tubular spaghetti.

zucchini (*Cucubita pepo*) Also known as 'courgette'. Slender baby marrows that are eaten when immature. The smaller the zucchini the better. They vary from grey-green, dark green, mottled or bright yellow. They are a good source of vitamin C. They usually do not need peeling and can be cut in half lengthways and stuffed; also sautéed, deep-fried, steamed, grilled or baked or used raw in salads. The bright yellow flowers, prepared soon after picking, are lightly sautéed, deep-fried in a light batter, or stuffed and baked.

zucchini flowers *see* ZUCCHINI.

zuccotto | ITALIAN | Dome-shaped dessert made by lining a pudding basin with sponge fingers moistened with Marsala. A mixture of amaretti biscuits and coffee ice-cream is then pressed against the sponge to form an even layer with a hollow, then frozen for two hours. The hollow is filled with a mixture of vanilla ice cream and grated chocolate and the zuccotto is placed in the freezer overnight. It is inverted onto a plate and decorated with chocolate curls.

zungenwurst | GERMAN | Black pudding sausage containing diced solid pork fat and pickled tongue.

zuppa | ITALIAN | Soup.

zuppa inglese | ITALIAN | Translates to 'English soup'. Cold dessert with many variations. It usually consists of light sponge soaked with Kirsch and covered with custard and crystallized fruit or toasted almonds. It may also be topped with Italian meringue and browned briefly in a hot oven.

zushi *see* SUSHI.

zwieback | GERMAN | Bread that is sliced and baked a second time until crispy and lightly browned.

BIBLIOGRAPHY

Aziz K, *The Encyclopedia of Indian Cooking*, Park Lane Press, London, 1983. Anderson K, *The Gourmet's Guide to Fish and Shellfish*, Quill, New York, 1984. *Australian Seafood Handbook*, CSIRO Marine Research, Australia, 1999.

Bailey A, and the Editors of Time-Life Books, *The Cooking of the British Isles*, Time-Life International, 1970.

Beck S, Bertholle L, and Child J, *Mastering The Art of French Cooking*, Penguin Books Ltd, England, 1966.

Bennani-Smires L, *Moroccan Cooking*. Editions Jean Pierre Taillandier. Berg G, and Waldo M, *The Molly Goldberg Jewish Cookbook*, Doubleday & Company, New York, 1955.

Bremness L, *The Complete Books of Herbs*, Dorling Kindersley Limited, London, 1988.

Brown D, and the Editors of Time-Life Books, *The Cooking of Scandinavia*, Time-Life International, 1969.

Brown D, and the Editors of Time-Life Books, *American Cooking*, Time-Life International, 1969.

Brissenden R, *South East Asian Food*, Penguin Books Ltd, England, 1972. Buglialli G, *The Taste of Italy*, Conran Octopus Limited, London, 1985. Chapman V J, *Seaweeds and Their Uses*, Methuen & Co Ltd, London, 1970. Claiborne C, and Virginia L, *The Chinese Cookbook*, Harper & Row, New York, 1972.

Colin R (ed), *Brennan's, A Souvenir Cookbook*, Brennan's Inc. USA, 1975.

Commercial Fish of Australia, Australian Government Publishing Service, Canberra, 1977

Constance M, *Raw Materials*, Sydney Morning Herald Books, Sydney, 1994. Cribb A B, and J W, *Wild Food in Australia*, Fontana, Sydney, 1976.

David E, *French Provincial Cooking*, Penguin Books Ltd, England, 1970. David E, *Italian Food*, Penguin Books Ltd, England, 1963.

Davidson A, *The Oxford Companion to Food*, Oxford University Press, New York, 1999.

Dekura H, *The Fine Art of Japanese Cooking*, Bay Books, Kensington, 1984. Durack T, *Noodle*, Allen & Unwin, Sydney, 1998.

Esbensen M B, *Thai Cuisine*, Nelson Publishers, Melbourne, 1986. Escoffier A, *Ma Cuisine*, Mandarin Paperback, London, 1991.

Feibleman P S, and the Editors of Time-Life Books, *The Cooking of Spain and Portugal*, Time-Life International, 1969.

Fisher M F K, and the Editors of Time-Life Books, *The Cooking of Provincial France,* Time-Life International, 1968.

Floyd K, *Floyd on Fish,* BBC Books, London, 1985.

Goode J, and Willson C, *Fruit and Vegetables of the World,* Lothian Publishing Company, Port Melbourne, 1987.

Gregory's Fishing Guide, 11th Edition, Gregory's Publishing Company, New South Wales, 1986.

Greig D, *The Book of Mint,* Kangaroo Press, Sydney, 1989. Grigson J, *Book of European Cookery,* Michael Joseph Limited, London, 1983.

Grigson J, *Charcuterie and French Pork Cookery,* Michael Joseph, London, 1967.

Grigson J, *The Mushroom Feast,* Penguin Books Ltd, England, 1978. Guerard M, *Cuisine Minceur,* Pan Books Ltd, London, 1978.

Hahn E, and the Editors of Time-Life Books, *The Cooking of China,* Time-Life International, 1970.

Hazan M, *The Classic Italian Cookbook,* Knopf, New York, 1987. Hazan M, *The Second Classic Italian Cookbook,* Macmillan, Papermac, London, 1983.

Hazelton, N S, and the Editors of Time-Life Books, *The Cooking of Germany,* Time-Life International, 1970.

Heath A, *The Penguin Book of Sauces,* Penguin Books Ltd, England, 1970. Hertlots G A C, *Vegetables in South East Asia,* Allen & Unwin, London, 1972.

Hicks R, *Mexican Cooking,* Quintet Publishing Limited, London, 1990. Hom K, *Ken Hom's Asian Ingredients,* Ten Speed Press, Berkeley, California, 1996.

Hosking R, *A Dictionary of Japanese Food,* Charles E Tuttle Company, Japan, 1996.

Herbst, S T, *The New Food Lover's Companion,* Barron's Educational Series, Inc, New York, 1995.

Isaacs J, *Bush Food,* Weldons Pty Ltd, Sydney, 1987.

Jenkins S, *Cheese Primer,* Workman Publishing, New York, 1996. Johns L, and Stevenson V, *Fruit for the Home and Garden,* Angus & Robertson, Sydney, 1985.

Kuiter R H, *Guide to Sea Fishes of Australia,* New Holland, Sydney, 1996. Kushi A, *Complete Guide to Macrobiotic Cooking,* Warner Books, New York, 1985.

Lambert M, *Cajun Cooking,* Quintet Publishing Limited, London, 1991.

Larousse Gastronomique, Paul Hamlyn, London, 1984.

Leigh L, *The Sunday Times Guide to Enlightened Eating,* Century Hutchinson Ltd, London, 1986.

Leonard L W, *Jewish Cookery,* Andre Deutsch Limited, London, 1968. Leonard, J N, and the Editors of Time-Life Books, *Latin American Cooking,* Time-Life International, 1970.

Leto M J, and Bode W K H, *The Larder Chef,* Third Edition, Heinemann Professional Publishing Ltd, 1989.

Macdonald R, and Westerman J, *Fungi of South-eastern Australia,* Thomas Nelson Australia Pty Ltd, Victoria, 1979.

MacMiadhachain A,*Spanish Regional Cookery* Penguin Books Ltd, England, 1976.

Ortiz E L, *The Complete Book of Caribbean Cooking*, Penguin Books Ltd, England, 1977.

Ortiz E L, *The Complete Book of Mexican Cooking*, Bantam Books, New York, 1968.

Papashvily H and G, and the Editors of Time-Life Books, *Russian Cooking*, Time-Life Books, New York, 1975.

Pellaprat H P, *L'Art Culinaire Moderne*, Collins, England, 1967.

Pepin J, *La Technique*, Papermac, London, 1982.

Phillips R, and Rix M, *Vegetables*, Macmillan Reference Books, London, 1995. Quimme P, *The Signet Book of Cheese*, Signet Books, New York, 1976.

Rau S R, and the Editors of Time-Life Books, *The Cooking of India*, Time-Life International, 1970.

Rinaldi A and T,Vassili, *Mushrooms and Other Fungi*, Hamlyn, London, 1974 Ripe C, *Goodbye Culinary Cringe*, Allen & Unwin, Sydney, 1993.

Roden C, *A New Book of Middle Eastern Food*, Penguin Books Ltd, England, 1986.

Rombauer I S, and Rombauer B M, *Joy of Cooking*, Bobbs-Merrill Company, 1975.

Root W, and the Editors of Time-Life Books, *The Cooking of Italy*, Time-Life International, 1969.

Ross J, *A Taste of Australia*, The Five Mile Press,Victoria, 1995.

Simon A, *A Concise Encyclopaedia of Gastronomy*, Collins, London, 1952. Solomon C, *Encyclopedia of Asian Food*, New Holland, Sydney, 2000.

Solomon C, *The Complete Asian Cookbook*, Lansdowne Press, Sydney, 1976. Sou San W, *Chinese Culinary in Plain English*, Brisbane, 1965.

Steinberg R, and the Editors of Time-Life Books, *The Cooking of Japan*, Time-Life International, 1969.

Stobart T, *The Cook's Encyclopaedia*, Batsford, London, 1980. Strahan R, *A Dictionary of Australian Mammal Names*, Angus & Robertson, Sydney, 1981.

Stuart A T, *Vietnamese Cooking*, Angus & Robertson (UK) Ltd, London, 1986.

Stud W, *Chalk and Cheese*, Purple Egg, South Melbourne, 1999. Thompson D, *Classic Thai Cuisine*, Simon & Schuster, Sydney, 1993. Thomas M, and Escoffey R, *The Penguin French Dictionary*, Penguin Books Ltd, England, 1985.

United Kingdom Bartenders Guild, *International Guide to Drinks*, Century, London, 1987.

Waugh A, and the Editors of Time-Life Books, *Wines and Spirits*, Time-Life International, 1969.

Wechsberg J, and the Editors of Time-Life Books, *The Cooking of Vienna's Empire*, Time-Life International, 1969.

272

Wells P, *The Food Lover's Guide to France*, Metheun, London, 1988. Werle L, *Australasian Ingredients*, Gore & Osment Publications, Sydney, 1997.

Wong E, *The Commonsense Indonesian & Malaysian Cookery Book*, Angus & Robertson, Sydney, 1978.

Wright J, *The Encyclopaedia of Italian Cooking*, Octopus Books, London, 1981.

Yamamoto K, and Hicks R W, *Sushi*, Quintet Publishing Ltd, London, 1990.